Charles Spurgeon, 1860

the LOST SERMONS *of*
C. H. SPURGEON

the LOST SERMONS *of*
C. H. SPURGEON

His Earliest Outlines and Sermons Between 1851 and 1854   *Vol. 2*

Edited with Introduction and Notes by CHRISTIAN T. GEORGE

NASHVILLE, TENNESSEE

The Lost Sermons of C. H. Spurgeon, Volume 2
Copyright © 2017 by Christian George and Spurgeon's College
Published by B&H Academic
Nashville, Tennessee

All rights reserved.

Standard Edition ISBN: 978-1-4336-8682-5
Collector's Edition ISBN: 978-1-4336-4990-5

Dewey Decimal Classification: 252
Subject Heading: SPURGEON, CHARLES H. \ SERMONS \ CHRISTIAN LIFE–SERMONS

Special thanks to Spurgeon's College, spurgeons.ac.uk

Unless otherwise indicated, Scripture quotations are taken from the King James Version.

Scriptures marked NIV are taken from THE HOLY BIBLE, NEW INTERNATIONAL VERSION®, NIV® Copyright © 1973, 1978, 1984, 2011 by Biblica, Inc.® Used by permission. All rights reserved worldwide.

Scriptures marked ESV are taken from the ESV® Bible (The Holy Bible, English Standard Version®) copyright © 2001 by Crossway, a publishing ministry of Good News Publishers. ESV® Text Edition: 2011. The ESV® text has been reproduced in cooperation with and by permission of Good News Publishers. Unauthorized reproduction of this publication is prohibited. All rights reserved.

The web addresses referenced in this book were live and correct at the time of the book's publication but may be subject to change.

The marbled paper for the cover of the collector's edition was created by Lesley Patterson-Marx, lesleypattersonmarx.com

Printed in China

1 2 3 4 5 6 7 8 9 10 · 22 21 20 19 18 17

RRD

In memory of

Justine (Kirby) Aliff (1991–2016)

My former research assistant at Oklahoma Baptist University, whose love for Jesus Christ and winsome perseverance improved not only this project but all who knew her. Justine's joy was evident in her recent battle with cancer, and though she did not live to see the publication of this present volume, she welcomed it from a distance and *lives eternally* in the unfailing arms of her savior.

CONTENTS

Foreword... xiii
Editor's Preface... xvii
Acknowledgments.. xxv
Abbreviations... xxxi

PART 1: *Introduction* 1

PART 2: *The Sermons, Notebook 2 (Sermons 78–134)* 22

Front Cover of Notebook 2		23
Opening Page of Notebook 2		24
Skeletons		26
Blank Page		32
Sermon 78	Self-Deception—Gal 6:3	34
Sermon 79	The Sword of the Spirit—Eph 6:17	40
Sermon 80	The Treasure in Earthen Vessels—2 Cor 4:7	46
Sermon 81	Take Heed How Ye Hear—Luke 8:18	50
Sermon 82	Final Perseverance Certain—Phil 1:6	52
Sermon 83	Count the Cost—Luke 14:28	64
Sermon 84	Jesus and His Acts—Heb 10:12–13	68
Sermon 85	The Dog and Swine—2 Pet 2:22	78
Sermon 86	The Lord Is a King—Jer 10:7	84
Sermon 87	The Thief's Prayer—Luke 23:42	90
Sermon 88	The Grace Received—John 1:16	92
Sermon 89	The Harvest of Souls—John 4:35	94
Sermon 90	Thou Art Too Light—Dan 5:27	104
Sermon 91	The Spirit Crying "Abba Father"—Gal 4:6	110
Sermon 92	Inventory and Title of Our Treasures—1 Cor 3:21–23	114
Sermon 93	Present Your Bodies, Etc.—Rom 12:1	130
Sermon 94	The Lost Saved—Luke 19:10	138

CONTENTS

Sermon 95	God the Father of Lights—Jas 1:17	142
Sermon 96	The Rending of the Veil—Mark 15:38	152
Sermon 97	The Tranquillity, Security, and Supplies Afforded to the Gospel Church—Isa 33:20–21	162
Sermon 98	The Invitation of Moses to Hobab—Num 10:29	164
Sermon 99	The Curse and the Blessing—Prov 3:33	176
Sermon 100	The Beloved of the Lord in Safety—Deut 33:12	184
Sermon 101	The Second Psalm—Psalm 2	190
Sermon 102	Justification, Conversion, Sanctification, Glory—Rom 6:22	200
Sermon 103	The Effect and Design of the Law—Gal 3:23	212
Sermon 104	The Children Cast Out—Matt 8:11–12	220
Sermon 105	Oh that Men Would Praise the Lord—Ps 107:8	232
Sermon 106	Religion, the Foundation of Confidence—Prov 14:26	244
Sermon 107	Jesus's Dead Body Whilst on the Cross—John 19:33–34	250
Sermon 108	Man's Weakness and God's Strength—Mark 10:27	270
Sermon 109	Prove Me Now Herewith—Mal 3:10	280
Sermon 110	The Minister's Commission—Matt 28:19–20	292
Sermon 111	Wise Men and Fools—Prov 3:35	302
Sermon 112	Envy Forbidden, Piety Commanded—Prov 23:17–18	308
Sermon 113	God's Visits and the Effects Thereof—Hos 14:5–7	316
Sermon 114	The Noble Bereans—Acts 17:11–12	326
Sermon 115	The Day of God—2 Pet 3:12	338
Sermon 116	David in the Cave of Adullam—1 Sam 22:2	348
Sermon 117	Justification by Imputed Righteousness—Job 25:4	356
Sermon 118	The Prodigal's Resolution—Luke 15:18–19	376
Sermon 119	Come Ye Out from Among Them—2 Cor 6:17–18	382
Sermon 120	The Watchman, His Work, Warning, and Promise—Ezek 3:17–19	396
Sermon 121	The Redeemer's Tears over Sinners—Luke 19:41	404
Sermon 122	Satan and His Devices—2 Cor 2:11	410
Sermon 123	Enduring Temptation—Jas 1:12	416
Sermon 124	The Downfall of Dagon—1 Sam 5:2–4	422
Sermon 125	The Best Feast—Isa 25:6–8	432
Sermon 126	Christ's Constant Intercession—Isa 62:1	440
Sermon 127	The Most Excellent Rock—Deut 32:31	446

CONTENTS

Sermon 128	The Corner Stone—Ps 118:22	452
Sermon 129	God, the Father of a Family—Jer 31:9	460
Sermon 130	Well with the Righteous—Isa 3:10	464
Sermon 131	The Church Needs the Spirit—Isa 32:13–15	472
Sermon 132	Christ's Sheep—John 10:28–29	474
Sermon 133	By Faith Jericho Fell—Heb 11:30	482
Sermon 134	Set Thine House in Order—Isa 38:1	490

Notebook Index 500
Doxology 502
Back Cover of Notebook 2 506
About the Editor 507
Scripture Index 509
Subject Index 521

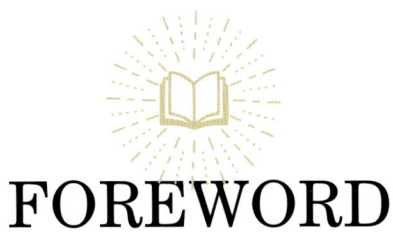

FOREWORD

"The history of the world is but the biography of great men," argued Thomas Carlyle, proponent of the Great Man Theory of history. Carlyle contended that the broader movements and contours of history can be traced to great leaders who exerted a unique, shaping influence on their times. Whether the Great Man Theory of history proves true is debatable, but that God providentially raises up certain individuals for kingdom work is not.

Throughout Scripture, God called forth individuals for consequential assignments. Figures like Moses, Joshua, David, Peter, and Paul dot the biblical landscape. In fact, Hebrews 11 is a biographical summation of the great lives of the Old Testament: men and women God appointed for his divine purposes. Church history is no different. In every era, God has raised up servants—men like Augustine, Luther, Calvin, Edwards, and Whitefield—granting them a double anointing and unleashing them to impact the world and strengthen his church. Charles Spurgeon was such a man.

Carl F. H. Henry labeled Spurgeon as "one of evangelical Christianity's immortals." And, for evangelicals, Spurgeon has become a paragon of faithful Christian ministry. Spurgeon ministered in London during the Victorian Era, when Great Britain reigned as the world's leading empire—thus amplifying Spurgeon's ministry and expanding his global fame and influence. Spurgeon was an accomplished pastor, author, apologist, leader, visionary, and school and ministry administrator. Yet, he was first and foremost a preacher. Spurgeon's auxiliary ministries flowed from his pulpit, and his weekly sermons were transcribed and dispensed around the world. Arguably, in the history of the church, there is no name in the English-speaking world more rightly associated with preaching than Charles Spurgeon. Spurgeon is commonly ranked, along with George Whitefield, as one of the two greatest preachers of the English language.

As a preacher, Spurgeon pastored the largest Protestant church in the world—the Metropolitan Tabernacle in London—where he preached for nearly 40 years to a congregation of some 6,000 members. In 1857, he preached to a crowd numbering 23,654 at London's Crystal Palace, and by the end of his ministry he had preached to more than 10 million people without the aid of modern technologies.

FOREWORD

As an author, Spurgeon possessed an indefatigable pen. He, on average, wrote 500 letters per week, and by the time of his death had authored approximately 150 books. His sermons, which he edited weekly, sold more than 56 million copies in his lifetime. In Spurgeon's day, they were translated into more than 40 languages and now total more than 62 hefty volumes. Additionally, Spurgeon wrote for various magazines and journals, including his own *Sword and Trowel*.

As an humanitarian, Spurgeon hurled himself at the great social ills of his day. He established two orphanages, a ministry for "fallen women," was an ardent abolitionist, started a pastors' college, and began a book distribution ministry for undersupplied pastors. He launched clothes closets and soup kitchens, for both his church members and nonmembers alike. By the age of 50, he had started no less than 66 social ministries, all of which were designed to meet both physical and spiritual needs.

As an apologist, Spurgeon ardently defended his Baptist, evangelical, and reformed convictions. He attacked hyper-Calvinism and Arminianism; Campbellism and Darwinism. Most especially, Spurgeon defended the person and work of Christ as well as the comprehensive inspiration and infallibility of Scripture. Spurgeon's apologetic efforts were most clearly witnessed through the prism of the Downgrade Controversy, where he challenged and ultimately withdrew from his own Baptist Union for their equivocation over these same issues.

As an evangelist, Spurgeon relentlessly preached the gospel and consistently won sinners to Christ. He remains an unsurpassed model for balancing the sovereignty of God and the responsibility of man in evangelism. In fact, one is hard-pressed to find any sermon Spurgeon ever preached that does not conclude with a gospel presentation. By the end of his ministry, Spurgeon had baptized 14,692 believers.

Spurgeon's ministry still owns a certain mystique. This is due, in part, to the fact that he was a genius. He devoured books, possessed a photographic memory, and once testified of simultaneously holding eight thoughts in his mind at once. His enormous influence, intriguing life and times, and his many physical and emotional travails factor in as well. Spurgeon's mystique is also due to his unflagging work ethic, which prompted David Livingstone to ask of Spurgeon, "How do you manage to do two men's work in a single day?" Spurgeon, referencing the Holy Spirit, replied, "You have forgotten there are two us."

Spurgeon was a phenom who preached in the largest Protestant church in the world within the context of the most powerful city in the world, London. Yet, his ministry coursed through and beyond the expansive tentacles of the British Empire. He embodied all that is right about biblical ministry and all that the contemporary

FOREWORD

church must recover in the 21st century: biblical faithfulness, evangelistic fervor, self-sacrificial ministry, power in the pulpit, social awareness, and defense of the faith.

Midwestern Baptist Theological Seminary is pleased to own Spurgeon's Library, which houses more than 6,000 books, letters, and artifacts once owned by Spurgeon. We are equally pleased to support the *Lost Sermons of C. H. Spurgeon* project and the scholar behind it all, Christian George. All of this points to a broader movement within the church, an even deepening appreciation of Spurgeon's work, and a growing realization of his contemporary relevance. This is fitting and right, and Midwestern Seminary is thankful to be at the center of this Spurgeonism.

Referencing important statesmen, the famed French leader Charles de Gaulle once quipped, "Graveyards are full of indispensable men." In Christ's kingdom no one is indispensable either, but certain men are irreplaceable. Charles Spurgeon was one such man, and, in his own way, Christian George is as well.

In the 19th century, God raised up Charles Spurgeon. In the 21st century, he has raised up Christian George to raise Spurgeon up anew. Christian George is Spurgeon-like in his gifting and in his tireless work ethic. He is a scholar who is also a pastor; a writer who is also a preacher; and, for all who know him, a colleague who is also a friend. He is the perfect man for this project and, by God's grace, will bless the church through this volume—and the entire 12-volume set—until Jesus returns.

JASON K. ALLEN
April 2017
Midwestern Baptist Theological Seminary

EDITOR'S PREFACE

In 1859, an American minister named "Rev. H." traveled to London to meet the famous pastor of the New Park Street Chapel. When Spurgeon discovered his guest was from Alabama, his "cordiality sensibly diminished." A six-month American preaching tour would expedite the construction of the Metropolitan Tabernacle, but could Southerners tolerate Spurgeon's stance against slavery? When Spurgeon asked his guest this question, the Alabamian said he "had better not undertake it."[1]

This advice might have saved Spurgeon's life. The same year, S. A. Corey, pastor of Eighteenth Street Baptist Church in New York City, invited the twenty-four-year-old to preach at the Academy of Music opera house for $10,000.[2] News of Spurgeon's visit was met with anticipation in the North and hostility in the South. According to an Alabama newspaper, Spurgeon would receive a beating "so bad as to make him ashamed."[3] On February 17, 1860,[4] citizens of Montgomery, Alabama, publicly protested the "notorious English abolitionist"[5] by gathering in the jail yard to burn his "dangerous books"[6]:

---

1 "Spurgeon's Anti-Slavery Mission to America," *The Times-Picayune* (October 22, 1859).
2 See "Spurgeon and His $10,000 Offer," *The Brooklyn Daily Eagle* (February 5, 1859).
3 "They Want Spurgeon," *Daily Confederation* (October 30, 1858).
4 There is some confusion about the date of the Montgomery burning. Some British newspapers claimed it occurred on January 17 ("Mr. Spurgeon's Sermons Burned by American Slaveowners," *The Southern Reporter and Daily Commercial Courier* [April 10, 1860]). American sources reveal the more likely date of February 17 ("Book Burning," *Pomeroy Weekly Telegraph* [March 13, 1860]).
5 The full quote is, "A gentleman of this city requests us to invite, and we do hereby invite all persons in Montgomery who possess copies of the sermons of the notorious English abolitionist, Spurgeon, to send them to the jail-yard to be burned, on next Friday (this day week). A subscription is also on foot to buy of our booksellers all copies of said sermons now in their stores to be burnt on the same occasion" (*Montgomery Mail*, repr. in "Spurgeon's Sermons—a Bonfire," *Nashville Patriot* [March 15, 1860]). See also "The Barbarism of Slavery," *The Cleveland Morning Leader* (July 3, 1860), and *Randolph County Journal* (July 5, 1860). The burning of Spurgeon's sermons in Montgomery solicited caustic responses in Northern states, such as in New York's *Poughkeepsie Eagle*: "There will—unless this fanaticism is soon checked—be a general bonfire of another Book, which has something of a circulation [in the] south, and which declares it to be every man's duty to 'let the oppressed go free'" (March 8, 1860).
6 For a more comprehensive account of the burning of Spurgeon's sermons at the Montgomery, Alabama, jail yard, see "Burning Spurgeon's Sermons," *The Burlington Free Press* (March 30, 1860).

EDITOR'S PREFACE

> Last Saturday, we devoted to the flames a large number of copies of Spurgeon's Sermons. . . . We trust that the works of the greasy cockney vociferator may receive the same treatment throughout the South. And if the Pharisaical author should ever show himself in these parts, we trust that a stout cord may speedily find its way around his eloquent throat.[7]

On March 22, a "Vigilance Committee"[8] in Montgomery followed suit and burned Spurgeon's sermons in the public square. A week later Mr. B. B. Davis, a bookstore owner, prepared "a good fire of pine sticks" before reducing about sixty volumes of Spurgeon's sermons "to smoke and ashes."[9] British newspapers quipped that America had given Spurgeon a warm welcome, "a literally brilliant reception."[10]

Anti-Spurgeon bonfires illuminated jail yards, plantations, bookstores, and courthouses throughout the Southern states. In Virginia, Mr. Humphrey H. Kuber, a Baptist preacher and "highly respectable citizen" of Matthews County, burned seven calf-skinned volumes of Spurgeon's sermons "on the head of a flour barrel."[11] The arson was assisted by "many citizens of the highest standing."[12] In North Carolina, Spurgeon's famous sermon "Turn or Burn"[13] found a similar fate when a Mr. Punch "turned the second page and burned the whole."[14] By 1860, slave-owning pastors were "foaming with rage because they [could not] lay hands on the youthful Spurgeon."[15] His life was threatened, his books burned, his sermons

---

[7] "Mr. Spurgeon's Sermons Burned by American Slaveowners." See also *The Morning Advertiser* (April 2, 1860). A similar statement is found in a letter from Virginia minister James B. Taylor: "Wonder that the earth does not open her mouth, and swallow up Spurgeon. . . . Pity that that cord from the South is not applied to his eloquent throat!" ("Review of a Letter from Rev. Jas. B. Taylor, of Richmond, Va.," *The Liberator* [July 6, 1860], 108).

[8] "News from All Nations," *The Bradford Reporter* (March 22, 1860).

[9] "Book-Burning in Montgomery, Ala.," *Randolph County Journal* (March 29, 1860). See also "Another Bonfire of Spurgeon's Sermons," *The Wilmington Daily Herald* (March 12, 1860).

[10] *The Morning Advertiser* (April 2, 1860). See also "The Rev. C. H. Spurgeon in Scotland," *The Morning Advertiser* (March 11, 1861).

[11] For a more accurate version of this account, see "Mr. Spurgeon's Sermons: Why They Were Burned by Virginians," *The New York Times* (July 9, 1860).

[12] "Virginia News," *Alexandria Gazette and Virginia Advertiser* (June 22, 1860). See also "Burning Spurgeon," *Richmond Dispatch* (June 5, 1860), and *Brooklyn Evening Star* (June 22, 1860).

[13] Spurgeon preached the sermon "Turn or Burn" (*NPSP* 2, Sermon 106) on December 7, 1856.

[14] "Our Politeness Exceeds His Beauty," *North Carolina Christian Advocate* (July 10, 1857).

[15] "Espionage in the South," *The Liberator* (May 4, 1860).

EDITOR'S PREFACE

censured,[16] and below the Mason-Dixon Line, the media catalyzed character assassinations. In Florida, Spurgeon was a "beef-eating, puffed-up, vain, over-righteous pharisaical, English blab-mouth."[17] In Virginia, he was a "fat, overgrown boy";[18] in Louisiana, a "hell-deserving Englishman";[19] and in South Carolina, a "vulgar young man" with "(soiled) sleek hair, prominent teeth, and a self-satisfied air."[20] Georgians were encouraged to "pay no attention to him."[21] North Carolinians "would like a good opportunity at this hypocritical preacher" and resented his "fiendish sentiments, against our Constitution and citizens."[22] *The Weekly Raleigh Register* reported that anyone selling Spurgeon's sermons should be arrested and charged with "circulating incendiary publications."[23]

Southern Baptists ranked among Spurgeon's chief antagonists.[24] *The Mississippi Baptist* hoped "no Southern Baptist will now purchase any of that incendiary's books."[25] The Baptist colporteurs of Virginia were forced to return all copies of his sermons to the publisher.[26] *The Alabama Baptist* and *Mississippi Baptist* "gave the Londoner 4,000 miles of an awful raking" and "took the hide off him."[27] The *Southwestern Baptist* and

---

16 The following reports suggest that the censuring of Spurgeon's sermons became widely publicized in American newspapers: "Beecher has charged that the American edition of Spurgeon's sermons, does not contain his sentiments on slavery as the English edition does. A comparison of the editions has been made, and the charge has been found correct" ("Spurgeon Purged," *Ashtabula Weekly Telegraph* [November 26, 1859]). In April of the following year, the newspaper reported that "grave charges have been made of interpolations and modifications in the American edition of his sermons, to suit American squeamishness, and secure currency to his works" (April 14, 1860). See also "Ex-Spurgeon," *Ohio State Journal* (November 29, 1859).

17 "A Southern Opinion of the Rev. Mr. Spurgeon," *The New York Herald* (March 1, 1860).

18 "The Great Over-Rated," *The Daily Dispatch* (August 17, 1858).

19 "Spurgeon on Slavery," *The Bossier Banner* (February 24, 1860).

20 "Spurgeon and the Lady," *Charleston Courier* (June 15, 1858).

21 *Macon Weekly Telegraph* (February 25, 1860).

22 "Rev. Mr. Spurgeon," *The North Carolinian* (February 18, 1860).

23 "Rev. Mr. Spurgeon," *The Weekly Raleigh Register* (February 15, 1860).

24 Spurgeon was ten years old when tensions over slavery resulted in Baptists from the Southern state conventions gathering in Augusta, Georgia, to form the Southern Baptist Convention in 1845 (see A. H. Newman, *A History of the Baptist Churches in the United States* [New York: The Christian Literature Co., 1894], 443–47). On June 20–22, 1995, the SBC adopted a resolution in Atlanta, Georgia, acknowledging that "our relationship to African-Americans has been hindered from the beginning by the role that slavery played in the formation of the Southern Baptist Convention," and "Many of our Southern Baptist forbears defended the right to own slaves, and either participated in, supported, or acquiesced in the particularly inhumane nature of American slavery." It also stated that they "unwaveringly denounce racism, in all its forms, as deplorable sin" ("Resolution on Racial Reconciliation on the 150th Anniversary of the Southern Baptist Convention," 1995; accessed May 18, 2016, www.sbc.net/resolutions/899/resolution-on-racial-reconciliation-on-the-150th-anniversary-of-the-southern-baptist-convention).

25 *The Weekly Mississippian* (March 14, 1860).

26 "Spurgeon Repudiated," *Newbern Weekly Progress* (March 20, 1860). See also "Spurgeon Rejected in Virginia," *Cincinnati Daily Press* (March 28, 1860).

27 "Prof. J. M. Pendleton of Union University, Tenn., and the Slavery Question," *The Mississippian* (April 4, 1860).

EDITOR'S PREFACE

other denominational newspapers took the "spoiled child to task and administered due castigation."[28]

In the midst of this mayhem, Spurgeon attempted to publish several notebooks of sermons from his earliest ministry. His promise to his readers in 1857 would not be fulfilled, however, due to difficult life circumstances in London. How poetic, then, that 157 years after *The Nashville Patriot* slandered Spurgeon for his "meddlesome spirit,"[29] a publishing house from Nashville would complete the task he failed to accomplish. How symmetrical that Spurgeon's early sermons would be published not by Passmore & Alabaster in London but by Americans. And not only Americans, but *Southern* Americans. And not only Southern Americans, but Southern *Baptist* Americans with all the baggage of their bespeckled beginnings.

As a Southern Baptist from Alabama, allow me to confess my own bias. I have spent the majority of my vocational life studying Spurgeon. I have found in him (and share with him) a genuine commitment to making Jesus Christ known to the nations. Like him, I too am deeply invested in the church and claim the same evangelical impulses that fueled Spurgeon's ministry. I admire his stance for social justice, love for the marginalized, and commitment to biblical orthodoxy.

Spurgeon's language is not always theologically precise. At times his colorful, allegorical, and experimental rhetoric make academic treatments challenging. However, Spurgeon was not a theologian in the systematic sense and never claimed to be. He was a preacher. And as such his ultimate concern was not crafting perfect manuscripts—though he spent a great deal of time redacting his sermons for publication. His greatest concern was, as his famous title hinted, becoming a *Soul Winner*. With pen and pulpit, Spurgeon indentured his literary and intellectual abilities to service of the church. His uncanny gift for rendering complex ideas in the working class vernacular distinguished him from many of his contemporaries and gave him instant audiences.

Spurgeon's preaching emerged not in the ivory towers of Cambridge but in the lowly villages surrounding it. He was more concerned with feeding sheep than giraffes.[30] Spurgeon started his ministry as a country, not city, preacher. His

---

28 "Mr. Spurgeon," *The Edgefield Advertiser* (February 22, 1860).
29 "Spurgeon's Sermons—a Bonfire," *Daily Nashville Patriot* (March 15, 1860).
30 "We must preach according to the capacity of our hearers. The Lord Jesus did not say, 'Feed my giraffes,' but 'Feed my sheep.' We must not put the fodder on a high rack by our fine language, but use great plainness of speech" (C.H. Spurgeon, *The Salt-Cellars: Being a Collection of Proverbs, Together with Homely Notes Thereon* [New York: A. C. Armstrong and Son, 1889], 56); "Some brethren put the food up so high that the poor sheep cannot possibly feed upon it. I have thought, as I have listened to our eloquent friends, that they imagined that our Lord had said, 'Feed my camelopards.' None but giraffes could reach the food when placed in so lofty a rack. Christ says, 'Feed my sheep,' place the food among them, put it close to them" (*MTP* 56: 406).

congregants at Waterbeach Chapel were farmers and laborers. Even after moving to London, Spurgeon retained his early earthy idioms and used illustrations common to the Victorian experience.

His preaching flourished in cholera-ravaged Southwark near London's warehouses, distilleries, and factories. This gave Spurgeon a finger on the pulse of the population that, when combined with his own physical and mental ailments, produced a level of empathy uncommon to his contemporaries. Spurgeon "never suffered from having never suffered."[31]

At the height of my illness in 2013, Spurgeon's earliest sermons had a profound effect on me. During a series of surgeries, my eyes chanced upon a phrase in Notebook 1: "Think much on grace, Christian."[32] Over the twelve months of my recovery, these words brought such encouragement that I doubt they shall ever be forgotten.

Whenever new discoveries are made—whether lost diaries, letters, hymns, poems, or sermons—there is an opportunity to further our knowledge of a particular subject or person. In 2011, only a handful of doctoral students in the world were writing on Spurgeon. Today roughly two dozen are entering the field. Much work is yet to be done. Caverns of untapped resources await exploration. My hope is that the publication of Spurgeon's lost sermons will inspire future generations of scholars to mine the theological treasures still untapped.

I am also hopeful that this project will promote a reinvigorated sense of unity, mission, and Christian witness throughout evangelicalism. The recent surge of interest in Spurgeon could and should be leveraged for the kingdom. Spurgeon can become an agent of healing. Everyone can, and does, claim him, regardless of theological stripe, tribe, or camp. Spurgeon's appeal extends not only across denominational barriers, but also into the broader evangelical tradition. With the upcoming accessibility of Spurgeon's sermons on the revamped website www.spurgeon.org and also with the advances in scholarship at The Spurgeon Library of Midwestern Baptist Theological Seminary, younger and older generations face exciting new opportunities to stand together as witnesses to the world in celebration of what God has accomplished in history. Who knows? Perhaps it was for this reason that the sermons were lost in the nineteenth century and found in the twenty-first.

In 1860, an article entitled "Mr. Spurgeon and the American Slaveholders" offered the following words: "Southern Baptists will not, hereafter, when they

---

31 Christian George, "Raising Spurgeon from the Dead," Desiring God, December 5, 2015; accessed May 18, 2016. http://www.desiringgod.com/articles/raising-spurgeon-from-the-dead.
32 See "God's Grace Given to Us" (Sermon 14).

visit London, desire to commune with this prodigy of the nineteenth century. We venture the prophecy that his books in [the] future will not crowd the shelves of our Southern book merchants. They will not; they should not."[33] In 1889, Spurgeon uttered a prophecy of his own: "For my part, I am quite willing to be eaten of dogs for the next fifty years; but the more distant future shall vindicate me."[34]

The more distant future *did* vindicate Spurgeon. His sermons *do* crowd the shelves of Southern bookstores. As Carl F. H. Henry rightly noted, Spurgeon has become "one of evangelical Christianity's immortals."[35] Throughout Alabama, Virginia, and the United States of America, the books of "the notorious English abolitionist" still burn—casting light and life in a dark and dying world.

After the Emancipation Proclamation of 1863, Spurgeon's reputation improved among Southern Baptists. Many of their churches were named after Spurgeon's Metropolitan Tabernacle, like Mark Dever's Capitol Hill Baptist Church in Washington, DC, which originally was called "Metropolitan Baptist Church."[36] Southern Baptists like John A. Broadus, founder of The Southern Baptist Seminary in Louisville, Kentucky, flocked to Elephant & Castle to hear Spurgeon preach. After his 1891 visit, Broadus said, "The whole thing—house, congregation, order, worship, preaching, was as nearly up to my ideal as I ever expect to see in this life."[37] In June 1884, the faculty of that seminary penned a collective letter of commendation to Spurgeon:

> We thank God for all that he made you and has by his grace enabled you to become and achieve. We rejoice in your great and wonderful work as preacher and pastor, and through your Orphanage and your Pastor's [sic] College; as also your numerous writings, so sparkling with genius, so filled with the spirit of the gospel.... And now, honored brother, we invoke upon you the continued blessings of our covenant God. May your life and health be long spared, if it be his will; may Providence still smile on your varied work, and the Holy Spirit richly bless your spoken and written messages to mankind.[38]

---

33 *The Christian Index*, repr. in "Mr. Spurgeon and the American Slaveholders," *The South Australian Advertiser* (June 23, 1860).
34 "The Preacher's Power, and the Conditions of Obtaining It" (*ST*, August 1889), 420.
35 Carl. F. H. Henry, quoted in Lewis Drummond, *Spurgeon: Prince of Preachers* (3rd ed.; Grand Rapids, MI: Kregel, 1992), 11.
36 See Timothy George, "Puritans on the Potomac," *First Things*, May 2, 2016; accessed May 18, 2016.
37 A. T. Robertson, *Life and Letters of John Albert Broadus* (Philadelphia: American Baptist Publication Society, 1910), 243.
38 Ibid., 342.

EDITOR'S PREFACE

In 1892, B. H. Carroll, founder of Southwestern Baptist Theological Seminary in Fort Worth, Texas, reflected on Spurgeon's enduring legacy: "The fire has tried his work. It abides unconsumed." He added, "When Bonaparte died, Phillips said: 'He is fallen.' When Spurgeon died, the world said: 'He is risen.'"[39] The notable theologian Augustus Hopkins Strong had such admiration for Spurgeon that, on June 17, 1887, he brought John D. Rockefeller to London to meet him. After two hours of fellowship, the two Americans concluded that "the secret of Mr. Spurgeon's success was his piety and his faith. Above all else, he seemed to be a man of prayer."[40]

In 1934, George W. Truett, pastor of First Baptist Church, Dallas, Texas, was the only speaker invited to deliver a fifty-five minute address at the Royal Albert Hall in London for the Centenary of Spurgeon's birth.[41] Truett's successor at First Baptist Dallas, W. A. Criswell, once claimed that Spurgeon was "the greatest preacher who has ever lived." He added, "When I get to Heaven, after I see the Saviour and my own dear family, I want to see Charles Haddon Spurgeon."[42] Billy Graham once applauded Spurgeon for being "a preacher who extolled Christ—everlastingly."[43]

Charles Spurgeon *has* come to America. Through the rotations of a thousand gears of grace, his early sermons have spanned a century and a sea to be read by new audiences. Like Abel, who "still speaks, even though he is dead" (Heb 11:4 NIV), Spurgeon still has something to say. "I would fling my shadow through eternal ages if I could,"[44] he once declared. And indeed, his shadow has spilled into our age. Few preachers are as frequently cited, "memed," tweeted, and quoted (or misquoted) as Spurgeon is. Future historians will be right to see the publication of his *Lost Sermons* as belonging to an extraordinary and unexpected narrative of redemption.

The publication of these sermons will reach full potential when they guide readers not just *to* Spurgeon but *through* Spurgeon to Jesus Christ. Insomuch as John the Baptist's words become our own, "[Christ] must increase, but I must decrease" (John 3:30 ESV), and insomuch as the sermons inform minds, reform hearts, and

---

39 These two quotations come from B. H. Carroll's 1892 address "The Death of Spurgeon" (J. B. Cranfill, comp., *Sermons and Life Sketch of B. H. Carroll* [Philadelphia: American Baptist Publication Society, 1895], 25, 44).

40 Crerar Douglas, ed., *Autobiography of Augustus Hopkins Strong* (Valley Forge, PA: Judson Press, 1981), 300. See also *ST*, July 1887: 369.

41 See Keith E. Durso, *Thy Will Be Done: A Biography of George W. Truett* (Macon, GA: Mercer University Press, 2009), 214. Truett had also delivered an address entitled "Spurgeon: Herald of the Everlasting Evangel" at the Marble Collegiate Church in New York City on May 8, 1934 (see "Centenary Program in Honor and Recognition of Charles Haddon Spurgeon" in The Spurgeon Library archives).

42 W. A. Criswell, quoted in *NPSP*, 1:book jacket.

43 Billy Graham, quoted in *NPSP*, 3:book jacket.

44 W. A. Fullerton, *C. H. Spurgeon: A Biography* (London: Williams and Norgate, 1920), 181.

EDITOR'S PREFACE

transform lives, then the energy will be worth the expenditure, and future generations will glimpse not only Spurgeon's shadow but the *Son* that caused the shadow.[45]

B. H. Carroll once said, "The great crying want of this day in our churches is *fire*."[46] If we can share Carroll's desire for fire, then Helmut Thielicke's words will still ring true of Spurgeon: "This bush from old London still burns and shows no signs of being consumed."[47]

Christian T. George
Assistant Professor of Historical Theology
Curator of The Spurgeon Library
Midwestern Baptist Theological Seminary
Kansas City, Missouri

---

45 I have used some of the verbiage in this paragraph and in the preceding one on numerous occasions in interviews, blogs, social media, and in my interview for Stephen McCaskell's documentary on Spurgeon, *Through the Eyes of Spurgeon*; accessed May 18, 2016, www.throughtheeyesofspurgeon.com. However, I originally wrote this material for the contextual introduction of the timeline "The Man and His Times: Charles Haddon Spurgeon" that hangs on the wall in the entrance of The Spurgeon Library at Midwestern Baptist Theological Seminary in Kansas City, Missouri.

46 Cranfill, *Sermons and Life Sketch of B. H. Carroll*, 42, emphasis added.

47 Helmut Thielicke, *Encounter with Spurgeon* (trans. John W. Doberstein; Stuttgart, Germany: Quell-Verlag, 1961), 4.

ACKNOWLEDGMENTS

Over the past eight years, I have become indebted to numerous individuals who have lent time and talent to the formation and publication of this project:

David Bebbington took an interest in this project from the beginning, and I am grateful for the encouraging way he has shepherded these sermons. Steve Holmes, my doctoral supervisor at the University of St. Andrews, has also provided timely advice and guidance over the years. Tom Wright, Ian Randall, Mark Elliot, and Ian Bradley were instrumental in sharpening my writing and honing my thoughts on Spurgeon's Christology. Timothy Larsen, Brian Stanley, Mark Hopkins, Michael Haykin, and Tom Nettles widened my understanding of nineteenth-century evangelicalism in ways that directly benefited this present volume.

J. I. Packer, Chuck Colson (1931–2012), and Mark Dever have offered broad direction to my research. I am indebted to their mentorship, support, and investment in my life. To those at St. Andrews who witnessed the embryonic stage of this research, I also remain grateful: Liam Garvey, pastor at St. Andrew's Baptist Church at the time; my doctoral colleagues at the Roundel; the students I tutored at St. Mary's College; and also Lawrence Foster (1991–2010), whose winsome conversations about Spurgeon on the Eden Golf Course made my frequent excavations of its bunkers always worth the dig.

When Nigel Wright and Andy Brockbank at Spurgeon's College first contracted with me in 2010 to publish Spurgeon's sermons, I could not have envisioned the scope of this project. Nigel's timely emails over the years are among my most cherished correspondences. Peter Morden, former acting principal of Spurgeon's College, is a Spurgeon scholar of the highest caliber whose friendship I value. I am also indebted to the librarian of the College for many years, Judy Powles, who aided my research in the Heritage Room Archives and, along with Mary Fugill, made arrangements for prolonged research visits.

Roger Standing, Helen Stokley, Annabel Haycraft, the board of governors, and all those who have served in the administration of Spurgeon's College have also

ACKNOWLEDGMENTS

garnished my gratitude. Their continued partnership with B&H Academic and The Spurgeon Library is accomplishing much in keeping Spurgeon's legacy alive for rising generations of scholars, pastors, and students. London-based photographer Chris Gander also deserves special acknowledgment for his indefatigable resolve in photographing every single page of Spurgeon's notebooks.

After I moved from St. Andrews to teach at Oklahoma Baptist University, the project benefited from the leadership of President David Whitlock, Provost Stan Norman, and Dean Mark McClellan. My colleagues in the Herschel H. Hobbs College of Theology and Ministry and in other departments offered helpful feedback in the initial editing and organization of the sermons. I am also grateful for the research assistants who offered their time in assisting me on the original proposal: Cara Cliburn Allen, Justine Kirby Aliff, Kasey Chapman, Raliegh White, and Christina Perry.

During my last semester in Shawnee, Oklahoma, Jim Baird, vice president of B&H Academic, expressed interest in publishing these sermons. Jim's enthusiasm, commitment to Christian publishing, and courage for undertaking a one-million-word project have not escaped me. He and his capable team in Nashville stand in direct continuity with Spurgeon's original London publisher, Passmore & Alabaster, who would have published these sermons in 1857–1858 if Spurgeon had completed his editing process. Special thanks goes to Chris Thompson, Dave Schroeder, Mike Cooper, Barnabas Piper, Audrey Greeson, Jade Novak, Heidi Smith, Steve Reynolds, India Harkless, Debbie Carter, Judi Hayes, Lesley Patterson-Marx, Jason Jones, Ryan Camp, Mandi Cofer, Jennifer Day, and Jessi Wallace for shaping the project thus far. I am also grateful for Trevin Wax, Chris Martin, and Brandon Smith. I am also deeply thankful for my literary agent, Greg Johnson, a friend and fellow laborer.

A turning point in the project came in 2014 when Jason Allen, president of Midwestern Baptist Theological Seminary, hired me to teach historical theology and serve as curator of The Spurgeon Library. His allocation of resources and excitement for these sermons allowed me to undertake a publication of this scope. I am grateful for his friendship, leadership, initiative, and vision for all that God has in store for this seminary. Connie and Bill Jenkins gave generously for the construction of The Spurgeon Library, and their support has provided a platform on which this project can stand. The opportunity to curate the thousands of volumes Spurgeon owned and often annotated has added innumerable layers of unexpected value to the research. Spurgeon owned some of the books in this collection during the writing of his early sermons.

ACKNOWLEDGMENTS

The faculty, administration, and staff of Midwestern Seminary have been instrumental in creating an environment where scholarship and collegiality excel. I am particularly grateful to Provost Jason Duesing, Deans Thor Madsen and John Mark Yeats, Vice President for Institutional Relations Charles Smith, and all those who work in the Communications Office, seminary library, and bookstore who daily embody the kind providence of God.

I have discovered a lifelong friend in Jared Wilson, director of content strategy and managing editor of "For the Church" (www.ftc.co). Jared is a wordsmith par excellence who won't shut up about grace and whose weekly conversations have sustained me through the editing of these sermons. I am grateful for Jared and the "thinklings" who join our weekly discussions and for all those associated with The Spurgeon Library. I am appreciative of Brian Albert, David Conte, and research assistants Ronni Kurtz, Phillip Ort, Tyler Sykora, Adam Sanders, Devin Schlote, Drake Osborn, Garrett Skrbina, and Savannah Nokes. I am also grateful for the team of Spurgeon Scholars who have worked in some capacity on the project: Allyson Todd, Cody Barnhart, Colton Strother, Austin Burgard, Gabriel Pech, Jordan Wade, Jacob Overstreet, Garet Halbert, and Andrew Marks. I am also thankful for Chad McDonald, my pastor at Lenexa Baptist Church, whose sermons rarely suffer from the absence of a poignant Spurgeon quotation.

During my research in Oxford, Cambridge, and London in November and December 2014, the following librarians offered me their expertise:

Emily Burgoyne, library assistant, The Angus Library and Archive, Regent's Park College, University of Oxford;

Yaye Tang, archives assistant, Cambridgeshire Archives and Local Studies, Shire Hall;

Josh E. Acton, Myles Greensmith, Celia Tyler, and Mary Burgess, local studies assistants with the Cambridgeshire Collection, Central Library;

Anne Taylor, head of the Map Department, and Ian Pittock, assistant librarian, Maps Room, Cambridge University Library;

Stephen Southall, Dorrie Parris, Marion Lemmon, and Anne Craig, Waterbeach Independent Lending Library;

John Matthews, archivist, St. Andrew's Street Baptist Church;

The librarians of Cherry Hinton Public Library, Bottisham Community Library Association, and Suffolk County Council Information and Library Service;

The librarians of Dr. Williams's Library and John Harvey Library, London.

ACKNOWLEDGMENTS

I am thankful for the tremendous hospitality of Osvaldo and Kristen Padilla, and their son Philip, during this season of research in the UK.

I am also grateful for assistance provided by Taylor Rutland, Pam Cole, and Amanda Denton of the New Orleans Baptist Theological Seminary, along with Jeff Griffin, Eric Benoy, and Kyara St. Amant. Numerous individuals also contributed to this project from a distance and deserve acknowledgment: Peter Williams at Tyndale House, Cambridge; Charles Carter, Robert Smith Jr., Gerald Bray, Paul House, Vickie Gaston, and Le-Ann Little at Beeson Divinity School; and David Dockery, Thomas Kidd, Nathan Finn, David Crosby, Fred Luter, and my longtime pilgrim friend, David Riker. I am also grateful for Stephen McCaskell, whose documentary *Through the Eyes of Spurgeon* (www.throughtheeyesofspurgeon.com) remains second to none, and Jeff Landon, who champions Spurgeon through www.missionalwear.com.

This project also found support in those who are historically and even biologically connected with Spurgeon. I am grateful for Darren Newman and Mary McLean, current residents of the Teversham cottage where Spurgeon preached his first sermon; Martin Ensell, pastor of Waterbeach Chapel, and his wife, Angela, for their hospitality; and also Peter Masters, senior pastor of the Metropolitan Tabernacle.

I am humbled to have known Spurgeon's living descendants: David Spurgeon (great-grandson), whom I met shortly before his passing in 2015. His wife, Hilary, and their two children, Susie (along with her husband, Tim, and children, Jonah, Lily, Juliet, and Ezra) and Richard (along with his wife, Karen, and daughter, Hannah), have become family to me.

I would especially like to acknowledge my father, who first inspired me to read Spurgeon on a pilgrimage to England and who continues to model scholarship, preaching, fatherhood, and Christian hospitality at their very best. My mother is one of the best writers I know, and her encouragements along the way have allowed me to better undertake this project. Bayne and Jerry Pounds have been prayer warriors for us from the beginning and would require additional paragraphs to acknowledge all they have done. Hannah and Jerry (and Luke and Caroline) Pounds are family who have become precious friends, and I am also grateful for the friendship of Stephanie and Nic Francis (and Andrew, Ella Grace, and Caleb). I am so thankful for Jane and Jack Hunter and for Dorothy Smith, an editor extraordinaire who worked tirelessly on the sermons during the early stages of editing.

The warmest words of gratitude I reserve for my wife, Rebecca—a writer, editor, and scholar of uncanny ability. Rebecca's companionship has made this road worth walking. When I first encountered the sermons in London, Rebecca was with me.

ACKNOWLEDGMENTS

Since then she has sacrificed greatly in donating hundreds of hours to copyediting, proofreading, researching, brainstorming, and improving every aspect of this project. Were it not for Rebecca's fearless resolve in 2013 during my illness, the *Lost Sermons* would have remained as lost today as when Spurgeon abandoned them in 1857 when his own life circumstances gridlocked the publication. To Rebecca I give full credit, not only for saving the life of this project, but also for saving the life of its editor.

When the first copy of his seven-volume commentary on the Psalms, *The Treasury of David*, was bound, Spurgeon "looked at it as fondly as he might have done at a favourite child."[1] The release of this present volume has solicited a similar sentiment in us and in many who have played roles in the stewardship of these sermons. To them, and to all those yet to join our journey, I remain a grateful bondservant.

---

1 Eric Hayden, introduction to *The Treasury of David*, by C. H. Spurgeon (London: Passmore & Alabaster ed.; Pasadena, TX: Pilgrim Publications, 1983), 1:iii.

ABBREVIATIONS

Autobiography   *C. H. Spurgeon's Autobiography. Compiled from His Diary, Letters, and Records, by His Wife, and His Private Secretary.* 4 vols. London: Passmore & Alabaster, 1899–1900. The Spurgeon Library.

Lectures   *Lectures to My Students: A Selection from Addresses Delivered to the Students of the Pastors' College, Metropolitan Tabernacle.* London: Passmore & Alabaster, 1893. The Spurgeon Library.

MTP   *The Metropolitan Tabernacle Pulpit: Sermons Preached and Revised by C. H. Spurgeon.* Vols. 7–63. Pasadena, TX: Pilgrim Publications, 1970–2006.

Notebook   *Spurgeon Sermon Outline Notebooks.* 11 vols. Heritage Room, Spurgeon's College, London. K1/5, U1.02.

NPSP   *The New Park Street Pulpit: Containing Sermons Preached and Revised by the Rev. C. H. Spurgeon, Minister of the Chapel.* 6 vols. Pasadena, TX: Pilgrim Publications, 1970–2006.

ST   *The Sword and the Trowel; A Record of Combat with Sin & Labour for the Lord.* 37 vols. London: Passmore & Alabaster, 1865–1902. The Spurgeon Library.

TD   *The Treasury of David: Containing an Original Exposition of the Book of Psalms; A Collection of Illustrative Extracts from the Whole Range of Literature; A Series of Homiletical Hints Upon Almost Every Verse; And Lists of Writers Upon Each Psalm.* 7 Vols. London: Passmore & Alabaster, 1869–1885. The Spurgeon Library.

INTRODUCTION

"GRACIOUS GOD, HELP ME WRITE
AND PREACH THESE SERMONS
JUST AS IF IT WERE MY LAST;
IF INDEED IT NOT BE."
Charles Spurgeon

(Notebook 2, Sermon 134, 1852)

In 1851, Charles Spurgeon transitioned from preaching itinerantly in the villages surrounding Cambridge to accepting the full-time pastorate of a chapel in Waterbeach. In a letter to his father on October 16 of that year, he wrote, "Last Sunday I went to a place called Waterbeach where there is an old established place, but not able to support a minister. I have engaged to supply to the end of the month."[1]

Charles remained pastor in Waterbeach until April 28, 1854. Every Sunday he walked "five or six honest miles"[2] to the village unless relieved by the passing of "a certain little pony and cart."[3] His congregation supplemented his annual salary, a meager forty-five pounds,[4] by hosting him on Sundays and providing for his material needs. "They do all they can," Charles wrote in a letter to his mother.[5] "I do not think there was a pig killed by any one of the congregation without my having some portion of it."[6]

Dating Notebook 2 is unproblematic given Charles's inscription on the inside back cover: "In health, contentment, and peace. June 19/52. Only feeling the thorns of sin and sin's effects."[7]

Yet Charles did not preach exclusively at Waterbeach Chapel in 1852. At the conclusion of his sermon "The Corner Stone" (Sermon 128), he recorded he had

---

1 Letter to his father (Angus Library and Archive, Regent's Park College, Oxford University, D/SPU 1, Letter 10). In her husband's autobiography, Susannah incorrectly dated this letter "October 15th" (*Autobiography* 1:228). Almost two weeks before Charles wrote this letter to his father, he preached for the first time in Waterbeach. See "Salvation from Sin" (Notebook 1, Sermon 33) preached on October 3, 1851.
2 *Autobiography* 1:316.
3 Ibid.
4 Ibid., 1:255.
5 Ibid., 1:249.
6 Ibid., 1:253.
7 A corresponding inscription is found on the front inside cover: "Finis. June 19. My 18th birthday." See Susannah's transcription of Charles's inscription (*Autobiography* 1:222).

preached in Cottenham,[8] Hythe, and Teversham—possibly in some of the same chapels he had visited while participating in the Lay Preachers' Association connected with St. Andrew's Street Baptist Church.[9]

Three years after Notebook 2, Charles's first biographer, E. L. Magoon, claimed the young preacher preached almost one dozen times each week: "On the week-dates, eleven villages shared the advantage of his sermons, which, in one year, amounted to as many as there are days in the year."[10] Charles's reputation as the "boy preacher of the fens"[11] soon spread throughout Cambridgeshire.

Yet the trajectory of his ministry was challenged by a pivotal decision: should Charles remain as the pastor of Waterbeach Chapel or instead enroll as a student in London's Stepney College? John Spurgeon "strongly advised"[12] both his sons to matriculate. In February 1852, a meeting was arranged between Charles and Joseph Angus, the tutor of the College. Charles recounted:

> I entered the house exactly at the time appointed, and was shown into a room where I waited patiently a couple of hours, feeling too much impressed with my own insignificance, and the greatness of the tutor from London, to venture to ring the bell, and make enquiries as to the unreasonably long delay. At last, patience having had her perfect work, and my school-engagements requiring me to attend to my duties as an usher, the bell was set in motion, and on the arrival of the servant, the waiting young man was informed that the Doctor had tarried in another room until he could stay no longer, and had gone off to London by train. The stupid girl had given no information to the family that anyone had called, and had been shown into the drawing-room; and, consequently, the meeting never came about, although designed by both parties.[13]

After departing from the mistimed appointment, Charles walked through Midsummer Common and "was startled by what seemed a loud voice, but which

---

8 According to Charles's inscription at the conclusion of "The Corner Stone" (Sermon 128), "three joined the Church at Cottenham."
9 *Autobiography* 1:200.
10 E. L. Magoon, ed., *'The Modern Whitfield': Sermons of the Rev. C. H. Spurgeon, of London, with an Introduction and Sketch of His Life* (New York: Sheldon, Blakeman, & Co., 1856), vi.
11 *Autobiography* 1:199.
12 Ibid. 1:241.
13 Ibid.

may have been a singular illusion. . . . 'Seekest thou great things for thyself? seek them not! [Jer 45:5].'"[14] This experience solidified Charles's decision not to pursue formal education, and unlike his brother James Archer, he did not move to London for a degree.

Charles wrote in a letter to his father, "I think then (with all deference to you) that I had better not go to college yet, at least not just now."[15] In November, Charles wrote to his mother: "I am more and more glad that I never went to College. God sends such sunshine on my path, such smiles of grace, that I cannot regret if I have forfeited all my prospects for it. . . . I had *rather be poor in His service than rich in my own.*"[16]

"You know what my style is," Charles further wrote. "I fancy it is not very college like."[17] The sermons contained in Notebook 2 reflect the accuracy of Charles's sentiment. With emotive and earnest rhetoric, he confronted the sins of his congregation:

> Fighter, God says, turn thy boxing gloves out.
> Swearer, wash thy foul mouth with blood divine.
> Unclean Fornicator, turn thy lust out.
> Sabbath Breaker, how wilt thou restore thy lost Sabbaths?
> Drunkard, turn thy glass bottom upwards.[18]

In his sermon on Luke 19:41, "The Redeemer's Tears over Sinners" (Sermon 121), Charles pleaded for Jesus to "stand up and weep over Waterbeach." He concluded by saying:

> Weep, oh preacher! Weep. Weep. Weep. Men, women! Now let Jesus stand up and weep over you, one by one:
>
> 1. Over the open reprobate, despisers, drunkards.
> 2. Over the unconverted, many-year hearer.
> 3. Over the hopeful young who yet will go aside.

---

14 Ibid., 1:242.
15 Letter to his father (Angus Library and Archive, Regent's Park College, Oxford University, D/SPU 1, Letter 12), underscore in the original.
16 *Autobiography* 1:248, italics in the original.
17 Letter to his father (Angus Library and Archive, Regent's Park College, Oxford University, D/SPU 1, Letter 12).
18 These quotes are found at the end of Charles's sermon "Set Thine House in Order" (Sermon 134). See also "Wise Men and Fools" (Sermon 111).

4. Over convinced sinners, wiping their tears away.
5. Over many feast-goers who go despite warnings.
6. Over old men on the brink of hell.
7. Over hypocrites, deceiving their own souls.
8. Over those who are given up and let alone.
9. Over careless, laughing, critical, etc., hearers.

"Dagon stands fast here," Charles said in his sermon "By Faith Jericho Fell" (Sermon 133). "But the ark is come." Charles's great question, "Would God save any souls through me?"[19] was sure to find immediate answers. His chapel "was not only full, but crowded with outside listeners at the open windows."[20] He wrote, "Providence has thrown me into a great sphere of usefulness, a congregation of often 450, a loving and praying church, and an awakened audience."[21]

Charles later reflected on the spiritual transformation that occurred under his ministry at Waterbeach:

> In a short time, the little thatched chapel was crammed, the biggest vagabonds of the village were weeping floods of tears, and those who had been the curse of the parish became its blessing. Where there had been robberies and villainies of every kind, all round the neighbourhood, there were none, because the men who used to do the mischief were themselves in the house of God, rejoicing to hear of Jesus crucified. I am not telling an exaggerated story, nor a thing that I do not know, for it was my delight to labour for the Lord in that village. It was a pleasant thing to walk through that place, when drunkenness had almost ceased, when debauchery in the case of many was dead, when men and women went forth to labour with joyful hearts,

---

[19] *Autobiography* 1:232.
[20] Ibid., 1:251.
[21] Letter to his father (Angus Library and Archive, Regent's Park College, Oxford University, D/SPU 1, Letter 12).

INTRODUCTION

singing the praises of the ever-living God; and when, at sunset, the humble cottager called his children together, read them some portion from the Book of Truth, and then together they bent their knees in prayer to God. I can say, with joy and happiness, that almost from one end of the village to the other, at the hour of eventide, one might have heard the voice of song coming from nearly every roof-tree, and echoing from almost every heart. I do testify, to the praise of God's grace, that it pleased the Lord to work wonders in our midst.[22]

In the fifty-seven sermons contained in Notebook 2, Charles incorporated a variety of literary habits: abbreviations,[23] dittography,[24] lines and stippling,[25] strike-throughs,[26]

---

22 *Autobiography* 1:228.

23 Examples of abbreviations are found in the following sermons: "The Sword of the Spirit" (Sermon 79); "Final Perseverance Certain" (Sermon 82); "Jesus and His Acts" (Sermon 84); "The Rending of the Veil" (Sermon 96); "The Invitation of Moses to Hobab" (Sermon 98); "Jesus's Dead Body Whilst on the Cross" (Sermon 107); "Justification by Imputed Righteousness" (Sermon 117); and "Come Ye Out from Among Them" (Sermon 119).

24 Examples of dittography are found in the following sermons: "The Dog and Swine" (Sermon 85); "Prove Me Now Herewith" (Sermon 109); and "The Downfall of Dagon" (Sermon 124).

25 Examples of lines and stippling are found in the following sermons: "Thou Art Too Light" (Sermon 90); "The Rending of the Veil" (Sermon 96); "Oh that Men Would Praise the Lord" (Sermon 105); "Religion, the Foundation of Confidence" (Sermon 106); "The Day of God" (Sermon 115); "Come Ye Out from Among Them" (Sermon 119); "The Watchman, His Work, Warning, and Promise" (Sermon 120); "The Redeemer's Tears over Sinners" (Sermon 121); "Christ's Constant Intercession" (Sermon 126); "The Most Excellent Rock" (Sermon 127); "The Corner Stone" (Sermon 128); "The Church Needs the Spirit" (Sermon 131); and "Set Thine House in Order" (Sermon 134).

26 Examples of strike-throughs are found in the following sermons: "The Lord Is a King" (Sermon 86); "The Grace Received" (Sermon 88); "The Harvest of Souls" (Sermon 89); "Inventory and Title of Our Treasures" (Sermon 92); "God the Father of Lights" (Sermon 95); "The Rending of the Veil" (Sermon 96); "The Invitation of Moses to Hobab" (Sermon 98); "The Beloved of the Lord in Safety" (Sermon 100); "Justification, Conversion, Sanctification, Glory" (Sermon 102); "The Effect and Design of the Law" (Sermon 103); "Religion, the Foundation of Confidence" (Sermon 106); "Jesus's Dead Body Whilst on the Cross" (Sermon 107); "Wise Men and Fools" (Sermon 111); "God's Visits and the Effects Thereof" (Sermon 113); "The Noble Bereans" (Sermon 114); "The Day of God" (Sermon 115); "David in the Cave of Adullam" (Sermon 116); "Justification by Imputed Righteousness" (Sermon 117); "The Prodigal's Resolution" (Sermon 118); "Come Ye Out from Among Them" (Sermon 119); "The Redeemer's Tears over Sinners" (Sermon 121); "Satan and His Devices" (Sermon 122); "The Downfall of Dagon" (Sermon 124); "The Corner Stone" (Sermon 128); "The Church Needs the Spirit" (Sermon 131); "Christ's Sheep" (Sermon 132); and "By Faith Jericho Fell" (Sermon 133).

superscripted text,[27] underscores,[28] marginal inscriptions,[29] inconsistent numbering techniques,[30] and extraneous notations.[31] He tended to refrain from crossing the letter

27 Examples of superscripted texts are found in the following sermons: "Take Heed How Ye Hear" (Sermon 81); "Jesus and His Acts" (Sermon 84); "The Lord Is a King" (Sermon 86); "Inventory and Title of Our Treasures" (Sermon 92); "The Rending of the Veil" (Sermon 96); "The Tranquillity, Security, and Supplies Afforded to the Gospel Church" (Sermon 97); "The Invitation of Moses to Hobab" (Sermon 98); "Justification, Conversion, Sanctification, Glory" (Sermon 102); "The Effect and Design of the Law" (Sermon 103); "Oh that Men Would Praise the Lord" (Sermon 105); "Man's Weakness and God's Strength" (Sermon 108); "Envy Forbidden, Piety Commanded" (Sermon 112); "David in the Cave of Adullam" (Sermon 116); "Justification by Imputed Righteousness" (Sermon 117); "Come Ye Out from Among Them" (Sermon 119); "The Watchman, His Work, Warning, and Promise" (Sermon 120); "Satan and His Devices" (Sermon 122); "The Downfall of Dagon" (Sermon 124); "The Most Excellent Rock" (Sermon 127); and "The Corner Stone" (Sermon 128).

28 Examples of underscores are found in the following sermons: "Jesus and His Acts" (Sermon 84); "The Spirit Crying 'Abba Father'" (Sermon 91); "Inventory and Title of Our Treasures" (Sermon 92); "Present Your Bodies, Etc." (Sermon 93); "The Lost Saved" (Sermon 94); "God the Father of Lights" (Sermon 95); "The Tranquillity, Security, and Supplies Afforded to the Gospel Church" (Sermon 97); "The Curse and the Blessing" (Sermon 99); "The Second Psalm" (Sermon 101); "Justification, Conversion, Sanctification, Glory" (Sermon 102); "The Effect and Design of the Law" (Sermon 103); "Oh that Men Would Praise the Lord" (Sermon 105); "Religion, the Foundation of Confidence" (Sermon 106); "Man's Weakness and God's Strength" (Sermon 108); "Prove Me Now Herewith" (Sermon 109); "The Minister's Commission" (Sermon 110); "God's Visits and the Effects Thereof" (Sermon 113); "The Noble Bereans" (Sermon 114); "The Day of God" (Sermon 115); "David in the Cave of Adullam" (Sermon 116); "The Prodigal's Resolution" (Sermon 118); "Come Ye Out from Among Them" (Sermon 119); "The Watchman, His Work, Warning, and Promise" (Sermon 120); "The Redeemer's Tears over Sinners" (Sermon 121); "The Downfall of Dagon" (Sermon 124); "The Best Feast" (Sermon 125); "Christ's Constant Intercession" (Sermon 126); "The Most Excellent Rock" (Sermon 127); "The Corner Stone" (Sermon 128); "Christ's Sheep" (Sermon 132); "By Faith Jericho Fell" (Sermon 133); and "Set Thine House in Order" (Sermon 134).

29 Examples of marginal inscriptions are found in the following sermons: "Self-Deception" (Sermon 78); "The Sword of the Spirit" (Sermon 79); "Treasure in Earthen Vessels" (Sermon 80); "Final Perseverance Certain" (Sermon 82); "The Dog and Swine" (Sermon 85); "The Lord Is a King" (Sermon 86); "The Grace Received" (Sermon 88); "The Harvest of Souls" (Sermon 89); "The Spirit Crying 'Abba Father'" (Sermon 91); "Inventory and Title of Our Treasures" (Sermon 92); "Present Your Bodies, Etc." (Sermon 93); "The Lost Saved" (Sermon 94); "God the Father of Lights" (Sermon 95); "The Rending of the Veil" (Sermon 96); "The Invitation of Moses to Hobab" (Sermon 98); "The Curse and the Blessing" (Sermon 99); "The Beloved of the Lord in Safety" (Sermon 100); "The Second Psalm" (Sermon 101); "Justification, Conversion, Sanctification, Glory" (Sermon 102); "The Effect and Design of the Law" (Sermon 103); "The Children Cast Out" (Sermon 104); "Oh that Men Would Praise the Lord" (Sermon 105); "Religion, the Foundation of Confidence" (Sermon 106); "Jesus's Dead Body Whilst on the Cross" (Sermon 107); "Man's Weakness and God's Strength" (Sermon 108); "Prove Me Now Herewith" (Sermon 109); "The Minister's Commission" (Sermon 110); "Wise Men and Fools" (Sermon 111); "Envy Forbidden, Piety Commanded" (Sermon 112); "God's Visits and the Effects Thereof" (Sermon 113); "The Noble Bereans" (Sermon 114); "The Day of God" (Sermon 115); "David in the Cave of Adullam" (Sermon 116); "Justification by Imputed Righteousness" (Sermon 117); "The Prodigal's Resolution" (Sermon 118); "Come Ye Out from Among Them" (Sermon 119); "The Watchman, His Work, Warning, and Promise" (Sermon 120); "The Redeemer's Tears over Sinners" (Sermon 121); "Satan and His Devices" (Sermon 122); "Enduring Temptation" (Sermon 123); "The Downfall of Dagon" (Sermon 124); "The Best Feast" (Sermon 125); "Christ's Constant Intercession" (Sermon 126); "The Corner Stone" (Sermon 128); "The Church Needs the Spirit" (Sermon 131); "Christ's Sheep" (Sermon 132); "By Faith Jericho Fell" (Sermon 133); and "Set Thine House in Order" (Sermon 134).

30 Examples of inconsistent numbering techniques are found in the following sermons: "The Dog and Swine" (Sermon 85); "David in the Cave of Adullam" (Sermon 116); and "Satan and His Devices" (Sermon 122).

31 Extraneous notations are found in the following sermons: "Thou Art Too Light" (Sermon 90); "The

INTRODUCTION

"t" and made common use of the Puritan "long s."[32] His sermons in his second notebook contain numerous exclamations,[33] final exhortations,[34] and concluding prayers.[35]

    Charles included extensive and diverse political, economic, cultural, and religious references: Muslims (Mahommetans),[36] Mormons,[37] Roman Catholicism,[38] Anglicanism,[39] Socinianism,[40] Quakers,[41] rationalism,[42] science,[43] morality,[44] philosophy,[45] Gypsies,[46]

    Curse and the Blessing" (Sermon 99); "The Minister's Commission" (Sermon 110); "Christ's Constant Intercession" (Sermon 126); and "The Most Excellent Rock" (Sermon 127).

32 In his sermon "The Prodigal's Resolution" (Sermon 118), Charles wrote: "The prodigal's ~~resol~~ resolution" as if to revise his use of the Puritan "s" in favor of the modern form of the letter.

33 See "The Noble Bereans" (Sermon 114) and "Come Ye Out from Among Them" (Sermon 119).

34 Examples of exhortations are found in the following sermons: "The Sword of the Spirit" (Sermon 79); "Treasure in Earthen Vessels" (Sermon 80); "Take Heed How Ye Hear" (Sermon 81); "Jesus and His Acts" (Sermon 84); "The Dog and Swine" (Sermon 85); "The Thief's Prayer" (Sermon 87); "The Harvest of Souls" (Sermon 89); "The Spirit Crying 'Abba Father'" (Sermon 91); "Inventory and Title of Our Treasures" (Sermon 92); "Present Your Bodies, Etc." (Sermon 93); "The Rending of the Veil" (Sermon 96); "The Tranquillity, Security, and Supplies Afforded to the Gospel Church" (Sermon 97); "The Effect and Design of the Law" (Sermon 103); "Oh that Men Would Praise the Lord" (Sermon 105); "Religion, the Foundation of Confidence" (Sermon 106); "Man's Weakness and God's Strength" (Sermon 108); "Envy Forbidden, Piety Commanded" (Sermon 112); "God's Visits and the Effects Thereof" (Sermon 113); "The Noble Bereans" (Sermon 114); "The Day of God" (Sermon 115); "David in the Cave of Adullam" (Sermon 116); "The Prodigal's Resolution" (Sermon 118); "Come Ye Out from Among Them" (Sermon 119); "The Watchman, His Work, Warning, and Promise" (Sermon 120); "The Redeemer's Tears over Sinners" (Sermon 121); "Satan and His Devices" (Sermon 122); "Enduring Temptation" (Sermon 123); "The Best Feast" (Sermon 125); "Christ's Constant Intercession" (Sermon 126); "The Most Excellent Rock" (Sermon 127); "The Corner Stone" (Sermon 128); "God, the Father of a Family" (Sermon 129); "The Church Needs the Spirit" (Sermon 131); "Christ's Sheep" (Sermon 132); "By Faith Jericho Fell" (Sermon 133); and "Set Thine House in Order" (Sermon 134).

35 Examples of prayers are found in the following sermons: "Treasure in Earthen Vessels" (Sermon 80); "Take Heed How Ye Hear" (Sermon 81); "The Harvest of Souls" (Sermon 89); "Present Your Bodies, Etc." (Sermon 93); "The Curse and the Blessing" (Sermon 99); "The Children Cast Out" (Sermon 104); "Religion, the Foundation of Confidence" (Sermon 106); "Jesus's Dead Body Whilst on the Cross" (Sermon 107); "The Minister's Commission" (Sermon 110); "God's Visits and the Effects Thereof" (Sermon 113); "The Noble Bereans" (Sermon 114); "The Day of God" (Sermon 115); "David in the Cave of Adullam" (Sermon 116); "Justification by Imputed Righteousness" (Sermon 117); "The Prodigal's Resolution" (Sermon 118); "Come Ye Out from Among Them" (Sermon 119); "The Watchman, His Work, Warning, and Promise" (Sermon 120); "The Redeemer's Tears over Sinners" (Sermon 121); "The Best Feast" (Sermon 125); "Christ's Constant Intercession" (Sermon 126); "The Most Excellent Rock" (Sermon 127); "The Corner Stone" (Sermon 128); "Christ's Sheep" (Sermon 132); "By Faith Jericho Fell" (Sermon 133); and "Set Thine House in Order" (Sermon 134).

36 See "Jesus and His Acts" (Sermon 84) and "Justification by Imputed Righteousness" (Sermon 117).

37 See "Jesus and His Acts" (Sermon 84) and "The Minister's Commission" (Sermon 110).

38 See "Self-Deception" (Sermon 78) and "The Second Psalm" (Sermon 101).

39 See "Prove Me Now Herewith" (Sermon 109); "The Second Psalm" (Sermon 101); and "Justification by Imputed Righteousness" (Sermon 117).

40 See "The Corner Stone" (Sermon 128).

41 See "Come Ye Out from Among Them" (Sermon 119).

42 See "Religion, the Foundation of Confidence" (Sermon 106).

43 See "Self-Deception" (Sermon 78).

44 See "Self-Deception" (Sermon 78) and "Thou Art Too Light" (Sermon 90).

45 See "The Noble Bereans" (Sermon 114).

46 See "Justification, Conversion, Sanctification, Glory" (Sermon 102).

heathens,[47] British currency,[48] military,[49] policemen,[50] agriculture,[51] homeopathy,[52] tropical environments,[53] suicide,[54] smoking tobacco,[55] and human anatomy.[56] The breadth of his references may best be explained by a statement in his letter to his father on April 6, 1852: "I have bought a great many books lately, for my constant work requires them."[57]

As in Notebook 1, Charles continued the practice of borrowing outlines and sermons from other preachers, including John Bunyan,[58] Charles Simeon,[59] Thomas Manton,[60] and Jean Claude.[61] His use of John Gill's commentaries is extensive.[62]

However, a puzzling mystery presented itself in the transcribing process of Notebook 2. At the top of six sermons, Charles inscribed a series of references without providing further attribution:

"V.1.91"	"Inventory and Title of Our Treasures" (Sermon 92)
"19V2" and "V.2.19"	"The Tranquillity, Security, and Supplies Afforded to the Gospel Church" (Sermon 97)
"2 Vol. II"	"The Invitation of Moses to Hobab" (Sermon 98)
"V2.42"	"Justification, Conversion, Sanctification, Glory" (Sermon 102)
"V3.52"	"Envy Forbidden, Piety Commanded" (Sermon 112)
"S. 97"	"God's Visits and the Effects Thereof" (Sermon 113)

An investigation into these sources revealed Charles had consulted a published

---

47 See "The Day of God" (Sermon 115) and "Come Ye Out from Among Them" (Sermon 119).
48 See "Inventory and Title of Our Treasures" (Sermon 92).
49 See "The Minister's Commission" (Sermon 110) and "David in the Cave of Adullam" (Sermon 116).
50 See "The Watchman, His Work, Warning, and Promise" (Sermon 120).
51 See "The Effect and Design of the Law" (Sermon 103) and "God's Visits and the Effects Thereof" (Sermon 113).
52 See "The Best Feast" (Sermon 125).
53 See "God's Visits and the Effects Thereof" (Sermon 113).
54 See "The Effect and Design of the Law" (Sermon 103).
55 See "The Noble Bereans" (Sermon 114).
56 See "Jesus's Dead Body Whilst on the Cross" (Sermon 107).
57 Letter to his father (Angus Library and Archive, Regent's Park College, Oxford University, D/SPU 1, Letter 13).
58 See "The Rending of the Veil" (Sermon 96) and "The Redeemer's Tears over Sinners" (Sermon 121).
59 See "The Invitation of Moses to Hobab" (Sermon 98).
60 See "God the Father of Lights" (Sermon 95).
61 See "The Treasure in Earthen Vessels" (Sermon 80).
62 The following sermons evidence the use of John Gill's commentaries: "The Tranquillity, Security, and Supplies Afforded to the Gospel Church" (Sermon 97); "The Beloved of the Lord in Safety" (Sermon 100); "The Second Psalm" (Sermon 101); "The Effect and Design of the Law" (Sermon 103); "Jesus's Dead Body Whilst on the Cross" (Sermon 107); "The Minister's Commission" (Sermon 110); "Envy Forbidden, Piety Commanded" (Sermon 112); "Justification by Imputed Righteousness" (Sermon 117); and "Enduring Temptation" (Sermon 123).

collection of sermons entitled *Sketches of Sermons*.[63] The translation of "V.1.91," for instance, is volume 1, sermon outline 91, and so forth. Four of his sermons in this notebook were taken directly from this publication (Sermons 92, 97, 102, and 112). The remaining two sermons bearing similar inscriptions (Sermons 98 and 113) were taken from Charles Simeon's *Horae Homileticae*.[64] Spurgeon inaccurately numbered these sources. The inscription "2 Vol. 11" should have been "2 Vol. 101" in Sermon 98, and the inscription "V.3.52" should have been "V.3.62." in Sermon 112.

In addition to referencing commentaries and sermon resources, Charles also displayed the unusual practice for him of selecting the entirety of a psalm for the scope of his sermon.[65] Also, for the first time in his early sermons, he deductively listed primary divisions at the beginning of a sermon after his introduction and before the first Roman numeral.[66] He later adopted this sermon structure in full measure. Throughout the pages of this notebook, Charles wrote his words to the edges, wasting little space as he often combined the conclusions of sermons with the beginnings of others.[67]

It is also evident that Charles's mind jumped ahead of his pen. On numerous occasions, he prematurely scribbled letters and words before completing the word he was finishing.[68] Also, unlike the pencil inscriptions in Notebook 1, purple ink

---

63 *Sketches of Sermons: Preached in Various Parts of the United Kingdom and on the European Continent Furnished by Their Respective Authors*, Vols. 1–4 (Philadelphia: Sorin and Ball, 1844). Special thanks to Ronni Kurtz and Phillip Ort for their months of tireless investigation hunting down this source.

64 Charles Simeon, *Horae Homileticae, or Discourses (in the Form of Skeletons) upon the Whole Scriptures*, Vol. 11 (London: printed by Richard Watts, 1819).

65 See "The Second Psalm" (Sermon 101).

66 See "Prove Me Now Herewith" (Sermon 109).

67 For examples of two sermons overlapping on the same page, see "Final Perseverance Certain" (Sermon 82); "The Grace Received" (Sermon 88); "The Harvest of Souls" (Sermon 89); "The Invitation of Moses to Hobab" (Sermon 98); "Jesus's Dead Body Whilst on the Cross" (Sermon 107); "Justification by Imputed Righteousness" (Sermon 117); "Well with the Righteous" (Sermon 130); and "Christ's Sheep" (Sermon 132).

68 For examples of Charles's writing of premature letters and words, see "The Sword of the Spirit" (Sermon 79); "Inventory and Title of Our Treasures" (Sermon 92); "The Second Psalm" (Sermon 101); "Man's Weakness and God's Strength" (Sermon 108); "Prove Me Now Herewith" (Sermon 109); "God's Visits and the Effects Thereof" (Sermon 113); "The Noble Bereans" (Sermon 114); "David in the Cave of Adullam" (Sermon 116); "The Watchman, His Work, Warning, and Promise" (Sermon 120); "Enduring Temptation" (Sermon 123); and "By Faith Jericho Fell" (Sermon 133).

markings suggest Charles began revising Notebook 2 after he moved to London when preparing his early sermons for publication in 1857.[69]

In the transcriptions, Charles's original punctuation has occasionally been adjusted to make the transcription more clear. While all efforts have been made to use Charles's actual King James Bible when quoting from Scripture, we have—on a very limited basis—applied more modernized methods of capitalization and punctuation to allow today's readers to easily recognize where a new sentence begins.

In contrast to the sermons contained in his first notebook, Charles included more autobiographical content in Notebook 2. At the conclusion of "Present Your Bodies, Etc." (Sermon 93), he wrote, "May God help me to do it personally." On his 100th sermon, he recorded the milestone in his ministry with the words "For this 100 I bless the Lord, for the good is his. May they be the seed of many a plant of the Lord."[70] In "Set Thine House in Order" (Sermon 134), he penned the prayer "Gracious God, help me to write and preach this sermon just as if it were my last, if indeed it be not." He also inscribed a personal challenge: "Thou art one year older. Search thy heart and see that you are right. Thou hast a large house entrusted to thee. Do all thou cans't and preach with all thy might, for thou shalt soon die and then thy hour is gone."

Charles may have even been speaking autobiographically in "God's Visits and the Effects Thereof" (Sermon 113) when he said, "Even when a Christian is gone, he leaves his scent behind him. In his life he smells as a cask of the fine old wine of Lebanon, and when poured out he leaves his scent in the cask. Yes, and like the wine of Lebanon if only put in a vessel for a little while it can be seen that it was there once."

A curious foreshadowing of the Surrey Garden Music Hall disaster in London is found in "The Curse and the Blessing" (Sermon 99): "In death. Often in its suddenness, in its darkness and sometimes terror." On October 19, 1856, Charles experienced a moment of terror when he preached from the same text (Prov 3:33, "The curse of the Lord is in the house of the wicked: but he blesseth the habitation of the just"). A balcony collapsed and resulted in a stampede that killed seven people and injured twenty-eight. Charles was "carried by a private garden into the street, and taken home

---

69 For examples of purple markings, see "The Minister's Commission" (Sermon 110); "The Noble Bereans" (Sermon 114); and "The Day of God" (Sermon 115). In 1857, Charles promised his readers: "I shall soon issue a volume of my earliest productions, while Pastor of Waterbeach . . . and would now bespeak for it a favourable reception" (*NPSP* 3:preface). His attempt at publication was unsuccessful.
70 See "The Beloved of the Lord in Safety" (Sermon 100).

more dead than alive."[71] Even the mention of Proverbs 3:33 solicited anxiety throughout Charles's later life.[72]

In the fifty-seven sermons contained in Notebook 2, Charles wrote thirty-two sermons (56 percent) on New Testament texts and twenty-five sermons (44 percent) on Old Testament texts. He preached more sermons from Isaiah and Luke than any other biblical books (six sermons each), followed by Proverbs and John (four sermons each). In total Spurgeon preached from twenty-six of the sixty-six books of the Bible (39 percent).

Of his twenty-five Old Testament sermons, 24 percent were from Isaiah (six sermons); 16 percent from Proverbs (four sermons); 12 percent from Psalms (three sermons); 8 percent (two sermons) each from Deuteronomy, 1 Samuel, and Jeremiah; and 4 percent (one sermon) each from Numbers, Job, Ezekiel, Daniel, Hosea, and Malachi. Spurgeon preached from twelve of the thirty-nine books of the Old Testament (31 percent). Charles did not preach any sermons from twenty-seven books in the Old Testament: Genesis, Exodus, Leviticus, Joshua, Judges, Ruth, 2 Samuel, 1 Kings, 2 Kings, 1 Chronicles, 2 Chronicles, Ezra, Nehemiah, Esther, Ecclesiastes, Song of Solomon, Lamentations, Joel, Amos, Obadiah, Jonah, Micah, Nahum, Habakkuk, Zephaniah, Haggai, or Zechariah (69 percent of the Old Testament books).

Of his thirty-two New Testament sermons, 19 percent were from Luke (six sermons); 13 percent from John (four sermons); 9 percent (three sermons) each from 2 Corinthians and Galatians; 6 percent (two sermons) each from Matthew, Mark, Romans, Hebrews, James, and 2 Peter; and 3 percent (one sermon) each from Acts, 1 Corinthians, Ephesians, and Philippians.[73] Charles did not preach from thirteen of the twenty-seven books of the New Testament: Colossians, 1 Thessalonians, 2 Thessalonians, 1 Timothy, 2 Timothy, Titus, Philemon, 1 Peter, 1 John, 2 John, 3 John, Jude, or Revelation (48 percent of the New Testament books).

A noticeable contrast is found between Charles's first and second notebooks in the expanding word count and page length for each sermon. In Notebook 1, Charles wrote one-page outlines (or "skeletons" as he called them). In this notebook, however, many of the fifty-seven sermons contain full paragraphs, descriptive introductions, and page-length prose.

---

71 *Autobiography* 2:207.
72 See W. Williams, *Personal Reminiscences of Charles Haddon Spurgeon* (2nd ed.; London, The Religious Tract Society, 1895), 46.
73 All percentages have been rounded.

The sermons in Notebook 2 range in word count from 91 words ("Well with the Righteous" [Sermon 130]) to 1,222 words ("Come Ye Out from Among Them" [Sermon 119]).[74] Below are the word counts for the sermons in Notebook 2:

Sermon 78 = 302 words	Sermon 107 = 1,107 words
Sermon 79 = 248 words	Sermon 108 = 766 words
Sermon 80 = 263 words	Sermon 109 = 1,090 words
Sermon 81 = 412 words	Sermon 110 = 719 words
Sermon 82 = 430 words	Sermon 111 = 530 words
Sermon 83 = 176 words	Sermon 112 = 400 words
Sermon 84 = 438 words	Sermon 113 = 814 words
Sermon 85 = 281 words	Sermon 114 = 898 words
Sermon 86 = 464 words	Sermon 115 = 798 words
Sermon 87 = 316 words	Sermon 116 = 1,142 words
Sermon 88 = 199 words	Sermon 117 = 1,189 words
Sermon 89 = 295 words	Sermon 118 = 480 words
Sermon 90 = 371 words	Sermon 119 = 1,222 words
Sermon 91 = 277 words	Sermon 120 = 850 words
Sermon 92 = 929 words	Sermon 121 = 490 words
Sermon 93 = 752 words	Sermon 122 = 493 words
Sermon 94 = 178 words	Sermon 123 = 466 words
Sermon 95 = 404 words	Sermon 124 = 902 words
Sermon 96 = 713 words	Sermon 125 = 658 words
Sermon 97 = 227 words	Sermon 126 = 458 words
Sermon 98 = 362 words	Sermon 127 = 443 words
Sermon 99 = 467 words	Sermon 128 = 386 words
Sermon 100 = 393 words	Sermon 129 = 484 words
Sermon 101 = 861 words	Sermon 130 = 91 words
Sermon 102 = 677 words	Sermon 131 = 237 words
Sermon 103 = 589 words	Sermon 132 = 346 words
Sermon 104 = 1,112 words	Sermon 133 = 666 words
Sermon 105 = 658 words	Sermon 134 = 544 words
Sermon 106 = 955 words	

74 These word counts include Roman numerals and other outlining mechanisms for headings and subheadings, but they do not include sermons titles, Scripture references, Scripture texts, references to villages or dates, or marginal notations written on the sermon page.

INTRODUCTION

    The average word count of the sermons in Notebook 1 was 196 words. However, in Notebook 2, the average word count is 569 words. This general trend suggests that until he moved to London, the longer Charles preached, the more words he wrote for each sermon.

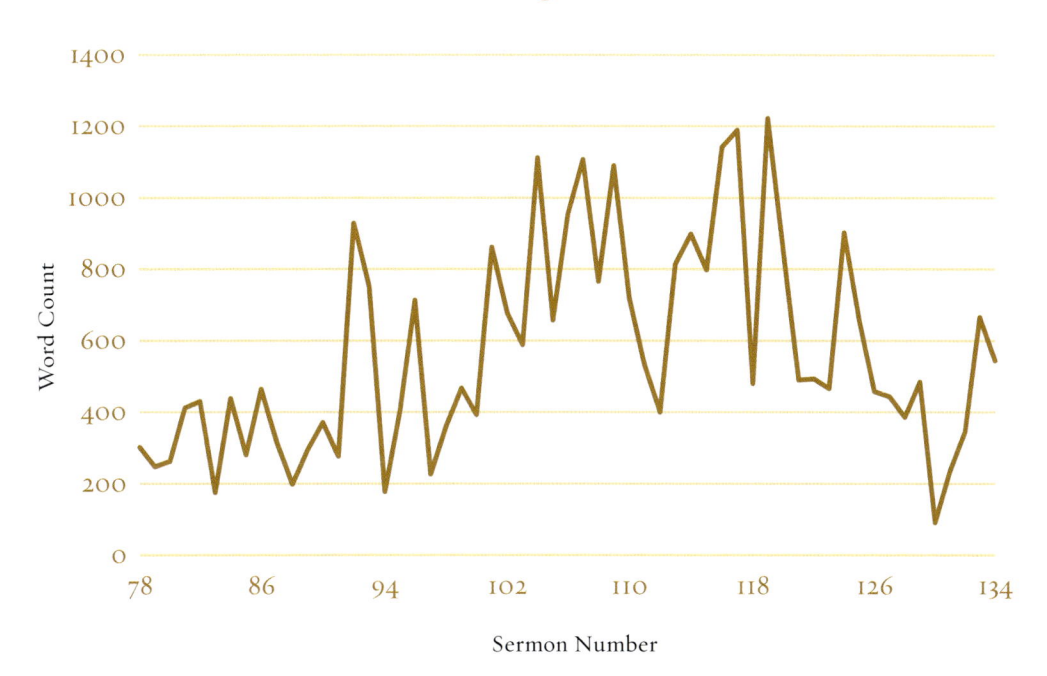

WORD COUNT *per* SERMON

the LOST SERMONS *of* C. H. SPURGEON

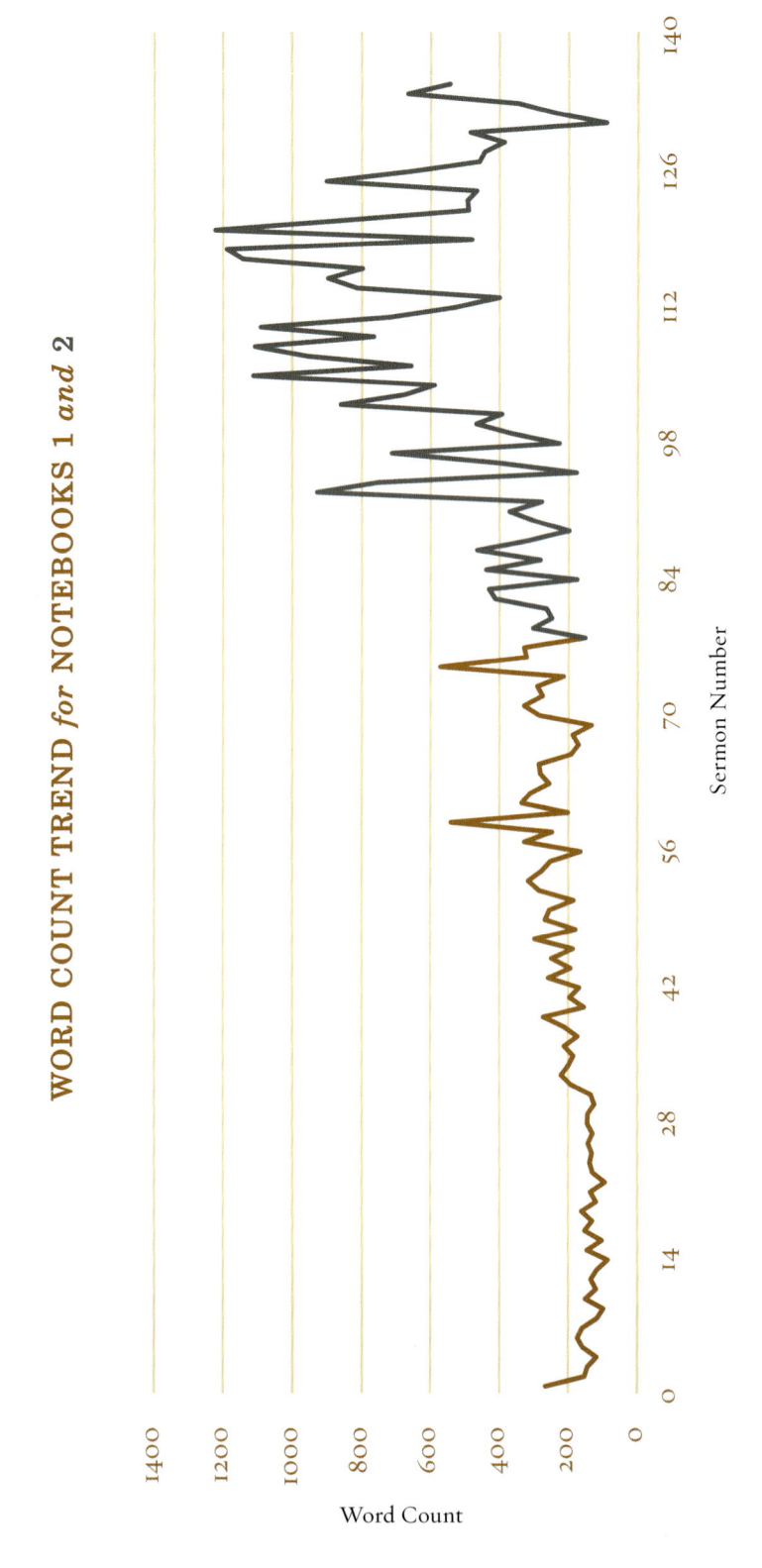

WORD COUNT TREND *for* NOTEBOOKS 1 *and* 2

INTRODUCTION

WORD COUNT DISTRIBUTION *of* SERMONS *in* NOTEBOOK 2[75]

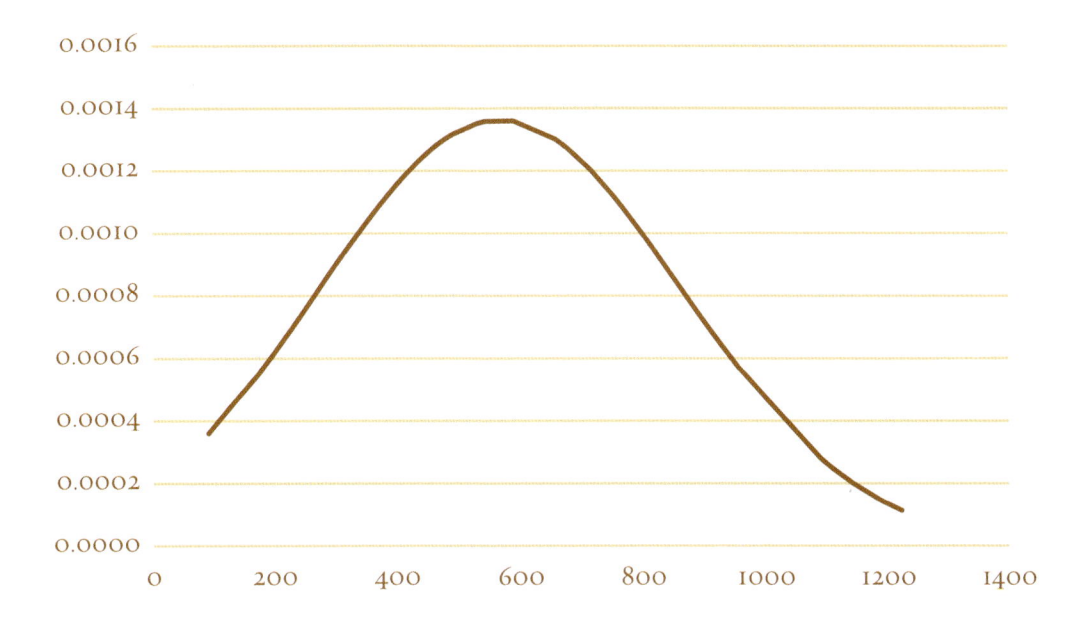

---

75 Of note to the statistician, the sermon word count in Notebook 2 forms a nearly perfect normal distribution ("bell curve") with a mean of 569 and a standard deviation of 293. This graph was plotted using Microsoft Excel. The x-axis represents word count and the y-axis represents probability.

PERCENTAGE *of* SERMONS *from* OLD *and* NEW TESTAMENTS

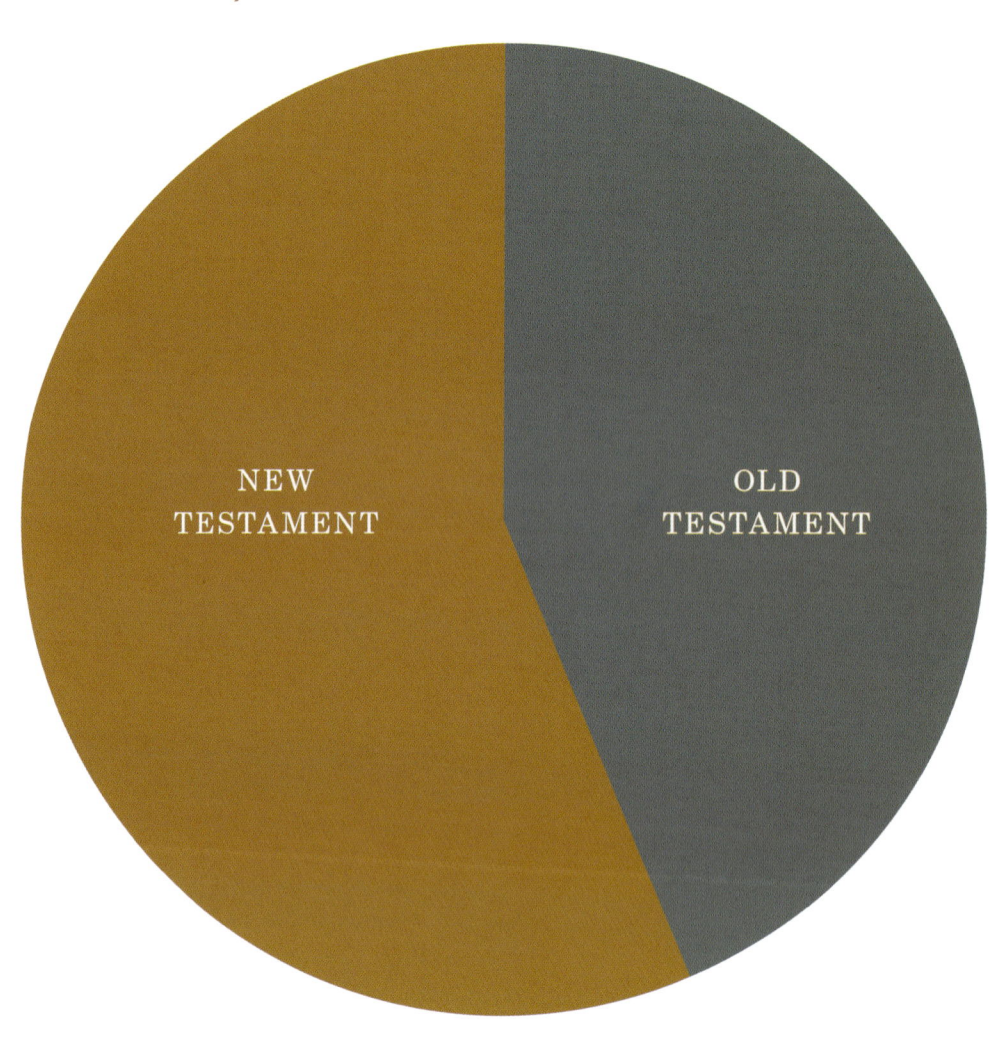

NEW TESTAMENT

OLD TESTAMENT

Percentage of Sermons:
- Old Testament – 44% (25 sermons)
- New Testament – 56% (32 sermons)

Books Most Frequently Preached:
Isaiah – 6 times
Luke – 6 times
Proverbs – 4 times
John – 4 times

Length of Sermons:
Longest Sermon – 1,222 words
Shortest Sermon – 91 words
Average Sermon – 569 words

INTRODUCTION

PERCENTAGE *of* OLD TESTAMENT SERMONS
Preached from Each Book

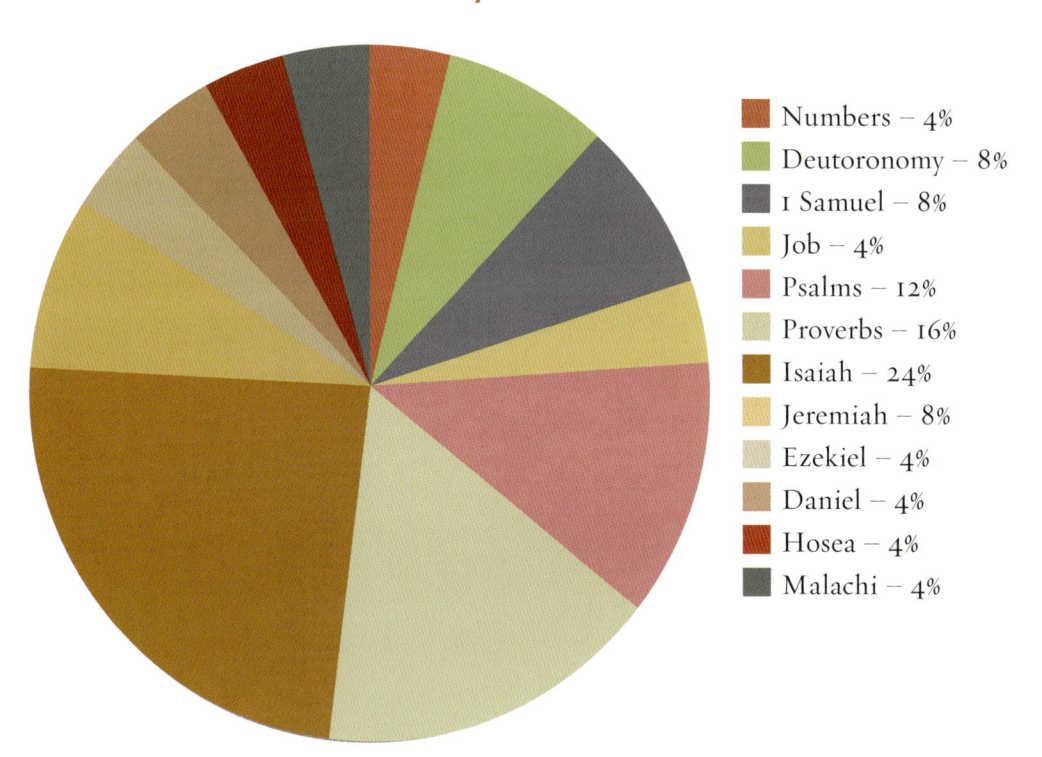

- Numbers – 4%
- Deuteronomy – 8%
- 1 Samuel – 8%
- Job – 4%
- Psalms – 12%
- Proverbs – 16%
- Isaiah – 24%
- Jeremiah – 8%
- Ezekiel – 4%
- Daniel – 4%
- Hosea – 4%
- Malachi – 4%

NUMBER *of* PREACHING OCCASIONS USING OLD TESTAMENT TEXTS

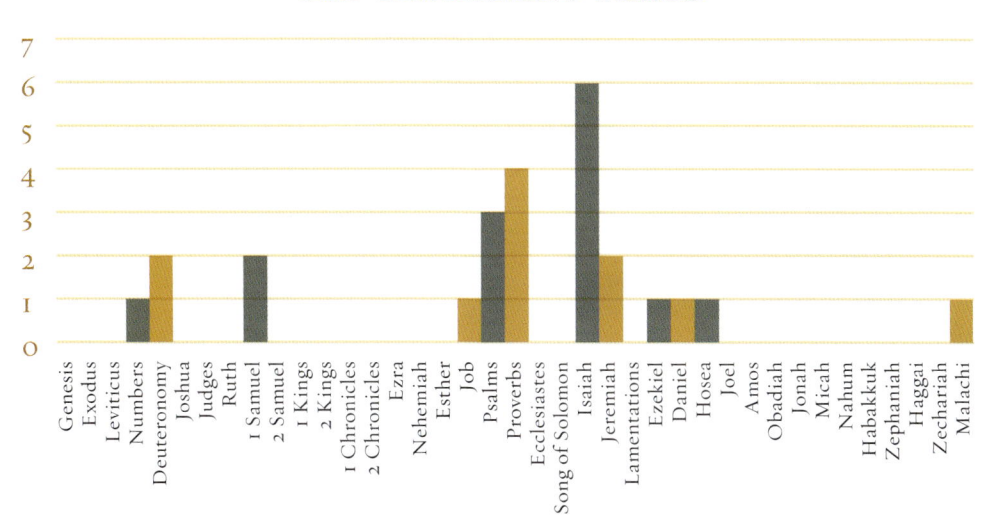

19

the LOST SERMONS *of* C. H. SPURGEON

PERCENTAGE *of* NEW TESTAMENT SERMONS
Preached from Each Book

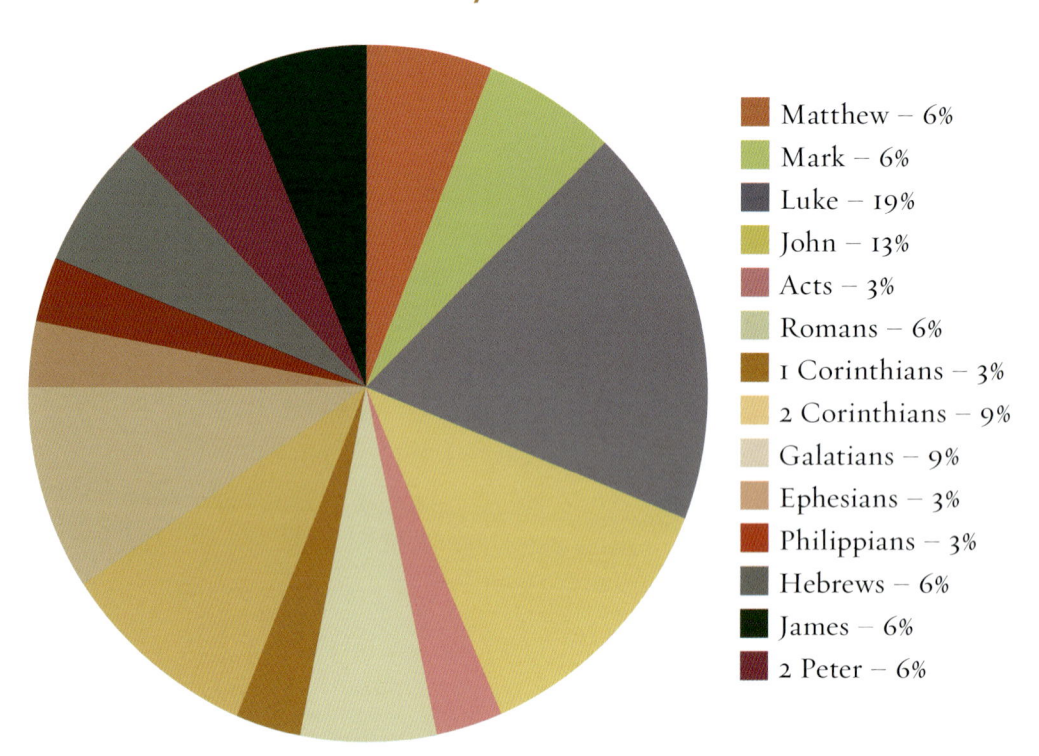

- Matthew – 6%
- Mark – 6%
- Luke – 19%
- John – 13%
- Acts – 3%
- Romans – 6%
- 1 Corinthians – 3%
- 2 Corinthians – 9%
- Galatians – 9%
- Ephesians – 3%
- Philippians – 3%
- Hebrews – 6%
- James – 6%
- 2 Peter – 6%

NUMBER *of* PREACHING OCCASIONS USING NEW TESTAMENT TEXTS

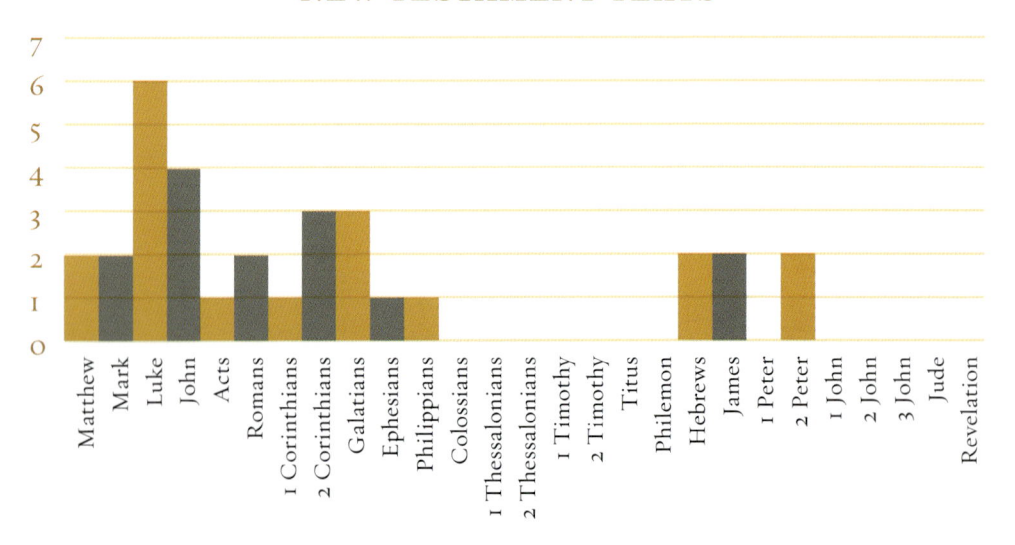

INTRODUCTION

WORD CLOUD *of* TOPICAL FREQUENCY

In this word cloud, the larger the word, the more frequently it appears in Notebook 2.

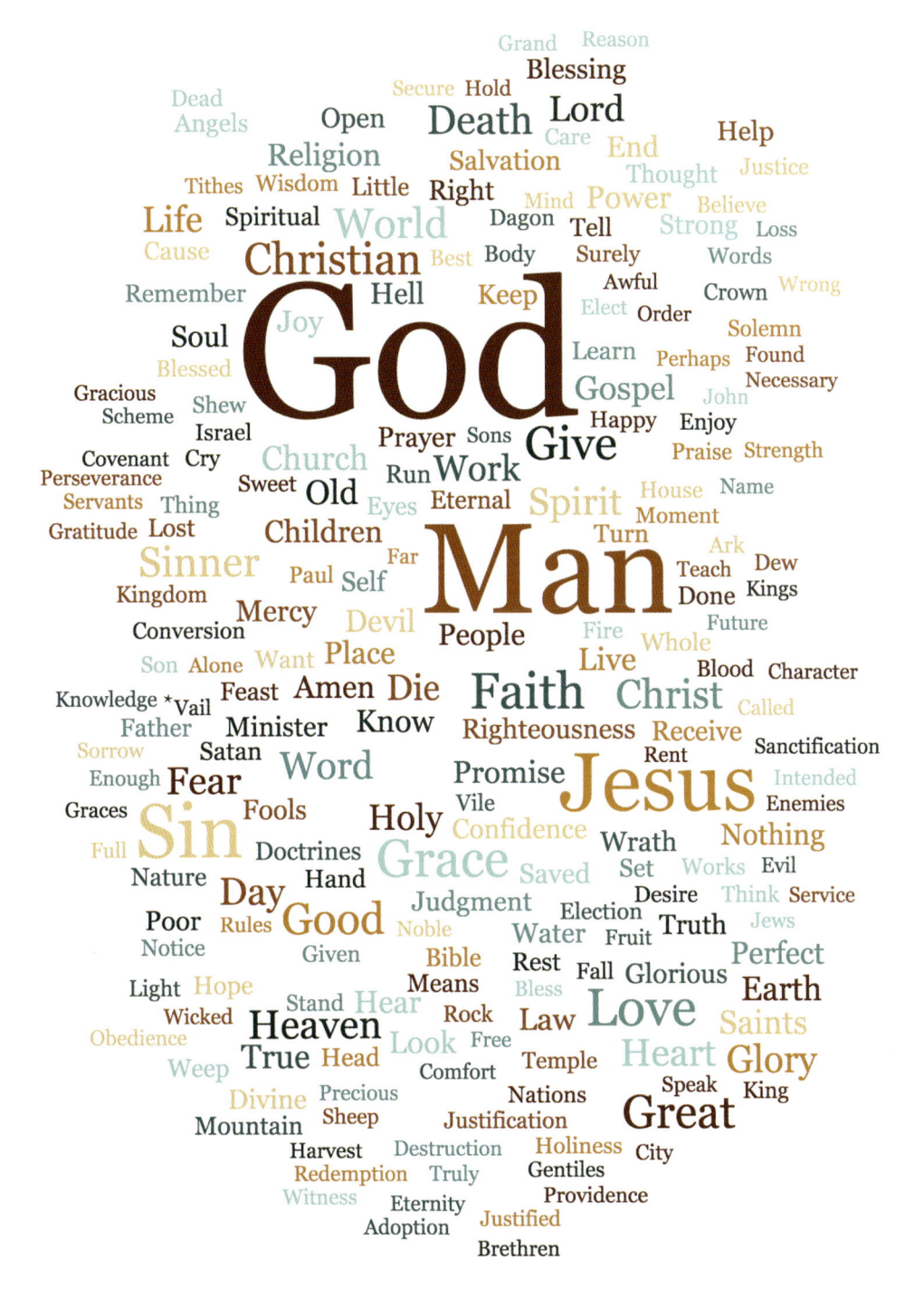

*In his sermons, Charles preferred the archaic spelling of the word "veil."

THE SERMONS

NOTEBOOK 2 (SERMONS 78–134)

FRONT COVER OF NOTEBOOK 2

OPENING PAGE OF NOTEBOOK 2

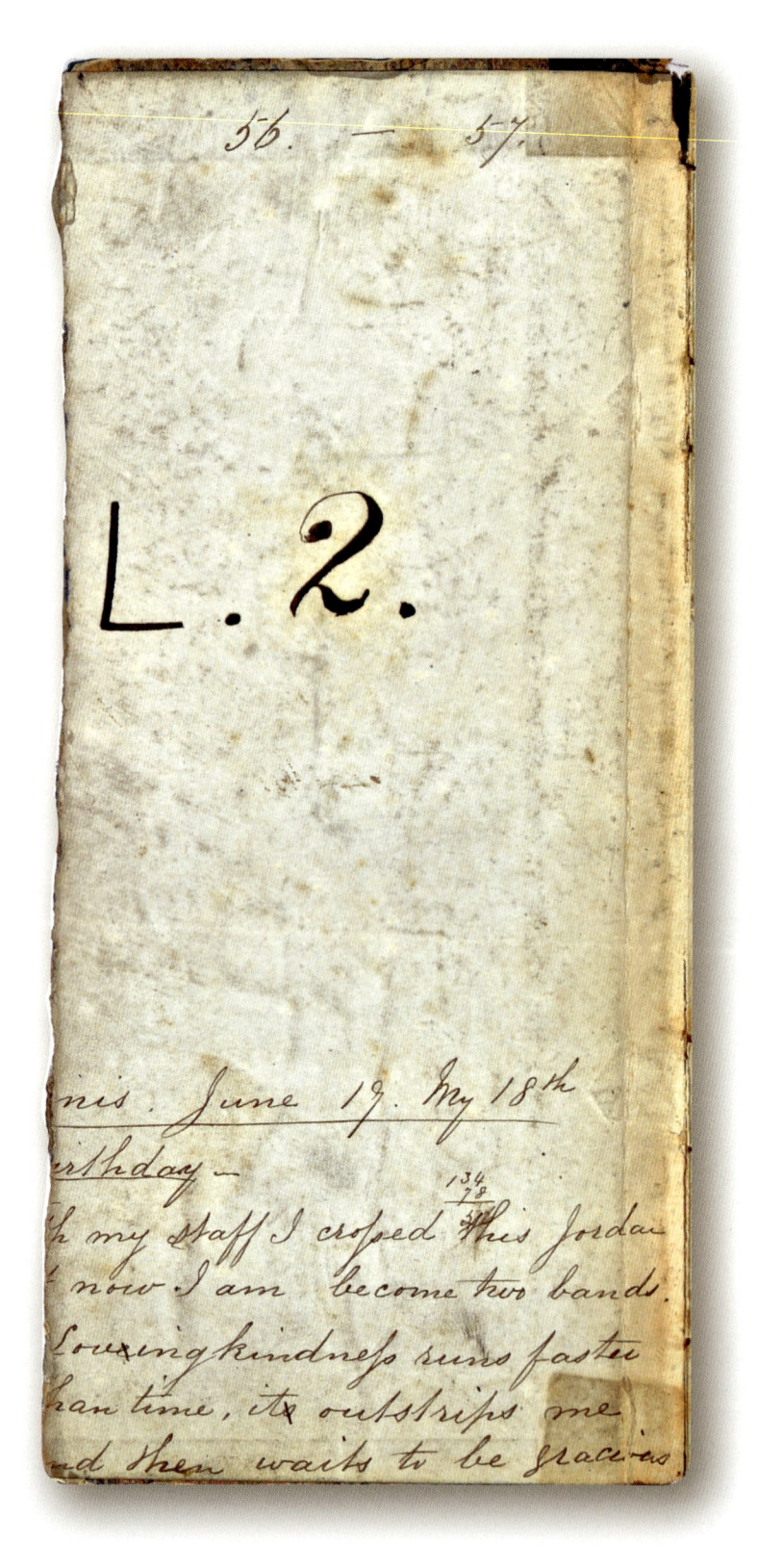

56.   57.

L. 2.

...nis June 19. My 18th
...rthday —
                    134
                    72
...h my staff I crossed this Jordan
... now I am become two bands.
...Lovingkindness runs faster
...han time, it outstrips me
...d then waits to be gracious

OPENING PAGE OF NOTEBOOK 2

56.–57.

[VO]L. 2.

[Fi]nis. June 19. My 18th
[b]irthday   134
                 78
                 56 1
[wit]h my staff I crossed this Jordan
[and] now I am become two bands.
Loveingkindness[2] runs[3] faster
[t]han time, its[4] outstrips me
[a]nd then waits to be gracious.[5]

Grace, free, sovereign, distinguishing,
rock, unsought, undeserved, infinite, unchanging,
abounding, embracing, eternal, boundless.

Saved from sin & the devil. Saved from hell.

Grace through Jesus
to me — to sinners

Skeletons
LXXVIII to CXXXIV

Praise ought to
and shall be given
to
God's free grace &
unchanging love for
these sermons given when
required to me, an undeserving one.

The Doctrines of Grace are the fountains of faith, Providence, love and all virtue, piety, charity, Absolute Sovereignty.

Grace: free, rich, unsought, abounding, constraining,[6] sovereign,[7] distinguishing,[8] entirely underserved, infinite,[9] unchanging, eternal, boundless.[10] Saved from sin, self, the devil.[11] Saved from hell.

Grace[12] through Jesus
to me, to sinners[13]

SKELETONS
LXXVIII *to* CXXXIV

Praise ought to
be and shall be given
to
God's free grace[14] and
unchanging love for
these sermons given when
required to me, an undeserving[15] one.[16]

I am the Rose of Sharon.[17] Thou art all fair my love.[18]
Man shall not live by bread alone.[19]
The Plant of Renown.[20]
Food for the saints in Jesus.
Altogether Lovely. Matchless.
The Leaves are for the healing of the nations.[21]
Better[22] than manna.[23]
Sweeter than honey or the Honeycomb.[24]
No mention shall be made of coral.[25]
The Doctrines of Grace are the fountains of virtue, piety, love, and all goodness.
They are truly practical.
Absolute Sovereignty, Providence, Justification by Faith,[26] Natural Depravity,[27]
Effectual Calling,[28] The Covenant of Redemption,[29] Perseverance,[30] Election,[31]
Imputed Righteousness.[32]
There is no lack[33] to the righteous.
Eat and be filled with fatness.[34]
Jesus makes us beautiful by putting his own[35] raiment on us.

SKELETONS—LXXVIII *to* CXXXIV

1. The mathematical equation 134−78=56 corresponds to the numbers 56.-57. at the top right corner of the flap. The equation suggests Charles sought to know how many sermons were contained in Notebook 2. By subtracting the total number of sermons contained in both notebooks from the number of sermons contained in Notebook 1, the number of sermons in Notebook 2 can be deduced (56). Why, then, did Charles write the number 57? The answer may have to do with the fact that Charles wrote two sermons labeled 37 in Notebook 1: "The Fight and the Weapons" (Sermon 37a) and "The Fight" (Sermon 37b). If Charles counted these two sermons individually, the equation would be 134−77=57.

2. Charles originally added the letter "e" after the "v" in the word "Loveingkindness." He struck through the letter "e" to correct the misspelling.

3. A partial fingerprint, likely belonging to Charles, appears above the word "runs." The source of the ink may be the number 56 above the letter "t" in the word "this" two lines above. For additional fingerprints see the front and end matter in Notebook 1 and "Election" (Notebook 1, Sermon 10).

4. Charles originally wrote the word "its." He struck through the letter "s" to correct the misspelling.

5. Half of the front flap of this notebook has been removed. However, Susannah recorded the text in her husband's autobiography when the front cover was still intact: "Finis. June 19. My 18th birthday. With my staff I crossed this Jordan, and now I am become two bands. Lovingkindness runs faster than time; it outstrips me, and then waits to be gracious" (*Autobiography* 1:222). Charles had Gen 32:10 in mind: "I am not worthy of the least of all the mercies, and of all the truth, which thou hast shewed unto thy servant; for with my staff I passed over this Jordan; and now I am become two bands." Charles may have believed the "two bands" represented Notebooks 1 and 2. On the inside of the back flap of this notebook he wrote a similar inscription: "In health, contentment, and peace. June 19/52." Both inscriptions were likely added after he had written the notebook.

6. Cf. "The Physician and His Patients" (Notebook 1, Sermon 74).

7. Cf. "God's Sovereignty" (Notebook 1, Sermon 18).

8. "The very marrow of the gospel lies in special, discriminating, distinguishing grace" (*MTP* 13:429).

9. The aging process of the right side of the page is detected in the discoloration of the paper caused by exposure to oxygen. The left side of the page was protected by the partial flap covering it and reflects more accurately the original color of the paper.

10. The exact order of these words is unclear; however, their directionality suggests a correct reading from top to bottom and left to right.

11. Cf. "The Fight and the Weapons" (Notebook 1, Sermon 37a).

12. A partial fingerprint, likely belonging to Charles, appears around the word "Grace." The source of the ink is likely the descending stroke in the letter "G."

13. The stylized letters in this line break from Charles's usual handwriting. The letter "s" is disconnected from the word "sinner" and is found to the right of the vertical phrase, "There is no lack to the righteous."

14. Cf. "Free Grace" (Notebook 1, Sermon 13) and Rom 3:24.

15. The letters "s" and "e" in the word "undeserving" are bolded. An illegible letter appears beneath the letter "e." Charles was likely correcting a misspelling.

16. In his diary entry on April 21, 1850, Charles wrote, "No merit in me, I am sure; vilest of the vile, for so long shutting mine eyes to this great salvation and glorious state of God's people" (*Autobiography* 1:132).

17. The following transcriptions will move vertically down the page, across from left to right, and then vertically up the right side. Each petal or leaf is transcribed on its own line. Song of Songs 2:1, "I am the rose of Sharon, and the lily of the valleys."

18. Song of Songs 4:7, "Thou art all fair, my love; there is no spot in thee."

19. Matthew 4:4, "But he answered and said, It is written, Man shall not live by bread alone, but by every word that proceedeth out of the mouth of God."

20. Cf. "The Plant of Renown" (Notebook 1, Sermon 20).

21. Revelation 22:2, "[A]nd the leaves of the tree were for the healing of the nations."

22. An illegible letter appears beneath the letter "B" in the word "Better."

23. Cf. Exodus 16.

24. Psalm 19:10, "[S]weeter also than honey and the honeycomb."

25. Job 28:18, "No mention shall be made of coral, or of pearls: for the price of wisdom is above rubies."

26. The words "by faith" likely correspond to "Justification" and are found in the two petals beneath "undeserving one." Cf. Rom 5:1; "The Saints' Justification and Glory" (Notebook 1, Sermon 68); "Justification, Conversion, Sanctification, Glory" (Sermon 102).

27. Cf. Charles Spurgeon, "An Essay on Depravity," 1851.

28. See James Smith's address at the Metropolitan Tabernacle entitled "Effectual Calling" in *Expositions of the Doctrines of Grace* (MTP 7:318–22).

29. Cf. Rom 3:24.

30. Cf. "Final Perseverance" (Notebook 1, Sermon 8); "Final Perseverance Certain" (Sermon 82).

31. Cf. "Election" (Notebook 1, Sermon 10); Rom 8:28–30; 11:5; Eph 1:4; 2 Thess 2:13.

32. Cf. "Justification by Imputed Righteousness" (Sermon 117).

33. Psalm 34:10, "The young lions do lack, and suffer hunger: but they that seek the Lord shall not want any good thing."

34. Isaiah 55:2, "[E]at ye that which is good, and let your soul delight itself in fatness."

35. Matthew 27:31, "And after that they had mocked him, they took the robe off from him, and put his own raiment on him, and led him away to crucify him."

BLANK PAGE

BLANK PAGE

[blank page][1]

1. The discoloration of the left side of this blank page is due to the aging process of the manuscript caused by exposure to oxygen. The right side of the page was protected by the partial flap covering it. It reflects more accurately the original color of the paper. Ink from illustrations on the back of the page can be seen at the top. The two creases on the lower left of the page and the fringed edge at the bottom of the page suggest at one time the page had been folded, possibly during the removal of half of the flap.

Gal. 6 – 3 – Self deception

Perhaps in the fall man lost some of the original acuteness of his intellect, without moral error it seems likely that he was free from mental error. But now man may easily be deceived, none dare claim infallibility save the Pope, and he is but a fool – How man's folly betrayed itself in the darker ages, in science & religion, and folly is not dead even now (particularly religious folly). In business men are deceived, how much more in religion. Many are deceived now and all Christians once were. Several circumstances render deception easy.
1. Our Ignorance, of sin, our hearts, the new birth.
2. The Custom of the world, judging with a wrong standard.
3. Partiality to ourselves, a hope for the best.
4. Suggestions of Satan, blinding of the eyes by him.
There may then be some deceived one here let him know that he deceives "himself". He bears the burden. God he cannot deceive, nor Saints, nor even the world long. The most common forms are.

I. An high opinion of Creature Capabilities, whereas we are "nothing". developed in the forms either of selfrighteousness or selfsufficiency – here the mischief ends in self.

II. A confidence in the young that their education, moral principles, &c – the educated heart like a tame tiger. How many have fallen – – nothing but conversion a real guard, without it – we are nothing.

III. The most hideous form is that of supposititious conversion when their ground of hope is either, doctrinal knowledge, impressions, ceremonies, morality – here the man's self most feels it — Yet let not God's children be downcast for faith in Jesus, love to God, secret devotion, meditation and good works are such evidences that with them full assurance may be enjoyed – Still searching of heart is at all times good. —

103

SELF-DECEPTION—*Galatians 6:3*

78

SELF-DECEPTION[1]
Galatians 6:3

"For if a man think himself to be something, when he is nothing, he deceiveth himself."

Perhaps in the Fall[2] man lost some of the original acuteness of his intellect.[3] Without moral error, it seems likely that he was free from mental error.

But now, man may easily be deceived. None dare claim infallibility save the Pope,[4] and he is but a fool. How man's folly betrayed itself in the darker ages in science and religion.[5] And folly is not dead even now, and particularly religious folly. In business men are deceived. How much more in religion? Many are deceived now, and all Christians once were.

Several circumstances render deception easy:

1. Our Ignorance of sin, our hearts, the new birth.

2. The Custom of the world, judging with a wrong standard.

3. Partiality to ourselves, a hope for the best.

4. Suggestions of Satan, blinding of the eyes by him.[6]

There may then be some deceived one here. Let him know that he deceives "himself."[7] He bears the burden.[8] God, he cannot deceive,[9] nor Saints, nor even the world long. The most common forms are:

I. AN HIGH OPINION OF CREATURE CAPABILITIES WHEREAS WE ARE "NOTHING."[10]

Developed in the forms either of self righteousness or self-sufficiency. Here, the mischief[11] ends in self.

II. A CONFIDENCE IN THE YOUNG.

That their education, moral principles, and etc.[12] The educated heart [is] like a tame tiger. How many have fallen?[13] Nothing but conversion [is] a real guard. Without it we are nothing.

SERMON 78

III. **THE MOST HIDEOUS FORM IS THAT OF SUPPOSITIOUS CONVERSION[14] WHEN THEIR GROUND OF HOPE IS EITHER DOCTRINAL KNOWLEDGE, IMPRESSIONS, CEREMONIES, MORALITY.**

Here the man's self most feels it.

Yet let not God's children be downcast, for faith in Jesus, love to God, secret devotion, meditation, and good works are such evidences that with them full assurance may be enjoyed. Still, searching of heart is at all times good.

103

SELF-DECEPTION—*Galatians 6:3*

1. This is the only time Charles preached a sermon on Gal 6:3. The discoloration on the right side of the page was caused by the aging process of the manuscript due to exposure to oxygen. The discoloration on this page is not as pronounced as that found on the title page. The noticeability of the discoloration decreases as the sermons in this notebook progress. However, traces of the damage, especially the dark vertical line bifurcating the page, can be detected in the first forty-two sermons of this notebook.

2. Cf. Genesis 3.

3. An ink blot, likely accidental, appears above the letter "e" in the word "intellect."

4. Pius IX. For additional references to the pope, see "Salvation in God Only" (Notebook 1, Sermon 24); "Pleasure in the Stones of Zion" (Notebook 1, Sermon 53); and his essay "Antichrist and Her Brood; or, Popery Unmasked."

5. "There have been eras and epochs in which gross heresies spread a contagion through the entire church. The period at which Arianism was so prominent comes at once to our recollection. That Christ was merely a man was almost the universal belief of Christendom. Only a few faithful ones maintained his Godhead at all hazards. But yet, to-day, where is Arianism? It has gone among the moles and the bats; the few that held the truth survived the deadly epidemic, and won the victory after all. God was with them, and in his name they became triumphant, and it will be so again. Error is like a hydra, as quickly as we cut off one of its heads another comes up in its place; but we must keep on killing till the last be slain. In the dark ages, Romanism was not only predominant, but it seemed to be and it really was all but universal: yet by the bright shining of his revealed word, did not God soon chase away the dense shades of ignorance and superstition?" (*MTP* 18:269). See also *MTP* 26:262 and *MTP* 37:454.

6. Cf. 2 Cor 4:4.

7. Galatians 6:3a, "For if a man think *himself*" (emphasis added).

8. An ink blot, likely accidental, appears above the word "burden."

9. Cf. Gal 6:7.

10. Galatians 6:3b, "[W]hen he is *nothing*" (emphasis added).

11. Charles originally hyphenated the word "mischief." For an additional example of this hyphenation, see "The Faith of Simon Magus" (Notebook 5, Sermon 237). In other instances Charles did not hyphenate the word, or the hyphen is barely visible, such as in "Zeal in Religion Commended" (Notebook 3, Sermon 154).

12. Charles may have intended to insert "&c." here instead of "&."

13. Charles's decision to remain pastor of Waterbeach Chapel and not become formally educated at Stepney College (unlike his brother James) may be relevant here (see *Autobiography* 1:241).

14. By using the phrase "suppositious conversion," Charles identified the act of false regeneration—one that is *supposed* but not authentic. "Like a foul bog covered over with greenest moss, our nature hides its rottenness beneath a film of suppositious righteousness" (*MTP* 18:484). "I find that advance in grace, if it be suppositious, can be rapid; but if it be real, it requires patience" (*MTP* 33:179). See also *MTP* 32:282.

79 | Ephes. 6. 17 — The Sword of the Spirit

In whatever light we regard God's children we shall find he has made ample provision for them. if they are plants, sheep, pilgrims, children or soldiers, he gives all necessaries. The Bible is meant not Jesus as it may be in Heb IV. 17.

I. It is called a "Sword" though its great mission is peace.
1. Because of its cutting, revealing, opening nature, its piercing and killing power.
2. It is a most useful defensive weapon to a Christian against Satan, his lusts, unbelief, the world —
3. It is the great conquering principle, subduing all things

II. "The Sword of the Spirit". 1) Because he is its maker a good maker is a great point. The Spirit is the great executive, he dictated the words of the glorious Trinity.
2. He has used it many a time, and still does —
3. He only can give us it and teach the use of it.

III. The apostle's advice "take it".—
1. Get it. the Bible is not ours till we have studied it, learnt it by true heart learning — get it by faith.
2. Gird it on your thigh — carry it every where never forget it, love it, have it at your finger's end.
3. Handle it, swords are meant to fight with not to look at _____

Caution. 1) Do not play with edged tools, nor this sword.
2. Do not alter the measure of the blade.
3. Often practise the cuts & drill —
   Cut thou Lord —

105. 146. 201. 203. 5¾

THE SWORD OF THE SPIRIT—*Ephesians 6:17*

79

The SWORD *of the* SPIRIT[1]
Ephesians 6:17

"And take the helmet of salvation, and the sword of the Spirit, which is the word of God."

In whatever light we regard God's children we shall find he has made ample provision for them. If they are plants,[2] sheep, pilgrims,[3] children, or soldiers, he gives all necessaries. The Bible is meant, not Jesus, as it may be in Heb. IV. 17.[4]

I. IT IS CALLED A "SWORD,"[5] THOUGH ITS GREAT MISSION IS PEACE.[6]

1. Because of its cutting, revealing, opening nature, its piercing[7] and killing power.[8]
2. It is a most useful defensive weapon to a Christian against Satan,[9] his lusts,[10] unbelief,[11] the world.
3. It is the great conquering principle subduing all things.

II. "THE SWORD OF THE SPIRIT."[12]

1.[13] Because he is its maker.[14] A good maker is a great point. The Spirit is the great executive. He dictated the words of the glorious Trinity.[15]
2. He has used it many a time, and still does.
3. He only can[16] give us it and teach the use of it.[17]

III. THE APOSTLE'S ADVICE, *"take it."*[18]

1. Get it. The Bible is not ours[19] till we have studied it,[20] learnt it by true heart learning.[21] Get it by faith.
2. Gird it on your thigh, carry it every where,[22] never forget it,[23] love it, have it at your finger's end.
3. Handle it.[24] Swords are meant to fight with, not to look at.

    Caution.
        1. Do not play with edged tools, nor this sword.[25]
        2. Do not alter the measure of the blade.[26]
        3. Often practise the cuts and drills.

            Cut thou, Lord.

105. 146. 201. 203. 520.[27]

SERMON 79

1. On April 19, 1891, Charles preached an additional sermon on Eph 6:17 entitled "The Sword of the Spirit" (*MTP* 37, Sermon 2201). There are enough structural similarities to suggest Charles had in mind the above outline when writing the later sermon.

2. See "Plant of Renown" (Notebook 1, Sermon 20).

3. For additional references to pilgrims see *MTP* 16:373–84; *MTP* 18:25–36; *MTP* 27:229–40; *MTP* 28:182; *MTP* 32:409–20; *MTP* 34:457–68; and *MTP* 37:73–84.

4. The number 2 was written in pencil over the number 7. The context of this sentence suggests Charles originally intended to write Heb 4:12, "For the word of God is quick, and powerful, and sharper than any two edged sword, piercing even to the dividing asunder of soul and spirit, and of the joints and marrow, and is a discerner of the thoughts and intents of the heart." See also "The Word a Sword" (*MTP* 34, Sermon 2010).

5. Ephesians 6:17, "[A]nd the sword of the Spirit."

6. "He is quiet as the dew, tender as the anointing oil, soft as the zephyr of eventide, and peaceful as a dove; and yet, under another aspect, he wields a deadly weapon. He is the Spirit of judgment and the Spirit of burning, and he beareth not the sword in vain" (*MTP* 37:230–31). See also Matt 10:34.

7. "That sword pursued you, and pierced you in the secrets of your soul, and made you bleed in a thousand places" (*MTP* 37:231).

8. "The Word gave you life; but it was at the first a great killer. Your soul was like a battle-field after a great fight, under the first operations of the divine Spirit, whose sword returneth not empty from the conflict" (*MTP* 37:231).

9. Cf. Matt 4:1–11.

10. Cf. Ps 119:9.

11. An illegible letter—likely "l"—appears after the letter "b" and before "l" in the word "unbelief." Charles likely prematurely wrote the letter "l" before adding the "e." "There is no such thing as the flat of the sword of the Spirit: it has a razor edge every way. Beware how you handle it, you critics; it may wound even you: it will cut you to your destruction. . . . We have seen this sword take

THE SWORD OF THE SPIRIT—*Ephesians 6:17*

off the head of many a Goliath doubt, and slay a horde of care and unbeliefs" (*MTP* 37:232, 234).

12. Ephesians 6:17, "and the sword of the Spirit."

13. The number 1 before the word "Because" suggests Charles intended to begin his list here. The repositioning of the first point beneath the words "The Sword of the Spirit" reflects this intention.

14. "*The Word is the sword of the Spirit because it is of his own making* . . . every portion of it bears his initial and impress; and thus he has a sword worthy of his own hand, a true Jerusalem blade of heavenly fabric" (*MTP* 37:232, 233, italics in the original).

15. "The Holy Ghost revealed the mind of God to the minds of holy men; he spake the word into their hearts, and thus he made them think as he would have them think and to write what he willed them to write: so that what they spoke and wrote was spoken and written as they were moved by the Holy Ghost. Blessed be the Holy Spirit for deigning to use so many writers, and yet himself to remain the veritable Author of this collection of holy books" (*MTP* 37:232).

16. The stem of an illegible letter, likely "t," appears over the letter "c" in the word "can." Charles likely began writing the word "teach" here as seen five words later.

17. Cf. 1 John 2:27.   18. Ephesians 6:17, "And take."

19. Charles likely added the letter "s" in the word "ours" afterward.

20. "It is a melancholy fact that there should be even a line of the sacred Scriptures which has never once come under your eye. . . . Study the Word, and work out its meaning. Go deep into the spirit of inspiration. He gets most gold who digs the deepest in this mine" (*MTP* 37:238).

21. Cf. Ps 119:11.

22. "I find, if I can lay a promise under my tongue, like a sweet lozenge, and keep it in my mouth or mind all the day long, I am happy enough" (*MTP* 37:240).

23. Cf. Ps 119:16.

24. "The raw recruit is not trusted with the general's sword; but here are you armed with the weapon of God the Holy Ghost, and called upon to bear that sacred sword which is so gloriously wielded by the Lord God himself" (*MTP* 37:235).

25. "Our warfare is not child's play: we mean business. We have to deal with fierce foes, who are only to be met with keen weapons. Buffets will not suffice in this context; we must come to sword-cuts" (*MTP* 37:235).

26. Cf. Rev 22:18.

27. The creases on the lower left of the page and also the fringed corner suggest at one time the page had been folded, possibly during the removal of half of the flap. See also the blank page that precedes the sermon "Self-Deception" (Sermon 78).

Claude's Essay.   2 Cor. IV. 7 –   The Treasure in earthen vessels.   80.

One great trial Paul had to endure was that ungenerous doubt of his apostleship which obtained in many churches. There were then as now many critics who if they could find no fault with treasure abused the vessel. But Paul stops them by this

I. God has committed his treasure to earthen vessels.

The gospel dispensation is a vast treasure, since it saves man's life, regenerates, moralizes, preserves the earth.

The Graces God gives are treasures for abundance, enduring superiority, immense cost. They need to be guarded with caution, watchfulness, jealousy —— This is in earthen &c

The preaching of the word is given to poor despised fishermen God's graces are given to men full of affliction & infirmities. They are only vessels – holders not makers – & earthen ones too.

II. The reason why "that the excellency &c"
1. The success of the gospel in conversion. Excellency of the power
2. The heavenly graces it produces

May appear to be of God. Men are apt to look at second causes, therefore God puts a poor thing there. It is of God in planning, providing & applying –

III. The Lessons we may learn hence –
1. Not to think lightly of the grace on account of the deformity — or beauty of the vessel –
2. Let us never admit a doctrine which dishonors God
3. We may see one reason why saints are so often sad.
4. None need think themselves too vile, for in this case there will be the more glory to the saving God.

Put this treasure in me Lord – more & more.

104.

Claude's Essay[1]

80

The TREASURE *in* EARTHEN VESSELS[2]
2 Corinthians 4:7

"But we have this treasure in earthen vessels, that the excellency of the power may be of God, and not of us."

One great trial Paul had to endure was that ungenerous doubt of his apostleship which [he] obtained in many churches.[3] There were then as now many critics who, if they could find no fault with treasure, abused the vessel. But Paul stops them by this:[4]

I. GOD HAS COMMITTED HIS TREASURE TO EARTHEN VESSELS.[5]

The Gospel dispensation is a vast treasure since it saves man's life, regenerates, moralizes, preserves the earth. The Graces God gives are treasures for abundance,[6] enduringness, superiority, immense cost.[7] They need to be guarded[8] with caution, watchfulness, jealousy.

This is in earthen, etc. The preaching of the word is given to poor, despised fishermen. God's graces are given to men full of affliction and infirmities.[9] They are only vessels—holders not makers—and earthen ones, too.

II. THE REASON WHY, *"that the excellency,* etc."[10]

1. The success of the gospel in conversion.[11] Excellency of the power.[12]
2. The heavenly graces it produces may appear to be of God. Men are apt to look at second causes.[13] Therefore, God puts a poor thing there. It is of God in planning, providing, and applying.

III. THE LESSONS WE MAY LEARN HENCE:

1. Not to think lightly of the grace on account of the deformity or beauty of the vessel.[14]
2. Let us never admit a doctrine which dishonors God.
3. We may see one reason why saints are so often sad.
4. None need think themselves too vile, for in this case there will be the more glory to the saving God.

Put this treasure in me, Lord, more and more.

104.

SERMON 80

1. This outline is original to Jean Claude (1619–1687), pastor of the French Reformed Church at Charenton, near Paris. This is the only time in Charles's ministry that he cited Claude or his posthumous publication *Traité de la Composition D'un Sermon*, which was originally part of Claude's *Œuvres Posthumus*, first published in Amsterdam in 1688. In 1778 Robert Robinson translated Claude's work into English and published an edition the following year that contained Claude's biography with extensive notations. For Charles's personal copy see Robert Robinson, *Miscellaneous Works of Robert Robinson, Late Pastor of the Baptist Church and Congregation of Protestant Dissenters, at Cambridge; in Four Volumes: To Which Are Prefixed Brief Memoirs of His Life and Writings, Vol. I* (Harlow: printed by B. Flower, 1807, The Spurgeon Library). In 1796 Charles Simeon published a less notated edition of Claude's *Essay*, followed in 1801 by a second edition (Charles Simeon, *Claude's Essay on the Composition of a Sermon: with Alterations and Improvements, by the Reverend Charles Simeon, M.A. Fellow of King's College, Cambridge*, second edition [Cambridge: printed by M. Watson, 1801]). Charles's personal copy of Claude's *Essay* is found in Charles Simeon, *Helps to Composition; or, Six Hundred Skeletons of Sermons; Several Being the Substance of Sermons Preached Before the University: By the Rev. Charles Simeon, M.A. Fellow of King's College, Cambridge, Vol. I, The Third Edition* (London: printed by Luke Hansard & Sons, for T. Cadell and W. Davies, in the Strand, 1815, The Spurgeon Library). See also "God's Visits and the Effects Thereof" (Sermon 113). For this sermon Charles consulted the section of Claude's *Essay* on 2 Cor 4:7 (70–76). Overlapping content is noted. In this sermon and "Final Perseverance Certain" (Sermon 82), Charles likely experimented with appropriating Claude's homiletical formula for dividing the Scripture text into the two parts: "[T]he first should be the apostle's *proposition*; and the second, the *reason*, which he gives for it" (Claude, quoted in Simeon, 70, italics in the original).

2. This is the only time Charles preached a sermon on 2 Cor 4:7.

3. Cf. 2 Corinthians 11; "God Glorified in the Saved" (Notebook 1, Sermon 56).

4. This contextual introduction is original to Charles. Claude did not include it in his exposition.

5. In his handling of this Scripture text, Charles appropriated Claude's instructions to the preacher to "examine 1. What is the *treasure*, and, 2. How it is *in earthen vessels*" (Claude, quoted in Simeon, 70, italics in the original).

THE TREASURE IN EARTHEN VESSELS—2 Corinthians 4:7

6. "Because of its *abundance*; for here are infinite riches, &c" (Claude, quoted in Simeon, 71, italics in the original).

7. "In this sense the Gospel in the parable is likened to *treasure hid in a field*, and to a *pearl of great price, &c*" (Claude, quoted in Simeon, 71, italics in the original).

8. Charles originally did not write the letter "u" in the word "guard." He corrected the misspelling by writing the letter "u" over the "a."

9. Cf. Claude's second and third points on 72–73.

10. Charles likely intended to close the quotation mark after the word "excellency." Charles followed Claude's instructions in this primary division: "Proceed now to the second part of the text, and examine two things: 1. The excellency of the power of the Gospel. 2. The design of God in putting such a treasure into earthen vessels, that the excellency of that power might be of him and not of men" (Claude, quoted in Simeon, 73).

11. "This consists, 1. In the happy *success* of the Gospel in the *conversion* of men, which may be represented as a victorious and triumphant power, and even as an excelling, that is, a prevailing and almighty energy" (Claude, quoted in Simeon, 73, italics in the original).

12. Charles switched Claude's ordering of these two phrases. In Claude's exposition, the phrase "*Excellency of the power*" comes before "In the happy *success* of the Gospel in the *conversion* of men" (Claude, quoted in Simeon, 73, italics in the original).

13. "St. Paul's reasoning proceeds upon this principle; that men are inclined to ascribe to second causes, effects, which belong only to the first cause. Whenever we see any great event which dazzles us, instead of elevating our thoughts to God, and giving him the glory, we meanly sink into creature attachments, as if the event were to be ascribed to instruments" (Claude, quoted in Simeon, 74).

14. "O happy *earthen vessels!* glory, in that ye were only dust and ashes; your weakness, brittleness, and nothingness, display a thousand times more the glory of the great Master who employed you, than the greatest dignity could have displayed it, had ye been golden vessels, angels or cherubims, dominions or thrones!" (Claude, quoted in Simeon, 76, italics in the original).

SERMON 81

81 Luke 8. 18. Take heed how ye hear.

Preaching is a divine institution. of old Enoch, Noah, the priests the prophets &c declared the law and now under grace the apostles, disciples, and ministers preach the gospel of Jesus.

As a divine ordinance it is generally blest, most conversions happen under its sound. We should then hear but take heed how we hear — This caution necessary in Christs time and now also, for as then & now there are captious, curious, careless hearers and Jesus knew their sad state and warns them for such are

1. Slighting precious truths.
2. Dishonoring a jealous God.
3. Putting away a glorious gospel.

we must not hear as they — in what manner we should hear we shall discuss under three heads.

I. Before hearing. preparation, desire, prayer.

1. Preparation — what day is it. where am I going — what for — what am I to hear — whose servant — whose word — dismiss all worldly thought — all evil thought of the preacher.
2. Earnest longing for the good word, food requires appetite. desire to be fed if a saint, to be converted if a sinner.
3. Earnest prayer for yourself, minister, congregation that they may be blessed by the Holy Spirit — pray believingly

II. During hearing. attention, candour, earnest prayer.

1. Attention without this good is seldom received. devils would attend if they might — do not lose any of it. turn all the sore carry away the sermon..
2. Candour — be open to conviction of sin or error in sentiment, do not shift it, judge but rightly — look not at the man, do not go out when your favorite preacher is not there. be willing to hear & feel.
3. Earnest prayer that you may have a blessing, sit expecting it, you need assistance. even in hearing do not hear without Christ and the Spirit.

TAKE HEED HOW YE HEAR—*Luke 8:18*

81

TAKE HEED HOW YE HEAR
Luke 8:18[1]

"Take heed therefore how ye hear: for whosoever hath, to him shall be given; and whosoever hath not, from him shall be taken even that which he seemeth to have."

Preaching is a divine institution of old. Enoch,[2] Noah,[3] the priests, the prophets, etc., declared the law. And now, under grace,[4] the apostles, disciples, and ministers preach the gospel of Jesus.[5]

As a divine ordinance it is generally blest; most conversions happen under its sound.[6] We should then hear, but take heed how we hear.[7] This caution [was] necessary in Christ's time and now also, for as then so now there are:

Captious
Curious } Hearers   And Jesus knew their sad state and warns them.
Careless[8] }   For such are:

    1. Slighting precious truth.
    2. Dishonoring a jealous God.[9]
    3. Putting away a glorious gospel.

We must not hear as they. In what manner we should hear we shall discuss under three heads.

I. BEFORE HEARING. PREPARATION, DESIRE, PRAYER.

1. Preparation.[10] What day is it? Where am I going? What for? What am I to hear? Whose servant? Whose word? Dismiss all worldly thought,[11] all evil thought of the preacher.
2. Earnest longing for the good word. Food requires appetite. Desire to be fed[12] if a saint, to be converted if a sinner.[13]
3. Earnest prayer for yourself, minister, congregation, that they may be blessed by the Holy Spirit. Pray believingly.[14]

II. DURING HEARING. ATTENTION, CANDOUR, EARNEST PRAYER.

1. Attention.[15] Without this, good is seldom received. Devils would attend if they might. Do not lose any of it. Turn all the soul.[16] Carry away the sermon.[17]
2. Candour.[18] Be open to conviction of sin or error in sentiment. Do not shift it. Judge, but rightly. Look not at the man. Do not go out when your favorite preacher is not there. Be willing to hear and feel.
3. Earnest prayer. That you may have a blessing. Sit expecting it.[19] You need assistance even in hearing. Do not hear without Christ and the Spirit.[20]

III. After hearing the work is not done, but we require.
1. Meditation, the sermon is nothing without it, but with it the poorest sermon is a good one, think on it all the week.
2. Application. See what applies to self. apply all however humbling. put it in your own heart.
3. Practise it. let it direct all the week, let it shine through, follow conscience, consent to the Spirit.
4. Pray again — yea at all times, wet the seed before you sow, wet it when it is sown, wet it afterwards —
Hear as damned souls would hear, as eternity would teach you to hear — God bless you all. amen —
17.

Phil. 1–6. — Final Perseverance certain.   82.
The text contains much important matter, it traces the work of salvation up to its true source as well in the Phillippians as others — but passing this over it expressly teaches the doctrine of Final Perseverance the "good work" is sanctification. "to perform" means "to complete". "the day of Jesus Christ" will be the day of his glory. —
Prop. All men who have had the work begun in them shall have it carried on and at last completed —
Invite to a candid investigation of the doctrine, remarking that by a calm enquiry may differences might be settled. —
Hint at the proof derivable from election and the covenant of redemption and pass on to establish it on grounds admitted by all Christians —
1. The joy of angels — these make no mistakes, if the repenting sinner fell away how disappointed would they be, how anxious must be their looks every day — they dare at best only hope.
2. The Intercession of Jesus, he prays now, and no doubt the same prayer as he did on earth. John XVII. he must be heard too. we are united, and the members must live as long as the head.
3. Pardon — granted forbids punishment. Justification declares glory certain. Adoption makes the man a son eternally. The witness of the Spirit seals them as God's own.

III. AFTER HEARING, THE WORK IS NOT DONE.

But we require:

1. Meditation. The sermon is nothing without it. But with it the poorest[21] sermon is a good one.[22] Think on it all the week.
2. Application. See what applies to self. Apply all, however humbling. Put it in your own heart.[23]
3. Practise it. Let it direct all the week. Let it shine through.[24] Follow conscience. Consent to the Spirit.
4. Pray again, yea, at all times.[25] Wet[26] the seed before you sow.[27] Wet it when it is sown. Wet it afterwards.

Hear as damned souls would hear, as eternity would teach you to hear.

God bless you all. Amen.

107.

82

FINAL PERSEVERANCE CERTAIN[1]
Philippians 1:6[2]

"Being confident of this very thing, that he which hath begun a good work in you will perform it until the day of Jesus Christ."

The text contains much important matter.[3] It traces the work of salvation up to its true source as well in the Philippians[4] as others. But passing this over, it expressly teaches the doctrine of Final Perseverance. The "good work" is sanctification.[5] "To perform" means "to complete." "The day of Jesus[6] Christ" will be the day of his glory.[7]

Prop.[8] All men who have had the work began in them shall have it carried on and at last completed.

Invite to a candid investigation of the doctrine, remarking that by a calm enquiry, many[9] differences might be settled.

Hint at the proof derivable from election[10] and the covenant of redemption[11] and pass on to establish it on grounds admitted by all Christians.

1. The joy of angels.[12] These make no mistakes. If the repenting sinner fell away, how disappointed would they[13] be? How anxious must be their looks every day? They dare at best only hope.
2. The Intercession of Jesus.[14] He prays now,[15] and no doubt the same prayer as he did on earth. John XVII. He must be heard, too. We are united[16] and the members must live as long as the head.[17]
3. Pardon granted forbids punishment.[18] Justification declares glory certain.[19] Adoption makes the man a son eternally.[20] The witness of the Spirit seals them[21] as God's own.[22]

4 God has done so much, in the gift of his son in the descent of his Spirit, in gracious revelations & helps that it is irrational to suppose that he will not go on.
5. Would not the attributes of God be dishonored?
6. Many Scriptures declare it — the Cov. Jer. 32. 39. John X. 28 — Pluck &c — John VI. 37 — Isaiah — 49. 14 — oath. Heb VI. 17 — John V. 24. Sam. woman John. IV. 14 — Jer. 31. 35. Isaiah 54. 10 — Rom. 8. 35 —

But as objections will arise let us answer them
1. Some texts. Heb VI. 4-8 — John XVII. 12 —
2. Suppose say they a man ceases to believe &c will he be saved — ans. this is a supposition that begs the question a man cannot leave off faith &c —
3. How can God punish sin in his people — By corrections affliction, the Spirit's desertion &c —
4. How can fear be maintained? Love is the great motive of the gospel — but fear may also be kept up by a fear lest we are not true believers. —
5. Does not this lead to licentiousness — The Puritans believed it — so do all abused, wrested doctrines.
6. Some do fall but 1. John 2. 19 —

1. How safe the saints are.
2. How much reason for joy.

106

FINAL PERSEVERANCE CERTAIN—*Philippians 1:6*

4. God has done so much in the gift of his son,[23] in the descent of his Spirit,[24] in gracious revelations and helps that it is irrational to suppose that he will not go on.
5. Would not the attributes of God be dishonored?[25]
6. Many[26] Scriptures declare it.[27] The Cov.[28] Jer. 32.39.[29] John X.28.[30] Pluck, etc. John VI.37.[31] Isaiah 49.14.[32] Oath. Heb. VI.17.[33] John V.24.[34] Sam.[35] woman. John IV.14.[36] Jer. 31.35.[37] Isaiah 54.10.[38] Rom. 8.35.[39]

But as objections will arise let us answer them.

1. Some texts. Heb. VI.4–8.[40] John XVII.12.[41]
2. Suppose, say they, a man ceases to believe, etc. Will he be saved? Ans[r]: This is a supposition that begs the question. A man cannot leave off faith, etc.
3. How can God punish sin in his people? By corrections, affliction, the Spirit's desertion, etc.
4. How can fear be maintained? Love is the great motive of the gospel, but fear may also be kept up by a fear lest we are not true believers.
5. Does not this lead to licentiousness? The Puritans believed it. So do all abused, wrested[42] doctrines.
6. Some do fall, but 1 John 2.19.[43]

    1. How safe the saints are.
    2. How much reason for joy.

106

SERMON 81

1. On August 23, 1868, Charles preached an additional sermon on Luke 8:18 entitled "Heedful Hearing" (*MTP* 59, Sermon 3357). Charles likely used the above outline when writing the first and second primary divisions in his later sermon.

2. Cf. Jude 1:14.

3. Cf. 2 Pet 2:5.

4. The phrase "under grace" is written above the word "now." Charles used a caret to show its insertion.

5. Cf. "Preach the Gospel" (*NPSP* 1, Sermon 34).

6. Cf. Rom 10:14.

7. "Take heed, take heed, and remember, then, that it is no trifling thing to hear a sermon if it be a gospel sermon" (*MTP* 59:267).

8. "Men never listen to a gospel sermon and remain as they were. They are either bettered by it, or—shall I say worsened?—if there be such a word. It is not possible that the gospel should have shone upon those eye-balls without either giving light or increasing the blindness" (*MTP* 59:268).

9. Cf. Exod 34:14; Deut 4:24.

10. The word "Preparation" is smeared toward the bottom of the page.

11. Cf. Col 3:2.

13. Cf. Acts 2:38; 3:19.

12. Cf. Job 23:12; Jer 15:16; 1 Pet 2:2.

14. Cf. Matt 21:22.

15. In his 1868 sermon Charles expanded upon this point. Cf. "The Text Implies Some Rules as to Hearing" (*MTP* 59:269).

16. The final two letters in this word are not clear. The word may also be "sort."

17. Charles wrote the words "Carry away the sermon" in smaller script beneath the line.

18. In his 1868 sermon Charles added the words "*hear believingly*" and "*hear obediently*" between the words "*attentively*" and "*candidly*" (*MTP* 59:270, italics in the original).

Charles also appended the following additional adjectives to his later list: "*hear devoutly and hear sincerely;*" hear "*earnestly,* and therefore *spiritually;*" "*hear feelingly;*" "hear *gratefully and prayerfully*" (MTP 59:271, 272, italics in the original). "Hear gratefully and prayerfully" is found in Charles's third and final point in the outline above.

19. "I wish it were a habit with you, when you get home, to take a few minutes in a quiet room, and pray for a blessing upon what has been heard. We might expect to see great results if this were your constant practice, to pray after your hearing, and even before, to get the ground ready, and when the seed is sown, to rake it, and water it, so that it may have congenial soil in which to take root" (MTP 59:272).

20. In his 1868 sermon Charles added "III. Certain Obvious Reasons for Taking Heed How You Hear" (MTP 59:272). In his later sermon Charles displayed more interest in answering the question *Why hear?* instead of the question he addresses in the above outline, *Now what?*

21. An illegible letter, likely "h," appears beneath the letter "p" in the word "poorest." Charles may have intended to write the word "humblest."

22. For one of the "poorest sermon[s]" Charles heard, see the account of his conversion in Colchester (*Autobiography* 1:105–8).

23. Cf. Ps 119:11.

24. Cf. Matt 5:16.

25. Cf. Luke 18:1; Eph 6:18; Phil 4:6.

26. An illegible letter was written beneath the "w" in "wet."

27. Cf. Matt 13:1–23.

SERMON 82

1. The subject matter of this outline—God's "good work"—was likely inspired by the line "*It is God who worked effectually in you, both to will and to do, of his own good pleasure*" in Jean Claude's *Essay on the Composition of the Sermon* that followed the outline Charles consulted two sermons prior ("The Treasure in Earthen Vessels" [Sermon 80]). See Charles Simeon, *Helps to Composition* 1:45, italics in the original.

2. On May 23, 1869, Charles preached an additional sermon on Phil 1:6 entitled "The Perseverance of the Saints" (*MTP* 15, Sermon 872). There is enough overlapping content, especially in *MTP* 15:294–97, to suggest Charles may have used the early outline when writing the later sermon. See also "Final Perseverance" (Notebook 1, Sermon 8).

3. Charles's contextual introduction in this outline evidences familiarity with Jean Claude's instructions on 2 Cor 4:7: "This passage is of this sort; the terms are easy, and the subject, of which St. Paul speaks, has no difficulty: but yet, on account of the importance of the matter, it must needs be explained, or, to speak more properly, extensively proposed" (Claude, quoted in Simeon, 70).

4. Charles originally spelled this word "Phillippians." He made no attempt to correct the misspelling.

5. Cf. "Salvation from Sin" (Notebook 1, Sermon 33).

6. The letter "C" was written beneath "J" in the word "Jesus." Charles likely began writing the word "Christ."

7. Cf. Acts 17:31.

8. Abbr. "Proposition." This is the first time Charles used the word "Proposition" in his sermons. Jean Claude's influence on the development of his homiletic is obvious here (see also "The Treasure in Earthen Vessels" [Sermon 80]). In his *Essay* Claude proposes, "I would then divide this text into two parts; the first should be the apostle's *proposition*; and the second, the *reason*, which he gives for it" (Claude, quoted Simeon, 70).

9. The letter "n" in the word "many" is difficult to detect.

10. See "Election" (Notebook 1, Sermon 10).

FINAL PERSEVERANCE CERTAIN—*Philippians 1:6*

11. See the inscription "The Covenant of Redemption" on the title page of this notebook. Cf. Rom 3:24.

12. Cf. Luke 15:10.

13. For clarity, the antecedent of the pronoun "they" is angels, not repenting sinners.

14. Cf. *MTP* 15:297.   15. Cf. Rom 8:34; Heb 7:25.

16. Cf. "Can Two Walk Together Unless They Are Agreed?" (Notebook 1, Sermon 76).

17. Cf. 1 Cor 12:27; Col 1:18.

18. An alternative reading of this line is "Pardon, [if] granted, forbids punishment."

19. Cf. Rom 5:1; Gal 2:16.

20. "I believe, my brethren, that if we realized the truth of our own adoption into the family of God, we should never leave off marvelling at it. That any man of mortal race should become a child of God might astound us; but that we ourselves should be such should amaze us beyond degree. We ought to cry 'Behold! Behold!' Let us begin to talk of it now, for we shall never cease to speak of it when we reach the New Jerusalem. Our regeneration and adoption are complex miracles of grace; a cluster of wonders condensed into one" (*MTP* 32:674). Cf. "Adoption" (Notebook 1, Sermon 1); Eph 1:5.

21. The tittle above the letter "e" and also the illegible letter beneath the letter "t" suggest Charles may have originally written the word "him."

22. Cf. 2 Cor 1:22; Eph 1:13.   23. Cf. John 3:16.

24. Cf. Luke 3:22.

25. "But further, in addition to the express testimonies of Scripture, we have to support this doctrine *all the attributes of God*, for if those who have believed in Christ are not saved, then surely all the attributes of God are in peril; if he begins and doth not finish his work, all the parts of his character are dishonoured. Where is his wisdom? Why did he begin that which he did not intend to finish? Where is his power? Will not evil spirits always say, 'that he *could not* do what he did not do'?

Will it not be a standing jeer throughout the halls of hell that God commenced the work and then stayed from it? Will they not say that the obstinacy of man's sin was greater than the grace of God, that the adamant of the human heart was too hard for God to dissolve? Would there not be a slur at once cast upon the omnipotence of grace? And what shall we say of the immutability of God, if he casts away those whom he loves—how shall we think that he doth not change? How will the human heart ever be able to look upon him again as immutable if after loving he hateth? And, my brethren, where will be the faithfulness of God to the promises which he has made over and over again, and signed and sealed with oaths by two immutable things, wherein it was impossible for God to lie? Where will be his grace if he casts away those that trust in him, if after having tantalised us with sips of love he shall not bring us to drink from the fountain head?" (*MTP* 15:295–96, italics in the original).

26. The letter "S" was written beneath "M" in the word "Many." Charles likely began writing the word "Scriptures."

27. "Our first ground shall be *the express teaching of Holy Scripture*. But, my dear friends, to quote all the scriptural passages which teach that the saints shall hold on their way, would be to quote a large proportion of the Bible, for, to my mind, Scripture is saturated through and through with this truth; and I have often said that if any man could convince me that Scripture did not teach the perseverance of believers, I would at once reject Scripture altogether as teaching nothing at all, as being an incomprehensible book, of which a plain man could make neither head nor tail, for this seems to be of all doctrines the one that lies most evidently upon the surface" (*MTP* 15:294, italics in the original). In his 1869 sermon Charles referenced the following additional verses in support of the doctrine of perseverance of the saints: Job 17:9; Ps 125:1–2; Rom 11:29; Heb 6:9–10; and 1 Pet 1:5. In both sermons Charles referenced John 10:28 and Isaiah 54.

28. Abbr. "Covenant."

29. An illegible number was written beneath the final number 3 in the Scripture reference "Jer. 32.39." Because this passage is in the context of the covenant, this interpretation is correct: "And I will give them one heart, and one way, that they may fear me for ever, for the good of them, and of their children after them."

FINAL PERSEVERANCE CERTAIN—*Philippians 1:6*

30. John 10:28, "And I give unto them eternal life; and they shall never perish, neither shall any man pluck them out of my hand."

31. John 6:37, "All that the Father giveth me shall come to me; and him that cometh to me I will in no wise cast out."

32. Isaiah 49:14, "But Zion said, The Lord hath forsaken me, and my Lord hath forgotten me."

33. Hebrews 6:17, "Wherein God, willing more abundantly to shew unto the heirs of promise the immutability of his counsel, confirmed it by an oath."

34. John 5:24, "Verily, verily, I say unto you, He that heareth my word, and believeth on him that sent me, hath everlasting life, and shall not come into condemnation; but is passed from death unto life."

35. Abbr. "Samaritan."

36. John 4:14, "But whosoever drinketh of the water that I shall give him shall never thirst; but the water that I shall give him shall be in him a well of water springing up into everlasting life."

37. Jeremiah 31:35, "Thus saith the Lord, which giveth the sun for a light by day, and the ordinances of the moon and of the stars for a light by night, which divideth the sea when the waves thereof roar; The Lord of hosts is his name."

38. Isaiah 54:10, "For the mountains shall depart, and the hills be removed; but my kindness shall not depart from thee, neither shall the covenant of my peace be removed, saith the Lord that hath mercy on thee."

39. Romans 8:35, "Who shall separate us from the love of Christ? shall tribulation, or distress, or persecution, or famine, or nakedness, or peril, or sword?"

40. Hebrews 6:4–8, "For it is impossible for those who were once enlightened, and have tasted of the heavenly gift, and were made partakers of the Holy Ghost, and have tasted the good word of God, and the powers of the world to come, if they shall fall away, to renew them again unto repentance; seeing they crucify to themselves the Son of God afresh, and put him to an open shame. For the earth which drinketh in the rain that cometh oft upon it, and bringeth forth herbs meet for them by whom it is dressed, receiveth blessing from God: But that

which beareth thorns and briers is rejected, and is nigh unto cursing; whose end is to be burned."

41. John 17:12, "While I was with them in the world, I kept them in thy name: those that thou gavest me I have kept, and none of them is lost, but the son of perdition; that the scripture might be fulfilled."

42. "To twist by violence; to extort by writhing or force" (Johnson's *Dictionary*, s.v. "wrest").

43. 1 John 2:19, "They went out from us, but they were not of us; for if they had been of us, they would no doubt have continued with us: but they went out, that they might be made manifest that they were not all of us."

Luke. 14 – 28 –   Count the cost.

Forethought is always requisite especially in religious decision – Either God or the devil –

I. The Cost of religion – Some say why tell it to young beginners, but Jesus did, this will sift them; no true one will turn back for all this cost but hypocrites will

1. Much trouble, repentance, daily & hourly, sickness of self. Satan's roarings, the worlds enmities –

2. Renounce all sin, great & small, the dearest, all inducements to sin, evil companions, all habits.

3. Renounce self righteousness. – be humbled. all the glory he demands –

4. Implicit obedience. Entire consecration. – Minute obedience, submission, activity & love him.

5. Thou must take him for better or worse – forever. How much the gain exceeds the loss –

II. The Cost of irreligion.
1. Through life, loss of solidity, enjoyment of Jesus.
2. At death a loss of joy –
3. At the judgment a loss of justification
4. In hell – vast loss –
5. Loss of heaven since, the requisites will be wanting – Oh awful cost – –

Heaven or Hell – are the only alternatives – Choose ye this day –

108.

COUNT THE COST—*Luke 14:28*

83

COUNT *the* COST
Luke 14:28[1]

*"For which of you, intending to build a tower, sitteth not down first,
and counteth the cost, whether he have sufficient to finish it?"*

Forethought is always requisite, especially in religious decision. Either God or the devil.

I. THE COST OF RELIGION.

Some say, why tell it to young beginners? But Jesus did. This will sift them.[2] No true one will turn back for all this cost, but hypocrites will.

1. Much trouble,[3] repentance,[4] daily and hourly, sickness of self,[5] Satan's roarings,[6] the world[']s enmities.[7]

2. Renounce all sin,[8] great and small, the dearest, all inducements to sin, evil companions,[9] all habits.[10]

3. Renounce self righteousness.[11] Be humbled.[12] All the glory he [de]mands.[13]

4. Implicit obedience.[14] Entire consecration.[15] Minute[16] obedience, submission,[17] activity, love him.[18]

5. Thou must take him for better or worse, for ever. How much the gain exceeds the loss.[19]

II. THE COST OF IRRELIGION.

1. Through life, loss of solidity, enjoyments of Jesus.

2. At death, a loss of joy.

3. At the judgment, a loss of justification.

4. In hell, vast loss.

5. Loss of heaven since the requisites will be wanting. Oh, awful cost.

Heaven or Hell are the only alternatives.[20]

Choose ye this day.[21]

108.

Sermon 83

1. On February 22, 1874, Charles preached an additional sermon on Luke 14:29–30 entitled "Counting the Cost" (*MTP* 20, Sermon 1159). Overlapping content is found between the first primary divisions of the outline and later sermon. Cf. "The Cost of Religion" and *"true religion is a costly thing"* (*MTP* 20:110, italics in the original).

2. "On this occasion our Lord spoke with a view to the winnowing of the great heap of nominal discipleship which lay before him, that the chaff might be driven away and only the precious corn might remain" (*MTP* 20:109).

3. Cf. John 16:33.

4. Cf. Matt 3:8; Luke 5:31–32; Acts 20:21.

5. "I am afraid there are some who would sooner hate father or wife than hate their own life. Yet such is the demand. It means this: that wherein my own pleasure, or my own gain, or my own repute, or even my own life shall come in the way of Christ's glory, I am so little to make any account of myself, that I must even hate myself if self shall stand in the way of Christ. I am to look upon father, mother, brother, sister, and myself also, as foes, so far as they are opposed to the Lord Jesus and this holy will" (*MTP* 20:115).

6. Cf. 1 Pet 5:8.

7. "If any man love the world the love of the Father is not in him, and he who has the smile of the ungodly must look for the frown of God" (*MTP* 20:115).

8. Cf. Prov 28:13.

9. "If you would be one with Christ, you must be separate from sinners" (*MTP* 20:120). Cf. 1 Cor 15:33.

10. "If you would walk the streets of gold above, you must walk the road of holiness below" (*MTP* 20:120).

11. Cf. Rom 10:13; 2 Cor 5:21; Phil 3:9.

12. Cf. Prov 11:2; Eph 4:2; Phil 2:3; Jas 4:10.

COUNT THE COST—*Luke 14:28*

13. Cf. 1 Cor 10:31. The letters "de" have been written in pencil before "mands" to construct the word "demands." This correction appears to be in the hand of Charles.

14. Cf. Luke 11:28; John 14:15; 2 John 1:6.

15. Cf. Josh 3:5.

16. Charles began writing the letter "M" in the word "Minute" after "consecration" in the line above. Due to the lack of space, he rolled the word onto the next line.

17. Cf. Jas 4:7.

18. Cf. Ps 18:1; Matt 22:37; 1 John 4:19.

19. Cf. Phil 3:8.

20. The latter half of the word "alternatives" is smeared downward.

21. Cf. Josh 24:15.

84. Heb X. 12.13 — Jesus and his acts.

The Remembrance of Jesus at all times profitable.
It is the very root of true spirituality, Xn love, and devotion
How good a thing it would be to have the Lord alway before us.
I. Jesus in humanity once offered a sacrifice.
Jesus was God, yet man, both, perfectly; not a composition of the two
but an union of both — he was less man than we, less because he
had no sin — more man than perfect Adam because he suffered
the sorrows of fallen humanity — his "one sacrifice" was
himself not in death only but in his self sacrificing life —
This he offered as man — God could not suffer, man too was
the condemned one, and justice could not be satisfied
unless man died — He died once — no more sacrifice,
none die more than once, — For sins of all colours,
degrees, or aggravation — for countless sins — He offered
the sacrifice, he was priest and offering too —

II. Jesus in humanity sits down in glory —
In human nature he ascended, flesh like ours but
spiritualized — in the humanity in which he suffered,
that he might be the first fruit of the resurrection.
When? — when he had done the work, not till then.
He sat down — he did not kneel, nor walk, nor does
he hang crucified, or lie buried in the tomb, this is
a posture implying.
1. That he had ceased offering for priests stand.
2. He had now rest from toil, all his work was done
   the conqueror has fought the fight and now rests.
3. His dignity in that others bow — but especially
   his kingly dignity, on his throne, the monarch sits —
   The place where he sits is at the right hand of God
which is a place of eminent dignity, and shews that he has great favour

JESUS *and* HIS ACTS
Hebrews 10:12–13[1]

"But this man, after he had offered one sacrifice for sins for ever, sat down on the right hand of God; from henceforth expecting till his enemies be made his footstool."

The Remembrance of Jesus [is] at all times profitable. It is the very root of true spirituality, Xn[2] love, and devotion. How good a thing it would be to have the Lord alway[3] before us.

I. JESUS IN HUMANITY ONCE OFFERED[4] A SACRIFICE.[5]

Jesus was God, yet man, <u>both</u> perfectly. Not a composition of the two[6] but an union of both. He was less man than we, less because he had no sin. More man than perfect Adam because he suffered the sorrows of fallen humanity.[7] His "one sacrifice"[8] was himself. Not in death only but in his self-sacrificing[9] life. This he offered as man.[10] God could not suffer.[11] Man too was the condemned one,[12] and justice could not be satisfied unless man died. He died once.[13] No more sacrifice. None die more than once. For sins of all colours, degrees, ch[14] aggravation, for countless sins. He offered the sacrifice. He was priest[15] and offering,[16] too.

II. JESUS IN HUMANITY SITS DOWN IN GLORY.[17]

In human nature he ascended,[18] flesh like ours but spiritualized in the humanity in which he suffered that he might be the first-fruit of the resurrection.[19] When? When he had done the work. Not till then. He sat down.[20] He did not kneel, nor walk, nor does he hang crucified or lie buried in the tomb.[21] This is a posture implying:

1. That he had ceased offering, for priests stand.[22]
2. He had now rest from toil.[23] All his work was done.[24] The conqueror has fought the fight[25] and now rests.
3. His dignity[26] in that others bow. But especially his kingly dignity. On his throne the monarch sits.

   The place where he sits is at the right hand of God[27] which is a place of eminent dignity and shows that he had[28] great favour from God, and friendship and sympathy with him. as also it is a sort of pledge that God's right hand of power, wisdom shall be employed on his behalf — he sits for ever —

III. Jesus' great expectations. —
Conqueror's tread on the necks of the vanquished, thrones have footstools, Jesus shall put his foot on his foe —
1. By the dissemination of the Gospel, Idolaters. Mahommedans, Catholics. Mormons all shall bow
2. At the last day his enemies shall wail because of him — Satan shall be bound and death shall die.
He expects — not hopes — knowing the certainty of the event, he thinks it a matter of course —

I. See Jesus crucified, and you shall see him for ever.
II. Despise Jesus and his mercy turns to wrath & you shall be his foe —
III. Remember him, who still remembers man.

III

JESUS AND HIS ACTS—*Hebrews 10:12-13*

from God, and friendship and sympathy with him. As also it is a sort of pledge that God's right hand of power, wisdom, shall be employed on his behalf. He sits for ever.

III. JESUS'[S] GREAT EXPECTATIONS.

Conquerors[29] tread on the necks of the vanquished.[30] Thrones have footstools. Jesus shall put his foot on his foes.[31]

1. By the dissemination of the Gospel. Idolaters, Mahommetans,[32] Catholics,[33] Mormons.[34] All shall bow.[35]

2. At the last day his enemies shall wail because of him.[36] Satan shall be bound[37] and death shall die.[38] He expects, not hopes. Knowing the certainty of the event, he thinks it a matter of course.

I. See Jesus crucified[39] and you shall see him for ever.

II. Despise Jesus and his mercy turns to wrath, and you shall be his foe.

III. Remember him who still remembers man.[40]

III

1. On July 6, 1856, Charles preached an additional sermon on Heb 10:12–13 entitled "Christ Exalted" (*NPSP* 2, Sermon 91). There is enough overlapping content among the primary divisions to suggest Charles had his early outline in mind when writing his later sermon.

2. Abbr. "Christian."

3. Charles used the word "alway" and "always" throughout his ministry. The former is found in the KJV, e.g., Matt 28:20. Cf. Charles Spurgeon, *Evening by Evening; or, Readings at Eventide for the Family or the Closet* (New York: Sheldon and Company, 1869, The Spurgeon Library), December 26 ; "The Spirit Crying 'Abba Father'" (Sermon 91).

4. Charles originally spelled this word "offeerred." The letters "e" and "r" are scribbled over in pencil to correct the misspelling.

5. Charles originally spelled this word "sacrafice." The letter "i" was written over the "a" in pencil to correct the misspelling. Throughout this sermon, Charles is inconsistent of the word "sacrifice."

6. "So that two whole, perfect, and distinct natures, the Godhead and the manhood, were inseparably joined together in one person, without conversion, composition, or confusion" (C. Matthew McMahon and Therese B. McMahon, eds., *The 1647 Westminster Confession of Faith with Scripture Proofs and Texts from the King James Bible* [Crossville, TN: Puritan Publications, 2011], 115). Charles's language also harkens back to the Council of Chalcedon (AD 451) when, according to the creed, Christ is acknowledged in two natures. "The orthodox doctrine maintains, against Eutychianism, the distinction of nature even after the act of incarnation, without confusion or conversion (ἀσυγχύτως, *inconfuse*, and ἀτρέπτως, *immutabiliter*), yet, on the other hand, without division or separation (ἀδιαιρέτως, *indivise*, and ἀχωρίστως, *inseparabiliter*), so that the divine will ever remain divine, and the human ever human, and yet the two have continually one common life, and interpenetrate each other, like the persons of the Trinity" (Philip Schaff, *A History of the Creeds of Christendom. With Translations* [London: Hodder and Stoughton, 1877, The Spurgeon Library], 31). Charles prefaced his 1855 republication of the 1689 Baptist Confession of Faith with the following words: "This ancient document is a most excellent epitome of the things most

surely believed among us" (*Thirty-Two Articles of Christian Faith and Practice; or, Baptist Confession of Faith, with Scripture Proofs, Adopted by the Ministers and Messengers of the General Assembly, Which Met in London in 1689, with a Preface by the Rev. C. H. Spurgeon*, [3rd ed.; London: Passmore & Alabaster, 1857]). The confession stated, "The Lord Jesus in his human nature thus united to the divine, in the person of the Son . . . Christ, in the work of mediation, acteth according to both natures, by each nature doing that which is proper to itself; yet by reason of the unity of the person, that which is proper to one nature sometimes in scripture, attributed to the person denominated by the other nature" (10–11). Throughout his ministry Charles's treatment of the hypostatic union was consistent with the language of Chalcedonian Christology. At times, however, his colorful and image-driven language results in theologically imprecise rhetoric. For instance, in speaking of the unity of Christ's human and divine natures, Charles said, "[D]eity espousing manhood" (*MTP* 9:700) and the two natures being "harmoniously blended" (*MTP* 23:685). In his 1859 sermon "Christ Precious to Believers," Charles said, "The precious gopher wood of his humanity is overlaid with the pure gold of his divinity" (*NPSP* 5:137). Clearly a reference to the ark of the covenant, Charles's language risked inverted Manichaeism, which kept Christ's divinity from penetrating his humanity (see Christian T. George, "Jesus Christ, The 'Prince of Pilgrims': A Critical Analysis of the Ontological, Functional, and Exegetical Christologies in the Sermons, Writings, and Lectures of Charles Haddon Spurgeon (1834–1892)" [PhD Thesis, University of St. Andrews, 2012], 78–84).

7. Cf. 2 Cor 5:21; *MTP* 52:146.

8. Charles originally spelled the word "sacrafice." He inserted the letter "i" over the "a" to correct the misspelling. Cf. Heb 9:28.

9. For additional instances of the hyphenation of the word "self-sacrifice," see *MTP* 22:402; *MTP* 27:499; and *MTP* 60:142.

10. "He has joys as God; but as the man-God, his joys spring from the salvation of the souls of men" (*NPSP* 2:299).

11. "I am told that deity cannot suffer. I am expected to subscribe to that because theologians say so. Well, if it be true, then I shall content myself with believing that the deity helped the humanity by strengthening it to suffer more than it

could otherwise have endured: but I believe that deity can suffer, heterodox as that notion may seem to be. I cannot believe in an impassive God as my Father" (*MTP* 26:162). See also *MTP* 20:597.

12. Cf. Rom 5:18.

13. "He has done so much, that it will never be needful for him again to be crucified. His side, once opened, has sent forth a stream deep, deep enough, and precious enough, to wash away all sin; and he needs not again that his side should be opened, or, that any more his hands should be nailed to the cross" (*NPSP* 2:298). Cf. 1 Pet 3:18.

14. Charles likely began writing the word "characteristics" before choosing to write the word "aggravations" instead.

15. Cf. Heb 4:14–15.

16. The emphasis in this sentence should fall on the word "He." It may best be read, "He was priest and offering too." Cf. *NPSP* 2:297–98; John 1:29; Heb 9:28; Rev 13:8.

17. Cf. Mark 16:19.   18. Cf. Acts 1:9.   19. Cf. 1 Cor 15:20; Jas 1:18.

20. "Christ would not sit down in heaven if he had more work to do. Sitting down is the posture of rest. . . . Oh! if the last thread had not been woven in the great garment of our righteousness, he would be spinning it now; if the last particle of our debt had not been paid, he would be counting it down now; and if all were not finished and complete, he would never rest, until, like a wise builder, he had laid the top-stone of the temple of our salvation. No; the very fact that he sits still, and rests, and is at ease, proves that his work is finished and is complete" (*NPSP* 2:298).

21. Cf. Matt 28:6; Luke 24:5–6.   22. Cf. 1 Kgs 8:11; Heb 10:11.

23. "But now he rests; there is no more toil for him now; there is no more sweat of blood, no more the weary foot, no more the aching head. No more has he to do" (*NPSP* 2:298).

24. Cf. John 19:30.

25. Cf. Col 2:15.

26. "The glorious dignity of our Saviour! I cannot talk of it in words, beloved: all I can say to you must be simple repetition" (*NPSP* 2:301).

27. Cf. Mark 16:19; Rom 8:34.

28. Charles inserted the phrase "and shows that he had" with a caret above and between the words "dignity" and "great."

29. Charles originally inserted an apostrophe between the letters "r" and "s" in the word "Conquerors." The context suggests he intended the word to be plural, not possessive.

30. "Then kings must bow their necks before his feet" (*NPSP* 2:304).

31. "In some sense that is already done; the foes of Christ are, in some sense, his footstool now. What is the devil but the very slave of Christ? for he doth no more than he is permitted against God's children. What is the devil, but the servant of Christ, to fetch his children to his loving arms?" (*NPSP* 2:303). See also *MTP* 22:363; Matt 24:44; and 1 Cor 15:25.

32. Cf. "The Little Fire and Great Combustion" (Notebook 1, Sermon 54).

33. "Not long shall anti-christ sit on her seven hills" (*NPSP* 2:303). Cf. "Salvation in God Only" (Notebook 1, Sermon 24).

34. Cf. "What Think Ye of Christ" (Notebook 1, Sermon 71).

35. Cf. Rom 14:11; Phil 2:10.

36. Cf. Matt 13:42; Luke 13:28.

37. Cf. Rev 20:1–3.

38. This is likely a reference to the last line of John Donne's sonnet "Death, Be Not Proud": "And Death shall be no more; Death thou shalt die" (John Carey, ed., *John Donne: The Major Works, Including* Songs and Sonnets *and Sermons* in Oxford World Classics [Oxford: Oxford University Press, 1990], 176). It may also be a reference to Isaac Watt's hymn "Guide Me O Thou Great Jehovah," which Charles cited at the conclusion of his 1856 sermon on Heb 10:12–13: "When

SERMON 84

I tread the verge of Jordan, / Bid my anxious fears subside: / Death of deaths, and hell's Destruction, / Land me safe on Canaan's side" (John T. Briscoe, ed., *The New Baptist Hymn Book Compiled from Steven's Selection, with Additions from the Old and New Hymnology of the Church of Christ* [London: Briscoe and Co., 1874, The Spurgeon Library], Hymn 496).

39. Cf. 1 Cor 2:2.

40. An alternative reading of this sentence is "Remember him, [the One] who still remembers man."

85 2 Pet. 2.22..   The Dog and Swine.

Here is
I. The Natural state of man he is a dog or sow
These are both unclean animals, the same figure occurs. Mat 7/6
dogs — violent, blaspheming men — swine, lascivious ones,
Man is depraved — so the best of men have said,
Investigate Scripture — ancient History — look now
at the Heathen, the Catholics and even here at those
who bursting the restraints of education, run wild.
  1. Selfishness is an animal propensity.
  2. Grovelling ideas unite men to brutes
  3. Sensuality — an animal characteristic.
II. There is a change which is not conversion.
the dog vomits, the sow is washed —
  I. There may be a conviction of sin, but.
    1. Common conviction denies God's justice
    2. Nor is it concerned for the loss of God's favour
    3. No hatred of sin as sin
    4. The sorrow arises from selflove not the love of God
    5. No discerning his depravity —
    6. No practical renunciation of self righteousness
  II. There may be a love of ordinances,
    1. Because of the scope & design of the gospel.
    2. Because of the pathos of the Speaker
    3. Because some sort of comfort is gained
but these do not care for spiritual communion
  III. Some reformation.
    1. The Man reforms from fear not love.
    2. Or he works for wages, for himself, not God

THE DOG AND SWINE—*2 Peter 2:22*

85

The DOG and SWINE
2 Peter 2:22[1]

"But it is happened unto them according to the true proverb, The dog is turned to his own vomit again; and the sow that was washed to her wallowing in the mire."

Here is:

I. THE NATURAL STATE OF MAN.

He is a dog or sow. These are both unclean animals. The same figure occurs [in] Matt. 7.6.[2] Dogs: violent, blaspheming men. Swine: lascivious ones. Man is depraved,[3] so the best of men have said. Investigate Scripture, ancient History. Look now at the Heathen, the Catholics,[4] and even here at those who, bursting the restraints of education, run wild.[5]

1. Selfishness is an animal propensity.
2. Grovelling ideas unite men to brutes.
3. Sensuality [is] an animal characteristic.

II. THERE IS A CHANGE WHICH IS NOT CONVERSION.

The dog vomits. The sow is washed.

I. There may be a conviction of sin, but:
   1. Common conviction denies God's justice.
   2. Nor is it concerned for the loss of God's favour.
   3. No hatred of sin as sin.
   4. The Sorrow arises from self-love, not the love of God.
   5. No discerning his depravity.
   6. No practical renunciation of self righteousness.

II. There may be a love of ordinances.[6]
   1. Because of the scope and design of the gospel.
   2. Because of the pathos of the speaker.
   3. Because some sort of comfort is gained.

   But these do not care for spiritual communion.

III. Some reformation.
   1. The Man reforms from fear, not love.
   2. Or he works for wages, for himself, not God.

III. This change is not enduring.
 1. Because it is not the design of the gospel.
 2. Love is absent —
 3. The Heart is untouched —

This does not interfere with the final perseverance of the saints, for they are sheep — these are still swine.

 1. Let us seek a change, lest we be among the goats.
 2. Let backsliders look to it —

110.

THE DOG AND SWINE—2 *Peter 2:22*

IV.[7] This change is not enduring.
> 1. Because it is not the design of the gospel.
> 2. Love is absent.
> 3. The Heart is untouched.

This does not interfere with the[8] final perseverance of[9] the saints,[10] for they are sheep. These are still swine.

> 1. Let us seek a change lest we be among the goats.
> 2. Let backsliders look to it.

SERMON 85

1. This is the only time Charles preached a sermon on 2 Pet. 2:22.

2. Matthew 7:6, "Give not that which is holy unto the dogs, neither cast ye your pearls before swine, lest they trample them under their feet, and turn again and rend you."

3. Cf. Ps 51:5; Rom 3:23; 5:12.

4. See previous sermon, "Jesus and His Acts" (Sermon 84).

5. Charles may have been referring to the college-educated students of Cambridge, though this is unlikely (Cf. *Autobiography* 1:241–48). His congregation at Waterbeach Chapel was composed mainly of uneducated farmers.

6. See "God's Estimation of Men" (Notebook 1, Sermon 41).

7. Charles originally inserted Roman numeral III instead of IV. There is no evidence to suggest he caught or corrected the misnumbering. An alternative interpretation is that Charles intended this section to be his third division.

8. Charles wrote the word "the" tightly between the words "with" and "final." He likely inserted this word after he had finished writing the line.

9. Charles wrote the word "of" as the last word of this line and also the first word of the next. This is an example of dittography.

10. It is evident that this doctrine, about which Charles preached three sermons prior in his sermon "Final Perseverance Certain" (Sermon 82), is still on his mind.

86   Jer X. 7 —   The Lord is a King —

The personage spoken of by Jeremiah as King is King now, had been then for a long time, even for ever, and will reign for ever — King of Nations, of Heaven, Hell and Earth he has 3 sorts of subjects —
  1. Those he rules in terrible justice, vengeance & wrath.
  2. Those he overrules by power, making their devices and even sins to work his will and purpose
  3. Those he rules by love, constraining them by gratitude
  These are willing subjects — among them he dwells in his great palace above, and his little ones below in men's hearts. his decrees are all made for them, his honor, wisdom love and power are their defense he ever smiles on them and gives audience to them they are happy some completely so, others partly so and that not because he is not equally loving to them but because they are not yet quite at one with him for they are not entirely holy as the angels &c are.
Angels, the saved one in heaven & some on earth are his subjects. and why not all.
    1. Because all do not know him, some are ignorant
    2. Some do not understand the way.
    3. All natural men dislike him.
But yet we ought to serve him and crown him for
    1. He is our Maker, father, strength.
    2. He is a Kingly personage, worthy to reign by reason of his holiness, wisdom, justice, truth, power.
    3. His past acts of kindness give him a claim.
    4. We live in his territory

THE LORD IS A KING—*Jeremiah 10:7*

86

The LORD *Is a* KING
Jeremiah 10:7[1]

"Who would not fear thee, O King of nations? for to thee doth it appertain: forasmuch as among all the wise men of the nations, and in all their kingdoms, there is none like unto thee."

The personage spoken of by Jeremiah as King is King now. [He] had been then for a long time, even for ever, and will reign for ever.[2] King of Nations,[3] of Heaven,[4] Hell, and Earth.[5]

He has 3 sorts of subjects:

1. Those he rules in terrible justice, vengeance, and wrath.
2. Those he over-rules by power, making their devices and even sins to work his will and purpose.[6]
3. Those he rules by love, constraining them by gratitude. These are willing subjects. Among them he dwells in his great palace above, and his little ones below in men's hearts. His decrees are all made for them. His honor, wisdom, love, and power are their defense. He ever smiles on them and gives audience to them. They are happy, some completely so. Others, partly so, and that not because he is not equally loving to them but because they are not yet quite at one with him. For they are not entirely holy as the angels, etc., are. Angels, the saved ones in heaven, and ~~they~~ some[7] on earth are his subjects. And why not all?

    1. Because all do not know him. Some are ignorant.
    2. Some do not understand the way.
    3. All natural men dislike him.

But yet, we ought to serve him and crown him,[8] for:

1. He is our Maker,[9] father,[10] strength.[11]
2. He is a Kingly personage, worthy to reign by reason of his holiness,[12] wisdom,[13] justice,[14] truth,[15] power.[16]
3. His past acts of kindness give him a claim.
4. We live in his territory.

Some will respond to this claim let them be thankful that they are willing in the day of his power, let them ever give to him.
1. Their humble homage of praise, honour and joy.
2. Strict, universal, obedience to his will
3. Entire resignation to his will
4. A trust implicit, and a love burning to increase his reign.

Some do not love submission let them know that he demands it of them, let me appeal.
1. To their conscience. is it just or right, is it not better to obey than to revolt.
2. To their fear. what is the use of rebellion, will it not bring heavy loss in time & eternity? do you not fear the great Lord of Hosts? Dare you give him a refusal.
3. To their hope — Does he not promise largely? he treats the submissive nobly, do not others prosper who obey will not you? Perhaps yea certainly you shall be happy for ever.
4. To their love, gratitude, generosity, to any spark of noble feeling — to induce them —

Cautioning them that a decree has passed. That Only through Jesus can obedience be accepted from creatures, fallen & depraved.

He. Prince Emanuel is sole ambassador —

112. 113.

THE LORD IS A KING—*Jeremiah 10:7*

Some will respond to this claim.

Let them be thankful that they are willing in the day of his power.[17] Let them ever give to him:

1. Their humble homage of praise, honour, and joy.[18]
2. Strict, universal obedience to his will.[19]
3. Entire resignation to his will.[20]
4. A trust implicit, and a love burning to increase his reign.

Some do not love submission.

Let them know that he demands it of them. Let me appeal:

1. To their conscience. Is it just or right? Is it not better to obey than to revolt?
2. To their fear. What is the use of rebellion? Will it not bring heavy loss in time and eternity? Do you not fear the great Lord of Hosts? Dare you give him ~~the~~ a refusal?[21]
3. To their hope. Does he not promise largely? He treats the submissive nobly. Do not others prosper who obey? Will not you? Perhaps, yea certainly, you shall be happy for ever.
4. To their love, gratitude, generosity, to any spark of noble feeling, to induce them, Cautioning[22] them that a decree has passed that Only through Jesus can obedience be accepted from creatures, fallen and depraved.

The Prince Emanuel is sole ambassador.

112. 113.[23]

SERMON 86

1. This is the only time Charles preached a sermon on Jer 10:7. For additional sermons on the kingly office of Christ, see "Jesus, the King of Truth" (*MTP* 18, Sermon 1086); "The King-Priest" (*MTP* 25, Sermon 1495); "Recruits for King Jesus" (*MTP* 30, Sermon 1770); "First King of Righteousness, and after That King of Peace" (*MTP* 30, Sermon 1768); "The Lowly King" (*MTP* 31, Sermon 1861); "The King in Pilate's Hall" (*MTP* 49, Sermon 2826); "The King of the Jews" (*MTP* 54, Sermon 3123); "Mocking the King" (*MTP* 55, Sermon 3138); and "A Vision of the King" (*MTP* 57; Sermon 3238).

2. Cf. Rev 11:15.

3. Cf. Rev 2:26.

4. Cf. Matt 28:18–19.

5. Cf. Zech 14:9.

6. Cf. Gen 50:20; John 17:12.

7. The word "some" is written above "on" and inserted with a caret. This change is in the hand of Charles. By "some" Charles could be referring to humans, as his following three points suggest. However, it is also possible Charles is continuing his train of thought by referring to angels. If so, perhaps he replaced "they" with "some" because Charles did not want to say *all* angels on earth are God's faithful subjects, for fallen angels "like ravenous lions go about seeking their prey" (*MTP* 11:76).

8. "None so majestic as he who wore the thorn-crown, but who shall put upon his head the crown of universal monarchy" (*MTP* 15:7).

9. Cf. Rev 4:11.

10. By using the word "father," Charles was likely referring to Jesus Christ, not God the Father. It is unusual for Charles to refer to the second person of the Trinity as "father." Cf. "Adoption" (Notebook 1, Sermon 1). See also the opening paragraphs of the sermon "His Name—the Everlasting Father" (*MTP* 12, Sermon 724).

11. Cf. Phil 4:13.

12. Cf. Heb 10:14.

13. Cf. 1 Cor 1:30.

14. Cf. Isa 42:1.

15. Cf. John 14:6.

16. Cf. Heb 1:3.

THE LORD IS A KING—*Jeremiah 10:7*

17. "We do not fear the day of judgment; we do not dread the thought of standing before our Lord Jesus, because we have a plea which we know will answer every purpose. Our plea is this: we have been tried, condemned, and punished already" (*MTP* 25:311).

18. Cf. Rev 5:12.   19. Cf. Luke 11:28.

20. Cf. *MTP* 12:39.

21. "He *will* reign over you, either by your own consent, or without it" (*MTP* 14:239, italics in the original).

22. The letter "g" in the word "cautioning" is smeared toward the bottom right of the page.

23. The number 113 is smeared toward the bottom right of the page.

87. Luke 23.42 — The thief's prayer —

This narrative though often improved is not exhausted.
The Circumstances briefly hinted at —

I. The thief's prayer, considered as an indication of real conversion — Sincere Prayer is an infallible sign — the difficulty is to know whether the prayer is real or no — we know the thief's was. we may presume that others will be like his. in his there was then —
  1. A confession of sin, and of the justness of the punishment
  2. A reliance on Jesus alone.
  3. Good works followed in proportion to his circumstances rebuke of his companion, an open confession, submission to Jesus, humility, a right estimation of heavenly things.

II. The greatness of the thief's faith as enhanced by various discouraging circumstances —
  1. Jesus circumstances. mocked, reviled, crucified, yet he calls him "Lord", and believes in his Kingdom, with clearer views than even Jesus disciples did. he did more than they, for they fled, he boldly confessed —
  2. The grounds of his faith, were small compared with what we enjoy, he probably had not attended his ministry, but perhaps was converted, by the Spirit, by means of Pilate's words, the exact fulfilment of prophecy. Jesus's quiet mien, prayer for his murderers, all united
  3. His own circumstances as a notorious, convicted sinner now at the point of death. in full view of depravity.

III. How far singular — in the circumstances of Jesus & in his own too — but as to the mode of salvation it is not at all singular — for all conversions are
  By grace acting on the heart — justification is still

87

The THIEF'S PRAYER
Luke 23:42[1]

"And he said unto Jesus, Lord, remember me when thou comest into thy kingdom."

This narrative, though often improved, is not exhausted.

The Circumstances briefly hinted at:

I. THE THIEF'S PRAYER CONSIDERED AS AN INDICATION OF REAL CONVERSION.[2]

Sincere Prayer is an infallible sign. The difficulty is to know whether the prayer is real or no[t]. We know the thief's was.[3] We may presume that others will be like his. In his there was this:

1. A confession of sin[4] and of the justness of the punishment.
2. A reliance on Jesus alone.
3. Good works followed in proportion to his circumstances. Rebuke of his companion,[5] an open confession, submission to Jesus, humility,[6] a right estimation of heavenly things.

II. THE GREATNESS OF THE THIEF'S FAITH AS ENHANCED BY VARIOUS DISCOURAGING CIRCUMSTANCES.

1. Jesus['s] circumstances. Mocked,[7] reviled, crucified.[8] Yet, he calls him "Lord" and believes in his kingdom with clearer views than even Jesus['s] disciples did.[9] He did more than they, for they fled.[10] He boldly confessed.
2. The Grounds of his faith were small compared with what we enjoy. He probably had not attended his ministry, but perhaps was converted by the Spirit, by means of Pilate's words, the exact fulfilment of prophecy.[11] Jesus'[s] quiet mien,[12] prayer for his murderers,[13] all united.[14]
3. His own circumstances as a notorious, convicted sinner now at the point of death[15] in full view of depravity.[16]

III. HOW FAR SINGULAR IN THE CIRCUMSTANCES OF JESUS, AND IN HIS OWN, TOO.

But as to the mode of salvation it is not at all singular,[17] for all conversions are By grace acting on the heart. Justification is at all

times by faith, no one has more merits than the thief. The same signs must be looked for in all conversions and all like prayers shall have like answers.
   1. Presume not. Sinner.
   2. Despair not. Sinner.
Let the thief's prayer help us in judging of ourselves and the sick — Let his faith shame our unbelief —
114.

John. 1–16.   The Grace received —   88.
The Evangelist is speaking not the Baptist.—
He is proceeding from what he says of Jesus in the 14th verse, where he speaks of what we shall speak of.
I. Jesus' fulness — not his divine fulness, but his mediatorial fulness as the head of a new covenant as the source of mercy — there was
   1. A fulness of grace — of the Spirit, of pardoning, justifying, upholding, persevering grace, as also of light, strength, wisdom and knowledge.
   2. A fulness of truth, he was the sum and substance, fulness of sincerity to man & integrity and faithfulness to God.
II. Our receivings. "grace for grace"—
not all men — not the apostles only, but all believers
   1. Grace instead of grace — the gospel instead of the fainter and less clear dispensation of Moses.
   2. ~~The Gos~~ Grace to produce grace in us — this was God's aim & design in giving grace.

THE THIEF'S PRAYER *and* THE GRACE RECEIVED

times by faith.[18] No one has more merits than the thief. The same signs must be looked for in all conversions, and all like prayers shall have like answers.

1. Presume not, sinner.
2. Despair not, sinner.[19]

Let the thief's prayer help us in [the] judging of ourselves and the sick.[20] Let his faith shame our unbelief.

114.

88

The GRACE RECEIVED
John 1:16[1]

"And of his fulness have all we received, and grace for grace."

The Evangelist is speaking, not the Baptist. He is proceeding from what he says of Jesus in the 14th verse, where he speaks of what we shall speak of.[2]

I. JESUS'[S] FULNESS.[3]

Not his divine fulness[4] but his mediatorial fulness as the head of a new covenant,[5] as the source of mercy. There was:

1. A fulness of grace. Of the Spirit,[6] of pardoning,[7] justifying,[8] upholding, persevering grace,[9] as also of light,[10] strength,[11] wisdom,[12] and Knowledge.[13]
2. A fulness[14] of truth.[15] He was the sum and substance,[16] fulness of sincerity to man and integrity and faithfulness to God.[17]

II. OUR RECEIVINGS, *"grace for grace."*

Not all men—not the apostles only, but all believer[s].

1. Grace instead of grace.[18] The Gospel instead of the fainter and less clear dispensation of Moses.[19]
2. ~~The Gos~~[20] Grace to produce grace in us.[21] This was God's aim and design in giving grace.[22]

3. Grace not for works but "for" on account of grace this is the great moving cause of all mercy –
4. Grace upon grace. mountains on mountains election, redemption, calling, regeneration, pardon &c.
 1. If we can say this how happy we are.
 2. If not how poor and miserable.
115.

---

89   John 4. 35.   The Harvest of souls.
How providential was this meeting with the woman. How wonderful the effect of a few words of conversation to one poor woman. – So is it still. by this is produced.
I. A whitening for harvest. What is it?
 1. Here was a congregation.
 2. Here were some convinced of sin.
 3. Some sort of reformation is a sign.
 4. Men were now desirous of knowing the truth.
II. A Harvest – whose harvest – ~~why a harvest~~. not the final gathering to glory but the gathering of grace – the reaping of the elect into the lower granary – It is
 1. Jesus harvest, the fruit of his agonies, the purchase of his life, the answer to his prayers.
 2. The Father's harvest, for to this end he gave his son, he longs to see righteousness extend.

3. Grace, not for works[23] but "for," on account, of grace. This is the great moving cause of all mercy.

4. Grace upon grace, mountains on mountains,[24] election,[25] redemption,[26] calling,[27] regeneration,[28] pardon,[29] etc.

    1. If we can say this how happy we are.

    2. If not, how poor and miserable.

115.

89

The HARVEST of SOULS
John 4:35[1]

"Say not ye, There are yet four months, and then cometh harvest? Behold, I say unto you, Lift up your eyes, and look on the fields; for they are white already to harvest."

How providential was this meeting with the woman. How wonderful the effect of a few words of conversation to one poor woman. So is it still. By this is produced:

I. A WHITENING FOR HARVEST. WHAT IS IT?

1. Here was a congregation.[2]

2. Here were some convinced of sin.

3. Some sort of reformation is a sign.

4. Men were now desirous of knowing the truth.[3]

II. A HARVEST.

Whose harvest?[4] ~~Why a harvest?~~[5] Not the final gathering to glory[6] but the gathering of grace, the reaping of the elect into the lower granary.[7] It is:

1. Jesus['s] harvest. The fruit of his agonies, the purchase of his life,[8] the answer to his prayers.

2. The Father's harvest. For to this end he gave his son.[9] He longs to see righteousness extend.

3. The Spirits' Harvest. for his is the seed, his to fit the sower for sowing, the ground for receiving, his to give life to the germ, to water, nourish, and mature.

4. A true Minister's harvest, for this he toils, not for applause or wealth, but for love to souls.

5. The Harvest of the Church. she travaileth, she is the machinery, the preacher the indicator. Of individual and collective exertion —

III. "Why a harvest?"
1. Because it is a thing desired and expected
2. It is a thing causing anxiety. will the crop be &c
3. It is a time of gladness & thankfulness.

IV. A few remarks.
1. Christians look. lift up your eyes with wonder, notice with attention.
2. Be instant with faith to keep off the blight with the clapping of prayer to keep off fowls.
3. Sinners. long to be reaped, see how heaven and earth are labouring for you.

Lord send a glorious harvest amen

116

3. The Spirit's Harvest. For his is the seed. His to fit the sower for sowing, the ground for receiving. His to give life to the germ, to water, nourish, and mature.

4. A true Minister's harvest. For this he toils. Not for applause[10] or wealth[11] but for love to souls.

5. The Harvest of the Church. She travaileth. She is the machinery, the preacher, the indicator of individual and collective exertion.

III. WHY A HARVEST?

1. Because it is a thing desired and expected.[12]

2. It is a thing causing anxiety.[13] Will the cross be good?

3. It is a time of gladness and thankfulness.

IV. A FEW REMARKS.

1. Christians, look. Lift up your eyes with wonder. Notice with attention.

2. Be instant with faith to keep off the blight[14] with the clapping of prayer to keep off fowls.

3. Sinners, long to be reaped. See how heaven and earth are labouring for you.

Lord, send a glorious harvest. Amen.

1. Charles preached two additional sermons on Luke 23:42. On January 31, 1886, he preached "The Dying Thief in a New Light" (*MTP* 32, Sermon 1881) and on April 7, 1889, he preached "The Believing Thief" (*MTP* 35, Sermon 2078). The former sermon overlaps in content with the first two Roman numerals of the outline above. The latter sermon, preached three years later, takes as its introductory and concluding subject the third Roman numeral. Charles likely had in mind this early outline when composing both later sermons.

2. "This robber breakfasted with the devil, but he dined with Christ on earth, and supped with him in Paradise" (*MTP* 32:59).

3. Cf. Luke 23:43.

4. "No one else was confessing Christ at that moment: no revival was around him with enthusiastic crowds: he was all by himself as a confessor of his Lord. After our Lord was nailed to the tree, the first to bear witness for him was this thief. The centurion bore witness afterwards, when our Lord expired; but this thief was a lone confessor, holding on to Christ when nobody would say 'Amen' to what he said. Even his fellow-thief was mocking at the crucified Saviour, so that this man shone as a lone star in the midnight darkness" (*MTP* 32:55).

5. Cf. Luke 23:40–41.

6. "[H]e did not say, 'Lord, let me sit at thy right hand;' or, 'Let me share of the dainties of thy palace;' but he said only, 'Remember me. Think of me. Cast an eye my way. Think of thy poor dying comrade on the cross at thy right hand. Lord, remember me. Remember me.' I see deep humility in the prayer, and yet a sweet, joyous, confident exaltation of the Christ at the time when the Christ was in his deepest humiliation" (*MTP* 32:55–56).

7. Cf. Luke 22:63.

8. Cf. Luke 23:33.

9. Cf. Mark 10:35–45; John 18:10; Acts 1:6.

10. "John might have been lingering at a little distance, and holy women may have stood farther off, but no one was present bravely to champion the dying Christ. Judas had sold him. Peter had denied him, and the rest had forsaken him; and it was then that the dying thief called 'Lord' and said, 'Remember me when thou comest into thy kingdom.' I call that splendid faith" (*MTP* 32:55). Cf. Mark 14:50.

11. Was Charles referring to an Old or New Testament prophecy about Pontius Pilate? Psalm 22:7 supports the former interpretation while John 8:28 and John 12:33 support the latter.

12. "Air; look; manner" (Johnson's *Dictionary*, s.v. "mien").

13. Cf. Luke 23:34.

14. "The robber wondered who this meek and majestic Personage could be. He heard the women weep, and he wondered in himself whether anybody would ever weep for him. . . . He himself, probably, had met his executioners with a curse; but he heard this man breathe a prayer to the great Father . . . . Peradventure, this dying thief read the gospel out of the lips of Christ's enemies. They said, '—He saved others.' 'Ah!' thought he, 'did he save others? Why should he not save me?' What a grand bit of gospel that was for the dying thief" (*MTP* 32:52–53).

15. "Remember, he was crucified. It was a crucified man trusting in a crucified Christ" (*MTP* 32:55).

16. "Here is a specimen of one who had gone to the extreme of guilt, and who acknowledged that he had done so; he made no excuse, and sought no cloak for his sin; he was in the hands of justice, confronted with the death-doom, and yet he believed in Jesus, and breathed a humble prayer to him, and he was saved" (*MTP* 35:183).

17. "The case of the dying thief is much more similar to our conversion than it is dissimilar; in point of fact, his case may be regarded as typical, rather than as an extraordinary incident" (*MTP* 35:181).

18. "If salvation had been by good works, he could not have been saved; for he was fastened hand and foot to the tree of doom. It was all over with him as to any act or deed of righteousness" (*MTP* 35:185). Cf. Rom 3:22; 5:1; Gal 2:16.

19. "Every sinner who has the will to do so may take the Lord home with him" (*MTP* 35:190).

20. An alternative reading of this line is "Let the thief's prayer help us in judging ourselves and the sick."

SERMON 88

1. Charles preached three additional sermons on John 1:16. On October 20, 1861, he preached "The Fulness of Christ Received!" (*MTP* 7, Sermon 415); on February 28, 1869, he preached "The Fulness of Jesus the Treasury of Saints" (*MTP* 15, Sermon 858); and his sermon "The Fulness and the Filling" (*MTP* 63, Sermon 3553) was published posthumously on March 1, 1917. Each of these sermons, and particularly the last, followed similar structures to the outline above, wherein Charles divided the sermon into the fullness of Christ and the filling of Christ's people. Charles possibly had his early outline in mind when writing his later sermons.

2. John 1:14, "And the Word was made flesh, and dwelt among us, (and we beheld his glory, the glory as of the only begotten of the Father), full of grace and truth."

3. "If I had no other text given to me to preach from until all preaching should be ended, this might suffice. *His fulness!*" (*MTP* 15:123, italics in the original)

4. In 1861 Charles contrasted this point with the words "The text informs us that there is a fulness in Christ. There is a fulness of essential Deity, for 'in him dwelleth all the fulness of the Godhead'" (*MTP* 7:537). In the sermon published in 1917, Charles echoed this emphasis: "Note this well; forget it not. Our Redeemer is essentially God. By nature he is divine" (*MTP* 63:99).

5. Cf. Heb 8:13.

6. Cf. 2 Cor 13:14.

7. Cf. Isa 55:7; 1 John 1:9.

8. Cf. Rom 5:1; "The Saints' Justification and Glory" (Notebook 1, Sermon 68).

9. Cf. "Final Perseverance" (Notebook 1, Sermon 8); "Final Perseverance Certain" (Sermon 82).

10. Cf. John 1:5; 8:12.

12. Cf. 1 Cor 1:24, 30.

11. Cf. Isa 40:29; Phil 4:13.

13. Cf. 1 Cor 2:16; 2 Pet 3:18.

14. An ink blot appears over the final three letters of the word "fulness" and also over the "c" and "e" of the word "substance" in the line below.

15. "We believe *in him*,—not merely in his words. *He* himself is Doctor and Doctrine, Revealer and Revelation, the Illuminator and the Light of Men" (*NPSP* 1:preface, italics in the original).

16. Charles used the phrase "sum and substance" with reference to Christ throughout his ministry. By this he meant, "Christ is the centre of the entire system

of the gospel, and all will be seen to move with regularity when you perceive that he is the chief fixed point; you cannot be right in the rest unless you think rightly of him. He is the centre and King of all truth" (*MTP* 17:634).

17. "In doing his Father's will, his action was so voluntary and so vicarious, that he has accumulated an inexhaustible fund of merit, which all of us who believe in his name may plead before the Father's throne" (*MTP* 63:100).

18. Charles may have used capitalization in the words "Grace" and "grace" to distinguish between the "Gospel" of the New Testament and "the fainter and less clear dispensation of Moses."

19. "Did none of them look to the works of the law? No, they all went to Jesus and his grace, and none to Moses and the law" (*MTP* 15:125).

20. Abbr. "Gospel."

21. "We receive from the fulness of Christ, of his grace, in order that it may be a living seed that shall produce grace in us as its natural fruit. The grace of gratitude should be produced in us by the grace of generosity from God" (*MTP* 63:108).

22. "If you have only got, as it were, an ounce of grace, that is a reason why you should then pray [to] God for a great weight of grace, and afterwards for a far more exceeding and eternal weight of glory. Believe that he gives grace for grace; that is, grace that you may open your mouth for more grace. The grace you have expands the heart, and gives you capacity for receiving yet more grace" (*MTP* 63:106).

23. Cf. Rom 3:28; Gal 2:16.

24. "The text is as [Mount] Tabor to us" (*MTP* 15:123).

25. Cf. "Election" (Notebook 1, Sermon 10); Eph 1:4; 2 Thess 2:13.

26. Cf. Gal 3:13; Eph 1:7.

27. Cf. "Jesus Calling" (*MTP* 48, Sermon 2781); "Calling and Election Sure" (Notebook 3, Sermon 135).

28. Cf. "Regeneration" (Notebook 1, Sermon 7); "Regeneration, Its Causes and Effects" (Notebook 1, Sermon 46).

29. Cf. Isa 55:7; 1 John 1:9.

SERMON 89

1. On July 29, 1866, Charles preached an additional sermon on John 4:35 entitled "Fields White for Harvest" (*MTP* 12, Sermon 706). In his later sermon Charles did not follow the primary structural divisions in the outline above. Instead his divisions were "*signs of harvest, wants of harvest,* and *fears of harvest*" (*MTP* 12:458, italics in the original). It is possible, though, given the large amount of overlapping content beneath the divisions, that Charles had this early outline in mind when writing his later sermon.

2. "We hear a great deal of strategy; it was our Saviour's strategy to bless the men of Samaria through this woman" (*MTP* 12:459). Cf. John 4:28.

3. "There they came, a whole troop of them from that little town, all anxious to listen to the Saviour" (*MTP* 12:460). Cf. John 4:30.

4. In his 1866 sermon Charles spoke to the cholera outbreak and death's harvest of bodies: "You cannot stop their dying, but oh! that God might help you to stop their being damned!" (*MTP* 12:466).

5. Charles likely struck through the phrase "why a harvest?" because he sought to save it for his third primary division on the following page.

6. Cf. Rev 14:15–16.

7. "The church of God is the barn, it is the Master's garner here; he has another garner yonder on the hill-top in heaven" (*MTP* 12:464).

8. Cf. Acts 20:28; Rev 5:9.

9. Cf. John 3:16.

10. Cf. Matt 6:1–5; John 5:41; 12:43.

11. Cf. Mark 10:23; Heb 13:15.

12. Cf. Matt 9:38.

13. "I cannot bear the thought that any of you should ever be bound in bundles to be burned" (*MTP* 12:467).

14. "Mildew; according to *Skinner*: but it seems taken by most writers, in a general sense, for any cause of the failure of fruits" (Johnson's *Dictionary*, s.v. "blight," italics in the original). In August 1852 British crops, particularly corn, suffered from unfavorable weather conditions (see "Review of the Corn Trade," *Manchester Examiner and Times*, September 8, 1852). These or similar blights may have been on Charles's mind. See also "Man's Weakness and God's Strength" (Sermon 108) and "God's Visits and the Effects Thereof" (Sermon 113).

90 —   Dan V. 27 —   Thou art too light.

Belshazzar feasts, defies the wrath of God, profanes his vessels, worships other God. He is jovial but sudden all his mirth is lost in terror — none can read but Daniel, hoar with 90 winters, bold in reproof he tells him that his gifts he disdains, tells him he was even worse than his grandfather, and then without exhorting him to repentance reads his irrevocable doom. —

No doubt I speak to Belshazzars who have turned their bodies, the vessels of Gods into pots for lust. Who have defied him, and that too under judgment.

I. The time when Tekel shall be uttered when Mene is said, thy days are numbered. the day of grace is sometimes over on earth. but in all cases at the day of judgment, all must be weighed, no shortweights allowed. —

II. The weights and scales —
1. The scales will hold all, even kings — mountains
2. They are very exact as the sufferings of Jesus the trials of the saints all testify, for these are by measure.
3. These are decisive, the standards, no appeal. —

The weights are not.
1. Our opinion of ourselves.
2. The opinion the church has of us
3. Nor the opinion of the world —

THOU ART TOO LIGHT
Daniel 5:27[1]

"TEKEL; Thou art weighed in the balances, and art found wanting."

Belshazzar feasts, defies the wrath of God, profanes his vessels, worships other God.[2] He is jovial, but sudden[ly] all his mirth is lost in terror.[3] None can read but Daniel, hoar[4] with 70 winters,[5] bold in reproof. He tells him that his gifts he disdains.[6] Tells him he was even worse than his grandfather.[7] And then, without exhorting him to repentance, [he] reads his irrevocable doom.[8]

No doubt I speak to Belshazzars who have turned their bodies, the vessels of Gods, into pots for lust, who have defied him, and that, too, under judgment.

I. THE TIME WHEN TEKEL SHALL BE UTTERED.

When Mene[9] is said, thy days are numbered. The day of grace is sometimes over on earth, but in all cases at the day of judgment all must be weighed.[10] No shortweights[11] allowed.

II. THE WEIGHTS AND SCALES.

1. The Scales will hold all, even Kings,[12] Mountains.

2. They are very exact, as: the sufferings of Jesus,
   the trials of the saints

   all testify. For these are by measure.[13]

3. These are decisive, the standards, no appeal.[14]

———————[15]

The weights are not:

1. Our opinion of ourselves.

2. The opinion the church has of us.

3. Nor the opinion of the world.

but the law of God, the Scriptures —

III. We will judge ourselves a little, that we may not be judged
We will put into the scale —
1. The whole human race by nature — short weight x
2. A selection of the very best, in themselves — too light x
3. Some of the poorest, least, believers in Jesus. all right ✓
4. Poor tempest-tost, Satan tempted sinner, up to the mark
  yet desiring to be saved by grace.
5. Hardly any need to try the Pharisee very light
  the swearer, drunkard, reprobate for these are x
6. Talkers, but not doers — short weight x
7. All Head, no heart, doctrine not practise short x
8. Shortwinded men. take it for a time short x
9. Half & Half — Hold with the hare, run with ye hounds short x
10. Sunday Man — no weekday religion short x
11. Morality but no change short x

None can sit in these scales, for all are as light as a feather. Yet Jesus will be weighed for his saints, we are complete in him.
117. 667.

But the law of God, the Scriptures.[16]

III. WE WILL JUDGE OURSELVES A LITTLE THAT WE MAY NOT BE JUDGED.[17]

We will put into the scale:

1. The whole human race by nature.[18] — short weight ☒
2. A selection of the very best in themselves. — too light ☒
3. Some of the poorest, least believers in Jesus.[19] — all right ☑
4. Poor tempest-tost,[20] Satan-tempted sinner, yet desiring to be saved by grace. — up to the mark ☑
5. Hardly any need to try the Pharisee, the swearer,[21] drunkard,[22] reprobate, for these are — very light ☒
6. Talkers but not doers. — short weight ☒
7. All Head no heart doctrine. Not practise. — short ☒
8. Shortwinded men take it for a time. — short ☒
9. Half and Half. Hold with the hare, run with ye hounds.[23] — short ☒
10. Sunday Man. No weekday religion. — short ☒
11. Morality, but no change. — short ☒

None can sit in these scales, for all are as light as a feather.[24] Yet Jesus will be weighed for his saints. We are complete in him.[25]

117. 667.

SERMON 90

1. On June 12, 1859, Charles preached an additional sermon on Dan 5:27 entitled "The Scales of Judgment" (*NPSP* 5, Sermon 257). The structural similarities between the title of the first primary division of the later sermon and the third in the outline above suggest Charles likely had in mind his early outline when writing his later sermon.

2. Cf. Dan 5:4.

3. Cf. Dan 5:6.

4. "White . . . grey with age . . . white with frost" (Johnson's *Dictionary*, s.v. "hoar").

5. Charles was referring to the seventy years of Judah's captivity in Babylon (Cf. Dan 9:2).

6. Daniel 5:17, "Then Daniel answered and said before the king, Let thy gifts be to thyself, and give thy rewards to another."

7. Daniel 5:22, "And thou his son, O Belshazzar, hast not humbled thine heart, though thou knewest all this."

8. Cf. Dan 5:24–28.

9. Daniel 5:26, "This is the interpretation of the thing: MENE; God hath numbered thy kingdom, and finished it."

10. Cf. Matt 12:36.

11. The word "shortweights" is not found in Johnson's *Dictionary* and may have been a colloquialism. The meaning of the word in singular form is constructed by combining the fifth definition of "short" ("not adequate; not equal: with *of* before the thing with which the comparison is made" [Johnson's *Dictionary*, s.v. "short," italics in the original]) with "weight" ("quantity measured by the balance" and "a mass by which, as the standard, other bodies are examined" [Johnson's *Dictionary*, s.v. "weight"]). In his 1883 sermon "The King's Weighings," Charles offered a context for the word "shortweight": "The Lord has gone on weighing all his acts as they have happened, and he has put them all aside as of short weight. As at the Bank all moneys are put through a process by which the light coins are detected, so

evermore our life passes over the great weighing-machine of the Lord's justice, and he separates that which is short in weight from that which is precious, doing this at the moment as infallibly as at the judgment day" (*MTP* 29:465).

12. "There is a weighing time for kings and emperors, and all the monarchs of earth" (*NPSP* 5:257).

13. This section, though broken, may most accurately read, "They are very exact, as the sufferings of Jesus [and] the trials of the saints all testify. For these are by measure." Charles likely added the phrases "the sufferings of Jesus" and "the trials of the saints" afterward. He may have originally intended the second point to read, "They are very exact as all testify. For these are by measure."

14. Cf. Matt 7:23.

15. Charles rarely divided his subpoints with a line of this length, especially in the middle of his sermon. He may have originally intended to place a conclusion here.

16. Cf. *NPSP* 5:260–61.

17. Cf. "Let Us Judge Ourselves That We May Not Be Judged" (*NPSP* 5:258).

18. Cf. Rom 3:23; 1 Cor 15:22.   19. Cf. Matt 25:40; 1 Cor 15:9.

20. The modernized spelling of "tempest-tost" is "tempest-tossed."

21. Cf. Matt 5:33–37; Jas 5:12.   22. Cf. 1 Cor 6:10.

23. The phrase "hold with the hare, run with the hounds" means to "play a double and deceitful game, to be a traitor in the camp" (Ebenezer Cobham Brewer, *Dictionary of Phrase and Fable. Giving the Derivation, Source, or Origin of Common Phrases, Allusions, and Words That Have a Tale to Tell* [17th ed., London, Paris & New York: Cassell & Company, 1885], 368).

24. "Do I descend in the scale with joy and delight, being found through Jesus'[s] righteousness to be full weight, and so accepted; or must I rise, light, frivolous, unsound in all my fancied hopes, and kick the beam?" (*NPSP* 5:263).

25. Cf. Col 2:10.

SERMON 91

91.   Gal 4.6 —   The Spirit crying "Abba Father."

The Epistle to the Galatians a great battering ram for the walls of Rome — as containing Justification by Faith. —

I. The Apostle Declaration. "God hath sent forth &c" not in a miraculous way, but still certain on all saints. Regeneration, conversion &c all require it, the personal safety, perseverance &c of the saints can only so be ensured. Of its influence on us we have internal evidence, in our souls, external in our lives. — In our "hearts" this is the original seat of action. it circulates from it to other parts — "sent forth" — implying that it does not rest in the word itself, nor in the heart of man naturally.

II. The Cause of his sending. "Ye are sons". Sonship, not service — that it might be of grace wholly. for sonship brought about by regeneration & adoption is manifestly the gift of God. — "Ye are" present things should be valued. we are not always to fret about what "we were", nor even always to sigh for "shall be"

III. The Effect — "crying Abba Father." "crying" not singing, or calling, or groaning. these are too high as evidences. all do not have them, but all have this. Abba. the word which slaves might not use to the free. — the Hebrews word, while the Gentile joins in & says Father. this is a short, unpolished, feeble cry: yet an eloquent, mighty and prevailing one. Jonah from the Fish. Moses without the utterance of a word, were heard and answered.

1. We must highly esteem the Spirit.
2. Let us take comfort, so shall the cry improve into the song.
3. How destitute of all are those who never cry. —

118.

91

The SPIRIT CRYING "ABBA FATHER"
Galatians 4:6[1]

"And because ye are sons, God hath sent forth the Spirit of his Son into your hearts, crying, Abba, Father."

The Epistle to the Galatians, a great battering ram for the walls of Rome,[2] as containing Justification by Faith.[3]

I. THE APOSTLE['S] DECLARATION. *"God hath sent forth, etc."*

Not in a miraculous way, but still certainly on all saints. Regeneration,[4] conversion,[5] etc. All require it. The personal safety, perseverance, etc. of the saints[6] can only so be ensured. Of its influence on[7] us we have internal evidence in our souls. External in our lives, in our "hearts." This is the original seat of action.[8] It circulates from it to other parts. "Sent forth:" implying that it does not rest in the word itself, nor in the heart of man naturally.

II. THE CAUSE OF HIS[9] SENDING. *"Ye are sons."*

Sonship,[10] not service, that it might be of grace wholly. For sonship brought about by regeneration and adoption[11] is manifestly the gift of God.[12] "Ye are." Present things should be valued. We are not always to fret about what "we were."[13] No, even always to sigh for "shall be."

III. THE EFFECT. *"Crying, Abba Father."*[14]

"Crying," not singing, or calling, or groaning. These are too high as evidences. All do not have them, but all have this: Abba. The word which slaves might not use to the free.[15] The Hebrews['] word. While the Gentile joins in and says, "Father." This[16] is a short, unpolished, feeble cry, yet an eloquent, mighty and prevailing one. Jonah from the Fish,[17] Moses without the utterance of a word,[18] were heard and answered.[19]

1. We must highly esteem the Spirit.[20]
2. Let us take comfort. So shall the cry improve into the song.
3. How destitute of all are those who never cry.

118.

SERMON 91

1. Charles preached two additional sermons on Gal 4:6. On September 22, 1878, he preached "Adoption—the Spirit and the Cry" (*MTP* 24, Sermon 1435), and on December 21, 1884, he preached "The Great Birthday and Our Coming of Age" (*MTP* 30, Sermon 1815). Both sermons share overlapping content with the above outline. In the former, Charles highlighted the doctrine of adoption. In the latter, he emphasized the incarnation. Between the two, the 1884 sermon more closely resembles the above outline and may have been inspired by it.

2. Cf. "Salvation in God Only" (Notebook 1, Sermon 24).

3. An alternative reading of this line is "The Epistle to the Galatians [is] a great battering ram for the walls of Rome [because it contains] Justification by Faith." Cf. "The Saints' Justification and Glory" (Notebook 1, Sermon 68); Rom 5:1.

4. Cf. "Regeneration" (Notebook 1, Sermon 7); 2 Cor 5:17; Titus 3:5.

5. Cf. "Repentance after Conversion" (*MTP* 41, Sermon 2419); "The Need and Nature of Conversion" (*MTP* 48, Sermon 2797).

6. The doctrine of perseverance of the saints is a dominant motif throughout Notebook 2. See "Final Perseverance Certain" (Sermon 82) and "The Corner Stone" (Sermon 128).

7. An illegible stem of a letter appears between the "o" and "n" in the word "on."

8. In Judaism, the heart "is the central point for the blood, and the seat of life" (Edward Robinson, trans., *Hebrew and English Lexicon of The Old Testament, Including the Biblical Chaldee. Translated from the Latin of William Gesenius, Doct. and Prof. of Theology in the University of Halle-Wittenberg* [Boston: Crocker and Brewster, 1836, The Spurgeon Library], 517).

9. An illegible letter is written beneath the letter "h" in the word "his."

10. Cf. John 1:12.   11. Cf. "Adoption" (Notebook 1, Sermon 1); Eph 1:5.

12. Our sonship comes by promise, by the operation of God as a special gift to a peculiar seed, set apart unto the Lord by his own sovereign grace, as Isaac was" (*MTP* 24:531).

13. This may be a reference to a 1793 remark by John Newton about 1 Cor 15:10: "1. I am not what I ought to be. Ah! how imperfect and deficient. 2. Not what

112

I might be, considering my privileges and opportunities. 3. Not what I wish to be. God, who knows my heart, knows I wish to be like him. 4. I am not what I hope to be; ere long to drop this clay tabernacle, to be like him and see him as He is. 5. Not what I once was, a child of sin, and slave of the devil. Though not all these, not what I ought to be, not what I might be, not what I wish or hope to be, and not what I once was, I think I can truly say with the apostle, 'By the grace of God I am what I am'" (Josiah Bull, *Letters by the Rev. John Newton of Olney and St. Mary Woolnoth. Including Several Never Before Published, with Biographical Sketches and Illustrative Notes* [London: The Religious Tract Society, 1869], 400).

14. Cf. Rom 8:15.

15. "According to ancient traditions no slave might say, 'Abba, Father'" (*MTP* 30:695). "Are you fond of wearing chains? Are you like Chinese women that delight to wear little shoes which crush their feet? Do you delight in slavery? Do you wish to be captives?" (*MTP* 30:696). "Rejoice that the free spirit dwells within you, and prompts you to holiness; this is a far superior power to the merely external command and the whip of threatening. Now no more are you in bondage to outward forms, and rites, and ceremonies" (*MTP* 24:534).

16. Excessive stippling surrounds the word "this."   17. Cf. Jonah 2:1.

18. Given his first reference to Jonah, Charles may have had in mind Moses's cry when rescued from the waters of the Nile River by Pharaoh's daughter (Cf. Exod 2:5–6).

19. An alternative reading of this line is "Jonah from the Fish [and] Moses without the utterance of a word were [both] heard and answered." In his 1878 sermon Charles said, "I want you now to notice a very sweet fact about this cry; namely, that *it is literally the cry of the Son.* . . . [O]ur Lord prayed in the garden, 'Abba, Father, all things are possible unto thee; take away this cup from me: nevertheless not what I will, but what thou wilt'" (*MTP* 24:538, italics in the original).

20. "Is it not ourselves that cry? Yes, assuredly; and yet the Spirit cries also. The expressions are both correct. The Holy Spirit prompts and inspires the cry. He puts the cry into the heart and mouth of the believer. It is his cry because he suggests it, approves of it, and educates us to it. We should never have cried thus if he had not first taught us the way. . . . There are times when *we* cannot cry at all, and then he cries in us" (*MTP* 24:537, italics in the original).

6.1.71.   1. Cor. 3. 21—23. Inventory & Title of our treasures. 92

The Church of Corinth lamentably divided, some choosing one minister and some another — now a preference for one more than another is natural and even innocent to some extent but when it induces contempt of other ministers it must be highly offensive to God. To idolize a minister is sin, to neglect others, is depriving ourselves of a part of the all which belongs to us and is blind folly — To reprove them for this Paul gives them —

I. An Inventory of their possessions: —
1. "Paul, or Apollos, or Cephas", all Gospel ministers; are not their own but the people can call them theirs. They seek not honour, emolument, or advancement, but God's glory by profiting his children. — They differ: "Paul" has a mind clear, strong, logical — He is deeply learned in all doctrine, is possessed of deep research & keen penetration. "Apollos", is elegant in person, musical in his voice, graceful in his action, he is less the logician, more the orator. "Cephas" is jealous, plain, and lively, he deals in unadorned truth, blunt and cutting. "Boanerges" is a son of thunder; damnation, wrath, hell, the law are sounded terribly, and with effect. "Barnabas" consoles us, by dwelling on Divine love and the softer, gentler, strains. "John" sends love out at every word. "Peter" cries "thou child of the devil &c" yet all these are God's — and so are ours to profit.
2. "The World" is ours, the only end of its existence is for us, when our end is served it will be burned. It is all ours and God deals out of its treasures to us by measure, we only enjoy it, others abuse it.

V.1.91[1]

92

INVENTORY *and* TITLE *of* OUR TREASURES
1 Corinthians 3:21–23[2]

"Therefore let no man glory in men. For all things are yours; whether Paul, or Apollos, or Cephas, or the world, or life, or death, or things present, or things to come; all are yours; and ye are Christ's; and Christ is God's."

The Church of Corinth [was] lamentably divided, some choosing one minister and some another. Now a preference for one more than another is natural, and even innocent to some extent.[3] But when it induces contempt of other ministers it must be highly offensive to God.[4] To idolize a minister is sin.[5] To neglect[6] others is depriving ourselves of a part of the all which belongs to us and is blind folly. To reprove them for this, Paul[7] gives them:

I. AN INVENTORY OF THEIR POSSESSIONS.[8]

   1. "Paul, or Apollos, or Cephas." All Gospel ministers are not their own, but the people can call them theirs.[9] They seek not honour, emolument,[10] or advancement, but God's glory by profiting his children. They differ:[11]

      "Paul" has[12] a mind clear, strong, logical.[13] He is deeply learned in all doctrine, is possessed of deep research and keen penetrations.
      "Apollos" is elegant in person, musical in his voice, graceful in his action.[14] He is less the logician, more the orator.[15]
      "Cephas" is zealous, plain, and lively. He deals in unadorned truth, blunt and cutting.[16]
      "Boanerges"[17] is a son of thunder. Damnation, wrath, hell, the law are sounded terribly, and with effect.[18]
      "Barnabas" consoles us by dwelling on Divine love and the softer, gentler strains.[19]
      "John" sends love out at every word.[20]
      "Peter" cries, "thou child of the devil,[21] etc."

Yet all these are God's, and so are ours to profit.

   2. "The World" is ours. The only end of its existence is for us.[22] When our end is served, it will be burned.[23] It is all ours, and God deals out of its treasures to us by measure. We only enjoy it; others abuse it.[24]

gods works in the world are ours to learn by, to teach us God — the earth is ours to conquer to Emmanuels dominion, we shall be kings and priests —

3. "Life". Is theirs as a lobby to dress in, for the grand entrée into the chamber of the Bridegroom. Theirs to enjoy the antepast of heaven in, theirs to glorify Jesus in. how sweet to have an opportunity of shewing our zeal. The seed-time of Eternity. The Saints purification time, with spices and with myrrh, to fit her for her Lord.

4. "Death" yes thou grim monster, hold thy tongue I am thy owner, frighten not thy master, but serve him. Tis a deliverance from sin, toil, trouble, care. Tis an entrance into Holiness, rest, joy, Jesus, Heaven. The gate of purity. The Perfecter of the Living.

5. "Things present" Prosperity should profit us by exciting to gratitude, joy, holiness. Adversity is doubly ours as the fire to consume the dross, and purify the gold. Providence is ours to guide, provide &c. Grace is ours to comfort, strengthen, constrain, restrain. [adoption justification] The ordinances, Sabbaths, Bible, Church all ours.

6. "Things to come" — death we have mentioned — all future life of whatever character. Resurrection we shall rise. Judgment, the confirmation of our state. Heaven. Eternity. God all the great unutterables are here summed up, without these things to come the list would not be complete, but all things conceivable, yea and inconceivable are ours for ever and ever since the title is Good and thus brings us to

INVENTORY AND TITLE OF OUR TREASURES—*1 Corinthians 3:21-23*

God[']s works in the world are ours to learn by, to teach us God. The earth is ours to conquer[25] to Emanuel[']s dominion. We shall be kings and priests.

3. "Life"[26] is theirs as a lobby to dress in for the grand entrée into the chamber of the Bridegroom. Theirs to enjoy the antepast[27] of heaven in. Theirs to glorify Jesus in. How sweet to have an opportunity of shewing our zeal. The Seed-time[28] of Eternity.[29] The Saint[']s purification[30] time, with spices and with myrrh to fit her for her Lord.[31]

4. "Death."[32] Yes, thou grim monster, hold thy tongue. I am thy owner. Frighten not thy master, but serve him.[33] Tis a deliverance from sin, toil, trouble, care.[34] Tis an entrance into Holiness, rest, joy, Jesus, Heaven.[35] The gate of purity.[36] The Perfecter of the Living.[37]

5. "Things[38] present." <u>Prosperity</u> should profit us by exciting to gratitude, joy, holiness. <u>Adversity</u> is doubly ours as the fire to consume the dross[39] and purify the gold.[40] <u>Providence</u> is ours to guide, provide, etc. <u>Grace</u> is ours to comfort, strengthen, constrain, restrain. <u>Adoption</u>,[41] <u>Justification</u>.[42] The ordinances,[43] Sabbaths, Bible, Church [are] all ours.

6. "Things to come." Death, we have mentioned. <u>All Future Life</u>[44] of whatever character. <u>Resurrection</u>, we shall rise.[45] <u>Judgment</u>,[46] the confirmation of our state. <u>Heaven</u>, <u>Eternity</u>, <u>God</u>, all the great unutterables are here summed up. Without these things to come, the list would not be complete. But all things conceivable, yea, and inconceivable, are ours for ever and ever since the title is Good. And thus brings us to:

II. The Title deed of the Inheritance.
"Ye are Christs, and Christ is Gods" – he, whose are all these, is Christs – 1. By the Father's gift to the Son.
2. By the Sons purchase on Calvary, with a bloody price.
3. By Consecration, to him – resigning their souls to him to be saved, their spirits to be renewed, their lives to be devoted – they are not their own but Christs
Unless you can say this you can't read your title for you have none – You must be his, his as he is 3 things. his as a disciple since he is a Prophet, as a humble suppliant he is a Priest, his as a subject for he is King. If you are his you are his <u>Brother</u>, his <u>Wife</u>, his <u>Bones & Flesh</u>
The Second part of the title deed runs thus, and is necessary to ~~his~~ its validity – "<u>Christ is Gods</u>"
"<u>Christ is Gods</u>" son – and therefore what shall be denied him
"<u>Christ is Gods</u>" heir, and who shall deny his right
"<u>Christ is Gods</u>" gift, will he not freely give us all things.
The Devil, the world, and old Unbelief with all their quibbles shall never hurt this title deed –
Burn it they cannot 'tis in heaven's archives. –
But if a man claim these, without the proper deed and writings, his case when tried will fail.
III. The proper behaviour of the possessor.
"Let no man glory in men." "Not to in <u>ministers</u>"
"You have all things do not be so dazzled with one.
"Ye are Christs" do not pin yourself to man.
"Christ is Gods" do not fancy he belongs to only one section of the Church, or to only one minister.

INVENTORY AND TITLE OF OUR TREASURES—*1 Corinthians 3:21-23*

II. THE TITLE DEED OF THE INHERITANCE.

"Ye are Christ[']s, and Christ is God[']s." He, whose are all these, is Christ[']s:

1. By the Father's Gift to the Son.[47]

2. By the Son[']s purchase on Calvary, with a bloody price.[48]

3. By consecration to him,[49] resigning their souls to him to be saved, their spirits to be renewed, their lives to be devoted.[50] They are not their own. but Christ[']s.[51]

Unless you can say this, you can't[52] read your title, for you have none. You must be his, his as he is 3 things:[53]

His as a disciple since he is a Prophet.[54]

[His] as a humble suppliant, [for] he is a Priest.[55]

His as a subject, for he is King.[56]

If you are his, you are his <u>Brother</u>,[57] his <u>Wife</u>,[58] his <u>Bones and Flesh</u>.[59]

The Second part of the title deed runs thus, and[60] is necessary to ~~his~~ its validity. "Christ is God's."[61]

"<u>Christ is God's</u>" son, and therefore what shall be denied him?

"<u>Christ is God[']s</u>" heir, and who shall deny his right?

"<u>Christ is God[']s</u>" gift. Will he not freely give us all things? The Devil, the world,[62] and old Unbelief with all their quibbles, shall never hurt this title deed. Burn it they cannot, 'tis in heaven's archives. But if a man claim[s] these without the proper deed and writings, his case when tried will fail.

III. THE PROPER BEHAVIOR OF THE POSSESSOR.[63]

"Let no man glory in men." "Not ~~to~~ in <u>ministers</u>."[64] You have[65] all things. Do not be so dazzled with one.[66] "Ye are Christ's." Do not pin yourself to man. "Christ is God[']s." Do not fancy[67] he belongs to only one section of the Church,[68] or to only one minister.

Glory not in self. You are nothing, have nothing except as self is lost and merged in Jesus.
Trust not your own strength, be humble, glory in God

1. Search for the deeds in the chest, in the heart, be sure if they are in heaven, you will have a copy of them.

2. If all things are ours. what fools we should be to murmur, the Possessor of the Earth must not cry for farthings — but be the happiest of beings.

3. Be liberal. If you have all things you can afford a little. If Christ gave you all sure you can give him some —

120. 237. 333. 440. 489.

INVENTORY AND TITLE OF OUR TREASURES—*1 Corinthians 3:21–23*

Glory not in <u>self</u>. You are nothing,[69] have nothing, except as self is lost and merged in Jesus.

Trust not your own strength.[70] Be humble,[71] glory in God.

1. Search for the deeds in the chest, in the heart.[72] Be sure, if they are in heaven, you will have a copy of them.[73]

2. If all things are ours, what fools we should be to murmur.[74] The Possessor of the Earth must not cry for farthings[75] but be the happiest of beings.

3. Be liberal. If you have all things, you can afford a little. If Christ gave you all, sure[ly] you can give him some.[76]

120. 237. 333. 440. 489.

SERMON 92

1. The inscription V.1.91 is the first of four inscriptions found in Notebook 2 corresponding to a collection of sermons entitled *Sketches of Sermons* (see also "The Tranquillity, Security, and Supplies Afforded to the Gospel Church" [Sermon 97]; "Justification, Conversion, Sanctification, Glory" [Sermon 102]; and "Envy Forbidden, Piety Commanded" [Sermon 112]). In 1851, Jabez Burns noted, "The practice of [d]isseminat[ing] those textual expositions generally known as an Analysis or Sketches of Sermons" had been lost for a century (Jabez Burns, *The Pulpit Cyclopædia, and Christian Minister's Companion; Containing Three Hundred and Sixty Skeletons and Sketches of Sermons, and Eighty-Two Essays on Biblical Learning, Theological Studies, and the Composition and Delivery of Sermons. By the Author of "Sketches and Skeletons of Sermons," "Christian's Daily Portion," and "Sermons for Family Reading"* [New York: D. Appleton & Company; Philadelphia: George S. Appleton, 1851], i). Two exceptions were Charles Simeon's *Horae Homileticae* and *Sketches of Sermons*, both of which Charles consulted when preparing his earliest sermons (for Charles's use of Simeon, see "The Son's Love to Us Compared with God's Love to Him [Notebook 1, Sermon 38] and "Regeneration, Its Causes and Effects" [Notebook 1, Sermon 46]). Burns described *Sketches* as "characterized by considerable fervor, . . . lively in their manner, and replete with evangelical doctrine; and will aid the student accurately to comprehend, and rightly to divide 'the word of truth'" (ii). According to *The London Catalogue of Books*, an earlier edition of *Sketches* had been published in 1821 by Holdsworth in eight volumes, each containing fifty sketches (see *The London Catalogue of Books, with Their Sizes, Prices, and Publishers. Containing the Books Published in London, and Those Altered in Size or Price, Since the Year 1810 to February 1831* [London: Robert Bent, 1831], 257, and *The Evangelical Magazine and Missionary Chronicle. 1821. Volume XXIX* [London: Francis Westley, 1821], 109). Charles did not use this eight-volume edition for his sermons. Instead, he consulted a later four-volume edition, which was also published in the United States (see *Sketches of Sermons: Preached in Various Parts of the United Kingdom and on the European Continent Furnished by Their Respective Authors*, vols. 1–4 [Philadelphia: Sorin and Ball, 1844]). The sermon outlines in this 1844 edition match identically Charles's volume and page numbers in his inscriptions with the exception of V.3.52 in "Envy Forbidden, Piety Commanded" (Sermon 112), which should instead be V.3.62. In the top left corner of the page, Charles inscribed the reference V.1.91 or volume 1, sermon outline 91, which corresponds to the sermon outline "The Riches of the Christian" in the first volume of *Sketches of Sermons* (329–32). Overlapping content is noted below.

INVENTORY AND TITLE OF OUR TREASURES—*1 Corinthians 3:21–23*

2. In 1856 Charles preached a sermon on 1 Cor 3:21–23 entitled "The Christian's Glorious Inventory" (*MTP* 44, Sermon 2589). This sermon was not included in the second volume of *New Park Street Pulpit* as it should have been. Instead, it was posthumously published in 1898. The structural divisions and overlapping content strongly suggest that Charles used the above outline when composing the later sermon.

3. "The Church of Corinth was divided into factions, each of which professed to love and admire one particular preacher, who was preferred to the utter exclusion of every other. To be more attached to one minister than another is natural, in some cases unavoidable, and perfectly innocent" (*Sketches of Sermons* 1:329).

4. "If it produces *contempt* of all other ministers, it is highly offensive to Him, whose ministers they are" (*Sketches of Sermons*, 1:329, italics in the original). "Now, beloved, the same thing that occurred in Corinth, has happened in London and elsewhere many a time. It is but right that persons should feel an attachment to those who preach the gospel to them; but when this grows to an overweening adoration, when it becomes almost a worship, and persons are led to despise all other ministers, and will hear none beside that one man whom they believe to be sent from God, then, indeed, they need a solemn reproof as did these Corinthians" (*MTP* 44:457).

5. "Their *sin* in *idolizing* any individual" (*Sketches of Sermons*, 1:330, italics in the original). Relevant here is Charles's opposition to the denomination that formed around his own ministry (see "Spurgeonism," *ST* March 1866:138).

6. Charles wrote an illegible letter beneath the "n" in the word "neglect."

7. Charles wrote an illegible letter beneath the "a" and "u" in the word "Paul."

8. "Nothing will tend so much to lessen your undue reverence for men, or to check your glorifying in them, as a vision of what you are yourselves worth. If you see your own property, your own possessions, you will not then be so much inclined to place too high a value upon one certain thing, though it may be in itself exceedingly precious" (*MTP* 44:458).

9. "All preachers are not Pauls, all are not like Apollos, and all cannot speak like Cephas; but ministers of all kinds are yours; they are not their own, they belong to the Church at large" (*MTP* 44:458).

SERMON 92

10. "Profit; advantage" (Johnson's *Dictionary*, s.v. "emolument").

11. Instead of a colon, this symbol could mean "because" or "therefore." See also "Future Judgment" (Notebook 1, Sermon 6).

12. Charles wrote the word "is" beneath the letter "h" in the word "has."

13. "*I am of Paul.*—I admire a learned minister, of a clear, strong, and logical mind" (*Sketches of Sermons*, 1:329, italics in the original).

14. "*I am of Apollos.*—I love a fine person, a musical voice, and graceful action" (*Sketches of Sermons*, 1:329, italics in the original). Cf. 1 Cor 2:4; 3:6; 2 Cor 11:6.

15. "[Apollos] cannot reason, perhaps, but he puts his thoughts into beautiful shapes, and delivers them well; go and hear Apollos" (*MTP* 44:458).

16. "*I am of Cephas.*—Logic, and the tinsel of oratory, I care nothing for; I love a zealous, plain, lively preacher, who deals in blunt unadorned truth" (*Sketches of Sermons*, 1:329, italics in the original). "[Cephas] never minces matters; what he says, he says out of his heart, *con amore;* his whole soul goes with every word" (*MTP* 44:458, italics in the original).

17. Boanerges was the name given to James and John, the two sons of Zebedee. Cf. Mark 3:17; Luke 9:54.

18. "Boanerges, sons of thunder. These chiefly dwell on the terrible; on the holiness of the law; the solemnities of a future judgment, the horrors of damnation" (*Sketches of Sermons*, 1:331). "[Boanerges] preaches, in a thundering manner, of the wrath to come; his sermons alarm you; he drags a harrow across your soul; he speaks as if he had just come from the top of Sinai, where the thunders of God were pealing, and the lightning flashing beneath his feet" (*MTP* 44:459).

19. "Others are only accessible chiefly by the passion of love. To these are sent Barnabas, a son of consolation; who dwells principally on the love of Christ, manifested in his death, his intercession, his invitations, and promises" (*Sketches of Sermons*, 1:331). "You seldom hear thunder from [Barnabas]; his preaching is like the soft evening breeze. He is like the sun that has healing beneath his wings; gently he speaks to the broken-hearted, and bindeth up their wounds" (*MTP* 44:459). Cf. Acts 4:36; 9:27; 11:22–24; Gal 2:13.

INVENTORY AND TITLE OF OUR TREASURES—*1 Corinthians 3:21–23*

20. "You can read love in [John's] eyes; he hath leaned his head on the bosom of Jesus" (*MTP* 44:459). Cf. John 13:23; 21:20; 1 John 4:7.

21. Acts 13:10, "And said, O full of all subtilty and all mischief, thou child of the devil, thou enemy of all righteousness, wilt thou not cease to pervert the right ways of the Lord?'"

22. "*2. The world is for their benefit.* But for the church the world would be destroyed. It is the scaffold which God uses in raising a temple of living stones in which he is to be eternally worshipped, the theatre in which he is to perform the wonderful operations of his grace" (*Sketches of Sermons*, 1:331, italics in the original). "Take *you* away, and the world would be turned into rottenness, and perish.... God bids the flames tarry till he has taken all his children home; he only keeps the world in existence for the sake of his elect" (*MTP* 44:460, italics in the original).

23. Cf. 1 Pet 3:7; 2 Pet 3:10.

24. "[Christians] alone properly enjoy the world. Others abuse it" (*Sketches of Sermons*, 1:331).

25. Cf. Gen 1:28.

26. "In life they obtain a meetness for 'the inheritance of the saints'" (*Sketches of Sermons*, 1:331).

27. "A foretaste; something taken before the proper time" (Johnson's *Dictionary*, s.v. "antepast").

28. See "Review of the Corn Trade: November," *Cambridge Chronicle and University Journal, Isle of Ely Herald, and Huntingdonshire Gazette*, November 13, 1852.

29. "In life they sow seed which will spring up to everlasting life, Gal. vi. 8. The longer the seed time, and the more seed sown, the greater and more glorious will be the harvest" (*Sketches of Sermons*, 1:331).

30. "With all its trials and sorrows, it is still a precious gem; it may be set in a ring of iron, but it is a gem notwithstanding" (*MTP* 44:461).

31. In his 1856 sermon Charles cited Esther, not Jesus, adorned with spices and myrrh (cf. Esth 2:12; John 19:39).

32. "*4. Death is for their benefit*" (*Sketches of Sermons*, 1:331, italics in the original).

33. "O Death! thy ghastly appearance hath sometimes frightened me, I have striven to run away from thee; but thou art my slave now, and I will not tremble at thee any more. Death, thou art mine! I write thee down among my goods and chattels, a part of my own property" (*MTP* 44:462).

34. "It terminates all his sufferings. The pilgrim ends his journey. The warrior retires victorious from the field of blood. The tempest-tost mariner enters a peaceful harbour" (*Sketches of Sermons*, 1:331).

35. "There are some books that have only plain black letters till you come to the 'Finis,' which is illuminated; so it is often with life, it is printed in black letters till you come to the last leaf, and that page is lit up with glory,—for that page is death" (*MTP* 44:462).

36. "His purity shall be spotless" (*Sketches of Sermons*, 1:331).

37. "It is good to die at last when we know what it is to die every day" (*MTP* 44:462).

38. The word "Things" is surrounded with stippling.

39. Charles is inconsistent with his use of the long "s." Cf. "possessor" on the following page with "poſsessor" on the fourth page of this outline.

40. Cf. Prov 17:3; Ezek 22:19–22; Zech 13:9; Mal 3:2–3; 1 Pet 1:7.

41. Cf. "Adoption" (Notebook 1, Sermon 1); Eph 1:5.

42. The words "Adoption, Justification" were written in smaller script beneath "ours to comfort." A less likely alternative location for these words is after "is."

43. Cf. "God's Estimation of Men" (Notebook 1, Sermon 41).

44. "Resurrection, judgment, heaven" (*Sketches of Sermons*, 1:331).

INVENTORY AND TITLE OF OUR TREASURES—*1 Corinthians 3:21–23*

45. Cf. Dan 12:2; 1 Corinthians 15; Rev 20:12–13.

46. Cf. "The Certain Judgment" (Notebook 3, Sermon 136); "The General Judgment" (Notebook 7, Sermon 323).

47. "1. *It is conveyed from God to Christ*" (*Sketches of Sermons*, 1:330, italics in the original). "Am I Christ's *by eternal donation*, because God the Father gave me to the Son?" (*MTP* 44:465, italics in the original). Cf. Eph 5:27.

48. Cf. Eph 1:7; 1 John 1:7.

49. Cf. Josh 3:5.

50. An illegible letter, likely "c," was written beneath the "d" in the word "devoted." Charles likely intended to write the word "consecrated." "If you consecrate yourselves to Jesus, you will never find him a hard Master. I have known him some little while, and he hath been exceedingly kind to his unworthy servant. I have nought to find fault with him, but much with myself" (*MTP* 44:466).

51. Cf. 1 Cor 6:19–20.

52. This is the first time Charles has used a contraction in his early notebooks.

53. An alternative reading of this line is "His, as he is. Three things:"

54. Cf. Matt 21:11.

55. Cf. Heb 4:14–16.

56. Cf. John 12:15; 18:37; 1 Tim 6:15; Rev 19:16.

57. Cf. Matt 12:48–49.

58. Cf. Isa 54:5; Eph 5:27; Rev 19:7–9; 21:9.

59. Cf. John 1:14; Gal 4:4; Phil 2:7.

60. Charles originally wrote the letter "i" beneath the "a" in the word "and." He likely wrote the word "is" prematurely.

61. "With one hand Christ links himself to men, with the other he is joined to God; and thus God and men are united" (*MTP* 44:466).

SERMON 92

62. Cf. "The Fight and the Weapons" (Notebook 1, Sermon 37a); "The Fight" (Notebook 1, Sermon 37b).

63. Charles reworded this third primary division in his later sermon: "III. Now, lastly, What Is the duty of a Man Who Has Such Large Possessions?" (*MTP* 44:467).

64. It is unclear why Charles inserted quotation marks around the phrase "Not ~~to~~ in ministers."

65. Charles originally wrote the letter "a" beneath "h" in the word "have." He likely began writing the word "all" prematurely.

66. Charles echoes here his earlier statement in the introduction to this outline: "To idolize a minister is sin." Charles originally did not include the final letter "r" in the word "ministers." He corrected this misspelling by inserting an "r" between the letters "e" and "s."

67. Cf. "The Men Possessed of the Devils" (Notebook 1, Sermon 70). In this context Charles used the word "fancy" synonymously with "think" or "believe." See also "The Unclean Spirit Returning" (Notebook 3, Sermon 168).

68. Cf. "Pleasure in the Stones of Zion" (Notebook 1, Sermon 53).

69. Cf. John 15:5.

70. Cf. 1 Chron 16:11; Pss 20:7–8; 27:1; Isa 41:10; Phil 4:13.

71. Cf. Matt 23:12; Phil 2:3; Jas 4:10; 1 Pet 5:6.

72. Cf. Matt 6:21; Luke 12:34.

73. "They believe his truth, feel his influence, obey his precepts, and copy his example" (*Sketches of Sermons*, 1:330). "If you have lost your copy, you can get another, for the old deed is up in the ark in heaven" (*MTP* 44:468).

74. "If all these belong to the Christian, it is a reproach to him to be the subject of murmuring and complaint" (*Sketches of Sermons*, 1:332). Cf. Phil 2:14; Jas 5:9; Jude 1:16.

INVENTORY AND TITLE OF OUR TREASURES—*1 Corinthians 3:21-23*

75. A farthing was a British coin worth one-fourth of a penny. Cf. "King of Righteousness and Peace" (Notebook 1, Sermon 42).

76. "Now, by way of a practical hint, I might say, if 'all things are yours,' *how willing you ought to be to give something to the cause of God!*" (*MTP* 44:468, italics in the original).

Rom. XII. 1 — "Present your bodies &c"

It is a foul piece of lying, and an abominable spawn of scandal to say "the doctrines of grace lead to licentiousness" for a belief of them lies at the root of all evangelical obedience & they are the very cause of holiness. The apostle who speaks of the loftiest heights of election is now climbing the heights of practise.

We shall notice, those of us who are Christians

I. What we are to do — "to present &c"
"to present" not give up when demanded, but freely to bring forward and freely give. and that every day, constantly — legal obedience resigns.
Spiritual obedience presents.
your bodies, the soul can only be presented in the body, the body can only be presented with the soul — the whole body, not the head, or hands, or ears alone. the whole time, talents — are to be presented — all.
a living sacrafice — in opposition to the dead ones of the law, death atones, but our sacrafice is not intended for that purpose. A living, not a formal heartless offering — a living. i.e. an active, lively one some Christians seem "dead and alive", not so ought it to be. a living, i.e. in life not delaying till the death bed. God loves not old dying bulls but without blemish sacrafice, here is consecration to him; as were the lambs of old, so must we be, dead to the world. here is self denial, self-sacraficing, the death of self, loving others better than self. a sac to man, to God

93

PRESENT YOUR BODIES, ETC.
Romans 12:1[1]

"I beseech you therefore, brethren, by the mercies of God, that ye present your bodies a living sacrifice, holy, acceptable unto God, which is your reasonable service."

It is a foul piece of lying and an abominable spawn of scandal[2] to say "the doctrines of grace lead to licentiousness," for a belief of them lies at the root of all evangelical obedience, and they are the very cause of holiness. The apostle who speaks of the loftiest heights[3] of election[4] is now climbing the heights of practise.

We shall notice, those of us who are Christians:

I. WHAT WE ARE TO DO, *"to present,* etc."

"To present." Not give up when demanded, but freely to bring forward and freely give. And that, every day, constantly.

> Legal obedience resigns.
> Spiritual obedience presents.

Your bodies. The soul can only be presented in the body. The body can only be presented with the soul—the whole body, not the head, or hands, or ears alone. The whole time, talents, are to be presented. All.

A living sacrifice[5] in opposition to the dead ones of the law.[6] Death atones, but our sacrifice[7] is not intended for that purpose. A living, not a formal, heartless offering. A living, i.e., an active, lively one. Some Christians seem "dead and alive." Not so ought it to be. A living, i.e., in life, not delaying till the death bed.[8] God loves not old dying bulls but [those] without blemish.[9]

Sacrifice.[10] Here is consecration to him. As were the lambs of old,[11] so must we be dead to the world. Here is self denial,[12] self-sacrificing,[13] the death of self, loving others better than self,[14] a sac[15] to man, to God.

II. How are we to do it. "Holy and acceptable &c.
Holy. Holiness is the only way of offering ourselves to God. a man has not made a full surrender until holiness predominates in him, — the ways of penance. mortification & adopted by Catholics are not the way God loves but it is holy. — God never requires us to do anything at variance with his law, and the best way of serving him is the way he has appointed acceptable, and to be so several things are required.
1. They must be slain by the priest. i.e. Jesus in us must destroy sin, if anything else makes a reform in us, it will not be acceptable.
2. They must be offered on the one altar. Jesus. the only acceptable works are those done by faith in him — we must offer only as his servants.
3. Mingled with salt. Jesus merit must be put with them, he must season them.
4. They must be wholly offered and be whole when offered, if but an inch of the tail be gone they cannot be accepted. — all or nothing

III. The arguments Paul employs.
1. your brother, God's ambassador, your minister beseech, strongly urge on you, more than desire or request. I beg and pray of you, even on my knees.
you. both Jews & Gentiles. for I have been speaking of both.
Therefore, because of your election. since if Jews ye are a remnant of a nation now given over to blindness of heart — if Gentiles that ye are

II. HOW ARE WE TO DO IT? *"Holy and acceptable, etc."*

Holy. Holiness is the only way of offering ourselves to God. A man has not made a full surrender until holiness predominates in him. The ways of penance, mortification, etc., adopted by Catholics are not the way God loves, but it is holy.[16] God never requires us to do anything at variance with his law, and the best way of serving him is the way he has appointed acceptable. And to be so, several things are required:

1. They must be slain by the priest, i.e., Jesus in us must destroy sin. If anything else makes a reform in us, it will not be acceptable.

2. They must be offered on the one altar. Jesus. The only acceptable works are those done by faith in[17] him.[18] We must offer only as his servants.

3. Mingled with salt. Jesus['s] merit must be put with them. He must season them.[19]

4. They must be wholly offered and be whole when offered. If but an inch of the tail be gone, they cannot be accepted. All or nothing.

III. THE ARGUMENTS PAUL EMPLOYS.

I, your brother, God's ambassador, your minister,

beseech, strongly urge on you, more than desire or request. I beg and pray of you, even on my knees.

You, both Jews and Gentiles, for I have been speaking of both.

Therefore, because of your election, since, if Jews, ye are a remnant of a nation now given over to blindness of heart;[20] if Gentiles, that ye are

not past by, as under the old dispensation and as the bulk of the world is even now at this time.
<u>brethren</u> — my brethren and brethren of Jesus, surely your dignified rank, demands such a sacrifice since, you remember, you are so only by grace. by the mercies of God — not by the terrors of Sinai, or the threatenings of law but by higher motives by the gratitude you owe to him — not for the mercies of God, not to obtain them, but by them, because you have received them — by your election, redemption effectual calling, justification, adoption, perseverance by the ills averted, by the good conferred, by the sin forgiven, by the holiness inwrought. I beseech do it <u>your reasonable service</u>, here is nothing at all exorbitant, you confess that you are purchased, it is only fare to serve the purchaser.
Creation, redemption, all grace received make it nothing but rational and right.
Let not this urgent appeal be in vain let us fall in with it, surely every child of God will.

1. This surrender will be impossible in our own strength, if Christ be not the slayer of lust, it will never die.
2. Let the Christian live in this Spirit for indeed it is a true Christian one.
3. Ye robbers of God, where shall ye stand when as felons ye are arraigned at his bar —
   May God help me — to do it personally Amen.

121. 241.

not pas[sed] by as under the old dispensation and as the bulk of the world is even now at this time.

<u>Brethren</u>, my brethren and brethren of Jesus, surely your dignified rank demands such a sacrifice[21] since, you remember, you are so only by grace.

<u>By the mercies of God</u>. Not by the terrors of Sinai,[22] or the threatenings of law, but by higher motives. By the gratitude you owe to him. Not <u>for</u> the mercies of God, not to obtain them, but by them[23] because you have received them by your election,[24] redemption, effectual calling, justification,[25] adoption,[26] perseverance,[27] and by the ills averted, by the good conferred, by the sin forgiven, by the holiness inwrought. I beseech ye[28] do it.

<u>Your reasonable service</u> here is nothing at all exorbitant. You confess that you are purchased. It is only fair[29] to serve the purchaser.

Creation, redemption, all grace received make it nothing but rational and right.

Let not this urgent appeal be in vain. Let us fall in with it. Surely every[30] child of God will.

---

1. This surrender will be impossible in our own strength.[31] If Christ be not the slayer of lust, it will never die.[32]

2. Let the Christian live in this Spirit, for indeed it is a true Christian one.

3. Ye robbers of God, where shall <u>ye</u> stand when as felons ye are arraigned at his bar?

May God help me to do it personally.
<u>Amen.</u>

121. 241.

SERMON 93

1. This is the only time Charles preached a sermon on Rom 12:1.

2. An illegible letter was written beneath the "c" in the word "scandal." If the letter is "a," it would explain why Charles originally did not write the "c" before he corrected the misspelling.

3. The word "heights" is surrounded by excessive stippling.

4. Cf. Rom 8:28–30; 11:5.

5. Charles originally spelled this word "sacrafice." No attempt was made to correct the misspelling. Throughout this sermon, Charles spelled the word "sacrafice." See also "Abraham Justified by Faith" (Notebook 1, Sermon 3) and "The Rending of the Veil" (Sermon 96).

6. Cf. Gal 2:19.

7. Charles originally spelled this word "sacrafice." No attempt was made to correct the misspelling.

8. "Death bed repentances [are] seldom genuine, and it is highly improbable that he who has lived in sin should be willing to give it up at the last moment" ("The Affliction of Ahaz" [Notebook 1, Sermon 57]); see also *MTP* 52:308.

9. Cf. Mal 1:8.

10. Charles originally spelled this word "sacrafice." No attempt was made to correct the misspelling.

11. Cf. Lev 14:13.   12. Cf. Matt 16:24.

13. Charles originally spelled this word "sacrafice." No attempt was made to correct the misspelling.

14. Cf. Phil 2:3.   15. Abbr. "sacrifice."

16. The word "holy" is smeared toward the right side of the page.

17. Charles may have originally written the word "on."

18. Cf. Eph 2:10; Jas 2:17–18.

19. Cf. Matt 5:13.

20. Cf. Rom 11:25.

21. Charles originally spelled this word "sacrafice." No attempt was made to correct the misspelling.

22. Cf. Exod 19:12; Heb 12:18.

23. The emphasis in this sentence should fall on the preposition: "But *by* them."

24. Cf. "Election" (Notebook 1, Sermon 10); Eph 1:4; 2 Thess 2:13.

25. Cf. "The Saints' Justification and Glory" (Notebook 1, Sermon 68); Rom 5:1.

26. Cf. "Adoption" (Notebook 1, Sermon 1); Eph 1:5.

27. Cf. "Final Perseverance" (Notebook 1, Sermon 8); "Final Perseverance Certain" (Sermon 82).

28. Charles wrote the word "ye" in superscript above the words "beseech" and "do" and indicated its location with a caret.

29. Charles originally spelled this word "fare." The context suggests, however, he intended to write the word "fair."

30. The letter "h" was written beneath the "e" in the word "every." Charles likely wrote the word "he."

31. Cf. "Self Sufficiency Slain" (*NPSP* 6, Sermon 345); Rom 8:2.

32. Cf. "Sin Slain" (*NPSP* 6, Sermon 337).

94.   Luke. 19. 10   The Lost Saved.

This verse contains in a few words the sum total of Jesus works of salvation — and may profitably be illustrated by taking man in all his progress from death to life —

To be lost — child in the wood, lamb on the mountains, sailors wrecked at sea — so is man

I. By nature, without the Gospel "lost."
In Adam — by natural depravity — by the first actual sin — by aggravated sin doubly lost. no hope — no way — but ruin stares him in the face

II. By nature, with the Gospel, but without the Spirit Naturally averse to good & prone to evil, hardened yet more by crime, unmelted by wrath or mercy by tears, by providences, he is "lost"

III. The First Stage of Salvation "sought"
By the word, by providence but especially by the effectual calling of the Holy Ghost — he seeks God in return, weeps, feels his sin & then comes

IV. The Effect of seeking "Saving"
He man believes & is saved. arrives in glory and is then completely saved. Christ does what he came to do.

122. 131.

94

The LOST SAVED
Luke 19:10[1]

"For the Son of man is come to seek and to save that which was lost."

This verse contains in a few words the sum total of Jesus['s] works of salvation and may profitably be illustrated by taking man in all his progress from death to life.

To be lost. Child in the wood, lamb on the mountains, sailors wrecked at sea.[2] So is man.

I. BY NATURE, WITHOUT THE GOSPEL, *"lost."*

In Adam, by natural depravity,[3] by the first actual sin,[4] by aggravated sin, doubly lost. No hope, no way, but ruin stares him in the face.[5]

II. BY NATURE, WITH THE GOSPEL, BUT[6] WITHOUT THE SPIRIT.

Naturally averse to good and prone to evil.[7] Hardened, yet more by crime,[8] unmelted by wrath or mercy, by tears, by providences. He is "lost."

III. THE FIRST STAGE OF SALVATION, *"sought."*[9]

By the word, by providence, but especially by the effectual calling of the Holy Ghost. He seeks God in return, weeps, feels his sin and then comes.

IV. THE EFFECT OF SEEKING, *"saving."*

The man believes and is saved, arrives in glory, and is then completely saved. Christ does what he came to do.

122. 131.

SERMON 94

1. Charles preached five additional sermons on Luke 19:10: "The Mission of the Son of Man" (*NPSP* 4, Sermon 204); "Good News for the Lost" (*MTP* 19, Sermon 1100); "Saving the Lost" (*MTP* 47, Sermon 2756); "The Errand of Mercy" (*MTP* 53, Sermon 3050); and "Christ the Seeker and Saviour of the Lost" (*MTP* 58, Sermon 3309). The sermon most closely resembling the above outline is his 1863 sermon "The Errand of Mercy." The structural similarities among the four primary divisions suggest Charles likely used this outline when writing his later sermon.

2. An alternative reading of this sentence is "To be [a] lost child in the wood, [a lost] lamb on the mountains, [lost] sailors wrecked at sea."

3. Cf. "Honey from a Lion" (*MTP* 27, Sermon 1591); Ps 51:5.

4. Cf. *MTP* 53:362–63.

5. "Man, in this world, is either in a state of condemnation or a state of salvation" (*MTP* 53:362).

6. A partial fingerprint is seen beneath the word "but." The fingerprint appears to be of the same color ink as the letters in the outline. The faint duplication of the dot at the end of the "t" may be the source of the imprint beneath the word. If so, it is likely this fingerprint belongs to Charles. For an additional fingerprint example, see "The Church Needs the Spirit" (Sermon 131).

7. "There is written upon human nature, by the finger of our first parent, this word, 'Lost'!" (*MTP* 53:362).

8. "When the gates of society are shut, the gates of mercy are not shut" (*MTP* 53:364).

9. "[Christ] does not sit still and pity men, does not stand up and propose a plan for them, but he is come to seek and to save them!" (*MTP* 53:366).

Martin James. 1. 17. — God. the Father of Lights. 95

James is contending against the infamous supposition that God can be the author of evil, and in this verse a secret yet mighty argument is couched, for if God be the author of Good and that immutably, he cannot be the cause of sin — We shall Observe.

I. That all good things are from above. i.e. from Heaven. from God. — there they are designed, by Jesus, the prince of Heaven, purchased, by the Spirit given all gifts from God are good. and if a thing be not so it came not from above but from beneath.— they "come" - not fall, come in measure, season, place this should keep us from self glory, vaunting over inferiors and envy of superiors & lead us to gratitude

II. All things from above are "gifts" Even if sinless. man could not deserve, the word is misapplied when used between a Creator & Creature much less now when man is a sinner can he merit anything — True in doing good we are rewarded & heaven is called a reward, but yet of grace. — dearly purchased yet freely given.— not as servants, but as sons, not wages but gifts.

III. Spiritual blessings are the best of blessings they are here called "good" and "perfect" those necessary to make us first good then perfect for that is their tendency — this passage does not mean temporal & spiritual as some think but Spiritual things in their degrees.—

Manton[1]

⬤ 95

GOD *the* FATHER *of* LIGHTS
James 1:17[2]

"Every good gift and every perfect gift is from above, and cometh down from the Father of lights, with whom is no variableness, neither shadow of turning."

James is contending against the infamous supposition that God can be the author of evil, and in this verse, a secret yet mighty argument is couched. For if God be the author of Good, and that immutably, he cannot be the cause of sin.[3] We shall Observe:

I. THAT ALL GOOD THINGS ARE FROM ABOVE, I.E., FROM HEAVEN, FROM GOD.

There, they are <u>designed</u> by Jesus, the prince of Heaven, <u>purchased</u> by the Spirit, <u>given</u>.[4] All gifts from God are good, and if a thing be not so, it came not from above but from beneath. They "come," not fall. Come in measure, season, place. This should keep us from self glory,[5] vaunting over inferiors,[6] and envy of superiors and lead us[7] to gratitude.

II. ALL THINGS FROM ABOVE ARE "GIFTS."[8]

Even if sinless, man could not deserve. The word is misapplied when used between a Creator and Creature. Much less now when man is a sinner[9] can he merit anything.[10] True, in doing good we are rewarded, and heaven is called a reward, but yet of grace. Dearly purchased yet freely given. Not as servants, but as sons. Not wages, but gifts.

III. SPIRITUAL BLESSINGS ARE THE BEST OF BLESSINGS.[11]

They are here called "good" and "perfect." Those necessary to make us first <u>good</u> then <u>perfect</u>.[12] For that is their tendency. This passage does not mean temporal and spiritual, as some think,[13] but spiritual things[14] in their degrees.[15]

they are very good because 1. only given to peculiar favorites of heaven. 2. they are eternal. 3 they never cloy and weary. — they are for our nobler part.

IV. God is "The Father of lights". Since he is the most resplendent, as he is the main source of light. — Light is used to express.
 1. His essence, and being, simple, sublime
 2. His glory. he is very light itself.
 3. His nature. happiness, wisdom, holiness.
 * All being, honor, wisdom, holiness is of him.
This should lead us to fly to God, and no more to abide his absence than the sun's departure. it tells us why wicked men hate God. we should walk like our Father. —

V. He is unchangeable — no parallax, declination eclipse — no motion, rising setting. —
In his attributes, all of them, holiness, mercy, love. Toward his Saints none — let them then strive to learn not to change so much. Get God to settle us. and trust in him as immutable. —

123. 124.

GOD THE FATHER OF LIGHTS—*James 1:17*

They are very good because:

    1. Only given to peculiar favorites of heaven.

    2. They are eternal.

    3. They never cloy and weary. They are for our nobler part.

IV. GOD IS "THE FATHER OF LIGHTS."

Since he is the most resplendent, as he is the main source of light. Light is used to express:

    1. His essence[16] and being,[17] simple, sublime.[18]

    2. His glory. He is very light itself.[19]

    3. His nature, happiness, wisdom, holiness.[20]

    4.[21] All being, honor, wisdom, holiness is of him.

This should lead us to fly to God[22] and no more to abide his absence than the sun's departure.[23] It tells us why wicked men hate God.[24] We should walk like our Father.[25]

V. HE IS UNCHANGEABLE.[26]

No parallax, declination, eclipse.[27] No motion, rising, setting in his attributes, all of them: holiness, mercy, love. Toward his saints, none.[28] Let them then strive to learn not to change so much. Get God[29] to settle us[30] and trust in him as immutable.[31]

123. 124.[32]

SERMON 95

1. This outline is original to Thomas Manton (1620–1677), an English clergyman and "one of the greatest divines among the Presbyterians" (James Grainger, *A Biographical History of England* [London: T. Davies, 1769], 210). Charles borrowed the above outline from Manton's exposition and notes on Jas 1:17 found in his *Commentary on James* (see *The Complete Works of Thomas Manton, D.D. Volume IV. Containing a Practical Commentary; or, an Exposition, with Notes, on the Epistle of James* [London: James Nisbet & Co., 1871, The Spurgeon Library], 109–14). Charles later wrote that Manton's exposition on James is in his "best style. An exhaustive work, as far as the information of the period admitted. Few such books are written" (C. H. Spurgeon, *Commenting and Commentaries: Two Lectures Addressed to the Students of the Pastors' College, Metropolitan Tabernacle, Together with a Catalogue of Biblical Commentaries and Expositions* [London: Passmore & Alabaster, 1876, The Spurgeon Library], 191). Charles became better acquainted with Manton's twenty-two-volume work in the composition of his commentary on the Psalms, entitled *The Treasury of David*. He wrote, "I have come to know him so well that I could pick him out from among a thousand divines if he were again to put on his portly form, and display among modern men that countenance wherein was 'a great mixture of majesty and meekness.'" Charles added, "Ministers who do not know Manton need not wonder if they are themselves unknown" (*Autobiography* 4:282).

2. For his first sermon at the New Park Street Chapel on December 18, 1853, Charles preached from a ten-page version of this sermon (see "The Father of Light" [Notebook 8, Sermon 351]). Susannah wrote, "The text of Mr. Spurgeon's first sermon in London has long been well known; but, until now, there does not appear to have been any printed record of the opening discourse in that marvellous Metropolitan ministry which was destined to exercise such a mighty influence, not only throughout London, and the United Kingdom, but 'unto the uttermost part of the earth'" (*Autobiography* 1:321). Susannah included a transcription of this sermon (321–26) but did not mention Manton. In the outline above and in the 1853 sermon, Charles borrowed heavily from—and at times quoted exactly—Manton's verbiage. Structural differences do exist between the early outline and Charles's later sermon at the New Park Street Chapel. In the outline the primary divisions follow closely Manton's "notes" or "Obs." located after the expositions. In the later sermon Charles's primary divisions follow Manton's loosely and are arranged as follows: "I. A Majestic Figure." "II. A Glorious Attribute." "III. A

3. "God is good, and immutably good, and therefore it cannot be from him, which was Plato's argument" (Manton, 110).

4. An alternative reading of this line is "There, they are designed by Jesus, the prince of Heaven, [and] purchased [and] given by the Spirit."

5. "Glorying in ourselves. Who would magnify himself in that which is from above?" (Manton, 111).

6. "Insultation, or vaunting it over others" (Manton, 111).

7. "Envy to those that have received most. Our eye is evil when God's hand is good. Envy is a rebellion against God himself, and the liberty and pleasure of his dispensations. God distributeth gifts and blessings as he will, not as we will; our duty is to be contented, and to beg grace to make use of what we have received" (Manton, 111).

8. Cf. 1 Cor 4:7.

9. "Some divines say, that in innocency we could not merit. When the covenant did seem to hang upon works, we could, in their sense, *impetrare*, but not *mereri*—obtain by virtue of doing, but not deserve. Merit and desert are improper notions to express the relationship between the work of a creature and the reward of a Creator; and much more incongruous are they since the fall" (Manton, 111, italics in the original).

10. An alternative reading of this sentence is "The word is misapplied when used between a Creator and Creature, much less now. When man is a sinner, can he merit anything?"

11. Cf. Matt 7:11.

12. "*Obs.* 3. That among all the gifts of God, spiritual blessings are the best: these are called here good and perfect, because these make us good and perfect" (Manton, 111–12, italics in the original).

Grateful Acknowledgement." Overlapping content between these two sermons, and also between Charles and Manton, are noted below.

13. "It is true some distinguish between the two clauses, δόσις ἀγαθὴ, or 'good gift,' to imply earthly blessings, and δώρημα τέλειον 'perfect gift,' to imply heavenly or spiritual blessings; but I suppose that is too curious. These two words imply the same mercies with a different respect" (Manton, 109).

14. Manton quoted St. Augustine: "*Nihil bonum sine summo bono*" (Manton, 112); however, the source of his citation is curious: "Aug. lib. Iv. contra Jul," or Michela Zelzer, editor, *Sancti Agustini Opera: Contra Iulianum (Opus Imperfectum) Tomus Posterior Libri IV–VI* (Verlag: Österreichischen Akademie der Wissenschaften, 2004) contained in *Corpus Scriptorum Ecclesiasticorum Latinorum: Editum Consilio et Impensis Academiae Scientiarum Austriacae Vol. LXXXV/2*. It appears the quote originated not with Augustine but instead with his disciple St. Prosper of Aquitaine, who condensed his views in his works *Sententia* and *Epigrammata* after Augustine's death in AD 430. Both James Ussher, Lord Archbishop of Armagh, and Thomas Cranmer, Archbishop of Canterbury, published Prosper's works. Cranmer's citation of *Sententia* and *Epigrammata* is: "Omnis infidelium vita peccatum est: et nihil est bonum sine summo bono. Ubi enim deest agnitio aeternae et incommunibilis veritatis, falsa virtus est, etiam in optimis moribus" (John Edmund Cox, ed., *Miscellaneous Writings and Letters of Thomas Cranmer, Archbishop of Canterbury, Martyr*, 1556 [Cambridge: Cambridge University Press, 1846], 522). Ussher's later citation matches that of Manton more closely. (James Ussher, *An Answer to a Challenge Made by a Jesuit in Ireland. Wherein the Judgment of Antiquity in the Points Questioned, Is Truly Delivered, and the Novelty of the Now Romish Doctrine Plainly Discovered* [London: printed for the Society of Stationers, 1625], 522, contained in *The Whole Works of the Most Rev. James Ussher, D.D. Lord Archbishop of Armagh, and Primate of All Ireland. Volume III*). Manton's citation "Aug. lib. Iv. contra Jul" likely came from either Cranmer's or Ussher's citation.

15. See the title page of Notebook 1 for an ink blot of similar size and shape.

16. Cf. 1 John 1:5.

17. Manton cited the Nicene-Constantinopolitan Creed (AD 381): "φῶς ἐκ φωτός, θεὸς ἀληθινὸς ἐκ θεοῦ ἀληθινοῦ" (Manton, 112). For Charles's personal copy of this creed, see Henry B. Smith and Philip Schaff, eds., *Theological and Philosophical Library: A Series of Text-Books, Original and Translated, for Colleges and Universities. The*

Creeds of the Greek and Latin Churches (London: Hodder and Stoughton, 1878, The Spurgeon Library), 57.

18. By using the word "sublime," Charles departed from following Manton's phrase "defecate quality" (Manton, 112).

19. Cf. 1 Tim 6:16.

20. "In short, reason, wisdom, holiness, happiness are often expressed by light, and they are all from God. As the stars shine with a borrowed lustre, so do all the creatures; where you meet with any brightness and excellency in them, remember it is but a streak and ray of the divine glory" (Manton, 112).

21. Charles likely struck through the number 4 because he had already made this point in the line above.

22. "We do not make [God] an occasional resort to be used only when we cannot help it, but we dwell in him, and morning by morning pour out our hearts before him; and so when adversity comes, we fly to God as naturally as the dove to its dovecote, or the coney to the rock, or the weary child to its mother's bosom" (*MTP* 20:387).

23. "We are dark bodies till the Lord fills us with his own glory. Oh! how uncomfortable should we be without God. In the night there is nothing but terror and error; and so it is in the soul without the light of the divine presence. When the sun is gone the herbs wither; and when God, who is the sun of spirits, is withdrawn, there is nothing but discomfort and a sad languishing in the soul. Oh! pray, then, God would shine in upon your soul, not by flashes, but with a constant light" (Manton, 113).

24. "It showeth the reason why wicked men hate God" (Manton, 113).

25. "Walk so as you may resemble the glory of your Father: faults in you, like spots in the moon, are soon discerned. You that are the lights of the world should not shine dimly; nay, in the worst times, like stars in the blackest night, you should shine brightest" (Manton, 113).

26. "*Obs.* 5. That the Lord is unchangeable in holiness and glory; he is a sun that shineth always with a like brightness. God, and all that is in God, is unchangeable;

SERMON 95

for this is an attribute that, like a silken string through a chain of pearl, runneth through all the rest" (Manton, 113, italics in the original).

27. "*With whom is no variableness,* παραλλαγὴ.—It is an astronomical word or term, taken from the heavenly bodies, which suffer many declinations and revolutions which they call parallaxes, a word that hath great affinity with this used by the apostle. The heavenly lights have their vicissitudes, eclipses, and decreases; but our sun shineth always with a like brightness and glory" (Manton, 110, italics in the original).

28. An alternative reading of this line is "In his attributes—all of them: holiness, mercy, love—[there is no motion, rising, or setting] toward his saints, none."

29. Charles originally did not capitalize the letter "g" in the word "god." He corrected the mistake by inserting a capital "G." For an additional example of this occurrence, see "The Rending of the Veil" (Sermon 96).

30. "Go to him to establish and settle your spirits" (Manton, 114).

31. "Carry yourselves to him as unto an immutable good" (Manton, 114).

32. See *Autobiography* 1:321.

SERMON 96

Mark 15. 38.   The rending of the veil.
The vail was one partition betwixt the Holy and most
Holy place. It was to keep from the eyes of the worshipper
the things most holy, when the high priest went in
thither, to accomplish the service of God.
It is described. Ex. 26. 31. 33 — mentioned Lev. 16. 2
2 Chron. 3. 14 —   It was made of blue, purple,
and crimson, and fine twined linen, embroidered
with figures of cherubim, "to show" says Bunyan
"that as the angels are with us here, and wait
upon us all the days of our pilgrimage in this world,
so, when we die, they stand ready even at the vail
at the door of heaven, to come, when bid, to fetch us
and carry us away into Abrahams bosom." Luke 16. 22.
It was a very thick piece of tapestry, a hand-
breadth is said to be its thickness, by one of the
Rabbi's —   of immense length. even 40 cubits
the breadth being twenty —   This gorgeous and
immense piece of tapestry, was rent in sunder
from the top to the bottom, in the midst (as
Luke adds), just when Jesus died — Because

I. Of the death of such an one — Jesus Christ.
1. It was a solemn act of mourning for his death
and horror at the blasphemous wickedness of the
murder — the temple, the sun, the earth, the rock
supplied mourners for his funeral. —
2. It was rent too, as an instance of his majesty,
even when in misery — the dying God-man did
what living man could not do —

96

The RENDING of the VEIL[1]
Mark 15:38[2]

"And the vail of the temple was rent in twain from the top to the bottom."

The vail[3] was one partition betwixt[4] the Holy and most Holy place. It was [there] to keep from the eyes of the worshippers the things most holy, when the high priest went in thither to accomplish the service of God.[5]

It is described [in] Ex. 26.31.33.[6] Mentioned [in] Lev. 16.2,[7] 2 Chron. 3.14.[8]

It was made of blue, purple, and crimson, and fine twined linen, embroidered with figures of cherubim, "to show," says Bunyan, "that as the angels are with us here and wait upon us all the days of our pilgrimage in this world, so, when we die, they stand ready even at the vail at the door of heaven, to come, when bid, to fetch us and carry us away into Abraham[']s bosom." Luke 16.22.[9]

It was a very thick piece of tapestry, a hand-breadth is said to be its thickness by one of the Rabbis.[10] Of immense length, even 40 cubits, the breadth being twenty. This gorgeous and immense piece of tapestry was rent in sunder from the top to the bottom, in the midst (as Luke adds),[11] just when[12] Jesus died. Because:

I. OF THE DEATH OF SUCH AN ONE, JESUS CHRIST.

1. It was a solemn act of mourning for his[13] death and horror at the blasphemous wickedness of the murder. The temple,[14] the sun, the earth, the rocks supplied mourners for his funeral.

2. It was rent, too, as an instance of his majesty. Even when in misery, the dying God-man did what living man could not do.[15]

3. The vail of the temple, was the barrier to the Holy place, and until rent none could even look within – so until this moment when Christ expired, the or unless he had died, none could have entered heaven, or the way of life –

II. At that moment the Mosaic System died –
1. This rending of so conspicuous an object was an excellent representative of the passing away of the whole. – This being the time of sacrifice the priest was at this moment standing by the brazen altar, which was situated near the vail – and as the day was an high one, probably Caiaphas was then sacraficing – this then would be a very conspicuous transaction.
2. It showed that God at that moment had withdrawn his presence from the Holy of Holies that it was no longer sacred, God had now no peculiar place for dwelling in on earth.
3. The Jewish nation had as it were been God's Sanctum Sanctorum, but the rent vail threw down the partition and gave Gentiles communion with them – He hath made both one.

III. The Birth of the Gospel took place at that instant. The rending of the vail just at its birth was prophetic –
1. Of the fuller revelation of Gospel Heaven

THE RENDING OF THE VEIL—*Mark 15:38*

    3. The vail of the temple was the barrier to the Holy place, and until rent, none could even look within. So until this moment when Christ expired,[16] ~~the~~ or unless he had died, none could have entered heaven or the way of life.[17]

II. AT THAT MOMENT THE MOSAIC SYSTEM DIED.

    1. This rending of so conspicuous an object was an excellent representative of the passing away of the whole. This, being the time of sacrifice,[18] the Priest was at this moment standing by the brazen altar, which was situated near the vail.[19] And as the day was an high one, probably Caiaphas[20] was then sacrificing.[21] This, then, would be a very conspicuous transaction.

    2. It showed that God at that moment had withdrawn his presence from the Holy of Holies, that it was no longer sacred. God[22] had now no peculiar place for dwelling in on earth.[23]

    3. The Jewish nation had, as it were, been God's Sanctum Sanctorum,[24] but the rent vail threw down the partition and gave Gentiles communion with them. He hath made both one.[25]

III. THE BIRTH OF THE GOSPEL TOOK PLACE AT THAT INSTANT.

The rending of the vail just at its[26] birth was prophetic:

    1. Of the fuller revelation of ~~Gospel~~ Heavenly[27]

mysteries — the things hidden are now laid open, the law was a system of mysteries and shadows, ours of revelations and light — The vail is rent.

2. Of the access with boldness — the sons of God enjoy then only the highpriest once a year, could enter now we all are kings and priests unto God and may at all times enter in. —

3. Of the sweet union between the saint and God. there is now no separation we are one with God.

4. Of the reception saints now receive when they die, they can enter heaven — the veil is rent they have none who can debar their entrance.

IV. From that time the destruction of Jerusalem was certain — and this was a sort of prophecy of it.

1. No privileges, ordinances, knowledge will save men; the temple is no bulwark, God rends its vail.

2. Judgment begins at the house of God, yea and in the very centre of the house, even this must all come down — where shall the ungodly appear.

3. God pays wrath at first by small instalments first the vail is rent then the temple — so now the man has some foretaste of future destruction.

———

1. Poor sinner, there is no vail, enter, cry, it is rent from top to bottom, not a small hole — nothing obstructs.

2. Christian — go boldly, live in communion with God have hope to enter heaven, but all by the rent vail. No way to see mysteries but through this rent —

126. 451.

THE RENDING OF THE VEIL—Mark 15:38

mysteries. The things hidden are now laid open.[28] The law was a system of mysteries and shadows;[29] our[s]of revelations and light.[30] The vail is rent.

2. Of the access with boldness[31] the sons of God enjoy. Then, only the high priest[32] once a year could enter.[33] Now we all are kings and priests[34] unto God, and may at all times enter in.

3. Of the sweet union between the saint and God.[35] There is now no separation.[36] We are one with God.[37]

4. Of the reception saints now receive when they die. They can enter heaven.[38] The vail is rent. They have none who can debar their entrance.

IV. FROM THAT TIME, THE DESTRUCTION OF JERUSALEM WAS CERTAIN,[39] AND THIS WAS A SORT OF PROPHECY OF IT.

1. No privileges, ordinances,[40] knowledge, will save men; the temple is no bulwark. God rends its vail.[41]

2. Judgment begins at the house of God,[42] yea and in the very centre of the house. Even this must all come down. Where shall the ungodly appear?

3. God pays wrath at first by small installments. First, the vail is rent, then the temple. So now, the man has some foretaste of future destruction.

---

1. Poor sinner, there is no vail. Enter, cry. It is rent from top to bottom. Not a small hole.[43] Nothing obstructs.

2. Christian, go boldly. Live in communion with God. Have hope to enter heaven, but all by the rent vail.

No way to see mysteries but through this rent.

126. 451.

SERMON 96

1. Charles borrowed heavily in this sermon from section LVII, "*Of the Vail of the Temple*," in John Bunyan's *Solomon's Temple Spiritualized* (see George Offor, ed., *The Works of John Bunyan. With an Introduction to Each Treatise, Notes, and a Sketch of His Life, Times, and Contemporaries. Volume Third. Allegorical, Figurative, and Symbolical* [Glasgow, Edinburgh, and London: Blackie and Son, 1856, The Spurgeon Library], 498, italics in the original). Charles did not follow closely Bunyan's primary divisions; however, his verbiage is often verbatim. Nor did Charles follow strictly Bunyan's spiritualizations, particularly in the instance when Bunyan compared the veil of the temple to the "visible heavens" Christ pierced during his ascension into the clouds (Bunyan, 498). Later in his ministry Charles applauded Bunyan's spiritualization in this outline. To the students of the Pastors' College he said, "You may allow much latitude in spiritualizing to men of rare poetical temperament, such as John Bunyan. Gentlemen, did you ever read John Bunyan's spiritualization of Solomon's Temple? It is a most remarkable performance, and even when a little strained it is full of a consecrated ingenuity. . . . Mr. Bunyan is the chief, and head, and lord of all allegorists, and is not to be followed by us into the deep places of typical and symbolical utterances. He was a swimmer, we are but mere waders, and must not go beyond our depth" (*Lectures* 1:112, 114).

2. On March 25, 1888, Charles preached a sermon on Matt 27:50–51 and Heb 10:19–20 entitled "The Rent Veil" (*MTP* 34, Sermon 2015). The primary divisions do not align precisely; however, substantial overlapping content suggests Charles may have had this early outline in mind when writing his later sermon.

3. The spelling of the word "vail" is not consistent in this outline. In the title Charles spelled the word with an "e." However, in the body of the sermon Charles spelled the word with an "a" as found in the KJV.

4. A modern translation of the word "betwixt" is "between."

5. "The vail of the temple was one partition, betwixt the holy and most holy place; and I take it, it was to keep from the sight of the worshippers the things most holy when the high-priest went in thither, to accomplish the service of God" (Bunyan, 498).

6. Exodus 26:31–33, "And thou shalt make a vail of blue, and purple, and scarlet, and fine twined linen of cunning work: with cherubims shall it be made. And

thou shalt hang it upon four pillars of shittim wood overlaid with gold: their hooks shall be of gold, upon the four sockets of silver. And thou shalt hang up the vail under the taches, that thou mayest bring in thither within the vail the ark of the testimony: and the vail shall divide unto you between the holy place and the most holy."

7. Leviticus 16:2, "And the LORD said unto Moses, Speak unto Aaron thy brother, that he come not at all times into the holy place within the vail before the mercy seat, which is upon the ark; that he die not: for I will appear in the cloud upon the mercy seat."

8. Second Chronicles 3:14, "And he made the vail of blue, and purple, and crimson, and fine linen, and wrought cherubims thereon."

9. "Upon the veil of the temple there were also the figures of cherubims wrought, that is, of angels; to show, that as the angels are with us here, and wait upon us all the days of our pilgrimage in this world; so when we die, they stand ready, even at the veil, at the door of these heavens, to come when bid, to fetch us, and carry us away into Abraham's bosom. Lu[ke] xvi. 22" (Bunyan, 498). Charles did not include the Scripture reference "Luke 16:22" within the quotation marks, likely because he added it afterward.

10. The son of Gamaliel (Acts 5:34), Rabbi Simeon bar-Gamaliel, wrote, "The veil was a handsbreadth thick, and was woven on a loom of seventy-two cords" (Jacob Nuesner, trans., *The Talmud of the Land of Israel, A Preliminary Translation and Explanation* [Chicago and London: University of Chicago Press, 1991, *Sheqalim*, vol. 15], 160).

11. The Gospel of Luke does not mention that the veil in the temple was torn from top to bottom. This detail is found instead in Matt 27:51 and Mark 15:38. Charles was likely referencing, as he does in his 1888 sermon, the fact that the veil was torn "in the midst" (Luke 23:45). See also *MTP* 34:173.

12. Charles originally did not include the letter "h" in the word "when."

13. An illegible letter was written beneath the "h" in the word "his."

14. "In the East men express their sorrow by rending their garments; and the temple, when it beheld its Master die, seemed struck with horror, and rent its veil. Shocked at the sin of man, indignant at the murder of its Lord, in its sympathy

with him who is the true temple of God, the outward symbol tore its holy vestments from the top to the bottom" (*MTP* 34:169–70).

15. Cf. Rom 8:3.

16. Cf. Exod 19:21.

17. "It is not only what we have *done*, but what we *are* that keeps us apart from God. . . . When grace makes us partakers of the divine nature, then are we at one with the Lord, and the veil is taken away" (*MTP* 34:170, italics in the original); cf. Heb 10:20.

18. Charles originally spelled this word "sacrafice." No attempt was made to correct the misspelling. For additional examples, see "Present Your Bodies, Etc." (Sermon 93).

19. Cf. Exod 39:38–39.

20. Cf. Matt 26:57–58; Luke 22:54.

21. Charles originally spelled this word "sacraficing." No attempt was made to correct the misspelling.

22. Charles originally did not capitalize the letter "g" in the word "god." He corrected the mistake by inserting a capital "G." For an additional example of this habit, see "God the Father of Lights" (Sermon 95).

23. Cf. John 4:21.

24. Trans., Latin, "holy of holies."

25. Cf. Rom 3:22; 10:12; Gal 3:28; Col 3:10.

26. An illegible letter, likely "a," was written beneath the "i" in the word "its." This is likely an example of dittography.

27. An ink blot, likely the result of a smudge, appears over the letters "ly" in the word "Heavenly."

28. Cf. Eph 3:1–13; Col 1:26.

29. Cf. Deut 29:29; Heb 10:1.

30. The phrase "revelations and light" suggests Charles had in mind his previous sermon, "God the Father of Lights" (Sermon 95).

31. "Look, look boldly through Jesus Christ: but do not content yourself with looking! Hear what the text says: 'Having boldness to *enter in*'" (*MTP* 34:174, italics in the original); cf. Eph 3:12; Heb 4:16.

32. Charles originally did not separate the words "high" and "priest." For consistency, these words have been separated.

33. Cf. Heb 9:7.

34. Cf. 1 Pet 2:9; Rev 5:10.

35. See C. H. Spurgeon, *The Saint and His Saviour: The Progress of the Soul in the Knowledge of Jesus* (London: Hodder and Stoughton, 1880, The Spurgeon Library).

36. "For believers the veil is not rolled up, but rent. The veil was not unhooked, and carefully folded up, and put away, so that it might be put in its place at some future time. Oh, no! but the divine hand took it and rent it from top to bottom. It can never be hung up again; that is impossible. Between those who are in Christ Jesus and the great God, there will never be another separation. 'Who shall separate us from the love of God?' Only one veil was made, and as that is rent, the one and only separator is destroyed" (*MTP* 34:173); cf. Rom 8:38–39.

37. "In heaven you will be with God; but on earth he will be with you" (*MTP* 34:175).

38. An alternative reading of this line is "Of the reception saints now receive. When they die, they can enter heaven."

39. Jerusalem was destroyed in AD 70 by the Roman armies under the command of Titus. For Jesus's prophecy of her destruction, see Matt 24:1–2 and Mark 13:1–2.

40. "The ordinances of an earthly priesthood were rent with that veil" (*MTP* 34:170); cf. "God's Estimation of Men" (Notebook 1, Sermon 41).

41. "I want you to notice that this veil, when it was rent, was rent by God, not by man. It was not the act of an irreverent mob; it was not the midnight outrage of a set of profane priests: it was the act of God alone" (*MTP* 34:174).

42. Cf. 1 Pet 4:17.

43. "If there had only been a small hole cut through it, the lesser offenders might have crept through; but what an act of abounding mercy is this, that the veil is rent in the midst, and rent from top to bottom, so that the chief of sinners may find ample passage! This also shows that for believers there is no hindrance to the fullest and freest access to God. Oh, for much boldness, this morning, to come where God has not only set open the door, but has lifted the door from its hinges; yea, removed it, post, and bar, and all!" (*MTP* 34:173).

97. Is. 33-20.21 — The tranquillity, security, and supplies afforded to the gospel church.

1822.

42.19

This prophecy immediately referred to the state of Jerusalem, when she should be delivered from Sennacherib but doubtless with fuller meaning it relates to the privileges of the church in gospel times.

I. The peace and tranquility of the Church. she shall be quiet, this shall result from.
1. the character of her governor.
2. The temper of her inhabitants.
3. The strength of her fortifications.
4. The subjugation of her enemies.
she shall be an "habitation" not lodginghouse.

II. Her permanency and security She is a tabernacle, for like it, she is
1. Of heavenly origin
2. Her artificers are divinely inspired
3. In her Gods glory rests.
She is not however a frail tent, she cannot move like the old tabernacle —
The stakes and cords are her ordinances & Gods promises which change not —

III. The nature of the supplies.
Herein the old Jerusalem is beaten, for she has no river
1. Our supplies are divine — "the glorious Lord"

THE TRANQUILLITY, SECURITY, AND . . . —*Isaiah 33:20–21*

97

<small>19V2[1]</small> # *The* TRANQUILLITY,[2] SECURITY, *and* SUPPLIES AFFORDED *to the* GOSPEL CHURCH[3] <small>V.2.19</small>
Isaiah 33:20–21[4]

> "Look upon Zion, the city of our solemnities: thine eyes shall see Jerusalem, a quiet habitation, a tabernacle that shall not be taken down; not one of the stakes thereof shall ever be removed, neither shall any of the cords thereof be broken. But there the glorious Lord will be unto us a place of broad rivers and streams; wherein shall go no galley with oars, neither shall gallant ship pass thereby."

This prophecy immediately referred to the state of Jerusalem when she should be delivered from Sennacherib.[5] But doubtless with fuller meaning it relates to the privileges of the church in gospel times.[6]

I. THE PEACE AND TRANQUILITY OF THE CHURCH.

She shall be quiet. This shall result from:

1. The character of her governor.[7]
2. The temper of her inhabitants.[8]
3. The strength of her fortifications.[9]
4. The subjugation of her enemies.[10]

She shall be an "habitation," not lodging house.

II. HER PERMANENCY AND SECURITY.[11]

She is a tabernacle,[12] for like it she is:

1. Of heavenly origin.[13]
2. Her artificers are divinely inspired.[14]
3. In her God[']s glory rests.[15]

She is not, however, a frail tent. She cannot move like the old tabernacle. The stakes[16] and cords are her ordinances[17] and God's promises, which change not.[18]

III. THE NATURE OF THE SUPPLIES.[19]

Herein the old Jerusalem is beaten, for she has no river.[20]

1. Our supplies are divine—"the glorious Lord."[21]

163

2. Our supplies are abundant – "broad rivers & streams"
3. Inexhaustible – rills may fail, rivers shall not
4. Ever near – "There", always at hand.
5. Unmolested. "no galley with oars &c"

Let this subject
1. Induce gratitude – that we live now rather than in persecuting, troublous times.
2. Inspire confidence – the Church is secure.
3. Excite expectation – who knows how broad the streams shall be. —

125.

---

2 bol II — Num. X. 29 – The invitation of Moses to Hobab. 98
It seems tolerably clear that Raguel or Reuel or Jethro (three names for one individual) was Moses' father in law & that Hobab was his brother in law. — Moses gives him this invitation. in it —

I. He reminds him of the occupation he must follow if he became one with Israel — "we are journeying."
1 You may not now make present things your object.
2 You must not count on ease, you must toil, you must be subject to many inconveniences.
3 You are never to be satisfied, it must ever be onward

he could have told him too that the journey they were taking was a singular one it was
1. Undertaken by divine command. 2. Continued under divine guidance

THE TRANQUILLITY, SECURITY, ... and THE INVITATION OF MOSES...

2. Our supplies are abundant—"broad rivers and streams."[22]
3. Inexhaustible—rills[23] may fail, rivers shall not.
4. Ever near—"There," always at hand.[24]
5. Unmolested—"No galley with oars, etc."[25]

Let this subject:

1. Induce gratitude—that we live now rather than in persecuting, troublous[26] times.[27]
2. Inspire confidence—the Church is secure.[28]
3. Excite expectation—who knows how broad the streams shall be?[29]

125.

---

2 Vol.II[1]

98

The INVITATION *of* MOSES *to* HOBAB
Numbers 10:29[2]

"And Moses said unto Hobab, the son of Raguel the Midianite, Moses' father in law, 'We are journeying unto the place of which the Lord *said, "I will give it you": come thou with us, and we will do thee good: for the* Lord *hath spoken good concerning Israel.'"*

It seems tolerably clear that Raguel, or Reul, or Jethro (three names for one individual) was Moses'[s] father-in-law and that Hobab was his brother-in-law. Moses gives him this invitation.[3] In it:

I. HE REMINDS HIM OF THE OCCUPATION HE MUST FOLLOW IF HE BECAME ONE WITH ISRAEL. *"We are journeying."*[4]

1. You may not now make present things your object.[5]
2. You must not count on ease; you must toil. You must be subject to many inconveniences.[6]
3. You are never to be satisfied; it must ever be onward. He could have told him too that the journey they were taking was a singular one. It was:
   1. Undertake[n] by divine command.
   2. Continued under[7] divine guidance.

3. Marked by God's miraculous and gracious care. Thus shall your journey be if ye will come with us.—

II. He informs him of the great object. Israel had in view "the place of which the Lord said, I will give it you". No less an object than Heaven itself which is desired
1. As the end of a toilsome & dangerous journey.
2. As a country amply stored with provision.
3. As the land promised. — a kingdom. Luke XII. 32. throne. Rev. 3. 21.— a crown. 2 Tim 4. 18. eternal life. 1 John. 2. 25.
4. As the gift of God, not as a debt, but a free gift.

III. He then gives him the invitation "Come &c"
1. Piety prompted Moses to desire this.
2. Benevolence prompted him.
3. Gratitude, for kindness shewn to him in ye wilderness.
4. His own interest, Hobab knew the wilderness. how useful may might be to us. We want men to give themselves to Christ and then openly to his church "come with us.—

IV. He backs up his request with the assurance that God had spoken good concerning Israel.
1. God has promised to find a good way for them
2. He has promised to lead find succours.—
3. He has declared them absolutely secure.
4. He has said glorious things concerning heaven. How happy! how honourable! how safe a thing it is to be a Christian!
The Church desires men's salvation, God desires that none should perish.—
129.

3. Marked by God's miraculous and gracious care. Thus shall your journey be if ye will come with us.

II. HE INFORMS HIM OF THE GREAT OBJECT ISRAEL HAD IN VIEW. *"The place of which the Lord said, 'I will give it [to] you.'"*

No less an object than Heaven itself, which is desired:

1. As the end of a toilsome and dangerous[8] journey.[9]

2. As a country amply stored with provision.

3. As the land promised. A kingdom. Luke XII.32.[10] Throne. Rev. 3.21.[11] A crown. 2 Tim 4.18.[12] Eternal life. 1 John 2.25.[13]

4. As the gift of God. Not as a debt but a free gift.[14]

III. HE THEN GIVES HIM THE INVITATION. *"Come, etc."*

1. Piety prompted Moses to desire this.

2. Benevolence prompted him.

3. Gratitude for kindness shewn to him in ye wilderness.[15] Hobab knew the wilderness.[16]

4. His own interest. How useful many might be to us. We want men to give themselves to Christ and then openly to his church.[17] "Come with us."[18]

IV. HE BACKS UP HIS REQUEST WITH THE ASSURANCE THAT GOD HAD SPOKEN GOOD CONCERNING ISRAEL.

1. God has promised to find a good way for them.[19]

2. He has promised to ~~lead~~ find succours.[20]

3. He has declared them absolutely secure.

4. He has said glorious things concerning heaven.

How happy! How honourable! How safe a thing it is to be a Christian![21]

The Church desires men's salvation. God desires that none should perish.[22]

129.

SERMON 97

1. This is the second of four sermons in Notebook 2 that Charles borrowed from the collection of sermon outlines entitled *Sketches of Sermons* (for information about this publication, see "Inventory and Title of Our Treasures" [Sermon 92]). See also "Justification, Conversion, Sanctification, Glory" (Sermon 102) and "Envy Forbidden, Piety Commanded" (Sermon 112). In the top right corner of the page, Charles inscribed the reference V.2.19 or volume 2, sermon outline 19, which corresponds to the nineteenth sermon outline, "The Tranquillity, Security, and Supplies Afforded to the Gospel Church," in the second volume of *Sketches of Sermons*, 79–84. Overlapping content is noted below.

2. Charles is inconsistent in this sermon in his spelling of the word "tranquility." In the title he spelled the word "Tranquillity"; however, in the body of the sermon he spelled it "tranquility." The former spelling of the word is found in *Sketches of Sermons*.

3. The horizontal line appears to be a seperation between the title and body of the sermon, not an underscore of the sermon title.

4. On January 18, 1863, Charles preached an additional sermon on Isa 33:20–23 entitled "Broad Rivers and Streams" (*MTP* 9, Sermon 489). There is not enough structural similarity or overlapping content to suggest Charles had in mind his early sermon when writing his later one.

5. Cf. Isa 33:19.

6. "It is a general opinion, that the prophecies contained in this chapter had a distinct reference to the period when Sennacherib invaded Judea, and besieged Jerusalem.... Many of the prophecies have a twofold accomplishment, and whatever reference the text might have had to Jerusalem literally, it must be understood spiritually as illustrative of the privileges conferred on the church of God under the New Testament dispensation" (*Sketches of Sermons*, 2:79–80).

7. "1. *The character of its governor*. We can easily conceive how much the tranquillity of a place depends on the wisdom, justice and peaceful disposition of him who governs it. Christ is the governor of his church" (*Sketches of Sermons*, 2:80, italics in the original).

168

8. "*2. The peaceful tempers of its inhabitants.* Men who are haughty, violent, and litigious, often light up the flames of discord, and create civil commotions among their tranquil neighbours. But Jerusalem shall be a quiet habitation; the members of the gospel church are all peaceable in their dispositions, however turbulent they were naturally; grace has tranquilized them" (*Sketches of Sermons*, 2:80, italics in the original).

9. "*3. The security of its fortifications.* Jerusalem was renowned for this; nature and art combined to render it a place of safety.... The gospel church is impregnable. Zion has been ploughed as a field, and Jerusalem literally become[s] heaps; but the gates of hell shall never prevail against the church of Christ" (*Sketches of Sermons*, 2:80–81, italics in the original).

10. "*4. The subjugation or destruction of its enemies.* The church of God has always had its enemies. The powers of darkness are the insidious and implacable foes of the people of God, but these he will bruise under their feet" (*Sketches of Sermons*, 2:81, italics in the original).

11. "II. Its Permanency and Security;—'a tabernacle that shall not be taken down.'... There were two tabernacles in the wilderness;—the tabernacle of the congregation, where the people assembled for the dispatch of their secular affairs; and the tabernacle of the Lord: here the Israelites offered sacrifices, performed religious service, &c" (*Sketches of Sermons*, 2:81).

12. In 1861, Charles's congregation at New Park Street Chapel relocated to Elephant and Castle. Significant to the sermon above is the fact that Charles named the new sanctuary the Metropolitan Tabernacle.

13. "*1. Of heavenly origin.* God planned the whole design, and deigned to adjust the most minute parts, and enjoined it upon Moses to make all things according to the original pattern" (*Sketches of Sermons*, 2:81, italics in the original). Cf. Rev 21:3.

14. "*2. Its artificers were divinely inspired.* God filled men with his Spirit in wisdom, understanding, and knowledge, for accomplishing the work of the tabernacle.... So in the gospel church, God chooses his own instruments, and qualifies them by his own Spirit" (*Sketches of Sermons*, 2:81, italics in the original).

15. "*3. It exhibited tokens of the Divine glory.* Here God met with his people, and communed with them from above the mercy-seat.... Thus in the gospel church, God displays

the glory of his grace, and power, and mercy, in the salvation of sinners, and this glory we beheld with open face" (*Sketches of Sermons*, 2:81–82, italics in the original).

16. Cf. Isa 54:2.

17. Charles may also have consulted John Gill on this point: "The *cords* with which these are all held together, which shall never be broken, are the everlasting love of God, electing grace, the covenant and its promises, the word and ordinances, which always remain firm and sure, and secure the stability and continuance of the church of God" (John Gill, *An Exposition of the Books of the Prophets of the Old Testament, Both Larger and Lesser, in Two Volumes. In Which, It Is Attempted to Give an Account of the Several Books, and the Writers of Them; a Summary of Each Chapter, and the Genuine Sense of Every Verse: And Throughout the Whole, the Original Text, and Various Versions are Inspected, and Compared; Interpreters of Best Note, Both Jewish and Christian, Consulted; and the Prophecies Shewn Chiefly to Belong to the Times of the Gospel, and a Great Number of Them to Times Yet to Come, Vol. I. Containing the Propheies of Isaiah, Jeremiah, and the Book of the Lamentations* [London: printed for author, and sold by G. Keith, at the Bible and Crown, in Grace-church-street; and by J. Robinson, at Dock-head, Southwark, 1757, The Spurgeon Library], 179, italics in the original).

18. "But the gospel church is 'a tabernacle that shall not be taken down; not one of the stakes thereof shall ever be removed, neither shall any of the cords thereof be broken.' May not these stakes and cords, which were used to give stability to the tabernacle, very fitly represent the ordinances of God, through which we receive grace to help in time of need, and the promises of the gospel which give security to the believing soul? the former shall never be removed, nor shall the latter ever be broken. The throne of grace remains accessible—the gospel continues to be preached—houses for worship multiply on every side—ordinances are still frequented—not one of these stakes is removed, nor ever shall be removed. Nor is any cord broken; the promises of grace are as immutable as their Author, who is without variableness or shadow of turning" (*Sketches of Sermons*, 2:82).

19. "III. The Nature of the Supplies Afforded to Us" (*Sketches of Sermons*, 2:82).

20. "The prophet might have designed to contrast Jerusalem literally, which was ill supplied with water, and through which an inconsiderable stream was accustomed

to flow, with the abundant supplies afforded to the gospel church" (*Sketches of Sermons*, 2:82).

21. "*Our supplies are divine*. . . . Jehovah is the glorious Lord—all is glorious that essentially belongs to him'" (*Sketches of Sermons*, 2:82, italics in the original).

22. "*Our supplies are abundant*. We shall not be supplied from a broken cistern, nor a stagnant pool, nor a mountain torrent, nor even a single river, but from 'broad rivers and streams'" (*Sketches of Sermons*, 2:83, italics in the original).

23. "A small brook; a little streamlet" (Johnson's *Dictionary*, s.v. "rill"). "A rill may dry up, and a current cease to flow, but broad rivers and streams hold on their majestic course. God's communications to his people are perpetual" (*Sketches of Sermons*, 2:83).

24. "*Our supplies are ever near*. 'There' (in the church,) 'the glorious Lord will be.' . . . [O]ur supplies are always at hand; we need not ascend up into heaven, nor descend into the deep, nor take the wings of the morning, to find God, or meet with these broad rivers, &c. No, God is ever with his people, and ever accessible by them" (*Sketches of Sermons*, 2:83, italics in the original).

25. "*Our supplies are unmolested*. There 'shall be no galley with oars,' &c. On these broad rivers and streams, no warlike ship shall sail, to invade the city, or cut off supplies from the inhabitants. This may serve to remind us that in the gospel church, they shall sit every man under his vine, and under his fig-tree, and none shall make them afraid" (*Sketches of Sermons*, 2:83, italics in the original).

26. Charles originally spelled this word "troblous." He inserted the letter "u" between the "o" and "b" to correct the misspelling. He indicated its location with a caret beneath the word.

27. "*Induce gratitude*. To us this prophecy is graciously accomplished; we live to see Jerusalem a quiet habitation. The fury of the persecutor never annoys us. We have heard of Bastiles, Inquisitions, and Smithfield fires, and bloody persecuting Bonners; we have heard of those who were stoned, sawn asunder, and slain with the edge of the sword; who, instead of having quiet habitations, wandered in deserts, and in mountains, and in dens, and in caves of the earth; but the storm has blown over, and the tempest has subsided. Hallelujah!" (*Sketches of Sermons*, 2:83–84, italics in the original).

28. "*Inspire confidence*. The church is secure, it is a 'tabernacle that shall not be taken down.' Men have striven to take it down, and have said, 'Rase it, rase it;'—the kings of the earth have set themselves, and the rulers have taken counsel together against it, but none of the stakes are yet removed, nor one of the cords broken. God will not take it down, and men cannot" (*Sketches of Sermons*, 2:84, italics in the original).

29. "*Excite expectation*. . . . Oh, what privileges we are called to realize!—What rich delights and exalted enjoyments lie before us!—Even in this world, God can do exceeding abundantly above all that we ask or think; but chiefly let us anticipate the period when we shall live in the new Jerusalem, where we shall be led to fountains of living waters, and where God shall wipe away all tears from our eyes" (*Sketches of Sermons*, 2:84, italics in the original).

THE INVITATION OF MOSES TO HOBAB—*Numbers 10:29*

1. This sermon is original to Charles Simeon. Spurgeon did not cite Simeon by name as he did in "The Son's Love to Us Compared with God's Love to Him" (Notebook 1, Sermon 38) and "Regeneration, Its Causes and Effects" (Notebook 1, Sermon 46). Instead, he wrote the inscription 2 Vol. II., which corresponds to Simeon's sermon entitled "Moses' Invitation to Hobab" (Charles Simeon, *Horae Homileticae, or Discourses (In the Form of Skeletons) upon the Whole Scriptures. Vol. II* [London: printed by Richard Watts, 1819], 10–17). However, Charles did not cite Simeon's sermon correctly. Instead of intending volume 2, sermon outline number 2, as his inscription suggests, Charles instead likely intended 2 vol. 11 or more accurately 2 vol. 101, which corresponds to the correct sermon number in volume 2 of *Horae Homileticae*, "Moses' Invitation to Hobab." For an additional referencing error in Notebook 2, see the inscription V.3.52 in "Envy Forbidden, Piety Commanded" (Sermon 112) which should instead be V.3.62. Overlapping content is noted below.

2. Charles preached an additional sermon on Num 10:29 entitled "A Generous Proposal" (*MTP* 16, Sermon 916). The emphasis of the later sermon is church membership and differs from that in the above outline. However, there is enough overlapping content and structural similarity to suggest Charles may have had this early outline in mind when writing his later sermon.

3. "Hobab, it should seem, was the son of Jethro, who is here called Raguel, and elsewhere Reuel. . . . But Moses besought him not to go, but to proceed with Israel to the promised land" (Simeon, *Horae Homileticae*, 2:10).

4. "That the journey of Israel in the wilderness was altogether typical of our journey heaven-ward, is well known" (Simeon, *Horae Homileticae*, 2:11).

5. "Nor let this sacrifice appear great: it is no other than was made by Abraham, and Moses, and the apostles of our Lord, and all the primitive Christians: nay, it is made daily even for the sake of a connexion with an earthly object: much more therefore may it be made for an union with Christ" (Simeon, *Horae Homileticae*, 2:12).

6. "There will be difficulties and obstructions which we must meet with; but we must meet them manfully: and, whatever be the cross that lies in our way, we must take it up, yea, and glory in it, and rejoice that we are counted worthy to bear it for His sake" (Simeon, *Horae Homileticae*, 2:12).

7. The words "continued under" are smeared toward the right side of the page.

8. An illegible letter appears beneath the "r" in the word "dangerous."

9. "All places are full of snares. Events, prosperous or adverse, expose you to temptation. All things that happen to you, though God makes them work for good, in themselves would work for evil. While here on this earth the world is no friend to grace to help you on to God. . . . Darkness prevails. It cannot minister to your safety or to your happiness. Neither can the sinful world minister light to the understanding, peace to the conscience, joy to the heart, or holiness to the life of the believer. You will have to fight continually. Till the last step you take it will be a conflict, and you will never be able to sheathe your sword until you are in the bosom of Christ" (*MTP* 16:100).

10. Luke 12:32, "Fear not, little flock; for it is your Father's good pleasure to give you the kingdom."

11. Revelation 3:21, "To him that overcometh will I grant to sit with me in my throne, even as I also overcame, and am set down with my Father in his throne."

12. Second Timothy 4:18, "And the Lord shall deliver me from every evil work, and will preserve me unto his heavenly kingdom: to whom be glory for ever and ever. Amen."

13. First John 2:25, "And this is the promise that he hath promised us, even eternal life."

14. Cf. Eph 2:8.

15. "God had undertaken to guide Israel through the wilderness, and to provide for and protect them in the way, yet there were many local circumstances which Hobab was acquainted with, by the communication of which, from time to time, he might render essential services to Moses and to all Israel" (Simeon, *Horae Homileticae*, 2:11). "He saw there every morning the pillar of cloud, and every night the pillar of fire. He heard the sound of the silver trumpets, he saw the uplifting of the sacred banners, and the marching of the chosen host of God" (*MTP* 16:105).

16. The sentence "Hobab knew the wilderness" was written between the words "interest" and "how" and beneath the phrase "kindness shewn." An alternative placement of this sentence is after "His own interest" in Charles's fourth point.

17. "First, dear hearer, thou must be one with Christ, reconciled to God, a believer in the precious blood, and then afterwards mayest thou come to the church of God" (*MTP* 16:101).

18. "Two considerations Moses proposed to Hobab: first, the benefit that would accrue to himself; and next, the benefit which he would confer on Israel. Similar considerations also may fitly be proposed to us. Consider then, if ye accept the invitation" (Simeon, *Horae Homileticae*, 2:13).

19. "God had undertaken to guide Israel" (Simeon, *Horae Homileticae*, 2:11); "Israel were altogether under the divine guidance, protection, and support" (Simeon, *Horae Homileticae*, 2:15).

20. "Aid; assistance; relief of any kind; help in distress" (Johnson's *Dictionary*, s.v. "succour").

21. "So, in the church of God there are the footprints of Deity, there are marks of the sublime presence of the Christ of God who abideth in the furnace with his afflicted people, signs of God's presence such as all the world besides cannot exhibit. You shall get good on the road" (*MTP* 16:105).

22. Cf. Ezek 18:23; 2 Pet 3:9.

Prov. 3. 33 — The Curse and the blessing. —

The grand distinction between the righteous and the wicked will be made in another world — yet in this world there is much that makes a sinner's state truly deplorable and the condition of the righteous truly blessed. —

A. The Curse is in the house, not at the door or the window. it is on all who are not truly converted for they are "wicked" the curse may evidently be seen

1. In their pleasures, — these are hollow at the best; if they are sinful pleasures the remorse following, and if allowable the disappointment are marks of the curse

2. On their projects — how often they fail, their tower is never finished. — if attained they are then seen to be unworthy of the labour of pursuit and so are cursed.

3. In their life — the want of true comfort, a consciousness of insecurity, a solitary friendlessness, and a sense of perpetual disappointment — are curses.

4. In death, often in its suddenness, in its darkness and sometimes terror, and in the calm death too is a curse.

5. In the children after them who too often inherit their vices, or turn out the grief of their eyes — no wonder — their parents are undutiful to God. —

Hardness of Heart, Final impenitence are too often curses. —

B. The blessing rests on the just — just in actions, and justified by the righteousness of Jesus Christ.
Even if to be just means only honest — Honesty is the best policy. Constantly the blessing rests on them.

1. Their pleasures are of a noble kind, they cloy not whether pleasures of sense or spirit, the Christian

THE CURSE AND THE BLESSING—*Proverbs 3:33*

99

The CURSE *and the* BLESSING
Proverbs 3:33[1]

"The curse of the Lord is in the house of the wicked: but he blesseth the habitation of the just."

The Grand distinction between the righteous and the wicked will be made in another world. Yet in this world there is much that makes a sinner's state truly deplorable and the condition of the righteous truly blessed.

A.[2] THE CURSE IS IN THE HOUSE.

Not at the door or the window. It is on all who are not truly converted, for they are "wicked."

The curse may evidently be seen:

1. In their pleasures. These are hollow at the best if they are sinful pleasures. The remor[s]e following, and, if allowable, the disappointment, are marks of the curse.[3]
2. On their projects. How often they fail; their tower is never finished.[4] If attained, they are then seen to be unworthy of the labour of pursuit and so are cursed.
3. In their life. The want of true comfort, a consciousness of insecurity, a solitary friendlessness, and a sense of perpetual disappointment are curses.
4. In death. Often in its suddenness, in its darkness and sometimes terror.[5] And in the calm death, too, is a curse.
5. In the children after them who too often inherit their vices[6] or turn out the grief of their eyes. No wonder—their parents are undutiful to God. Hardness of Heart,[7] Final impenitence[8] are too often curses.

B. THE BLESSING RESTS ON THE JUST.

Just in actions, and justified by the righteousness of Jesus Christ. Even if to be just means only honest. Honesty is the best policy.[9] Constantly, the blessing rests on them.

1. Their pleasures are of a noble kind. They cloy not.[10] Whether pleasures of sense or spirit, the Christian

177

enjoys such a share of them as do him good, they are his stepping stones to God — gratitude is excited by them.

2. When the habitation is in trouble, he has a God to comfort and strengthen him, a friend into whose bosom he pours all his grief — this too is so sanctifie that it becomes a first class blessing. —

3. In their projects, of earthly concern so far as they are lawful God assists — the blasting of their unlawful ones is a blessing — in spiritual concerns, God gives them their desire —

4. In their life — a quiet conscience, a firm faith in providence — a heavenly security, a calm resignation, & sweet communion bless him

5. In death — its horrors are mitigated, or the soul is nerved to meet them cheerfully, after it death is swallowed up in life — here are blessings.

6. In his family, God's promise is fulfilled the sons spring up in their father's place. God shows mercy to tens of thousands. —

1. Since men know the fruit of their doings, there will be no excuse of ignorance for them.

2. Lay the two clauses to heart — choose ye whom ye will serve — <u>Bless. bless. bless.</u>
130. 132.

THE CURSE AND THE BLESSING—*Proverbs 3:33*

      enjoys such a share of them as do him good. They are his stepping stones to God. Gratitude is excited by them.

2. When the habitation is in trouble, he has a God to comfort and strengthen him,[11] a friend[12] into whose bosom he pours all his grief.[13] This, too, is so sanctified that it becomes a first class blessing.[14]

3. In their projects of earthly concern, so far as they are lawful, God assists. The blasting of their unlawful ones is a blessing. In spiritual concerns, God gives them their desire.[15]

4. In their life, a quiet conscience, a firm faith in providence,[16] a heavenly security,[17] a calm resignation, and sweet communion bless him.

5. In death, its horrors are mitigated,[18] or the soul is nerved to meet them cheerfully.[19] After it, death is swallowed up in life.[20] Here are blessings.[21]

6. In his family, God's promise is fulfilled. The sons spring up in their father's places.[22] God shows mercy to tens of thousands.

1. Since men know the fruit of their doings, there will be no excuse of ignorance for them.[23]

2. Lay the two clauses to heart. Choose ye whom ye will serve.[24] <u>Bless. Bless. Bless.</u>

130. 132.

1. The second and only additional sermon Charles preached on Prov 3:33 occurred on the evening of October 19, 1856, at the Surrey Garden Music Hall in London (see Sermon 109 for the text Charles preached on that morning). Charles's congregation had outgrown the New Park Street Chapel and was forced to rent secular halls to hold the large audiences. That evening an estimated 12,000 persons gathered inside with an equal number on the outside of the building. According to the autobiography, the words Charles said on the evening of the disaster were not what he had intended. His sermon, eventually truncated, was not included in the second volume of *The New Park Street Pulpit* as it would have been. A transcription of his brief sermon, however, was taken down by a stenographer during the event: "Many were afraid to stop here, because they thought, if they stayed, they might die, and then they would be damned. They were aware—and many of you are aware—that, if you were hurried before your Maker to-night, you would be brought there unshriven unpardoned, and condemned. But what are your fears now to what they will be on that terrible day of reckoning of the Almighty, when the heavens shall shrink above you, and hell shall open her mouth beneath you?" (*Autobiography* 2:205–6). Not long after he said these words, someone in the audience shouted "'Fire!' 'The galleries are giving way!' 'The place is falling!'" (*Autobiography* 2:204). The resulting stampede left seven dead and twenty-eight injured. Charles was "carried by a private garden into the street, and taken home more dead than alive" (*Autobiography* 2:207). Charles never again preached on Prov 3:33. According to William Williams, his friend and future biographer, even the mention of Prov 3:33 solicited a change in Charles's countenance: "'What are you going to preach from to-morrow?' he once asked me. 'The curse of the Lord is in the house of the wicked, but He blesseth the habitation of the just.' He gave a deep sigh; his countenance changed even before I had finished the verse, brief as it was; and he said in tones of deep solemnity, *'Ah Me!'* 'What is the matter, sir?' 'Don't you know,' he replied, 'that is the text I had on that terrible night of the accident at the Surrey Music Hall?' I did not know it, but I learned from the mere mention of it how permanent was the effect upon his mind of that awful night's disaster" (W. Williams, *Personal Reminiscences of Charles Haddon Spurgeon* [2nd ed.; London, The Religious Tract Society, 1895], 46, italics in the original). Charles avoided preaching from or writing about this verse. In his 1887–88 devotional *Cheque Book of the Bank of Faith*, published approximately thirty-two years after the disaster, Charles ignored the first

part of the verse, "The curse of the LORD is in the house of the wicked," and only commented on the second part, "He blesseth the habitation of the just" (see *Cheque Book of the Bank of Faith: Daily Readings by C. H. Spurgeon* [Ross-shire, Scotland: Christian Focus Publications, 1996], March 5). Did Charles preach the same sermon in 1856 as he did in the above 1852 outline? A comparison reveals traces of overlapping content. However, given the absence of Charles's later sermon, it is unclear if he intended to follow the primary divisions of the above outline.

2. This is the first time in Notebook 2 that Charles used capital letters to signify his primary divisions.

3. Cf. Genesis 3.

4. Cf. Ps 127:1; Luke 14:28.

5. In his 1856 sermon Charles said, "My friends, there is a terrible day coming, when the terror and alarm of this evening shall be as nothing. That will be a time when the thunder and lightning and blackest darkness shall have their fullest power, when the earth shall reel to and fro beneath us, and when the arches of the solid heavens shall totter to their centre. The day is coming when the clouds shall reveal their wonders and portents, and Christ shall sit upon those clouds in glory, and shall call you to judgment. Many have gone away to-night, in the midst of this terrible confusion, and so shall it be on that great day" (*Autobiography* 2:205).

6. Cf. Exod 34:7.

7. Cf. Exod 10:20; Ps 95:8–9; Eph 4:18; Heb 3:7–9.

8. An early definition of the doctrine of "final impenitence" (*finalem impoenitentiam*) is found in Thomas Aquinas's use of Augustine: "That blasphemy or sin against the Holy Ghost is final impenitence, when, namely a man perseveres in mortal sin until death. Sin, moreover, not confined to utterance by word of mouth, but covering also word of heart and deed, not once but repeatedly" (Augustine, quoted in Thomas Aquinas, *Summa Theologicae*, vol. 32 [London: Blackfriars in Conjunction with Eyre & Spottiswoode; New York: McGraw-Hill Book Company, 1975], 119). For additional references to final impenitence in Charles's later sermons, see *MTP* 15:214; 20:471; 55:561.

9. The adage "Honesty is the best policy" was common to the Victorians. See "To Correspondents," *Cambridge Chronicle and University Journal, Isle of Ely Herald, and Huntingdonshire Gazette*, March 15, 1851.

10. Charles may have in mind Thomas Manton's line "They never cloy and weary" (see "God the Father of Lights" [Sermon 95]).

11. Cf. Ps 27:1.

12. Cf. Matt 11:19; John 15:15; Jas 2:23.

13. Cf. Ps 55:22; 1 Pet 5:7.

14. Charles here used "first class" to describe blessings; however, in his 1856 sermon he also used the word but in the context of social order: "Although, my hearers, you may suppose that there are *fifty different classes of persons* in the world, there are, in the eyes of God, but two. God knows nothing of any save the righteous and the unrighteous, the wicked and the just" (*Autobiography* 2:206, italics in the original).

15. Cf. Pss 20:4; 37:4; 145:19.

17. Cf. John 6:37; 10:28; 2 Cor 1:22.

16. Cf. Ps 103:19.

18. Cf. 1 Cor 15:15.

19. In his 1856 sermon Charles said, "But know you not, my friends, that grace, sovereign grace, can yet save you? Have you never heard the welcome news that Jesus came into the world to save sinners? Even if you are the chief of sinners, believe that Christ died for you, and you shall be saved. Do you not know that you are lost and ruined, and that none but Jesus can do helpless sinners good? You are sick and diseased, but Jesus can heal you; and He will if you only trust Him" (*Autobiography* 2:206).

20. Cf. Isa 25:8; 1 Cor 15:54.

21. "I would rather that you retired gradually, and may God Almighty dismiss you with His blessing, and carry you in safety to your homes! If our friends will go out by the central doors, we will sing while they go, and pray that some good may, after all, come out of this great evil. Do not, however, be in a hurry. Let those nearest the door go first" (*Autobiography* 2:206).

22. Cf. Ps 128:3.

23. Cf. Rom 1:20; 2:1.

24. Joshua 24:15, "And if it seem evil unto you to serve the Lord, choose you this day whom ye will serve; whether the gods which your fathers served that were on the other side of the flood, or the gods of the Amorites, in whose land ye dwell: but as for me and my house, we will serve the Lord."

Deut. 33.12. — The Beloved of the Lord in Safety.

How noble a sight is an old man, who has served God for many a year, how glorious to see with his children around, just starting on his journey across the Jordan. See Jacob leaning on his staff or Moses even a more conspicuous character bidding farewell to all — The whole of this book is a sermon and this last chapter is a song. how sweet to die singing such a song — The Israelites had often provoked him but he is not angry, he dies in a fine spirit, blessing all —

I. To whom is he speaking — Literally to Benjamin Jacob's youngest darling son — he styles him "the beloved of the Lord". Spiritually he speaks to the elect, loved with special love, called by peculiar grace — specially beloved by God for such love from God is at the root of all our love. But election can only be known by marks & evidences let us look at them — some are these.
1. Love to God — am I found on my knees, reading his word.
2. Love to God's people, and cause, desire to spread his name.
3. Hatred alike to sin & self righteousness — carelessness for the world.
4. Fear to offend God, a longing to please him.
5. Am I hated by the world, jeered & scoffed at. —

II. What Moses says — Literally to Benj — that the temple shall be in his borders, God shall rest between his hills. Spiritually to God's beloved that they ~~Lord shall~~ dwell in safety — Not they shall dwell in ease & pleasure. Not they shall dwell in plenty & riches — Nor even does he say they shall dwell safely every where but only "by him" —
"The Lord shall cover him" &c — as a cloud guiding them. as a mist concealing — as armour protecting — as a

THE BELOVED OF THE LORD IN SAFETY—*Deuteronomy 33:12*

100[1]

The BELOVED of the LORD in SAFETY
Deuteronomy 33:12[2]

"And of Benjamin he said, The beloved of the LORD *shall dwell in safety by him; and the Lord shall cover him all the day long, and he shall dwell between his shoulders."*

How noble a sight is an old man who has served God for many a year. How glorious to see with his children around just starting on his journey across the Jordan.[3] See Jacob leaning on his staff,[4] or Moses, even a more conspicuous character, bidding farewell to all.[5] The whole of this book is a sermon, and this last chapter is a song. How sweet to die singing such a song.[6] The Israelites had often provoked him,[7] but he is not angry. He dies in a fine spirit blessing all.

I. TO WHOM IS HE SPEAKING?

Literally to Benjamin, Jacob's youngest darling son. He styles him "the beloved of the Lord." Spiritually, he speaks to the elect, loved with special love,[8] called by peculiar grace,[9] specially beloved by God.[10] For such love from God is at the root of all our love.[11] But election can only be known by marks and evidences. Let us look at them. Some are these:

1. Love to God. Am I found on my knees reading his Word?
2. Love to God's people and cause, desire to spread his name.
3. Hatred alike to sin and self righteousness, carelessness for the world.[12]
4. Fear to offend God.[13] A longing to please him.
5. Am I hated by the world,[14] jeered and scoffed at?

II. WHAT MOSES SAYS, LITERALLY TO BENJ.[15]

That the temple shall be in his borders. God shall rest between his hills. Spiritually, to God[']s beloved that they ~~Lord~~ shall dwell in safety.

Not they shall dwell in ease and pleasure.
Not they shall dwell in plenty and riches.

Nor even does he say they shall dwell safely everywhere, but only "by him."

"The Lord shall cover them," etc., as a cloud guiding them,[16] as a mist concealing, as armour protecting, as an

ornament adorning. as a robe in the day of judgment. "all the day long" as long as he shall live anywhere. he shall cover him from the heat of the sun of prosperity, the cold damps of affliction, the arrows of the devil, the eye of justice — To have God in our foreheads is to show him — in our hearts is to love him, between our shoulders is to strengthen us. where the burden is the blessing is — this strength is needed to preserve from sin & guide & help in prayer.
133. 137. 142. 195. 198. 288. 290. 445.

For this 100 I bless the Lord for the good is his. may they be the seed of many a plant of the Lord.

THE BELOVED OF THE LORD IN SAFETY—*Deuteronomy 33:12*

ornament adorning, as a robe in the day of judgment.[17]

"All the day long." As long as he shall live anywhere, he shall cover him from the heat of the sun of prosperity,[18] the cold damps of affliction, the arrows of the devil,[19] the eye of justice.[20]

To have God in our foreheads is to show him,[21] in our hearts is to love him,[22] between our shoulders is to strengthen us. Where the burden is, the blessing is. This strength is needed to preserve from sin and guide and help in prayer.

133. 137. 142. 195. 198. 288. 290. 445.

For this 100 I bless the Lord, for the good is his.

May they be the seed of many a plant of the Lord.[23]

SERMON 100

1. Charles bolded the number 100 likely because he perceived the preaching of this sermon to be a milestone in his ministry. See the concluding remarks at the end of this sermon.

2. This is the only time Charles preached on Deut 33:12.

3. The sentence "How glorious to see with his children around just starting on his journey across the Jordan" may have been a reference to Christian, the main character in John Bunyan's *The Pilgrim's Progress*. At the end of the allegory, Christian crosses the Jordan River (death) before arriving at the Celestial City. "You must go through [the river], or you cannot come at the Gate. . . . They then addressed themselves to the Water; and entering, *Christian* began to sink, and crying out to his good friend *Hopeful*; he said, I sink in deep Waters, the Billows go over my head, all his Waves go over me, *Selah*. Then said the other, Be of good chear, my Brother, I feel the bottom, and it is good" (John Bunyan, *The Pilgrim's Progress from This World to That Which Is to Come. Delivered Under the Similitude of a Dream. Wherein Is Discovered, the Manner of His Setting Out; His Dangerous Journey, and Safe Arrival at the Desired Country* [ed. George Offor; London: printed by J. Haddon, 1847, The Spurgeon Library], 186–87, italics in the original). See also "David in the Cave of Adullam" (Sermon 116).

4. Cf. Gen 47:31; Heb 11:21.   5. Cf. Deuteronomy 33.

6. On the title page of Notebook 4 Charles wrote, "I hope to die singing." See also "Oh That Men Would Praise the Lord" (Sermon 105).

7. Cf. Exod 16:2–3; Num 11:1–15; 14:2.

8. This phrase, "loved with special love," is similar to one in John Gill's exposition of Heb 8:10: "whether *Jews* or *Gentiles*; and who are such whom God has loved with a special love, has chose in Christ, and given to him, and with whom he has made a covenant in him" (John Gill, *An Exposition of the New Testament, in Three Volumes. In Which the Sense of the Sacred Text Is Given; Doctrinal and Practical Truths Are Set in a Plain and Easy Light, Difficult Places Explained, Seeming Contradictions Reconciled; and Whatever Is Material in the Various Readings, and Several Oriental Variations, Is Observed. The Whole Illustrated with Notes Taken from the Most Ancient Jewish Writings. Vol. III* [London: printed for the author, 1748, The Spurgeon Library], 401, italics in the original).

9. Cf. Col 3:12; 1 Pet 2:9.

10. Cf. Song 6:1–3; Rom 1:7; 9:25.

11. Cf. 1 John 4:19.

12. Cf. 1 John 2:15.

13. Cf. Matt 10:28.

14. Cf. Matt 10:22; Mark 13:13; Luke 21:17; John 15:18.

15. Abbr. "Benjamin."

16. Cf. Exod 13:21.

17. Cf. Isa 61:10; Rev 19:8.

18. "They say that persecution after all does not hurt the church; it only winnows her and drives away her chaff: but these are far worse days, for prosperity undermines piety" (*MTP* 22:483).

19. Cf. Ps 91:5; Eph 6:16.

20. Cf. Rom 3:25.

21. Cf. Rev 22:4.

22. Cf. Eph 3:17.

23. The phrase "May they be the seed of many a plant of the Lord" is reminiscent of Charles's letter to his father on October 16, 1851. After explaining his initial call to fill the pulpit of Waterbeach Chapel he wrote, "I am glad you have such good congregations. I feel no doubt there is a great work doing there. The field[s] are ripe unto the harvest. The seed you have sown has yielded plenty of green. Let us hope there will be abundance of wheat" (Angus Library and Archive, Regent's Park College, Oxford University, D/SPU 1, Letter 10).

The Second Psalm.—

This Psalm was written by David and doubtless with an eye to Christ in every word of it — it may easily be divided into

I. An account of the world's opposition to Christ's empire — 1 to 3.

1. This opposition was very fierce, they raged; next they imagined evil, then the kings set themselves against it both in counsel and act — This opposition is base, caused by man's love of sin, the humbling nature of the gospel &c —

2. It was general, all ranks from the people up to the king, all nations both the "heathen" and the "people" the Jews. every individual by nature abhors it & in some way resists — Jewish Persecution, Romish, English Church, the Mob, churls.

3. This opposition was caused not only by a hatred to the Gospel, but to the God of the gospel, to God and Christ too. they did not then and do not now love the "cords" & "bands" the mercies & blessings they would like but no duties —

II. A declaration of God's anger on account of it — 4. 5 —

1. God is no unconcerned spectator of this stir, he sees, and seeing he is wrath, because of their ingratitude & rebellion.

2. He is not wrath because he fears in the least any of these attempts for he "laughs" at them, to show his own security and his own contempt of them — he sees that they are in his hand, he knows the madness of the attempt and moreover when they rave the most they are but working out his divine purposes and to defeat themselves —

3. This wrath is not stifled in his bosom, nor does his contempt of them suffer them to pass unpunished. "he speaks" in judgments here & sooner or later he will "vex" them, by baffling their designs and crushing their persons.

III. A boast of what God has done already. 6. 7.

1. He has chosen the hated one to be a king, yea "my king" says God, my beloved above all, I have given him a kingdom too even Zion, I have "set" him there by my own hand

THE SECOND PSALM

101

The SECOND PSALM[1]
Psalm 2

This Psalm was written by David, and doubtless with an eye to Christ in every word of it.[2] It may easily be divided into:

I. AN ACCOUNT OF THE WORLD'S OPPOSITION TO CHRIST'S EMPIRE (1 TO 3).[3]

1. This opposition was very fierce. They <u>raged</u>. Next, they <u>imagined</u> evil.[4] Then the kings set themselves against it, both in counsel and act. This opposition is base, caused by man's love of sin, the humbling nature of the gospel, etc.
2. It was general. All ranks from the people up to the king.[5] All nations, both the "heathen" and the "people," the Jews. Every individual by[6] nature abhors[7] it and in some way resists.[8] Jewish Persecution, Romish, English Church, the Mob,[9] churls.[10]
3. This opposition was caused,[11] not only by a hatred to the Gospel but to the God of the gospel, to God and Christ, too. They did not then and do not now love the "cords" and "bands."[12] The mercies and blessings they would like, but no duties.

II. A DECLARATION OF GOD'S ANGER ON ACCOUNT OF IT (4 . 5).

1. God is no unconcerned spectator of this stir. He sees, and seeing he is wrath[ful][13] because of their ingratitude and rebellion.
2. He is not wrath[ful] because he fears in the least any of these attempts, for he "laughs" at them[14] to show his own security and his own contempt of them. He sees that they are in his hand. He knows the madness of the attempt. And moreover, when they rave the most they are but working out his divine purposes and so defeat themselves.
3. This wrath is not stifled in his bosom, nor does his contempt of them suffer them[15] to pass unpunished. "He speaks" in judgments here and sooner or later he will "vex" them[16] by baffling their designs and crushing their persons.

III. A BOAST OF WHAT GOD HAS DONE ALREADY (6 . 7).

1. He has chosen the hated one to be a king. Yea, "my king," says God,[17] my beloved[18] above all. I have given him a kingdom, too, even Zion. I have "set" him there by my own hand

in my own fair and sacred Zion. the beauty of the whole earth.
2. He has despite all opposition made his kingdom secure, he has "set" him, on a "hill" beyond all reach on a "hill" and so secure. the decree shall never change.
3. Jesus is God's son, and all the rage of man cannot undo that. this same Jesus is both Lord and God, above all kings and angels he is exalted both by the "sonship" he possesses through divine generation and that which as God-man he has, through God's exaltation.—

IV. A promise to the opposed Son, of yet greater things. 8.9. The world thinks lightly of what God has done, Zion say they is a paltry empire, a mere hill, well God gives more.
1. He gives him an "inheritance" to save, and that too from among the "heathen" from the "uttermost parts" with a promise that in latter days these shall be most numerous.
2. He gives him, the whole earth that he may use all to aid his grand design, all men are now the property of Christ, though not to be saved by grace yet to be forced by providence to render service & by his overruling power to contribute to the spread of his Kingdom.
3. He gives him his foes, as victims to his just anger, to be governed with a rod not of sweet love, but of iron. to be dashed to shivers like a potter's vessel in helpless destruction, rendered unable to unite their shattered parts, & beaten in fierce wrath small as the dust of heaven.

V. A counsel to all deduced from this. 10. 11. 12.
1. It is nothing but the dictate of common prudence that the enemies of God should submit, they cannot defeat Christ, he has a kingdom now, that kingdom is eternally secure. they themselves are unwittingly

in my own fair and sacred Zion, the beauty of the whole earth.[19]
2. He has, despite all opposition, made his kingdom secure. He has "set" him on a "hill" beyond all reach. On a "hill," and so secure. The decree shall never change.[20]
3. Jesus is God's son,[21] and all the rage of man cannot undo that. This same Jesus is both Lord and God above all kings and angels. He is exalted both by the "sonship["] he possesses through divine generation[22] and that which as God-man he has through God's exaltation.[23]

IV. A PROMISE TO THE OPPOSED SON, OF YET GREATER THINGS (8 . 9).

The world thinks lightly of what God has done. Zion, say they, is a paltry empire, a mere hill. Well, God gives more.

1. He gives him an "inheritance" to save, and that, too, from among the "heathen" from the "uttermost parts"[24] with a promise that in latter days these shall be most numerous.
2. He gives him the whole earth that he may use all to aid his grand design. All men are now the property of Christ, though not to be saved by grace, yet to be forced by providence to render service, and by his overruling power to contribute to the spread of his Kingdom.[25]
3. He gives him his[26] foes as victims to his just anger, to be governed with a rod,[27] not of sweet love but of iron, to be dashed to shivers like a potter's vessel[28] in helpless destruction, rendered unable to unite their shattered parts, and beaten in fierce[29] wrath, small as the dust of heaven.

V. A COUNSEL TO ALL DEDUCED FROM THIS (10 . 11 . 12).

1. It is nothing but the dictate of common prudence that the enemies of God should submit. They cannot defeat Christ. He has a kingdom now. That kingdom is eternally secure. They, themselves, are unwillingly

his vassals, to be used on earth against their wills and at last to be subdued by wrath — the task is hopeless — give it up —

2. Considering their sinful opposition — they must be expected to serve him with fear of wrath & when led in Jesus to rejoice yet then trembling must season joy — considering how great the Holy one is we have need ever to fear, & tremble.

3. A dread of consequences should lead to immediate submission & compliance with the required service for suppose you are cut down now, that would be solemn — sudden destruction is however "but a little" of the kindling of his wrath — what will the "great day of his wrath" be —

4. The thought of the blessed state of those who trust in him should induce it — for truly this subject renders them doubly blessed. their kingdom is secure, for theirs it is as coheirs with Christ — their salvation is certain the kingdom cannot be moved. Christ's promise to his people, has his father's oath to back it. Thrice blessed are all they that put their trust in him — Look unto him then & enjoy the same.

134.

his vassals to be used on earth against their wills and at last to be subdued by wrath. The task is hopeless. Give it up.

2. Considering their sinful opposition, they must be expected to serve him with fear of wrath[30] and when led in Jesus to rejoice. Yet then trembling must season joy. Considering how great the Holy one is, we have need ever to fear and tremble.[31]

3. A dread of consequences should lead to immediate submission and compliance with the required service, for suppose you are cut down now. That would be solemn. Sudden destruction is, however, "but a little" of the kindling of his wrath.[32] What will the "great day of his wrath"[33] be?

4. The thought of the blessed state of those who trust in him should induce it. For truly, this subject renders them doubly blessed. Their kingdom is secure. For theirs it is as coheirs with Christ.[34] Their salvation is certain. The kingdom cannot be moved.[35] Christ's promise to his people has his father's oath to back it.

Thrice blessed are all they that put their trust in him. Look unto him[37] then and enjoy the same.

134.

SERMON 101

1. In this sermon Charles selected the entire second psalm as the scope of his biblical text. Other occasions for this wide scope are found in "The Seven Cries on the Cross (Notebook 3, Sermon 142); "Jacob's Dream" (Notebook 4, Sermon 194); "I Have Found a Ransom" (Notebook 4, Sermon 224); and "Vision of the Man with the Inkhorn" (Notebook 5, Sermon 256). In his later ministry Charles preached four additional sermons on the second psalm: "An Earnest Invitation" (*NPSP* 5, Sermon 260); "The Greatest Trial on Record" (*MTP* 9, Sermon 495); "Christ's Universal Kingdom, and How It Cometh" (*MTP* 26, Sermon 1535); and "An Earnest Entreaty" (*MTP* 63, Sermon 3550). To preserve space on this page, the lengthy biblical text has not been included beneath the title of this sermon. However, individual verses quoted by Charles are written in full in the footnotes.

2. On March 13, 1859, Charles preached the sermon "Christ Precious to Believers," in which he revealed his Christological hermeneutic by recounting a conversation between a Welsh minister and his friend Jonathan George: "And my dear brother, your business is when you get to a text, to say, 'Now what is the road to Christ?' and then preach a sermon, running along the road towards the great metropolis—Christ. And,' said he, 'I have never yet found a text that had not got a road to Christ in it, and if I ever do find one that has not a road to Christ in it, I will make one; I will go over hedge and ditch but I would get at my Master, for the sermon cannot do any good unless there is a savour of Christ in it'" (*NPSP* 5:140). On July 6, 1873, Charles preached a sermon entitled "The Apple Tree in the Wood" in which he articulated a similar hermeneutical principle: "Whatever we do not preach, let us preach Jesus Christ. I have found, wherever I have been during the last month, that though there might not be a road to this place or that, there was sure to be a London road. Now, if your sermon does not happen to have the doctrine of election, or the doctrine of final perseverance in it, let it always have Christ in it. Have a road to London, a road to Christ, in every sermon" (*MTP* 19:381).

3. For clarity and consistency, the Scripture verses in this sermon are enclosed within parentheses.

4. Psalm 2:1, "Why do the heathen rage, and the people imagine a vain thing?"

5. Psalm 2:2, "The kings of the earth set themselves, and the rulers take counsel together, against the LORD."

6. An illegible letter appears beneath the word "by."

7. Charles may have misspelled the second part of the word "abhors" and sought to correct the misspelling.

8. Cf. Eph 2:3.

9. Charles's reference to the "Mob" is unclear; however, mob activity was rampant throughout England during the mid-1850s (see "Election Exposures," *The [London] Daily News*, May 30, 1853).

10. "A rustick; a countryman; a labourer . . . a rude, surly, ill-bred man" (Johnson's *Dictionary*, s.v. "churl").

11. An illegible mark or letter appears above the letter "a" in the word "caused."

12. Psalm 2:3, "Let us break their bands asunder, and cast away their cords from us." In his *Exposition of the Old Testament*, John Gill wrote, "But of the heathen, the people, the kings of the earth, and rulers, who with one voice say this and what follows, *and cast their cords from us*; with relation to the Lord and his Anointed, whole laws, ordinances and truths, they call *bands* and *cords*" (John Gill, *An Exposition of the Old Testament, in Which Are Recorded the Original of Mankind, of the Several Nations of the World, and of the Jewish Nation in Particular: the Lives of the Patriarchs of Israel; the Journey of That People from Egypt Through the Wilderness to the Land of Canaan, and Their Settlement in That Land; Their Laws Moral, Ceremonial, and Judicial; Their Government and State Under Judges and Kings; Their Several Captivities, and Their Sacred Books of Devotion. In the Exposition of Which, It Is Attempted to Give an Account of the Several Books, and the Writers of Them; a Summary of Each Chapter; and the Genuine Sense of Every Verse: And Throughout the Whole, the Original Text, and the Versions of It, Are Inspected and Compared; Interpreters of the Best Note, Both Jewish and Christian, Consulted; Difficult Places at Large Explained; Seeming Contradictions Reconciled; and Various Passages Illustrated and Confirmed by the Testimonies of Writers, as Well Gentile as Jewish, Vol. III. Containing I. 1 Chronicles. II. II Chronicles. III. Ezra. IV. Nehemiah. V. Esther. VI. Job. VII. Psalms, Part I* [London: printed for the author, and sold by George Keith, at the Bible and Crown in Grace-church-street, 1765, The Spurgeon Library], 496, italics in the original).

13. Psalm 2:5a, "Then shall he speak unto them in his wrath."

14. Psalm 2:4, "He that sitteth in the heavens shall laugh: the LORD shall have them in derision."

15. Charles originally wrote the word "them"; however, he struck through the letter "t" possibly to form the word "him." The context suggests the word "them" is correct.

16. Psalm 2:5b, "[A]nd vex them in his sore displeasure."

17. Psalm 2:6, "Yet have I set my king upon my holy hill of Zion."

18. The word "beloved" is not found in Ps 2:6–7. Charles may have had in mind Matt 3:17, "And lo a voice from heaven, saying, This is my beloved Son, in whom I am well pleased."

19. Psalm 48:2, "Beautiful for situation, the joy of the whole earth, is mount Zion, on the sides of the north, the city of the great King."

20. Psalm 2:7, "I will declare the decree: the LORD hath said unto me, Thou art my Son; this day have I begotten thee."

21. Cf. Matt 3:17; John 3:16; Heb 5:5; 1 John 4:15.

22. Cf. Matt 1:18–20.   23. Cf. Acts 5:31; Phil 2:9.

24. Psalm 2:8, "Ask of me, and I shall give thee the heathen for thine inheritance, and the uttermost parts of the earth for thy possession."

25. Charles did not hold to the concept of unmerited reprobation. In his 1861 sermon "Expositions of the Doctrines of Grace" (*MTP* 7, Sermon 385), Charles said, "But we are next met by some who tell us that we preach the wicked and horrible doctrine of *sovereign and unmerited reprobation*. 'Oh,' say they, 'you teach that men are damned because God made them to be damned, and that they go to hell, not because of sin, not because of unbelief, but because of some dark decree with which God has stamped their destiny.' Brethren, this is an unfair charge again. Election does not involve reprobation. There may be some who hold unconditional reprobation. I stand not here as their defender, let them defend themselves as best they can; I hold God's election, but I testify just as clearly that if any man be lost he is lost for sin; and this has been the uniform statement of

Calvinistic ministers.... If any of you have ever uttered that libel against us, do it not again, for we are as guiltless of that as you are yourselves.... If he be lost, damnation is all of man; but, if he be saved, still salvation is all of God" (*MTP* 7:301, italics in the original). In his sermon "Jacob and Esau" (*NPSP* 5, Sermon 111), he spoke about himself in the third person, saying, "'He gives God all the glory for every soul that is saved, but he won't have it that God is to blame for any man that is damned.' That teaching I cannot understand. My soul revolts at the idea of a doctrine that lays the blood of man's soul at God's door. I cannot conceive how any human mind, at least his Christian mind, can hold any such blasphemy as that. I delight to preach this blessed truth—salvation of God, from first to last—the Alpha and Omega; but when I come to preach damnation, I say, damnation of man, not of God; and if you perish at your own hands must your own blood be required" (*NPSP* 5:119).

26. The illegible markings written beneath "his" could be the letters "v" and "i" in the word "victims." If correct, Charles accidently or prematurely wrote this word.

27. Psalm 2:9a, "Thou shalt break them with a rod of iron."

28. Psalm 2:9b, "[T]hou shalt dash them in pieces like a potter's vessel."

29. Charles wrote the letter "e" prematurely beneath "i" in the word "fierce."

30. Psalm 2:11, "Serve the Lord with fear, and rejoice with trembling."

31. Cf. Pss 97:4; 99:1; 114:7; 119:120; Prov 1:7; Isa 64:2; Joel 3:16; Amos 3:6.

32. Psalm 2:12a, "Kiss the Son, lest he be angry, and ye perish from the way, when his wrath is kindled but a little."

33. Revelation 6:17, "For the great day of his wrath is come; and who shall be able to stand?" See also Isa 8:22; Joel 2:31; Zeph 1:15.

34. Cf. Rom 8:17.   35. Cf. Heb 12:28.

36. Charles may have had Isa 45:22 in mind: "Look unto me, and be ye saved, all the ends of the earth: for I am God, and there is none else" (see *Autobiography* 1:105–10).

102. Rom. VI. 22. Justification, Conversion, Sanctification, Glory.
v. 42.

The fault of men is to look abroad when home wants them much more; the Bible always recommends us to look at home, so let us turn from others and just look at ourselves and see if here is somewhat for us.— though, perhaps, restricting the expression we notice

I. Justification. "now being made free from sin".—
This is a blessing enjoyed by all true believers, they are all perfectly justified — by pardon & imputed righteousness.
1. We are freed from the guilt of sin, it need not now cause such distress and fear, the soul is washed.
2. Freed from all the losses it caused, sinners lost God's favour, peace of conscience, security, heaven but now we are not counted as sinners, but as righteous and so we lose none of these things.
3. Freed from ills incurred — such as the wrath of God, the sentence of the law, loss of the promises, hell.—
We <u>are made</u>, we did not make ourselves so.
<u>now</u>, that is at the first moment, faith exists.

II. Conversion "and become servants to God" the two are concomitant, commencing at one time. conversion is the first acting of grace, sanctification the subsequent ones — justification never exists in an unconverted man — in conversion man has somewhat of activity "become" not "are made" yet the term still allows & implies that Divine

JUSTIFICATION, CONVERSION, SANCTIFICATION, GLORY—*Romans 6:22*

102

V2.42[1]

JUSTIFICATION, CONVERSION, SANCTIFICATION, GLORY[2]
Romans 6:22[3]

"But now being made free from sin, and become servants to God, ye have your fruit unto holiness, and the end everlasting life."

The fault of men is to look abroad when home wants them much more. The Bible always recommends us to look at home.[4] So let us turn from others and just look at ourselves and see if here is somewhat[5] for us. Though perhaps restricting the expression, we notice:

I. JUSTIFICATION, *"now being made free from sin."*[6]

This is a blessing enjoyed by all true believers. They are all perfectly justified by pardon and imputed righteousness.[7]

1. We are freed from the guilt of sin.[8] It need not now cause such distress and fear.[9] The soul is washed.[10]

2. Freed from all the losses it caused. Sinners lost God's favour, peace of conscience, security, heaven. But now we are not counted as sinners but as righteous,[11] and so we lose none of these things.

3. Freed from ills incurred such as the wrath of God,[12] the sentence of the law, loss[13] of the promises, hell. We <u>are made</u>. We did not make ourselves so. <u>Now</u>—that is, at the first moment—faith exists.

II. CONVERSION, *"and become servants to God."*

The two are concomitant, commencing at one time. Conversion is the first acting of grace; sanctification, the subsequent ones. Justification never exists in an unconverted man. In[14] conversion man has somewhat of activity. "Become," not "are made." Yet the term still allows and implies that Divine,

supernatural grace is necessary. in conversion as servant
1. We submit to God's will — before we brooked no servitude
our own wild will was our only Lord, now we agree to submit
to God's will in all our affairs, sufferings, actions, we are his.
2. We agree that our support shall come from him, we
being his servants we expect he will maintain us.
we give up our old beggarly gipsying habits and settle down
with a good Master, who supplies, clothes, strengthens, keeps even to hair
3. We are interested in his cause. as good servants we
like our master to prosper. we long to see Jesus King of all.
Let none imagine they are justified if not thus converted.

<u>III</u>. Sanctification. "ye have your fruit unto holiness"
This follows the others, and cannot come before them
or exist without them —   any sanctification which
is ~~not~~ antecedent to justification & conversion is but a
sham, painted, Pharasaical one — a mere guy. —
Sanctification is not the root but the fruit. there is
1. The Fruit of the heart, which is a holy fear of sin,
a longing for perfect holiness, all desire is now counted
sin and is as such striven against.
2. The Fruit of the lips. In prayer, striving for it,
in singing extolling its God, in conversation chaste,
seasoned with salt — lying, anger, filthy speech is gone.
3. The Fruit of their lives. they cannot do as others.
they avoid all ~~sin~~ and so far as in them lies are holy
Christians are holier than others, whilst they feel
themselves greater sinners, than others allow themselves to be.
this because they count many things sin which others do not.

JUSTIFICATION, CONVERSION, SANCTIFICATION, GLORY—*Romans 6:22*

supernatural grace is necessary in conversion, As servant[s]:[15]

1. We submit to God's will.[16] Before, we brooked[17] no servitude. Our own wild will was our only Lord. Now, we agree to Submit to God's will in all our affairs, sufferings, actions. We are his.[18]

2. We agree that our support shall come from him. We, being his servants, we expect he will maintain us.[19] We give up our old, beggarly, gipsying[20] habits and settle down with a good Master who supplies clothes,[21] strengthens,[22] keeps [us] even to hoar hairs.[23]

3. We are interested in his cause. As good servants we like our master to prosper.[24] We long to see Jesus King of all. Let none imagine they are justified if not thus converted.

III. SANCTIFICATION, *"ye have your fruit unto holiness."*[25]

This follows the others and cannot come before them or exist without them. Any sanctification which is ~~not~~ antecedent to justification and conversion[26] is but a sham, painted, Pharasaical one—a mere goy.[27] Sanctification is not the root but the fruit. There is:

1. The Fruit of the heart, which is a holy fear of sin, a longing for perfect holiness.[28] All desire is now counted sin and is as such striven against.

2. The Fruit of the lips.[29] In prayer, striving for it. In singing, extolling its God. In conversation, chaste,[30] seasoned with salt.[31] Lying, anger, filthy speech is gone.

3. The Fruit of their lives.[32] They cannot do as others. They avoid all sin, and so far as in them lies are holy.[33] Christians are holier than others, whilst they feel themselves greater sinners than others allow themselves to be. This [is] because they count many things sin which others[34] do not.

4. This is their great object — they press toward it, they grow and increase in it or should do daily.

Ye have, that is all truly converted men, unless we have this in part: we have not the two first nor may we expect the "end"

IV. Glory — "and the end everlasting life"
1. The only end to our journey is Canaan, we rest not here, our end is not this life, but the everlasting one.
2. An endless state of being is promised, no death because no body to die. A sea without a shore.
3. A state of unutterable joy, life is the word for joy — death causes sorrow. gladness, activity, enjoyment.

1. As we desire the end so must we desire to be found in all the stages of the road. man must
be justified by faith in Jesus, or no glory for him
be converted by sovereign grace or no glory for him
be sanctified, body, soul, & spirit or he cannot see it.
135.

JUSTIFICATION, CONVERSION, SANCTIFICATION, GLORY—*Romans 6:22*

4. This is their great object. They press toward it. They grow and increase in it, or should do daily.

Ye[35] <u>have</u>. That is, all truly converted men. Unless we have this in part, we have not the two first, nor may we expect the "end."

IV. GLORY, *"and the end everlasting life."*[36]

1.[37] The only end to our journey is Canaan. We rest not here. Our end is not this life but the everlasting one.[38]

2. An endless state of being is promised.[39] No death because no body to die.[40] A[41] sea without a shore.

3. A state of unutterable joy.[42] Life is the word for Joy. Death causes sorrow. Gladness, activity, enjoyment.

1. As we desire the end, so must we desire to be found in all the stages of the road. Man must:

> Be Justified by faith in Jesus,[43] or no glory for him.
>
> Be converted by sovereign grace,[44] or no glory for him.
>
> Be sanctified, body, soul, and spirit,[45] or he cannot see it.

135.

SERMON 102

1. This is the third of four sermons in Notebook 2 that Charles borrowed from the collection of sermon outlines entitled *Sketches of Sermons* (for information about this publication, see "Inventory and Title of Our Treasures" [Sermon 92]). See also "The Tranquillity, Security, and Supplies Afforded to the Gospel Church" (Sermon 97) and "Envy Forbidden, Piety Commanded" (Sermon 112). In the top right corner of the page, Charles inscribed the reference "V2.42," or volume 2, sermon outline 42, which corresponds to the forty-second sermon outline, "The Blessed State of Believers," in the second volume of *Sketches of Sermons*, 185–89. Overlapping content is noted below.

2. For similar sermons on the doctrine of justification, see "The Saints' Justification and Glory" (Notebook 1, Sermon 68); "Justification by Grace" (*NPSP*, Sermon 126); "Justification and Glory" (*MTP* 11, Sermon 627); and "Justification by Faith" (*MTP* 60, Sermon 3392). For similar sermons on the practice of conversion, see "Repentance unto Life" (*NTPS* 1, Sermon 44); "The Conversion of Saul of Tarsus" (*NPSP*, Sermon 202); "Conversions Desired" (*MTP* 22, Sermon 1282); "Conversions Encouraged" (Sermon 1283); "Converts, and Their Confession of Faith" (*MTP* 41, Sermon 2429); and "Conversion and Character" (*MTP* 59, Sermon 3372). For similar sermons on the doctrine of sanctification, see "Threefold Sanctification" (*MTP* 8, Sermon 434); "The God of Peace and Our Sanctification" (*MTP* 23, Sermon 1368); and "Perfect Sanctification" (*MTP* 26, Sermon 1527). For similar sermons on the doctrine of glorification, see "The Glory, Unity, and Triumph of the Church" (*MTP* 25, Sermon 1472) and "Glory!" (*MTP* 29, Sermon 1721).

3. This is the only time Charles preached a sermon on Rom 6:22.

4. Cf. Phil 3:20; Heb 11:10; 13:14.

5. An alternative reading of this line is "See if here is some[thing] for us."

6. "1. Believers are free from sin. By believers we are to understand those who, under the influence of the Holy Spirit, have repented truly for their sins, and believed with the heart unto righteousness" (*Sketches of Sermons* 2:185).

7. Cf. "Abraham Justified by Faith" (Notebook 1, Sermon 3).

8. "*The accumulated guilt of sin*.... Having believed on Jesus as their substitute and

ransom, they enjoy redemption through his blood, the forgiveness of sins, Eph. i. 7" (*Sketches of Sermons* 2:185, italics in the original).

9. "The curse of Mount Sinai does not alarm them, justice has ceased to threaten them, and conscience to accuse them. Being justified by faith, they have peace with God" (*Sketches of Sermons* 2:185).

10. Cf. Isa 1:18.

11. Cf. Gen 15:6; Rom 4:5.

12. See the previous sermon, "The Second Psalm" (Sermon 101).

13. An illegible letter was written beneath the letter "l" in the word "loss." An alternative explanation of this revision is the reinforcement of the arm of the letter "l."

14. It appears Charles originally wrote the letter "c" beneath "i" in the word "in." Charles possibly intended to begin the phrase with the word "conversion."

15. An alternative reading of this phrase is "In conversion, as servants."

16. "*They are governed by his will.* The servant of God is in covenant with his Maker; he has made a surrender of his person and services to the Lord, resolving to serve him faithfully till death: and as the master's will is the law of the servant, so the persons in question have no greater pleasure than in doing the good, and perfect, and acceptable will of the Most High. His statutes are their songs" (*Sketches of Sermons* 2:186–87, italics in the original). Cf. Rom 12:2; Jas 4:7; 1 Pet 5:6.

17. "To bear; to endure; to support" (Johnson's *Dictionary*, s.v. "brook").

18. An alternative reading is "Now, we agree to submit to God's will. In all our affairs, sufferings, actions, we are his."

19. "2. Supported by his grace. The Servant looks to his master for support and protections, and Christians to their Lord. In the covenant agreement they have avouched the Lord to be their God" (*Sketches of Sermons* 2:187, italics in the original). An alternative reading of this line is "We agree that our support shall come from him. We, being his servants, we expect he will maintain us."

20. This is the second time Charles referred to Gypsies (cf. "Imitation of God" [Notebook 1, Sermon 69]). In his personal library Charles owned a copy of George Smith, *Gipsy Life: Being an Account of Our Gipsies and Their Children, with Suggestions for Their Improvement* (London: Haughton & Co., 1880, The Spurgeon Library). For additional references to Gypsies, see *MTP* 23:287; 27:322; 36:616; and 39:291.

21. Cf. Matt 6:31–32.

22. Cf. Pss 28:7; 46:1; 119:28; Isa 40:29; Hab 3:19; Mark 12:30; Eph 6:10.

23. Isaiah 46:4a, "And even to your old age I am he; and even to hoar hairs will I carry you."

24. "3. *Interested in his cause.* The faithful servant is concerned to promote his master's interest: this is the object of his unremitting study and labour; and the servant of God has no greater pleasure than in spreading the common Saviour's fame. It is not a matter of indifference to him whether the Church is clothed with mourning, or garments of praise; whether the number of Zion's travellers is increasing or diminishing; no, he feels the work of God of paramount importance; hence his time, talents, influence, and pecuniary aid, are most cheerfully devoted to God. The love of Christ constraineth him while he labours to accelerate the spread of the gospel" (*Sketches of Sermons* 2:187, italics in the original).

25. "III. Their fruit is unto holiness. Before, they were servants of sin, and free from righteousness, ver. 20; but now, being free from sin, and servants of God, their fruit is unto holiness" (*Sketches of Sermons* 2:187).

26. The stem of an illegible letter is written on the "v" in "conversion."

27. "A Jewish designation of a non-Jew, a Gentile" [Heb. gōy people, nation pl. gōyím]" (*The Oxford English Dictionary*, s.v. "goy").

28. "1. *The fruit of their hearts.* Having experienced the power of regenerating grace, the stream of nature's tide is turned; the understanding being enlightened, and the conscience purged from dead works, the affections are heavenly, the imaginations chaste, the desires pure, and the motives sincere and upright" (*Sketches of Sermons* 2:187, italics in the original).

29. "*2. The fruit of their lips.* The grace of God keeps the tongue from evil speaking, lying, and slander: in their lips is no guile" (*Sketches of Sermons* 2:188, italics in the original).

30. "Their conversation is modest and chaste, not frivolous, light, trifling, and obscene, calculated to pollute and disgust, rather than edify. The principles of religion in the heart govern the lips. Their conversation being as becometh the gospel of Christ, is calculated to administer grace to the hearers" (*Sketches of Sermons* 2:188).

31. Colossians 4:6, "Let your speech be always with grace, seasoned with salt, that ye may know how ye ought to answer every man."

32. "*3. The fruit of their lives.* Holiness to the Lord is the Christian's motto. If the tree be good, the fruit will be good, Matt. vii. 17. An ungodly life is the evidence of an unrenewed heart, though a moral life is not always the result of a renewed heart: a man may be moral without religion, but no man can be religious and immoral. The servants of God are true and just in their dealings, peaceable in their demeanour, merciful according to their power, and useful as talents and opportunity will admit; the law of God is their rule, and not the maxims of the world. What God hates, they disapprove; what he forbids, they avoid; and what he commands, they do" (*Sketches of Sermons* 2:188, italics in the original).

33. An alternative reading of this line is "They avoid all sin and so far as in them lies, [they] are holy."

34. The final "h" in the word "which" and the "o" in the word "others" are smeared toward the right of the page.

35. It is likely Charles originally wrote the word "We" and then added a tail to the letter "y" to form the word "Ye."

36. "Their end is everlasting life. This is consummation of blessedness, of which at present we know but in part" (*Sketches of Sermons* 2:188).

37. Charles originally wrote Roman numeral I before changing it to the number 1 to be consistent with his second and third points in the lines below.

38. The theme of pilgrimage is evidently on Charles's mind here. Cf. "The Fight and the Weapons" (Notebook 1, Sermon 37a).

39. "1. *A state of uninterrupted and eternal union with Christ.* The language of a Christian on earth is, 'I live, yet not I, but Christ liveth in me,' Gal. ii. 20; and as the branch derives its nourishment from the vine, so the believer lives in Christ, Col. iii. 3,4; and death, which separates soul and body, will render this union complete: they shall be for ever with him" (*Sketches of Sermons* 2:188, italics in the original).

40. Charles is not arguing against the concept of bodily resurrection here (cf. "If There Be No Resurrection—" [*MTP* 38, Sermon 2287]). A better interpretation of this line is "[There will be] no death because [there will be] no body [that dies]."

41. An illegible letter is written over the terminal of "a."

42. "3. *A state of the highest enjoyment* . . . which is already begun in the peace, joy, satisfaction, and comfort he feels; but it is in proportion to the enjoyment of heaven, only as a drop compared with the ocean, the light of a taper with the sun, or a grain of sand with the terraqueous globe. The powers of the mind will no doubt be vastly expanded, and though it doth not yet appear what we shall be, we know that when he shall appear, we shall be like him" (*Sketches of Sermons* 2:189, italics in the original).

43. Cf. Rom 5:1.

44. Cf. Eph 2:5.

45. Cf. Rom 12:2; 1 Thess 4:3.

Gal 3. 23 — The Effect and design of the Law.

It is highly important that we should rightly understand the use and design of the law, since by misunderstanding it, men have been led into dangerous errors.

I. The law is here called a garrison, by whom we are kept under guard and vigilantly eyed — it is a guard

1. It made rigorous rules for all actions of worship under the Mosaic economy, it thereby prevented all presumption, unholy daring, or irreverent approach — the minutest particulars were ruled.

2. It keeps unregenerate man from those lengths of sin into which he would run unless restrained by its threatenings and so preserves society from immediate destruction — while by its restraints the elect are prevented from committing those sins which would put them beyond the reach of mercy such as suicide, unpardonable sin — murder since death follows it.

3. It prevents boasting, the prisoners hair is shorn, none of us dare boast, we are "kept under".

II. The law is not only a guard, but at last a prison. the slave toils at its mill by day, and is put in the pit at night — "shut up" —

1. In itself, without Jesus, it shuts the whole world up in the condemned cell — hopeless, barred in for death.

2. By the Holy Spirit, it is used as a prison for the elect to bring them to a sense of sin, it is a pound for the wandering sheep. Here the whip, the chain, the cheerless damp cold floor, the high wall, the bread and water, bring the rebel on his knees. the sentence of death shakes his hardened soul, and he humbly cries for mercy.

3. He uses it too as a prison for the regenerate when they grow self righteous, or when licentious, or when they undervalue their spiritual mercies — This is the place for an appetite, this gives a sweet to liberty —

THE EFFECT *and* DESIGN *of the* LAW[1]
Galatians 3:23[2]

"But before faith came, we were kept under the law, shut up unto the faith which should afterwards be revealed."

It is highly important that we should rightly understand the use and design of the law, since by misunderstanding it, men have been led into dangerous errors.

I. THE LAW IS HERE CALLED A ~~PRISON, WHEREIN~~ GARRISSON BY WHOM[3] WE ARE KEPT UNDER GUARD AND VIGILANTLY EYED.

<u>It is a guard.</u>

1. It made rigorous rules for all actions of worship under the Mosaic economy. It thereby prevented all presumption, unholy daring, or irreverent approach. The minutest particulars were ruled.
2. It keeps unregenerate man from those lengths of sin into which he would run unless restrained by its threatenings,[4] and so preserves society from immediate destruction while by its restraints the elect are prevented from committing those sins which would put them beyond the reach of mercy, such as suicide.[5] Unpardonable sin, murder, since death follows it.[6]
3. It prevents boasting. The prisoner[']s hair is shorn.[7] None of us dare boast.[8] We are "kept under."[9]

II. THE LAW IS NOT ONLY A GUARD, BUT AT LAST A PRISON.

The slave toils at its mill by day and is put in the pit at night[10]—"shut up."

1. In itself, without Jesus, it[11] shuts the whole world up in the condemned cell.[12] Hopeless, barred in for death.[13]
2. By the Holy Spirit it is used as a prison for the elect to bring them to a sense of sin. It is a pound for the wandering sheep. Here the whip,[14] the chain, the cheerless damp cold floor, the high wall, the bread and water bring the rebel on his knees. The sentence of death shakes his hardened soul and he humbly cries for mercy.
3. He uses it, too, as a prison for the regenerate when they grow self righteous, or when licentious, or when they undervalue their spiritual mercies. This is the place for an appetite. This gives a sweet to liberty.

III. As a guard or as a prison, its dominion lasts only till faith comes, its design is to lead us to faith.

1. The law was given by God to shew us the impossibility of salvation by working, even by the most holy workings & so to prepare us to value salvation by grace through believing.

2. When a poor sinner feels himself in prison, he is not put there for ever, but only till the appointed time when faith is to be revealed. Its object is not to distress but by distress to save.

3. When a child of God gets in this prison, there is some end to be answered by it, old nature is thus destroyed.

IV. From the nature, effect, and design of the law we argue

1. That though seemingly diverse & contrary, yet as made by one God, the law & gospel do harmonize and work together for the salvation of the elect — the law preparing men for the gospel and the gospel fulfilling the law.

2. Those are wrong who speak against the law, since it is God's law and serves such important purposes.

3. They err who seek to be justified by the law since it was only intended to shut up & not to give liberty.

4. Those persons are far from right, who, when their conscience is touched, and their sin revealed do therefore suppose that they are past mercy, whereas these are indications of grace & preparations for mercy.

1. Let them tremble who never were in this prison.
2. Let those who are prisoners take heart.
3. Rejoice, believer in thy glorious liberty. —

138.

THE EFFECT AND DESIGN OF THE LAW—*Galatians 3:23*

III. AS A GUARD OR AS A PRISON ITS DOMINION LASTS ONLY TILL FAITH COMES. ITS DESIGN IS TO LEAD US TO FAITH.

1. The law was given by God to shew us the impossibility of salvation by working,[15] even by the most holy workings, and so to prepare us to[16] value salvation by grace through believing.
2. When a poor sinner[17] feels himself in prison, he is not put there for ever, but only till the appointed time when faith is to be revealed.[18] Its object is not to distress, but by distress to save.
3. When a child of God gets in this prison, there is some end to be answered by it. Old nature is thus destroyed.

IV. FROM THE NATURE, EFFECT, AND DESIGN OF THE LAW WE ARGUE:

1. That though seemingly diverse and contrary yet as made by one God, the law and Gospel do harmonize and work together for the salvation of the elect. The law [is] preparing men for the gospel, and the gospel [is] fulfilling the law.[19]
2. Those are wrong who speak against the law since it is God's law and serves such important purposes.
3. They err who seek to be justified by the law[20] since it was only intended to shut up and not to give liberty.
4. Those persons are far from right, who, when their conscience is touched and their sin revealed, do therefore suppose that they are past mercy. Whereas these are indications of grace and preparations for mercy.

1. Let them tremble who never were in this prison.
2. Let those who are prisoners take heart.
3. Rejoice, believer, in thy glorious liberty.

138.

1. For additional sermons on the law, see "The Uses of the Law" (*NPSP* 3, Sermon 128); "The Perpetuity of the Law of God" (*MTP* 28, Sermon 1660); "The Law Written on the Heart" (*MTP* 28, Sermon 1685); "The Law's Failure and Fulfilment" (*MTP* 37, Sermon 2228); and "God's Law in Man's Heart" (*MTP* 43, Sermon 2506).

2. On March 3, 1887, Charles preached an additional sermon on Gal 3:23 entitled "Under Arrest" (*MTP* 41, Sermon 2402). Noticeable similarity are found in the second primary division of the later sermon and the first in the above outline. There is enough overlapping content and structural similarity to suggest Charles had in mind this early outline when writing his later sermon.

3. It is unclear why Charles struck through the words "prison, wherein." He possibly preferred the words "garrisson" and "by whom," which he wrote in superscript. There is no evidence Charles corrected the misspelling of the word "garrisson." The correct spelling is "garrison." The differences between a prison and a garrison are minor enough to conclude Charles's revision had more to do with phraseology than theology. However, Charles might have struck through the word "prison" because he sought to expound upon the idea in a different location, namely in the second Roman numeral: "The law is not only a guard, but at last a prison."

4. "Alas, I did sin; but my sense of the law of God kept me back from a great many sins. I could not, as others did, plunge into profligacy, or indulge in any of the grosser vices, for that law had me well in hand" (*MTP* 41:102).

5. Charles preached passionately against suicide—an act he considered tantamount to murder. The following quotes are taken from his later ministry. "He that commits suicide to get out of trouble leaps into a gulf to escape from the water; drowns himself to prevent himself from getting wet; leaps into the fire because he is scorched. Do it not; do it not. He that kills himself goes with his hands red with blood before his Maker, and goes thence to his own damnation" (*MTP* 7:528). "Thoughts of suicide! Why, my brethren, they are awful, they are not to be allowed; there is murder in them; he that even thinks of them hath committed murder already in his heart" (*MTP* 15:608). Suicide is the "crime of all crimes . . . the crime of self-murder" (*MTP* 22:701). "In your worst moment, should Satan whisper in your ear a suggestion concerning

rope, or knife, or poison bowl, or sullen stream, flee from it with all your soul. Obey the apostolic word, 'Do thyself no harm.' . . . Self-destruction, if done by a man in his senses, is a daring defiance of God, and the sealing of damnation" (*MTP* 24:347). Charles's strongest words on suicide may be found in his 1874 sermon "Fear of Death": "If a man in his sober senses were to commit suicide we would entertain no hope of eternal life for him" (*MTP* 55:1). These quotations must be balanced with Charles's own thoughts of suicide during his struggle with sin prior to his conversion in January 1850. In his autobiography he reflected, "I felt the weight of sin, and I did not know the Saviour; I feared God would blast me with His wrath, and smite me with His hot displeasure! From chapel to chapel I went to hear the Word preached, but never a gospel sentence did I hear: but this one text preserved me from what I believe I should have been driven to,—the commission of suicide through grief and sorrow. It was this sweet word, 'Whosoever shall call upon the name of the Lord shall be saved'" (*Autobiography* 1:95). There is no evidence to suggest Charles was speaking with hyperbole. From an early age he had immersed himself in John Bunyan's allegory *The Pilgrim's Progress* in which Christian experienced suicidal thoughts while remaining in the prison of Doubting Castle. Christian asks his friend Hopeful, "What shall we do? The life we now live is miserable. For my part, I know not whether is best, to live thus, or to die out of hand. . . . [T]he Grave is more easy for me than this Dungeon." Hopeful replied, "*Indeed our present condition is dreadful, and death would be far more welcome to me than thus for ever to abide: But yet let us consider, the Lord of the Country to which we are going, hath said, Thou shalt do no mur[d]er, not to another man's person; much more then are we forbidden to take his counsel to kill our selves. Besides, he that kills another, can but commit murder upon his body; but for one to kill himself, is to kill body and soul at once. And moreover, my Brother, thou talkest of ease in the Grave; but hast thou forgotten the Hell, whither for certain the murderers go? for no murderer hath eternal life*" (Bunyan, *Pilgrim's Progress*, 138, italics in the original).

6. An alternative reading of this line is "such as suicide[,] [an] unpardonable sin. [It is] murder since death follows it."

7. Charles may have had Samson in mind here (see Judg 16:15–21). More likely he was referencing the common practice of inmates being forced to shave their heads. For instance, in 1848 Prussian soldiers assaulted a freed prisoner, John

Rakowaki, who showed his assailants his shaven head as proof he had been incarcerated (see "Dastardly and Atrocious Conduct of Prussian Soldiers," *The Hull Advertiser*, June 30, 1848).

8. Cf. 1 Cor 4:7; 2 Cor 11:30; Eph 2:8–9.

9. "The word for 'kept' means that we were arrested, and given in charge, or that we were taken under the care of a garrison. The ten commandments of God, like ten armed legionaries, took us into custody, and held us fast" (*MTP* 41:101).

10. Charles likely consulted John Gill's commentary on Gal 3:23: "Also the allusion may be to the custom of the *Eastern* nations, in the usage of their slaves and captives; who in the day-time used to grind at a mill in a prison-house, and in the night-time were put down into a pit and shut up, and a mill-stone put to the mouth of the pit" (Gill, *Exposition of the New Testament*, 3:23, italics in the original).

11. Charles likely wrote the word "in" beneath "it."

12. "The whole world was one vast prison to [David], for he could not get out of the reach of the imperial power" (*MTP* 41:101).

13. Cf. Rom 5:18.

14. In his exposition on Gal 3:23–24, Charles said, "This is an unfortunate translation; it should be, 'The law was our pedagogue.' That was a slave, who was employed by the father of a family, to take his boy to school, and bring him home again. He often also was permitted to whip the boy if he did not learn his lessons well" (*MTP* 41:108).

15. Cf. Rom 3:20.

16. The close proximity of the words "us" and "value" suggest Charles likely wrote the word "to" between them afterward.

17. Charles likely added the letters "ner" to the word "sinner" afterward.

18. The letter "g" was written beneath the "d" in the word "revealed." Charles likely wrote the word "revealing" before his revision.

19. An alternative reading of this line is "That though seemingly diverse and contrary yet as made by one God, the law and Gospel do harmonize and work together for the salvation of the elect: the law, preparing men for the gospel and the gospel, fulfilling the law."

20. Cf. Gal 2:16.

SERMON 104

Matt. 8. 11. 12.   The children cast out.

These words were words of Jesus. the tender one who therefore speaks these most solemn words only for our good. So kind a being could not cause us unnecessary sorrow, he worked a miracle of mercy the moment after, to shew that his hardest blows are the wounds of a friend. Here is

I. A glorious promise "many shall come &c."

1. Glorious in relation to the number of the saved "many" — few in any one place, but a countless throng in the mass. Few now but a crowd, a flock, in the latter day. Many they shall be despite man, the world, the devil.

2. Glorious as to the certainty of the salvation of these "shall come" Not they may if they will which would be gracious, but I will make them willing "they shall". wondrous gracious. God's oath & promise makes it sure. Election, the covenant of redemption and Jesus death demand it — While God's omnipotence, the vast provision of grace, & the Spirit's power supply all requisites to effect the work.

3. Glorious as to the extent of gospel grace "the east & the west" Not the Jews but Gentiles too, not of one tribe or nation but universal man. Sin locked realms shall open wide Some in a figurative sense are at the very ends of the earth least likely to come, most in sin, most hardened in crime.

4. Glorious as to the state of the glorified "sit down." or recline — a posture of ease, rest from toil, dignity too they sit down to feast, not as they ate the passover. Holy familiarity and fulness of communication & in a kingdom

5. As to the society of heaven "with Abraham, Isaac & Jacob. Saved by the same grace they shall enjoy the same glory. The Jews would not allow Gentiles to eat with them,

104

The CHILDREN CAST OUT
Matthew 8:11–12[1]

"And I say unto you, That many shall come from the east and west, and shall sit down with Abraham, and Isaac, and Jacob, in the kingdom of heaven. But the children of the kingdom shall be cast out into outer darkness: there shall be weeping and gnashing of teeth."

These words were words of Jesus, the tender one, who therefore speaks these most solemn words only for our good. So kind a being could not cause us unnecessary sorrow. He works a miracle of mercy the moment after to shew that his hardest blows are the wounds of a friend. Here is:

I. A GLORIOUS PROMISE, *"many shall come,* etc."

1. Glorious in relation to the number of the saved, "many." Few in any one place, but a countless throng in the mass. Few now, but a crowd, a flock, in the latter day. Many they shall be despite man, the world, the devil.[2]
2. Glorious as to the certainty of the salvation of these, "shall come." Not, they may if they will, which would be gracious. But, I will make them willing, "they shall." Wondrous, gracious. God's oath and promise makes it sure. Election,[3] the covenant of redemption,[4] and Jesus['s] death demand it. While God's omnipotence,[5] the vast provision of grace, and the Spirit's power supply all requisites to effect the work.
3. Glorious as to the extent of gospel grace, "the east and the west." Not the Jews, but gentiles, too.[6] Not of one tribe or nation, but universal man.[7] Sin[-]locked realms shall open wide. Some, in a figurative sense, are at the very ends of the earth,[8] least likely to come, most in sin, most hardened in crime.[9]
4.[10] Glorious as to the state of the glorified. "Sit down," or recline. A posture of ease, rest from toil, dignity, too. They sit down to feast. Not as they ate the passover. Holy familiarity and fulness of communication, and in a kingdom.
5. As to the society of heaven, "with Abraham, Isaac and Jacob." Saved by the same grace, they shall enjoy the same glory. The Jews would not allow Gentiles to eat with them.[11]

but there we shall eat with the chiefs of their nation. The honour we enjoy will be great if we sit with them, how sweet the conversation of such men, we shall eat their dainties
II. A solemn warning. "but the children of the kingdom &c"
1. Solemn as it regards the persons, for such composed the congregation then surrounding Jesus — the Jews were. Such are found in all congregations and are
(1). Children of pious parents. (2). Regular attendants (3). All in this land of gospel (4). Professors. (5). The Learned in Doctrine.
If such are lost where must the far off appear? The character described is a most common one.
2. Solemn as it respects their reception in heaven. They are rolled into another world, they seem sure of glory they knock, they stand on the threshold — but not for a moment — they are not gently dismissed or even chided away but "cast out" with violence & abhorrence and that because they had not come in the way of faith — with the robe of righteousness.
3. Solemn as to the place to which they are driven "outer darkness" — in allusion to the darkness of the street even when the festal board flames with light, such darkness — that not one ray of mercy, one beam of hope, one glance of joy or flash of comfort shall ever enliven it. Egyptian darkness. Hellish darkness — only illumined by the lurid flames of hell revealing dancing devils, howling fiends, damned souls, and immense preparation for future exquisite torture.

But there, we shall eat with the chiefs of their nation. The honour we enjoy will be great if we sit with them. How sweet the conversation of such men. We shall eat their dainties.

II. A SOLEMN WARNING, *"but the children of the kingdom, etc."*[12]

1. Solemn as it regards the persons, for such composed the congregation then surrounding Jesus—the Jews were.

   Such[13] are found in all congregations, and are:

   (1).[14] Children of pious parents.[15]

   (2). Regular attendants.

   (3). All in this land of gospel.

   (4). Professors.

   (5). The Learned in Doctrine.

   If such are lost, where must the far off appear? The character described is a most common one.

2. Solemn as it respects their reception in heaven. They are rolled into another world. They seem sure of glory, they knock, they stand on the threshold, but not for a moment. They are not gently dismissed or even chided away, but "cast out" with violence and abhorrence, and that because they had not come in the way of faith with the robe of righteousness.[16]

3. Solemn as to the place to which they are driven, "outer darkness." In[17] allusion to the darkness of the street, even when the festal board flames with light,[18] such darkness that not one ray of mercy, one beam of hope, one glance of joy or flash of comfort shall ever enliven it. Egyptian darkness.[19] Hellish darkness,[20] only illumined by the lurid flames of hell[21] revealing dancing devils, howling fiends, damned souls, and immense preparation for future exquisite torture.

4. Solemn as to the occupation of the damned "weeping &c
"Weeping" — tears would not flow in penitence before but remorse will do it ⸺ hell fire will make men weep floods of tears but those tears shall be oil to the fire — briny tears shall increase their thirst weep! they shall at the recollection of grace and glory lost, at the remembrance of sinful joy, and mirthful jollity. weep! at the thought of past torture, and the expectation of future woe. with the horrid thought of hell's eternity. "gnashing of teeth" — chattering in the midnight air when excluded from the glowing genial air of the marriage banquet, all the parts of body and soul shall be in convulsion. Devils & men shall gnash in impotent wrath at the avenging God — Devils shall gnash with malice on men. Men shall gnash on devils cursing the tempter once loved. Women shall gnash at men, Men at women. Fathers on sons while sons shall grind their teeth on their own parents as the author of so cursed a being and as the neglecters of their training or even their tutors in vice. the saints shall weep no more these weep for ever. the saints sing for joy these gnash their teeth in anguish.

III. A cutting aggravation — arising from,
1. A sight of the saints in glory sitting at royal tables in regal company, in ease and plenty. they will no doubt see for so Dives saw Lazarus. while they hunger the saints feast, while they are parched these are satisfied. the one racked in unutterable pain, the other sitting in happiness.
2. To see so many. If few were saved then they might get some consolation from the fact — but when multitudes escape for me to be damned; and that by my own sin.

THE CHILDREN CAST OUT—*Matthew 8:11–12*

4. Solemn as to the occupation of the damned, "weeping, etc."

"Weeping." Tears would not flow in penitence before, but remorse will do it. Hell fire will make men weep floods of tears, but those[22] tears shall be oil to the fire. Briny tears shall increase their thirst. Weep! they shall at the recollection of grace and glory lost, at the remembrance of sinful joy and mirthful jollity. Weep! at the thought of past torture, and the expectation of future woe with[23] the horrid thought of hell's eternity. "Gnashing of teeth." Chattering in the midnight air when excluded from the glowing genial air of the marriage banquet, all the parts of body and soul shall be in convulsion.[24] Devils and men shall gnash in impotent wrath at the avenging God.

Devils shall gnash with malice on men. Men shall gnash on devils, cursing the tempter once loved. Women shall gnash at men. Men at women. Fathers on sons, while sons shall grind their teeth on their own parents as the author of so cursed a being and as the neglecters of their training, or even their tutors in vice.

The saints shall weep no more.[25] These weep for ever. The saints sing for joy. These gnash their teeth in anguish.

III. A CUTTING AGGRAVATION ARISING FROM:

1. A sight of the saints in glory sitting at royal tables in regal company, in ease and plenty. They will no doubt see, for so Dives[26] saw Lazarus.[27] While they hunger, the saints feast. While they are parched, these are satisfied. The one racked in unutterable pain, the other sitting in happiness.

2. To see so <u>many</u>. If few were saved, then they might get some consolation from the fact, but when multitudes escape for me to be damned, and that[28] by my own sin.

3. To see such a kind of men "from the east & the west." Oh! how the Jews now in hell do rave at the sight of saved Gentiles. How the self-righteous do vex themselves at the sight of Publicans and harlots in the Kingdom. The vile hireling preacher shall see the poor despised minister. the clever scholar, the disputer, the rich, the mighty shall have double damnation when they see the ignorant the childish, the poor, the fool in glory —

4. To have been "a child of the Kingdom" to have known the way of life, to have gone some way in it by profession will inflict many stripes on a sinner.

5. To find one's self in hell when we thought to find ourselves in heaven, to be cast out when we thought ourselves "children" — to be disappointed —

6. To sit down and think on their lost state will add intensity to woe. thought is good here, but there it shall be a stinging adder — consider what it is to be damned — how long — by whom — for what.

1. Having as God's ambassador made this known I hope to be able to warn them once more in God's name telling them the way of salvation & urging them by God's Spirit to run in that way.

Touching the "children of the Kingdom" especially.

The Lord save me and all who hear me from this most awful woe, through the blood of Jesus. Amen

140. 141. 192. 274. 345. 405. 431. 478. 580

THE CHILDREN CAST OUT—*Matthew 8:11–12*

3. To see such a kind of men "from the east and the west."

   Oh! how the Jews now in hell do rave at the sight of saved Gentiles. How the self-righteous do vex themselves at the sight of Publicans[29] and harlots in the Kingdom. The vile, hireling[30] preacher shall see the poor, despised minister. The clever scholar, the disputer, the rich, the mighty shall have double damnation when they see the ignorant, the childish, the poor, the fool in glory.[31]

4. To have been "a child of the kingdom." To have known the way of life, to have gone some way in it by profession, will inflict many stripes on a sinner.

5. To find one's self in hell when we thought to find ourselves in heaven, to be cast out when we thought ourselves "children," to be disappointed.

6. To sit down and think on their lost state will add intensity to woe. Thought is good here, but there it shall be a stinging adder.[32] Consider what it is to be damned. How long? By whom? For what?

I.[33] Having as God's ambassador[34] made this known, I hope to be able to warn them once more in God's name, telling them the way of salvation and urging them by God's Spirit to run in that way.

Touching the "children of the kingdom" especially.

The Lord save me and all who hear me from this most awful woe, through the blood of Jesus.[35]

Amen

140. 141. 192. 274.[36] 345. 405.[37] 431. 478. 580

SERMON 104

1. On the evening of September 4, 1855, "in a field" in Hackney, Charles preached an additional sermon on Matt 8:11–12 entitled "Heaven and Hell" (*NPSP* 1, Sermon 39/40). The following words were appended to the conclusion of his sermon: "P.S. This sermon was watered by many prayers of the faithful in Zion. The preacher did not intend it for publication, but seeing that it is now in print, he will not apologize for its faulty composition or rambling style" (*NPSP* 1:310). A comparison of Charles's early sermon outline and his 1855 sermon reveals overlapping content in the first two primary divisions. The concluding statements in his 1855 sermon were more extemporaneous than those in his early outline; however, there is enough structural similarity to suggest Charles had the outline in mind during the later sermon's composition.

2. Cf. "The Fight and the Weapons" (Notebook 1, Sermon 37a); "The Downfall of Dagon" (Sermon 124).

3. Cf. "Election" (Notebook 1, Sermon 10); Rom 8:28–30; 11:5; Eph 1:4; 2 Thess 2:13.

4. See the inscription on the title page of this notebook, "The Covenant of Redemption." Cf. Rom 3:24.

5. See "Prove Me Now Herewith" (Sermon 109).

6. Cf. Rom 1:16; 3:29; 10:12; 1 Cor 1:24.

7. Cf. Rev 7:9.

8. "But Jesus Christ said there will be many that will come from the east and from the west. There will be a multitude from that far off land of China, for God is doing a great work there, and we hope that the gospel will yet be victorious in that land. There will be a multitude from this western land of England; from the western country beyond the sea, in America; and from the south in Australia; and from the north, in Canada, Siberia, and Russia" (*NPSP* 1:303).

9. Crime was rampant throughout Cambridgeshire in the years leading up to Charles's first pastorate (see "The Approaching Execution," *Cambridge Independent Press and Huntingdon, Bedford, & Peterborough Gazette*, April 6, 1850). Charles's ministry had a transformative effect on the crime in Waterbeach (see *Autobiography* 1:227–28).

THE CHILDREN CAST OUT—*Matthew 8:11–12*

10. Charles originally misnumbered the list by writing the number 3.

11. Cf. Acts 10:14–15, 28.

12. "II. The second part of my text is heart-breaking. I could preach with great delight to myself from the first part; but here is a dreary task to my soul, because there are gloomy words here. But, as I have told you, what is written in the Bible must be preached whether it be gloomy or cheerful" (*NPSP* 1:306).

13. Charles originally did not capitalize the word "Such."

14. This is the first time in Notebook 2 that Charles used parentheses for numbering his subpoints.

15. "I can conceive of no one entering hell with a worse grace than the man who goes there with drops of his mother's tears on his head, and with his father's prayers following him at his heels. Some of you will inevitably endure this doom, some of you young men and women shall wake up one day and find yourselves in outer darkness, while your parents shall be up there in heaven, looking down upon you with upbraiding eyes, seeming to say, 'What! after all we did for you, all we said, are ye come to this!'" (*NPSP* 1:306).

16. Cf. Job 29:14; Ps 132:9; Isa 61:10; Zech 3:4; Rev 19:8.

17. Charles originally wrote the word "In." However, the context suggests he intended to write the word "An."

18. The "festal board" referred to the celebration of a festival often associated with light. A popular British melody is found in Thomas Harttree Cornish's *British Melodies*: "Come to my festal board with glee, / Come to my festal board; / My hall's lit up and we'll merry be" (T. H. Cornish, *British Melodies* [London: published for the author, 1831], Melody—LXVIII, 76). See also "The Education of the Masses," *The Hull Advertiser*, January 13, 1855; "Miscellanea," *The Drogheda Argus, and Leinster Journal*, May 19, 1849; and "Poet's Corner, 'King Art's Harper,'" *The Nation* (Dublin), October 26, 1950. Throughout Charles's three-year pastorate, the streets of Waterbeach were illuminated by gas lamps. Across the street from his chapel was, in fact, the village "Gas works" (Denis Cheason and Joan Danby, comp., *The Waterbeach Chronicle: Events in the Life of a Fen-Edged Village Between 1779 and*

1899, as Reported in the Cambridge Chronicle [London: Plaistow Press Magazines Ltd, published for the Waterbeach Village Society, 1984, repr. 2014], map, n.p.). Controversies about gas lighting were common throughout England in the 1850s. Several months before Charles preached from this sermon outline, gas companies in London were accused of excessive profits (see "Gas.—Street Lights," *Reading Mercury, Oxford Gazette, Newbury Herald, and Berks County Paper*, January 18, 1851).

19. Cf. Exod 10:21–23.
20. Cf. 2 Pet 2:4; Jude 1:6.

21. Cf. Matt 13:50; Rev 14:11; 20:15; 21:8.

22. Charles may have originally written the word "now" before changing it to "those."

23. An illegible letter was written beneath "w" in the word "with."

24. Cf. Matt 10:28; Luke 12:5.
25. Cf. Isa 30:19; Rev 21:4.

26. The word "Dives" is not found in Johnson's or Worcester's dictionaries; however, the word was commonly used on both sides of the Atlantic Ocean to describe the rich men in Luke 16:19–31. For instance, nineteen years prior to Charles's preaching the outline above, a pastor in Portland, Maine, said: "*Why* pleads then the wretched Dives with father Abraham, saying, Send him therefore, send Lazarus, to my father's house, that he may testify to my brethren, lest they also come into this place of torment?" (Menzies Rayner, *Parable of the Rich Man and Lazarus; Illustrated in Nine Lectures, Delivered in the First Universalist Church in Portland, Maine, 1833* [Boston: Marsh, Capen & Lyon, 1833], 83, italics in the original).

27. Cf. Luke 16:19–31.

28. Charles originally wrote the word "they" before changing it to "that."

29. Tax collectors. Cf. "Election" (Notebook 1, Sermon 10); "The Physician and His Patients" (Notebook 1, Sermon 74); Matt 9:9–13; Luke 18:13; 19:1–10.

30. This is the second time Charles has used the word "hireling." Cf. "Offending God's Little Ones" (Notebook 1, Sermon 67).

31. Cf. 1 Cor 1:27.

THE CHILDREN CAST OUT—*Matthew 8:11–12*

32. "A serpent, a viper, a poisonous reptile; perhaps of any species" (Johnson's *Dictionary*, s.v. "adder").

33. Charles also concluded his sermon "Justification, Conversion, Sanctification, Glory" (Sermon 102) by writing the number 1.

34. Cf. 2 Cor 5:20; Eph 6:20; "Christ's Ambassadors" (*MTP* 55, Sermon 3148).

35. In the conclusion of his 1855 sermon Charles said, "May he show you that you are dead, that you are lost, ruined. May he make you feel what a dreadful thing it would be to sink into hell! May he point you to heaven!" (*NPSP* 1:310).

36. The significance of the ink stroke above the number 4 is unclear. Charles possibly intended to write a question mark.

37. The number 405 is smeared toward the upper left of the page.

Ps. 107. 8 — Oh that men would praise the Lord.

This verse was the chorus to a song, and truly one in which every creature may with safety join — they who sing this may do so without fear of hypocrisy. It is good for all to join in the worship at least spiritually — Surely this is the desire of angels & glorified saints

I. Why are we desirous that men should praise God
 1. Because we love him ourselves, and therefore we want all to do the same, we increase not his real glory we only expose it to view — this we love.
 2. Because when men do this truly — they are the sons of God & converted — prayer & praise are the signs of piety, that heart is right which sings to the Most High.
 3. Because this exercise is highly beneficial to those employed in it — It keeps off worldly carnal fleshly thought — it bids adieu to care, trouble, anxiety, it draws off the soul alike from flattering & condemning others; gives exercise to faith and love.
 4. Because New Jerusalem then comes down, or rather this earth goes up — we come near angels & the glittering ranks in white robes. — by praise

II. What men are to praise God for.
 1. His goodness, his own nature, his attributes for what he is — as the Holy One inhabiting eternity
 2. For his kindness to man as a <u>creature</u>
<u>Frail</u> he is and yet what costly ware what cunning workmanship are shown, what forethought to provide him with a body wondrously adapted

105

OH *that* MEN WOULD PRAISE *the* LORD[1]
Psalm 107:8[2]

"Oh that men would praise the LORD *for his goodness, and for his wonderful works to the children of men!"*

This verse was the chorus to a song, and truly one in which every creature may with safety join. They who sing this may do so without fear of hypocrisy. It is good for all to join in[3] the worship, at least spiritually. Surely, this is[4] the desire of angels and glorified saints.

I. WHY ARE WE DESIROUS THAT MEN SHOULD PRAISE GOD?

1. Because we love him ourselves, and therefore we want all to do the same. We increase not his real glory, we only expose it to view. This we love.

2. Because when men do this, truly they are the sons of God and[5] converted.[6] Prayer and praise are the signs of piety. That heart is right which sings to the Most High.[7]

3. Because this exercise is highly beneficial to those employed in it. It keeps off worldly, carnal, fleshly thought. It bids adieu to care, trouble, anxiety. It draws off the soul alike from flattering and condemning others, gives exercise to faith and love.

4. Because New Jerusalem thus comes down, or rather this earth goes up. We come near angels and the glittering ranks in white robes[8] by praise.

II. WHAT MEN ARE TO PRAISE GOD FOR.

1. His goodness,[9] his own nature, his attributes,[10] for what he is as the Holy One inhabiting eternity.

2. For his kindness to man as a <u>creature</u>.
<u>Frail</u> he is, and yet what costly ware,[11] what cunning workmanship[12] are shown. What forethought to provide him with a body wondrously adapted.[13]

Weak he is and yet he is Lord of the whole earth.
he is vicegerent — how strong reason makes him.
rides the wave. bridles the wind, confines the lightning
Insignificant — compared with many might beasts
of earth — compared with stars the Sun &c — with angels
yet not forgotten — all seems made for him.
3. For his goodness to men as <u>sinners</u>
<u>Reprieving</u> them when justice might claim imme
— diate execution — <u>Sparing</u> their lives even
when exposed to great perils. <u>Birth</u> in a X'n land.
<u>Restraining</u> them from some sins, Keeping them
from committing the most awful crimes
giving them <u>temporal</u> mercies in abundance
supplying all their wants unwearied by their sins.
4. For his goodness to men as his <u>elect</u>.
To <u>choose</u> them for no merit of their own, to
<u>redeem</u> them & that with his only son. to give
a <u>covenant</u> attested by oath. To send the
<u>Holy Spirit</u>. To fulfil all too. —
5. His kindness to men as <u>born again</u>.
Their <u>regeneration</u> consequently their <u>pardon</u> &
complete <u>justification</u>. their <u>sanctification</u> by the
<u>restraints</u> and <u>constraints</u> of the adorable Spirit
Their <u>adoption</u> — their joys, yea and <u>troubles</u>
all their <u>graces</u>, their <u>deliverances</u>, the promises
the <u>ordinances</u>, his answers of their prayer,
his <u>visits</u>, his strength, his forbearing love.

OH *that* MEN WOULD PRAISE THE LORD—*Psalm 107:8*

<u>Weak</u> he is,[14] and yet he is Lord of the whole earth. He is vicegerent.[15] How strong reason makes him. [He] rides the wave, bridles the wind, confines the lightning.[16] <u>Insignificant</u> compared with many might[y] beasts of earth.[17] Compared with stars,[18] the sun, etc., with angels. Yet not forgotten.[19] All seems made for him.

3. For his goodness to men as <u>sinners</u>.

   <u>Reprieving</u> them when justice might claim immediate execution. <u>Sparing</u> their lives, even when exposed to great perils. <u>Birth</u> in a Xn[20] land.[21] <u>Restraining</u> them from some sins. Keeping them from committing the most awful crimes.[22] Giving them <u>temporal</u> mercies in abundance. Supplying all their wants.[23] Unwearied by their sins.

4. For his goodness to men as his <u>elect</u>.[24]

   To <u>choose</u> them for no merit of their own.[25] To <u>redeem</u> them,[26] and that, with this only son.[27] To give a <u>covenant</u> attested by oath.[28] To send the <u>Holy Spirit</u>.[29] To fulfil all, too.[30]

5. His kindness to men as <u>born again</u>.[31]

   Their <u>regeneration</u>,[32] consequently, their <u>pardon</u> and complete <u>justification</u>.[33] Their <u>sanctification</u>[34] by the <u>restraints</u> and <u>constraints</u> of the adorable Spirit. Their <u>adoption</u>,[35] their <u>joys</u>, yea, and <u>troubles</u>. All their <u>graces</u>, their <u>deliverances</u>,[36] the promises,[37] the <u>ordinances</u>,[38] his <u>answers</u> of their prayer, his <u>visits</u>, his <u>strength</u>,[39] his forbearing love.[40]

SERMON 105

6. For his goodness to men as those who are to be <u>glorified</u> making final <u>perseverance</u> immutably secure. Giving grace to meet the grand enemy and conquer. Justifying at the day of judgment and throughout eternity imparting fresh measures of rapturous joy.

III. How can men praise God?

1. By a devout hymning of his praise; ascribing all glory to him by adoration in prayer, by grateful feeling and expression, as also by holy joy in him.

2. By thank offerings it was of old and so now, the Christian should give sometimes a special token by special devotion and sometimes by contributions.

3. By walking in faith — leaning all on him, he loves to be trusted, confide in his love

4. By holy living, "singing as you shine" by shining men can see what they will not believe when they hear. Follow Jesus closely — in all points

- -

Praise him because else you are worse than the brutes
Praise him because thus you are like angels.
Praise him for you do so praise your Father.
Praise him thus shall you learn heaven's tune.
Praise him then shall you be honoured.
Crown him! Crown him! King of Kings!

139. 153. 251.

OH *that* MEN WOULD PRAISE THE LORD—*Psalm 107:8*

6. For his goodness to men as those who are to be glorified.[41]

    Making final perseverance[42] immutably secure. Giving grace to meet the grand enemy and conquer. Justifying at the day of judgment and throughout eternity, imparting fresh measures of rapturous joy.[43]

III. HOW CAN MEN PRAISE GOD?

1. By a devout hymning[44] of his praise, ascribing all glory to him by adoration in prayer, by grateful feelings and expression, as also by holy joy in him.

2. By thank offerings.[45] It was of old and so now, the Christian should give sometimes a special token by special devotion, and sometimes by contributions.

3. By walking in faith,[46] leaning all on him. He loves to be trusted. Confide in his love.

4. By holy living, "singing as you shine."[47] By shining, men can see what they will not believe when they hear. Follow Jesus closely in all points.

Praise him, because else you are worse than the brutes.

Praise him, because thus you are like angels.[48]

Praise him, for you do so praise your Father.

Praise him, thus shall you learn heaven's tune.

Praise him, then shall you be honoured.

    Crown him! Crown him! King of Kings![49]

139. 153. 251.

SERMON 105

1. For additional sermons on praise, see "Public Praise" (Notebook 6, Sermon 318); "Praise Ye the Lord" (Notebook 7, Sermon 327); "The Power of Prayer and the Pleasure of Praise" (*MTP* 9, Sermon 507); "Jesus, the Example of Holy Praise" (*MTP* 14, Sermon 799); "Praises and Vows Accepted in Zion" (*MTP* 17, Sermon 1023); "The Philosophy and Propriety of Abundant Praise" (*MTP* 25, Sermon 1468); "The Happy Duty of Daily Praise" (*MTP* 32, Sermon 1902); "Open Praise and Public Confession" (*MTP* 45, Sermon 2604); "The Garment of Praise" (*MTP* 59, Sermon 3349); and "Praise Comely to the Upright" (*MTP* 61, Sermon 3460).

2. This is the only time Charles preached a sermon on Ps 107:8.

3. The word "in" was written above the line in superscript and indicated by a caret.

4. The source of the stain surrounding the word "is" is unknown.

5. The words "God &" were written above the line in superscript and indicated by a bolded caret.

6. An alternative reading of this sentence is "Because when men do this truly, they are the sons of God and converted."

7. Cf. "I hope to die singing" (Notebook 4, title page). See also "The Beloved of the Lord in Safety" (Sermon 100).

8. Revelation 6:11, "And white robes were given unto every one of them."

9. Cf. "God's Goodness Leading to Repentance" (*MTP* 49, Sermon 2857).

10. Cf. "Faith Precious" (Notebook 1, Sermon 23); "Ignorance, Its Evils" (Notebook 1, Sermon 31); "The King of Righteousness and Peace" (Notebook 1, Sermon 42).

11. "Commonly something to be sold" (Johnson's *Dictionary*, s.v. "ware").

12. Cf. Eph 2:10.

13. Cf. Ps 139:13.

14. Cf. Ps 8:5; Heb 2:7.

15. See "The Improvement of Our Talents" (Notebook 1, Sermon 61, footnote 5) and "The Unclean Spirit Returning" (Notebook 3, Sermon 168).

16. The phrase "confines the lightning" is likely a reference to electricity. The mid-nineteenth century saw the invention and patenting of numerous electrical machines. In 1852, Charles may have read the advertisement in a Cambridge newspaper about the newly patented "Hydro-Electric Chain," a self-administered device that claimed to be able to cure nervousness. "The Discovery, that mild, but continuous Electric Currents, as evolved from these Portable Chains, exercise the most *decisive influence* on the whole System, will, when generally known, range among the greatest blessings that we owe to Science, and will prove even more conducive to individual happiness than that other Marvel of the Day, the *Electric Telegraph* ("Patent Hydro-Electric Chain, for Personal Use," *Cambridge Chronicle and University Journal, Isle of Ely Herald, and Huntingdonshire Gazette*, July 10, 1852, italics in the original).

17. Cf. Job 40:15–24; 41.

18. Cf. Ps 8:3.

19. An alternative reading of this line is "Compared with stars, the sun, etc. [Man is compared] with angels, yet [he is] not forgotten."

20. Abbr. "Christian."

21. Charles was not alone in his view that England was a Christian nation. In 1850, a dispute arose in the House of Commons over the production of British sugar in comparison with sugar manufacturing in foreign countries where slave labor prevailed. A resolution was voiced by Sir E. Buxton who said, "If there was one principle which this country had maintained more than another, at home and abroad, it was this—that, having once abolished slavery in our own colonies, it endeavoured to do all that was incumbent *upon a great and Christian nation* to put it down in other countries" ("House of Commons—Friday. The Sugar Duties," *Nottingham Review, and General Advertiser for the Midland Counties*, June 7, 1850, emphasis added). From his earliest ministry in Waterbeach, Charles regarded England as a "land of gospel" ("The Children Cast Out" [Sermon 104]). He retained this opinion throughout his later London ministry, though he occasionally lamented

the combative advancement of the British Empire: "The progress of the arms of a Christian nation is not the progress of Christianity, and that the spread of our empire, so far from being advantageous to the Gospel, I will hold, and this day proclaim, hath been hostile to it" (*NPSP* 3:334). He added, "I should pray to God, if such a thing could be, that he would give me a black face and make me like a Hindoo; for otherwise I should feel that when I preached I should be regarded as one of the lords—one of the oppressors" (*NPSP* 3:335). Charles loved his country and had a great amount of national pride, but his love of country did not stop him from frankly acknowledging the flaws of the British Empire.

22. The doctrine of restraining grace was clearly on Charles's mind, as it was three sermons prior: "It keeps unregenerate man from those lengths of sin into which he would run unless restrained by its threatenings" ("The Effect and Design of the Law" [Sermon 103]). See also Charles's fifth point in this outline, "by the restraints and constraints of the adorable Spirit."

23. Philippians 4:19, "But my God shall supply all your need according to his riches in glory by Christ Jesus." Cf. Ps 23:1.

24. Cf. "Election" (Notebook 1, Sermon 10).

25. Cf. Deut 7:7; John 15:16.

28. Cf. Heb 6:13.

26. Cf. Rom 3:24; 1 Cor 1:30.

29. Cf. John 14:15–17.

27. Cf. Eph 1:7.

30. Cf. Acts 13:33.

31. Cf. John 3:3. The letter "n" in the word "again" and also the period are smeared toward the right side of the page.

32. Cf. "Regeneration" (Notebook 1, Sermon 7); "Regeneration, Its Causes and Effects" (Notebook 1, Sermon 46); Rom 5:1.

33. Cf. "Justification, Conversion, Sanctification, Glory" (Sermon 102).

34. Cf. "Salvation from Sin" (Notebook 1, Sermon 33).

35. Cf. "Adoption" (Notebook 1, Sermon 1); Eph 1:5.

36. Cf. "Salvation from Sin" (Notebook 1, Sermon 33).

37. Cf. "Certain Fulfilment of Promises" (Notebook 1, Sermon 36).

38. Cf. "God's Estimation of Men" (Notebook 1, Sermon 41).

39. Cf. 1 Chron 16:11; Pss 20:7–8; 27:1; Isa 41:10; 1 Cor 12:9–10; Phil 4:13.

40. Cf. Exod 34:6; Rom 2:4.

41. Cf. "Justification, Conversion, Sanctification, Glory" (Sermon 102).

42. Cf. "Final Perseverance" (Notebook 1, Sermon 8); "Final Perseverance Certain" (Sermon 82).

43. An alternative reading of these lines is "Justifying at the day of judgment. And throughout eternity, imparting fresh measures of rapturous joy."

44. Hymnody played a significant role in Charles's later ministry. In his personal library Charles owned numerous hymnals and books about hymns, including Isaac Watts, *Psalms, Hymns, and Spiritual Songs. A New Edition, with Copious Indexes Carefully Revised* (London: T. Nelson and Sons, 1860, The Spurgeon Library); John Rippon, *A Selection of Hymns from the Best Authors, Including a Great Number of Originals; Intended as an Appendix to Dr. Watts' Psalms and Hymns. A New Edition, with a Number of Additional Hymns, and Suitable Tune[s] Adapted to the Whole from "The Psalmist"* (London: Arthur Hall, Virtue, & Co., 1858, The Spurgeon Library); and C. H. Spurgeon, *Our Own Hymn-Book. A Collection of Psalms and Hymns for Public, Social, and Private Worship* (London: Passmore & Alabaster, 1885, The Spurgeon Library). Of particular importance to Charles's pastorate in London at New Park Street Chapel was the legacy John Rippon left when he served as its minister. Charles included nine of Rippon's hymns in his own hymnal: "Gethsemane" (Hymn 272); "Divine Drawings Implored" (Hymn 463); "Against Self-Destruction" (Hymn 528); "Contention Within" (Hymn 628); "Trust in God" (Hymn 629); "Jesus' Presence Desired" (Hymn 771); "Longing for the Spread of the Gospel" (Hymn 973); "Re-opening" (Hymn 1022); and "Show Me a Token for Good" (Hymn 1047).

45. Cf. Lev 7:15; 22:29; 2 Chron 29:31; Ps 107:21–22; Jer 33:11.

46. Cf. Eph 5:2; 2 John 1:6.

47. This is a reference to the final lines of the hymn "An Ode" by Joseph Addison (1672–1719): "What though, in solemn silence, all / Move round the dark terrestrial ball; / What though no real voice, nor sound / Amidst their radiant orbs be found: / In reason's ear they all rejoice, / And utter forth a glorious voice; / For ever singing as they shine: / 'The hand that made us is divine'" (*The Poetical Works of Joseph Addison; Gay's Fables; and Somerville's Chase. With Memoirs and Critical Dissertations by the Rev. George Gilfillan* [Edinburgh: James Nichol; London: James Nisbet & Co; Dublin: W. Robertson, 1859, The Spurgeon Library], 140).

48. Cf. Pss 103:20; 148:2.

49. Cf. 1 Tim 6:15; Rev 19:16.

106.   Prov. 14.26.   Religion the foundation of confidence.
Uncertainty in temporal things, if we consider them important, cannot be borne — and in spiritual matters it is not to be endured for one moment — or if it be suffered it is the cause of great distress and sorrow. Solomon here points to the source of certainty, & promises that it is not only a harbour now but that it shall be a refuge to "God's children."—

I. What is meant by fear? "the fear of the Lord"? By it is not intended a slavish fear of God as punishing, nor a sinful dread of him, nor base distrust of him, for these things are never the cause of "confidence" but quite the reverse. but by it is meant a fear of God entirely consistent with perfect love — a fear of giving cause of grief (speaking humanly) to our tender Father. This is often put for the whole of religion. because though faith be the root, love the sweetest flower, yet fear of God is the sap of all religion. It is the fear of God as opposed to the fear of man, the fear of punishment, the fear of losing character, and many other fears which may produce a partial reformation. The "Fear of God", as the sap of Piety, means True Religion.

II. What is the "Strong Confidence" here spoken of? It is not rashness which makes men run into danger, nor presumption which leads men to imagine God will not punish, nor carnal security, the strong delusion which men have when they falsely conclude themselves to be sons of God — for these being unholy emotions

106

RELIGION, *the* FOUNDATION *of* CONFIDENCE
Proverbs 14:26[1]

"In the fear of the Lord is strong confidence: and his children shall have a place of refuge."

Uncertainty in temporal things, if we consider them important, cannot be borne. And in spiritual matters it is not to be endured for one moment. Or if it be suffered, it is the cause of great distress and sorrow.

Solomon here points to the source of certainty and promises that it is not only a harbour now but that it shall be a refuge to God's children.

I. WHAT IS MEANT BY FEAR? "<u>The fear of the Lord</u>?"

By it is not intended a slavish fear of God as punishing,[2] nor a sinful dread of him, nor base distrust of him. For these things are never the cause of "confidence," but guide the reverse. But by it is meant a fear of God entirely consistent with perfect love. A fear of giving cause of grief (speaking humanly) to our tender Father. This is often put for the whole of religion because though faith be the root, love [is] the sweetest flower.[3] Yet fear of God is the sap of all religion. It is the fear of God as opposed to the fear of man,[4] the fear of punishment, the fear of losing character, and many other fears which may produce a partial reformation. The "Fear of God," as the sap of Piety, means <u>True Religion</u>.

II. WHAT IS THE "<u>STRONG[5] CONFIDENCE</u>" HERE SPOKEN OF?[6]

It is not rashness which makes men run into danger. Nor [is it] presumption which leads men to imagine God will not punish. Nor carnal security, the strong delusion which men have when they falsely conclude themselves to be sons of God. For these, being unholy emotions,

SERMON 106

cannot be caused by the holy grace "fear of the Lord". But the "strong confidence" produced by religion consists in.

1. The settling of the mind with regard to what truth is. The Infidel, the freethinker, the rationalist, in fact all seekers after truth by nature's candle get bewildered — They become fools their creed is doubting — their faith is unbelief — but religion is sure.

2. In a holy calmness under all trouble — in poverty, in sickness, in persecution, strong temptation. in fact in all there is "strong confidence"

3. In a sense of perfect security, if by faith we be saved. In the hour of death, in judgment we have strong confidence that we are saved — secure for ever — this is more than others dare say, we confide in Jesus — this is the fruit of religion.

III. How does religion give confidence?

It is called fear and some Christians seem to imagine assurance to be unattainable, and almost sinful — but this arises from a mistaken use of the word "fear", and a misunderstanding of the design of the gospel which is to produce "**confidence**". Religion does not produce confidence by fixing salvation to some easy duties, nor by advocating lawlessness — nor by preaching up the absolute and infinite mercy of God —

But yet the <u>fear of the Lord</u> is the parent of <u>strong confidence</u>

1. The doctrines true religion builds on are so consistent with divine justice, mercy and every other attribute of God's character — so consistent with the revelation made by God's works — and with the known nature & condition of man — that the mind which receives them may well be settled. Besides the precious promises which religion lives on are so exceedingly nourishing that she should be strong. Witness election by grace, perseverance by grace, justification by faith, continual providence and then say shall not a man loving such a religion be full of "strong confidence".

cannot be caused by the holy grace, "fear of the Lord." But the "strong confidence" produced by religions consists in:

1. The settling of the mind with regard to what truth is. The Infidel, the freethinker, the rationalist, in fact all seekers after truth by nature's candle get bewildered. They become fools. Their creed is doubting. Their faith is unbelief. But religion is sure.

2. In a holy calmness under all trouble. In poverty, in sickness, in persecution, strong temptation.[7] In fact, in all there is "strong confidence."

3. In a sense of perfect security, if[8] by faith we be saved. In the hour of death, in judgment, we have strong confidence that we are saved, secure for ever. This is more than others dare say. We confide in Jesus. This is the fruit of religion.

III. HOW DOES RELIGION GIVE CONFIDENCE?

It is called fear and some Christians seem to imagine assurance to be unattainable and almost sinful. But this arises from a mistaken use of the word "fear" and a misunderstanding of the design of the gospel which is to produce "confidence."

Religion does not produce confidence by fixing salvation to some easy duties, nor by advocating lawlessness,[9] nor by preaching up the absolute and infinite mercy of God.

But yet, the <u>fear of the Lord</u> is the parent of <u>strong confidence</u>.

1. The doctrines true religion builds on are so consistent with divine justice, mercy, and every other attribute of God's character.[10] [They are] so consistent with the revelation made by God's works and with the known nature and condition of man that the mind which receives them may well be settled. Besides, the precious promises which religion lives on are so exceedingly nourishing that she should be strong. Witness election by grace,[11] perseverance by grace,[12] justification by faith,[13] continual providence, and then say, shall not a man loving such a religion be full of "strong confidence"?

2. The Fear of the Lord or true religion becomes in a Christian so prominent an object, that what is to others great and terrible is to him a mere molehill — the man is abstracted absorbed — Like kills like. Fear kills fear.

3. The Fear of offending God will make a man fear to distrust God and so will tend to strengthen faith. The Graces are divine sisters, they are like a shock of wheat the sheaves lean on each other, while each produces a heavenly crop of "confidence"

4. The Holy Ghost, the presence of Jesus, the love of God must ever be a cause of strong confidence

Before leaving this we may notice from this

1 That the man who is yet uncertain has not realized the great object of the gospel "strong confidence"

2. That Doubting Christians are not to be preferred to those who have more faith, for these are nearer to the true gospel state. "Strong confidence"

3. Although difficult of attainment yet if we have true religion it behoves us to seek this "confidence" and to this end we notice.

IV. The Grand Promise here made.
He promises a refuge and ask the Jewish manslayer, ask Lot in Zoar, ask the warrior or the sailor what a refuge means & they will answer.

All creatures have some refuge provided.

All men imagine some but since we have left all — shall not God give us a better.

We are God's property, bought at an immense price will he not find us a refuge.

We have been beloved with eternal love, we are

RELIGION, THE FOUNDATION OF CONFIDENCE—*Proverbs 14:26*

2. The Fear of the Lord, or true religion, becomes in a Christian so prominent an object that what is to others great and terrible is to him a mere molehill. The man is abstracted, absorbed. Like kills like. Fear kills fear.[14]

3. The Fear of offending God will make a man fear to distrust God and so will tend to strengthen faith. The Graces are divine sisters. They are like a shock of wheat. The sheaves lean on each other while each produces a heavenly crop of "confidence."

4. The Holy Ghost, the presence of Jesus, the love of God must ever be a cause of strong confidence.

Before leaving this, we may notice from this:

1. That the man who is yet uncertain has not realized[15] the great object of the gospel, "strong confidence."

2. That Doubting Christians[16] are not to be preferred to those who have more faith, for these are nearer to the true gospel state. "Strong confidence."

3. Although difficult of attainment, yet if we have true religion it behoves us to seek this "confidence." And to this end we notice:

IV. THE GRAND PROMISE HERE MADE.

He promises a refuge.[17] And ask the Jewish manslayer.[18] Ask Lot in Zoar.[19] Ask the warrior or the sailor what a refuge means and they will answer.

All creatures have some refuge provided.

All men imagine some, but since we have left all, shall not God give us a better?

We are God's property, bought at an immense price.[20] Will he not find us a refuge?

We have been beloved with eternal love.[21] We are,

in fact his children – and shall children perish while the Father has an arm to save. The children must be taken care of this is a prime object of paternal solicitude.

You have had a refuge he now says you shall have in death, in judgment. Imagine more, Conceive more Write more precious things than God has written. Ah! 'tis past your power – what more can he say or you desire? Trust him. In his Fear have confidence Begone dull fear come rapturous security.

This is the tendency of religion – you are warranted in the strongest faith –

143   Lord encrease our Faith. Amen

John XIX. 33.34. Jesus' dead body whilst on the cross. 107
Every step Jesus took was fraught with meaning, there is something grand in littles, fulfilment of prophecy, or else some lesson for unborn ages. Jesus has cried "It is finished" he is dead, but even now some prophecies are to be fulfilled by the lifeless corpse ere it be taken down John seems to be the only witness, but or at least the only evangelist who records it, his tender love binds him to the spot, just as it carried him into the hall of judgment with him, made him the guardian of Mary and helped him to outrun even Peter – John saw it so clearly that he says "he knoweth that he saith true," and perhaps in these words he is invoking God himself as evidence of the truth of the wonderful fact. The facts being thus attested, they bear upon us a

RELIGION, THE FOUNDATION . . . *and* JESUS'S BODY . . .

in fact, his children.[22] And shall children perish while the Father has an arm to save?[23] The children must be taken care of. This is a prime object of paternal solicitude.

You have had a refuge.[24] He now says you shall have [it] in death, in judgment. Imagine more. Conceive more. Write more precious things than God has written. Ah! 'tis past your power. What more can he say or you desire? Trust him. In his Fear, have confidence.

Begone, dull fear. Come, rapturous security. This is the tendency of religion. You are warranted in the strongest faith.

143 Lord, increase[25] our Faith.[26] Amen

107

JESUS'[S][1] DEAD BODY WHILST *on the* CROSS
John 19:33–34[2]

"But when they came to Jesus, and saw that he was dead already, they brake not his legs: but one of the soldiers with a spear pierced his side, and forthwith came there out blood and water."

Every step Jesus took was fraught with meaning. There is something grand in littles, fulfilment of prophecy, or else some lesson for unborn ages. Jesus has cried, "It is finished."[3] He is dead, but even now some prophecies are to be fulfilled by the lifeless corpse ere[4] it be taken down.

John seems to be the only witness, ~~but~~ or at least the only evangelist who records it.[5] His tender love binds him to the spot, just as it carried him into the hall of judgment with him, made him the guardian of Mary,[6] and helped him to outrun even Peter.[7] John saw it so clearly that he says, "he knoweth that he saith true."[8] And perhaps in these words he is invoking God himself as evidence of the truth of the wonderful fact.

The facts being thus attested, they bear upon us a

SERMON 107

great weight of importance demanding consideration and promising amply to repay it.

I The not breaking of his legs — The Romans allowed the crucified to remain on the cross, to rot, or be the prey of ravenous birds, this however was contrary to Jewish law, and would in this instance have been peculiarly obnoxious as a defilement of their great sabbath. They request that the death of the condemned may be hastened by breaking their legs, which seems to have been done by blows from an iron bar. The Soldiers, devoid of humanity, break the legs of the wretch on one side and then do the same to the dying saint on the other. Reserving Jesus for the last, perhaps through a sort of reverence of one whose death was so mysterious and so attended with miracle. But now they must execute the command — but no Providence prevents, they turn their eyes aloft, and by his drooping head, his ghastly countenance, and fallen jaws they clearly perceive that Jesus is dead. The pain he had endured, the emaciated condition of his body and the intense agony of his mind had hastened on his death — Malice now comes too late, and there is ~~now~~ no necessity for the use of the bar — Thus Providence kept his bones not one of them was broken great weight of importance,[9] demanding consideration and promising amply to repay it.

I. THE NOT BREAKING OF HIS LEGS.

The Romans allowed the crucified to remain on the cross to rot or be the prey of ravenous birds.[10] This, however, was contrary to Jewish law and would, in this instance, have been peculiarly obnoxious as a defilement of their great sabbath.[11]

They request that the death of the condemned may be hastened by breaking their legs, which seems to have been done by blows from an iron bar.[12] The Soldiers, devoid of humanity, break the legs of the wretch on one side and then do the same to the dying saint on the other. Reserving Jesus for the last, perhaps through a sort of reverence of one whose death was so mysterious and so attended with miracle.[13] But now they must execute the command. But no, Providence prevents. They turn their eyes aloft, and by his drooping head,[14] his ghastly countenance, and fallen jaws they clearly perceive that Jesus is dead. The pain he had endured, the emaciated condition of his body, and the intense agony of his mind had hastened on his death. Malice now comes too late, and there is ~~now~~ no necessity[15] for the use of the bar. Thus, Providence kept his bones. Not one of them was[16] broken.

This was done – for many reasons.

1. To shew that Jesus was the true Lamb of God's passover. as all the old types centred in him so did this. and the preservation of his bones entire proved his identity with the type, his true Messiahship.

2. To shew that his death was voluntary, He had power to give or withhold and here he exercises his sovereignty over himself – in reserving his bones –

3. To manifest that he did well sustain the burden of our guilt and God's wrath – what would have crushed us to powder and shall dash in pieces the wicked he bore without the breaking of a bone.

4. As the champion of God. though dignified with scars in his flesh, the great enemy gave him no thrust so powerful as to break a bone – he reserved his body entire for a glorious resurrection – whereby he crushed the serpent in his head.

5. Just as the visible body of Jesus was never broken so never can one bone of his body mystical be in the least impaired or severed from the head.

II. The piercing of his side.

But Providence though it stays the breaking of his bones permits the rough soldier to pierce the side with the cruel spear, in wanton sport. but even this deep wound gapes wide with meaning to our view.

1. This Proved him to be the Messiah. Zech XII. 10 as also that he is Jehovah for God is speaking therefore Jesus is God.

2. This proved that he was dead – even if he had been still alive, that thrust would have ended his life. It was necessary that he should be clearly proved

JESUS'[S] DEAD BODY WHILST ON THE CROSS—*John 19:33–34*

This was done for many reasons:[17]

1. To shew that Jesus was the true[18] Lamb of God's passover. As all the old types centred in him,[19] so did this, and the preservation of his bones entire[ly] proved his identity with the type,[20] his true Messiahship.[21]

2. To shew that his death was voluntary. He had power to give or with-hold,[22] and here he exercises his sovereignty over himself in reserving his bones.

3. To manifest that he did well sustain the burden of our guilt and God's wrath. What would have crushed us to powder and shall dash in pieces the wicked, he bore without the breaking of a bone.

4. As the champion of God. Though dignified with scars in his flesh,[23] the great enemy gave him no thrust so powerful as to break a bone. He reserved his body entire[ly] for a glorious resurrection whereby he crushed the serpent in his head.[24]

5. Just as the visible body of Jesus was never broken, so never can one bone of his body mystical be in the least impaired or severed from the head.[25]

II. THE PIERCING OF HIS SIDE.

But Providence, though it stays the breaking of his bones, permits the rough soldier to pierce the side with the cruel spear in wanton sport. But even this deep wound gapes wide with meaning to our view.

1. This Proved him to be the Messiah, Zech. XII.10.[26] As also that he is Jehovah, for God is speaking. Therefore, Jesus is God.

2. This proved that he was dead. Even if he had been still alive, that thrust would have ended his life. It was necessary that he should be clearly proved

to be really dead or else his resurrection was not actual and his enemies might say the disciples stole his body while yet alive and by natural means restored him. Let us remember too that on the fact of his resurrection the whole gospel scheme hinges. As also that if Jesus died not then redemption is not complete and we shall have yet to bear the tremendous sentence. That death-thrust is the grand witness that "it is finished". —

3. Herein was centred the sin of ages — this the epitome of sin — is chargeable on all though not the actual piercers — all shall bear the guilt or share the gain. Let us weep that this lovely body e'er should be so mangled — let us rejoice in the effects flowing therefrom.

III. The effusion of blood and water. Supernatural no doubt, but it possibly be accounted for on natural grounds. perhaps the pericardium was pierced a vessel near the heart containing a small quantity of water. — when this was pierced water followed and the blood accompanying showed that the spear had actually entered the heart — or it may mean that by death the small globules of blood were coagulated and separated from the liquor sanguinis which was the water.

But however this was here too is instruction. Some have said Baptism and the Lord's supper were intended, and certainly both of them derive

JESUS'[S] DEAD BODY WHILST ON THE CROSS—*John 19:33–34*

to be really dead or else his resurrection was not actual and his enemies might say the disciples stole his body while yet alive and by natural means restored him.[27] Let us remember, too, that on the fact of his resurrection, the whole gospel scheme hinges. As also, that if Jesus died not, then redemption is not complete and we shall have yet to bear the tremendous sentence. That death-thrust is the grand witness that "it is finished."

3. Herein was centred the sin of ages. This, the epitomé of sin, is chargeable on all.[28] Though not the actual piercers,[29] all shall bear the guilt or share the gain. Let us weep that this lovely body ere should be So mangled. Let us rejoice in the effects flowing therefrom.

III. THE EFFUSION OF BLOOD AND WATER.

Supernatural, no doubt, but it possibly [could] be accounted for on natural grounds. Perhaps the pericardium was pierced, a vessel near the heart containing a small quantity of water.[30] When this was pierced,[31] water followed, and[32] the blood accompanying showed that the spear had actually entered the heart. Or it may mean that by death, the small[33] globules of blood were coagulated and separated from the liquor sanguinis,[34] which was the water.

But however this was, here, too, is instruction.

Some have said Baptism and the Lord's supper were intended,[35] and certainly both of them derive

SERMON 107

their meaning from the water and blood but still they are only emblems of the two precious liquids which are the double cure of sin – Christ's great catholicons–

1. Blood – the price of our purchase – the atonement for sin – the offering for guilt – the remission of sin. Precious Heart's blood – no blood of bulls like this – the blood of armies fats the soil, may this fertilize my soul.

2. Water. For the cleansing of sin's defilement, applied to us in sanctification – the filth is washed away Here's the true holy water – Here's the water cure. Better than mineral springs, of Bath or Tunbridge A drop of this would cure a million – quench a world, or make a desert blossom –

Here the two flow together, What Christ has joined let no man sunder – Baptismal Regeneration water does not come from this source. the devil fetched this from the waters of the Styx in the skull of Simon Magus – It tastes of the gall of bitterness, it comes from the Dead Sea and smells of Sodom –

But now let us gaze, admire, wonder, adore weep, melt, die – yet live anew at the sight. Sinner behold him whom thou hast pierced. Saint behold thy substitute – Be crucified with him – Not as the Jews said it – say we –

44   The blood be on us and on our children to cleanse our guilt away

<u>Amen</u>

their meaning from the water and blood. But still, they are only emblems[36] of the two precious liquids which are the double cure of sin—Christ's great catholicons.[37]

1. Blood, the price of our purchase,[38] the atonement for sin, the offering for guilt, the remission of sin.[39] Precious Heart's blood. No blood of bulls[40] like this. The blood of armies fats the soil.[41] May this fertilize my soul.

2. Water for the cleansing of sin's defilement applied to us in sanctification. The filth is washed away. Here's the true[42] holy water.[43] Here's the water cure. Better than mineral springs of Bath or Tunbridge,[44] a drop of this would cure a million, quench a world,[45] or make a desert blossom.[46]

Here, the two flow together. What Christ has joined let no man sunder.[47] Baptismal Regeneration water does not come from this source.[48] The devil fetched this from the waters of the Styx[49] in the skull of Simon Magus.[50] It tastes of the gall of bitterness.[51] It comes from the Dead Sea and smells of Sodom.[52]

But now let us gaze, admire, wonder, adore, weep, melt, die, yet live anew at the sight.

Sinner, behold him whom thous hast pierced.

Saint, behold thy substitute.[53] Be crucified with him.[54] Not as the Jews said it, say we:

144

> The blood be on us and on our children
> to cleanse our guilt away.[55]

<u>Amen</u>

SERMON 106

1. In 1876 Charles preached an additional sermon on Prov 14:26 entitled "Godly Fear and Its Goodly Consequence" (*MTP* 22, Sermon 1290). The overlapping content, particularly in the primary divisions and subpoints, suggests Charles likely had his early outline in mind in the writing of his later sermon.

2. "The fear of the slave who dreads a task-master we have now escape from. At least we ought to be free from such bondage, for we are not under the law, which is the task-master, but we are under grace, which is a paternal spirit, and has given us the liberty of sons" (*MTP* 22:231).

3. Cf. 1 Cor 13:13.

4. Cf. Matt 10:28.

5. Charles likely intended to reinforce the middle stroke of the letter "S."

6. In the second primary division of his 1876 sermon, Charles highlighted the confidence of biblical and historical heroes of the faith, including Job, Habakkuk, Abraham, Shadrach, Meshach, Abednego, Micah, Peter, John, and Hugh Latimer (*MTP* 22:234–37).

7. Charles misspelled the word "temptation" by adding the letter "t" before "p." No attempt was made to correct the misspelling.

8. An illegible letter, possibly "a," was written beneath "i" in the word "if."

9. Cf. Matt 13:41; 2 Cor 6:14; 1 John 3:4.

10. Cf. "Faith Precious" (Notebook 1, Sermon 23) and "The Saints' Justification and Glory" (Notebook 1, Sermon 68).

11. Cf. "Election" (Notebook 1, Sermon 10); Rom 8:28–30; 11:5; Eph 1:4; 2 Thess 2:13.

12. Cf. "Final Perseverance Certain" (Sermon 82).

13. Cf. Rom 5:1; "The Saints' Justification and Glory" (Notebook 1, Sermon 68); "Justification, Conversion, Sanctification, Glory" (Sermon 102).

14. The phrase "Like kills like" was a Victorian idiom. An example is found in *The Gouty Philosopher*: "The homeopathists tell us that like kills like, and that poisons

RELIGION, THE FOUNDATION OF CONFIDENCE—*Proverbs 14:26*

which create headache cure headache" (Charles Mackay, 2nd ed.; *The Gouty Philosopher; or, The Friends, Acquaintances, Opinions, Whims, and Eccentricities of John Wagstaff, Esq., of Wilbye Grange, J.P., and Ex-M.P.* [London: Saunders, Otley, and Co., 1864], 109). Though the phrase is still used in the field of homeopathy, an approximation of this idiom today may be "fight fire with fire."

15. Two letters appear beneath and after the "d" in the word "realized." Charles originally wrote the word "realizes" before striking through the letter "s" to construct the past tense.

16. Charles inserted an apostrophe between the letters "n" and the "s" in the word "Christians"; however, the context suggests Charles did not intend the word to be possessive.

17. Cf. Pss 46:1–3; 91:2; Jer 16:19.

18. According to Joshua 20, if a Jew committed murder accidently, he could flee to one of six cities of refuge and find safety. In his 1876 sermon, Charles did not allude to this practice.

19. Genesis 19:30, "And Lot went up out of Zoar, and dwelt in the mountain, and his two daughters with him; for he feared to dwell in Zoar: and he dwelt in a cave, he and his two daughters." "God cannot burn Sodom and Gomorrah till he has got Lot safe out of the way. He must find a refuge for his children" (*MTP* 22:239).

20. First Corinthians 6:20, "For ye are bought with a price: therefore glorify God in your body, and in your spirit, which are God's;" 1 Cor 7:23, "Ye are bought with a price; be not ye the servants of men."

21. Cf. Jer 31:3. 22. Cf. Gal 3:26; 1 John 3:2.

23. "Oh, dear friends, there is a heaven lying asleep inside those words—*his children*. There is paradise eternal couched within that word—Abba, Father. If you know how to say it with the spirit of adoption, you have the earnest of the inheritance within you: you have got a heaven, a young heaven within your spirit" (*MTP* 22:238, italics in the original).

24. "There is a refuge for you somewhere, Christian, even in the matter of ordinary providence, and there is always a mercy-seat for you to go to. There is always the bosom of Christ for you to fly to. The fear of the Lord does not drive you from him. It drives you to him, and when it drives you to him you have got a place of refuge" (*MTP* 22:240).

25. Charles originally spelled the word "encrease."

26. Luke 17:5, "And the apostles said unto the Lord, Increase our faith."

JESUS'[S] DEAD BODY WHILST ON THE CROSS—*John 19:33–34*

1. Charles originally spelled the word "Jesus'"; however, the letter "s" has been added to the end of this word for consistency.

2. Charles preached two additional sermons on this biblical text: "The Water and the Blood" (*MTP* 58, Sermon 3311) and "The Pierced Heart of Jesus" (*MTP* 63, Sermon 3559). There is enough overlapping content to suggest Charles may have used material from the outline above in both later sermons. Charles also likely consulted the second volume of John Gill's *Exposition of the New Testament* for this sermon (John Gill, *An Exposition of the New Testament, in Three Volumes: In Which the Sense of the Sacred Text Is Given; Doctrinal and Practical Truths Are Set in a Plain and Easy Light, Difficult Places Explained, Seeming Contradictions Reconciled; and Whatever Is Material in the Various Readings, and Several Oriental Variations, Is Observed. The Whole Illustrated with Notes Taken from the Most Ancient Jewish Writings, Vol. II* [London: printed for the author; and sold by Aaron Ward, at the King's-Arms in Little-Britain, 1747, The Spurgeon Library]). Overlapping content is noted below.

3. Cf. John 19:30.

4. "Before" (Johnson's *Dictionary*, s.v. "ere").

5. See also 1 John 5:6–8.

6. Charles was referring to Jesus's instruction to John to take care of his mother, Mary (John 19:26).

7. John 20:4, "So they ran both together: and the other disciple did outrun Peter, and came first to the sepulchre."

8. John 19:35, "And he that saw it bare record, and his record is true: and he knoweth that he saith true, that ye might believe."

9. A blot of ink appears above the letter "m" in the word "importance."

10. In his *Exposition of the New Testament in Three Volumes*, John Gill noted, "According to *Roman* laws, such bodies hung until they were putrified, or eaten by birds of prey; wherefore [the Jews asked that the bones be broken] that their land might not be defiled, and especially their sabbath, by their remaining on the cross" (Gill, *Exposition of the New Testament*, 2:109, italics in the original).

11. Cf. Lev 21:11; Num 19:11, 14.

12. "This seems to have been done by striking the legs of those that were crucified, which were fastened to the cross, with a bar of iron, or some such instrument" (Gill, *Exposition of the New Testament*, 2:109).

13. Charles was referring to the darkening of the sun, earthquakes, and dead rising from tombs (Cf. Matt 27:45, 50–54).

14. John 19:30, "When Jesus therefore had received the vinegar, he said, It is finished: and he bowed his head, and gave up the ghost."

15. Charles originally wrote the word "necessities." A tittle appears above the final serif of the letter "y." Additionally, Charles struck through the letter "s."

16. Charles originally wrote the word "are" beneath "was."

17. An ink blot, similar to that on the previous page, appears after the word "reasons." It is unclear whether the blot was intentional or accidental.

18. A tittle appears above the letter "u" in the word "true."

19. In *Commenting and Commentaries*, Charles criticized Benjamin Keach's *Tropologia*: "This is a vast cyclopaedia of types and metaphors of all sorts, and was once very popular. It is a capital book, though too often the figures not only run on all-fours but on as many legs as a centipede" (Spurgeon, *Commenting and Commentaries*, 61). See also "The Peculiar People" (Notebook 1, Sermon 25).

20. Ps 34:20, "He keepeth all his bones: not one of them is broken"; John 19:36, "For these things were done, that the scripture should be fulfilled, A bone of him shall not be broken."

21. An alternative reading of this sentence is "And the preservation of his bones [intact, or whole] proved his identity with the type, his true Messiahship."

22. Charles originally spelled the word without the hyphen. However, after forming the ascender of the letter "h," he inserted the hyphen. Cf. John 19:11.

23. Cf. John 20:27.

24. Cf. Gen 3:15; Rom 16:20.

JESUS'[S] DEAD BODY WHILST ON THE CROSS—*John 19:33–34*

25. Cf. Rom 12:4–5; 1 Cor 12:27; Eph 4:4; Col 1:18.

26. Zechariah 12:10, "And I will pour upon the house of David, and upon the inhabitants of Jerusalem, the spirit of grace and of supplications: and they shall look upon me whom they have pierced, and they shall mourn for him, as one mourneth for his only son, and shall be in bitterness for him, as one that is in bitterness for his firstborn."

27. "The very central point of the atonement was death; there was no way of making atonement for sin except by the shedding of the precious blood of Jesus, as of a lamb without blemish and without spot. There must be life to atone for sin, and that life sacrificed; and, therefore, Christ 'was dead.' It was no dream, no delusion, no sleep, no swoon, no coma; he 'was dead'" (*MTP* 46:402).

28. Cf. Rom 3:23; 1 Cor 15:22.

29. It is unclear why Charles bolded the letter "r" in the word "piercers."

30. See Gill, *Exposition of the New Testament* 2:109–10.

31. A series of dots appears above the word "pierced."

32. It is unclear why Charles added the letter "t" at the end of the word "and."

33. An illegible letter, possibly a "b," was written beneath the "s" in the word "small." It is possible Charles originally intended to write the word "blood."

34. In his 1834 *Manual of Chemistry*, Lewis C. Beck explained, "The blood, when circulating, is mechanically distinguishable into two parts, one essentially liquid, which may be called *liquor sanguinis*, the other essentially solid, which is merely suspended in the former, and imparts its red colour to the mixture.... The *liquor sanguinis* when set at rest coagulates, and forms a uniform jelly of precisely the same volume as when it was liquid, and possesses the exact figure of the containing vessel; and in a short time, by the contraction of the mass of coagulated fibrin, a yellowish liquid appears, which is the true *serum* of the blood. It is the liquor sanguinis, thus shown to be spontaneously separable into fibrin and serum, which forms a yellowish liquid stratum at the surface of blood" (Lewis C. Beck, *A Manual of Chemistry; Containing a Condensed View of the Present State of the Science, with Copious References to the More Extensive Treatises, Original Papers, &c. Intended as a Text Book for Medical Schools, Colleges and Academies, Second Edition, Revised and Enlarged*

[Albany, NY: E.W. & C. Skinner, 1834], 414–15, italics in the original). See also Charles's personal copy of *The Bridgewater Treatises on the Power, Wisdom, and Goodness of God as Manifested in the Creation in which William Prout Wrote Chemistry Meteorology and the Function of Digestion Considered with Reference to Natural Theology* (London: William Pickering, 1834, The Spurgeon Library), 466–80, 514–29.

35. "This water and blood some make to signify baptism and the Lord's supper, which are both of Christ's appointing, and spring from him, and refer to his sufferings and death" (Gill, *Exposition of the New Testament* 2:109–10).

36. See Charles's lecture from the Pastors' College, "Books of Fables, Emblems, and Parables" in *The Art of Illustration: Being Addresses Delivered to the Students of the Pastors' College, Metropolitan Tabernacle* (London: Passmore & Alabaster, 1894, The Spurgeon Library), 93–143.

37. "An universal medicine" (Johnson's *Dictionary*, s.v. "catholicon"). Cf. "The Physician and His Patients" (Notebook 1, Sermon 74).

38. Cf. Acts 20:28; 1 Cor 6:20; 7:23; 1 Pet 1:19.

39. Cf. Matt 26:28; Heb 9:22.

40. Charles originally inserted an apostrophe before the final letter "s" in the word "bulls." The context suggests, however, that he intended the word to be plural, not possessive.

41. Isaiah 34:7, "And the unicorns shall come down with them, and the bullocks with the bulls; and their land shall be soaked with blood, and their dust made fat with fatness."

42. Charles wrote the letter "l" beneath the "e" in the word "true." He likely intended to write "truly"; however, it is unclear why he inserted the tittle above the letter "u." This is the second time in this sermon Charles wrote a tittle above the word "true" (cf. "to shew that Jesus was the *true* Lamb of God's passover," emphasis added).

43. Charles is likely contrasting the water flowing from Christ's side and the "holy" water used in the Roman Catholic tradition. See *MTP* 20:625.

44. Cf. "The Physician and His Patients" (Notebook 1, Sermon 74).

45. Cf. John 4:14; 7:38.

46. Isaiah 35:1, "The wilderness and the solitary place shall be glad for them; and the desert shall rejoice, and blossom as the rose."

47. Mark 10:9, "What therefore God hath joined together, let not man put asunder."

48. On June 5, 1864, Charles preached a sermon entitled "Baptismal Regeneration" (*MTP* 10, Sermon 573) in which he denounced the belief that pedobaptism instilled regeneration. The primary thesis of his sermon was "BAPTISM WITHOUT FAITH SAVES NO ONE" (*MTP* 10:315, capitalization in the original). Charles also spoke against the use of the Book of Common Prayer, which he believed clearly taught baptismal regeneration. Ten years after the delivery of his 1864 sermon, Charles recounted that it "was delivered with the full expectation that the sale of the sermons would receive very serious injury; in fact, I mentioned to one of the publishers that I was about to destroy it at a single blow" (*Autobiography* 3:82). He was not mistaken in his anticipation of criticism from the established church. However, the widespread exposure of the controversy surrounding this sermon increased the sales of his sermon and bolstered his reputation throughout the nation. Immediately following the sermon, 100,000 copies of it were sold. By the end of the nineteenth century, that number rose to 230,000, and by the publication of Charles's autobiography, the sermon was "still in constant demand" (*Autobiography* 3:82). For two academic treatments of the Baptismal Regeneration Controversy, see Tom Nettles, *Living by Revealed Truth: The Life and Pastoral Theology of Charles Haddon Spurgeon* (Ross-shire, Scotland: Christian Focus Publications, 2013), 513–17; and Larry Michael, "The Effects of Controversy on the Evangelistic Ministry of C. H. Spurgeon" (PhD diss., The Southern Baptist Theological Seminary, 1988), 148–86. Fifteen years after the controversy, Charles said, "Of all transparent falsehoods surely that of baptismal regeneration is the grossest. It is a marvel that men who live and walk among sane persons should ever fall into it" (*MTP* 25:55).

49. The word "Styx" comes from the Greek Στύξ, "hate" (Matina Psyhogeos, *English Words Derived from Greek Language* [New York: Page Publishing, Inc., 2016], s.v. "styx"). Charles's personal copy of the *Greek and English Lexicon to the New Testament* offers the following etymology: "Στυγναζω, from στυγνος *odious, hateful, sorrowful,* which from στυγος *hate, hated,* and this from στυγεω *to hate*" (John Parkhurst, *Greek and English Lexicon to the New Testament: In Which the Words and Phrases Occurring in Those Sacred Books Are Distinctly Explained; and the Meanings Assigned to Each Authorized*

SERMON 107

by References to Passages of Scripture, and Frequently Illustrated and Confirmed by Citations from the Old Testament and from the Greek Writers. To This Work Is Prefixed, a Plain and Easy Greek Grammar, Adapted to the Use of Learners, and Those Who Understand No Other Language Than English. A New Edition, Corrected, Enlarged, and Improved* [London: printed for William Baynes and Son, 1822, The Spurgeon Library], 524–25, italics in the original). According to Greek mythology, the River Styx separated the traveling soul from the Underworld. In his *Divine Comedy*, Dante presented Styx as the fifth circle of hell—a slimy quagmire or slough through which souls pass (I. C. Wright, trans., *Dante, Translated into English Verse. Third Edition. Illustrated with Engravings on Steel After Designs by Flaxman* [London: Henry G. Bohn, 1854, The Spurgeon Library], 27).

50. Simon Magus, also called Simon the Sorcerer, is referenced in Acts 8:9–24. Irenaeus wrote, "All those who in any way corrupt the truth, and injuriously affect the preaching of the Church, are the disciples and successors of Simon Magus of Samaria. Although they do not confess the name of their master, in order all the more to seduce others, yet they do teach his doctrines" (Irenaeus, *Against Heresies* in Alexander Roberts and James Donaldson, eds., *Ante-Nicene Fathers, Vol. 1, The Apostolic Fathers, Justin Martyr, Irenaeus* [Peabody, MA: Hendrickson Publishers, 2012], 353; see also 347–48). Jacobus de Voragine, the thirteenth-century archbishop of Genoa, recorded in *Legenda Aurea* that Simon Magus cracked his skull on the pavement in Rome after being suspended in the air by demons at the command of Simon Peter in the presence of Emperor Nero (Alberto Ferreiro, *Simon Magus in Patristic, Medieval and Early Modern Tradition* in Studies in the History of Christian Traditions [Leiden, The Netherlands: Brill, 2005], 297–99).

51. Charles may have had Exod 15:23 in mind: "And when they came to Marah, they could not drink of the waters of Marah, for they were bitter: therefore the name of it was called Marah."

52. Cf. Genesis 19; Matt 11:24.

53. Charles struck through an illegible letter, likely "s," after "i" in the word "substitute."

54. Cf. Luke 9:23; Gal 2:20.

55. Matthew 27:25, "Then answered all the people, and said, His blood be on us, and on our children."

108. Mark. 10. 27. Man's weakness & God's strength.
The young man by his love of riches is hindered from following Christ. Jesus then declares how difficult it is for rich men to be saved, and in the next verse explains himself as meaning those who "trust in" or love riches. He then compares the entrance to heaven to a needle's eye as hard to hit and hard to get through. and the rich he calls camels who bear other's burdens, their gold must be taken off at the journey's end. These huge creatures can never enter the needle's eye unless by some extraordinary manifestation of Divine power. The disciples were much astonished, for their rabbi's had taught that Messiah's kingdom would mostly consist of rich men — "Well" say they "if the rich are so hardly saved, who then can be". But Jesus tells them that the salvation of any man on the foot of human nature is impossible. but that God will do impossibilities. —

I. Many things in nature are beyond man's power, and all things in spiritual affairs are specially so. Man has done much but there is a limit to his power and let him not boast of what he can do for his strength is but derived from the Omnipotent But let him launch into spiritual things and there he is out done.
  1. The planning of salvation excels human wisdom.
  2. The procuring salvation exceeds all his merit.
  3. The embracing of grace, by the simple act of faith never has been done by man alone in a single instance

MAN'S WEAKNESS *and* GOD'S STRENGTH[1]
Mark 10:27[2]

"And Jesus looking upon them saith, With men it is impossible, but not with God: for with God all things are possible."

The young man by his love of riches is hindered from following Christ. Jesus then declares how difficult it is for rich men to be saved,[3] and in the next verse explains himself as meaning those who "<u>trust in</u>" or love riches.[4] He then compares the entrance to heaven to a needle's eye[5] as hard to hit and hard to get through.[6] And the rich he calls camels who bear other's burdens. Their gold must be taken off at the journey's end.

These huge creatures can never enter the needle's eye unless by some extraordinary manifestation of Divine power. The disciples were much astonished, for their rabbis[7] had taught that Messiah's Kingdom would mostly consist of rich men.[8] "Well," say they, "if the rich are so hardly saved, Who then can be?"[9]

But Jesus tells them that the[10] salvation of any man on the foot of human nature is impossible, but that God will do impossibilities.

I.[11] MANY THINGS IN NATURE ARE BEYOND MAN[']S POWER, AND ALL THINGS IN SPIRITUAL AFFAIRS ARE SPECIALLY SO.

Man has done much, but there is a limit to his power and let him not boast of what he can do,[12] for his strength is but[13] derived from the Omnipotent.[14]

But let him[15] launch into spiritual things and there he is out done.

1. The planning of salvation excels human wisdom.
2. The procuring [of] salvation exceeds all his merit.[16]
3. The embracing of grace by the simple act of faith never has been done by man alone in a single instance.

4. The performance of holy actions day by day, and especially perseverance unto the end is impossible to man alone. otherwise why does God put his hand to the work? why did Jesus die? why is the Holy Spirit needed.

His Spirit well inwrought into the mind, would blast all creature boastings, while it would not lead men to sit still but to cry out in anguish.

Without me ye can do nothing — man is powerless.

II. God by his almighty power has already done much that was impossible to man.

Not to mention the great act of creation, the leading of stars and of this globe in their orbits; the deluge, earthquakes or storms or even the growing of corn — we will notice acts which refer more to God as the deliverer of our race.

1. He has planned a glorious scheme, mapped out the design.
2. He has in the person of his son, vindicated justice and magnified mercy, so that now heaven, unattainably by human merit, is laid wide open by the righteousness of Jesus.
3. He has overcome by his Holy Spirit the stoutest sinner, the proudest Pharisee, the proudest king, the meanest slave, the most ignorant, the most abominable.
4. He has delivered his people when all hope was gone. witness. Jacob preserved from famine. Joseph led to grandeur. The iron bars of Egypt's dungeon opened to the chosen race. The red sea divided. Water and manna found where none were seen before. The gigantic nations crushed. Gideon. Samson. David, the lion's den. the burning furnace. the Jews' return from Babylon. Peter. Paul.
5. He has enabled many so to hold on, that now they have attained the goal.
6. His promises have been so far fulfilled that

4. The performance of holy actions day by day, and especially perseverance unto the end,[17] is impossible to man alone. Otherwise, why does[18] God put his hand to the work? Why did Jesus die? Why is the Holy Spirit needed?

This Spirit, well inwrought[19] into the mind, would blast[20] all creature boastings, while it would not lead men to sit still but to cry out in anguish, Without me, ye can do nothing.[21] Man is powerless.

II. GOD, BY HIS ALMIGHTY POWER, HAS ALREADY DONE MUCH THAT WAS IMPOSSIBLE TO MAN.

Not to mention the great act of creation,[22] the leading of stars and of this globe in their orbits,[23] the deluge,[24] earthquakes,[25] or storms,[26] or even the growing of corn.[27] We will notice acts which refer more to God as the deliverer of our race.

1. He has planned a glorious scheme, mapped out the design.[28]

2. He has, in the person of his son, vindicated justice and magnified mercy so that now heaven, unattainably by human merit, is[29] laid wide open by the righteousness of Jesus.

3.[30] He has overcome by his <u>Holy Spirit</u>[31] the stoutest sinner, the proudest Pharisee,[32] the proudest king,[33] the meanest slave, the most ignorant, the most abominable.

4. He has delivered his people when all hope was gone. Witness Jacob preserved from famine,[34] Joseph led to grandeur,[35] the iron bars of Egypt's dungeon opened to the chosen race,[36] the Red Sea divided,[37] water and manna found where none were seen before,[38] the gigantic nations crushed,[39] Gideon,[40] Samson,[41] David,[42] the lion's den,[43] the burning furnace,[44] the Jews's[45] return from Babylon,[46] Peter,[47] Paul.[48]

5. He has enabled many so to hold on that now they have attained the goal.

6. His promises have been so far fulfilled that

SERMON 108

nations have bowed before him and kings have licked ye dust. Never yet has sinner been beyond his grace or saint beyond his love or enemy too great for his power.

"**With God all things have been possible.**"

III. All things yet to come are possible — God's decrees and promises shall all be fulfilled.

1. The salvation of the vilest sinners is possible with him
2. The final perseverance of all saints and their support in the most fiery trial until they shall be perfect in glory is most certainly possible.
3. The deliverance of an immense multitude the final conquest of the whole earth, the destruction of the most haughty enemies of our religion, and the chaining of Satan with all evil spirits is possible.
4. Support for us in death, the resurrection of our bodies, our exaltation in glory and eternal victory in heaven is certain.
5. The burning of the earth, the judgment of quick and dead, the burnings of hell, and its perpetual smokings are possible with God.

1. Sinner quit vain confidence, look to the Strong One.
2. Saint cease to look in broken cisterns.
3. Have faith in God — for he is omnipotent.

When I am weak — then I am strong. I can do nothing alone, but all things through God.

147. 177

MAN'S WEAKNESS AND GOD'S STRENGTH—*Mark 10:27*

nations have bowed before him[49] and kings have licked ye dust.

Never yet has [a] sinner been beyond his grace, or [a] saint beyond his love, or [an] enemy too great for his power.[50]

<u>"With God all things have been possible."</u>[51]

III. ALL THINGS YET TO COME ARE POSSIBLE.

God's decrees and promises shall all be fulfilled.

1. The salvation of the vilest sinners is possible with him.
2. The final perseverance of all saints and their support in the most fiery trial until they shall be perfect in glory, is most certainly possible.
3. The deliverance of an immense multitude, the final conquest of the whole earth, the destruction of the most haughty enemies of our religion, and the chaining of Satan with all evil spirits,[52] is possible.
4. Support for us in death, the resurrection of our bodies,[53] our exaltation in glory, and eternal victory in heaven, is certain.
5. The burning of the earth,[54] the judgment of quick and dead,[55] the burnings of hell,[56] and its perpetual smokings, are possible with God.

1. Sinner, quit vain confidence. Look to the Strong One.
2. Saint, cease to look in broken cisterns.[57]
3. Have faith in God,[58] for he is omnipotent.

When I am weak, then I am strong.[59]
I can do nothing alone, but all things through God.[60]

147. 177

1. For additional sermons on God's strength, see "As Thy Days, So Shall Thy Strength Be" (*NPSP* 4, Sermon 210); "The Joy of the Lord, the Strength of His People" (*MTP* 17, Sermon 1027); "Strengthening Medicine for God's Servants" (*MTP* 21, Sermon 1214); and "Increased Faith the Strength of Peace Principles" (*MTP* 22, Sermon 1318).

2. This is the only time Charles preached a sermon on Mark 10:27.

3. Mark 10:23, "And Jesus looked round about, and saith unto his disciples, How hardly shall they that have riches enter into the kingdom of God!"

4. Mark 10:24, "And the disciples were astonished at his words. But Jesus answereth again, and saith unto them, Children, how hard is it for them that trust in riches to enter into the kingdom of God!"

5. The phrase "to a needle's eye" is written above the line and indicated with a caret between the words "heaven" and "as."

6. Mark 10:25, "It is easier for a camel to go through the eye of a needle, than for a rich man to enter into the kingdom of God."

7. Charles originally wrote an apostrophe before the letter "s" in the word "rabbi's." However, the context suggests he intended the word to be plural, not possessive.

8. Charles may have consulted Matthew Henry's *Exposition of the New Testament*: "They knew what were generally the sentiments of the Jewish teachers, who affirmed that the Spirit of God chooses to reside in rich men; nay, they knew what abundance of promises there were, in the Old Testament, of temporal good things; they knew likewise that all either are rich, or fain would be so, and that they who are rich, have so much the larger opportunities of doing good, and therefore were amazed to hear that it should be so hard for rich people to go to heaven" (Matthew Henry, *An Exposition of the New Testament: Wherein Each Chapter Is Summed Up in Its Contents: The Sacred Text Inserted at Large in Distinct Paragraphs: Each Paragraph Reduced to Its Proper Heads: The Sense Given, and Largely Illustrated: With Practical Remarks and Observations. With Preface by the Rev. C. H. Spurgeon. Vol. III. Mark, Chaps. X.–XVI. Luke, Chaps. 1.–XVI* [London: Thomas C. Jack; Edinburgh: Grange Publishing Works, n.d., The Spurgeon Library], 9).

MAN'S WEAKNESS AND GOD'S STRENGTH—*Mark 10:27*

9. Mark 10:26, "And they were astonished out of measure, saying among themselves, Who then can be saved?"

10. Two letters, likely "s" and "a," appear beneath "t" and "h" in the word "the." Charles likely began writing the word "salvation" prematurely.

11. Charles likely bolded Roman numerals I, II, and III for emphasis.

12. Cf. Prov 27:1; 1 Cor 1:31; 2 Cor 12:5–10.

13. The letter "y" appears beneath the "u" in the word "but." Charles originally wrote the word "by."

14. Cf. Pss 27:1; 37:39; Phil 4:13; 1 Tim 1:12.

15. A stroke appears between the words "let" and "him." Charles may have intended to write the word "The."

16. See "Regeneration" (Notebook 1, Sermon 7) and "The Saints' Justification and Glory" (Notebook 1, Sermon 68).

17. See "Final Perseverance Certain" (Sermon 82).

18. The word "does" was written above the line and between the words "why" and "God." Charles indicated its location with a caret.

19. "Adorned with work" (Johnson's *Dictionary*, s.v. "inwrought"). Cf. "God the Father of a Family" (Sermon 129).

20. The ink pattern beneath the letters "s" and "t" in the word "blast" originates from the bolded Roman numeral III that bled from the back side of the page.

21. John 15:5, "I am the vine, ye are the branches: He that abideth in me, and I in him, the same bringeth forth much fruit: for without me ye can do nothing."

22. Cf. Gen 1:1; Isa 45:12; John 1:3.

23. Cf. Gen 1:16; Neh 9:6; Ps 148:3–6; Isa 40:26.

24. Cf. Genesis 7.

25. Cf. Matt 28:2; Acts 16:26; Heb 12:26.

26. Cf. Job 28:25–27; Pss 135:7; 147:8; Matt 8:26–27.

27. Throughout 1852, numerous articles on the failure of English corn crops appeared. See "Review of the Corn Trade," *Manchester Examiner and Times*, September 8, 1852. See also "The Harvest of Souls" (Sermon 89) and "God's Visits and the Effects Thereof" (Sermon 113).

28. Cf. Rev 13:8.

29. The letter "a" appears beneath the "i" in the word "is." Charles originally wrote the word "as."

30. Charles originally wrote the number 2.

31. The bolded ascender of the letter "h" suggests Charles originally did not capitalize the word "Holy."

32. Cf. Acts 9:1–9.

33. Cf. Jonah 3:6–9.

34. Cf. Gen 45:4–7.

35. Cf. Gen 41:41–46.

36. Charles was referring to the Israelite exodus out of bondage in Egypt. Cf. Exod 13:17–18.

37. Cf. Exod 14:21.

38. Cf. Exod 17:1–7, 16.

39. Cf. Judges 1.

40. Cf. Judges 6.

41. Cf. Judges 13–16.

42. Cf. 1 Samuel 17.

43. Cf. Daniel 6.

44. Cf. Daniel 3.

45. Charles inserted the apostrophe before the letter "s" in the word "Jews." However, the context suggests he intended the word to be in the plural possessive, not the singular.

46. Cf. Ezra 1.

47. Cf. Acts 12:7.

48. Cf. Acts 16:25–26; 2 Cor 1:10; 2 Tim 4:18.

49. Cf. Ps 72:11; Rev 7:9.

50. An alternative reading of this sentence is "Never yet ha[ve] sinner[s] been beyond his grace, or saint[s] beyond his love, or enem[ies] too great for his power."

51. Charles bolded and underscored the sentence "<u>**With God all things have been possible**</u>" for emphasis. Charles changed the verb tense from the present progressive tense "are" to the present perfect progressive tense "have been."

52. Cf. Jude 1:6; Rev 20:1–3.

53. Cf. 1 Cor 15:35–58.

54. Cf. 2 Pet 3:10.

55. First Peter 4:5, "Who shall give account to him that is ready to judge the quick and the dead." Charles may have also had in mind the Apostles' Creed (for Charles's personal copy of the Apostles' Creed in its original language, see Henry B. Smith and Philip Schaff, eds., *Theological and Philosophical Library: A Series of Text-Books, Original and Translated for Colleges and Universities: The Creeds of the Greek and Latin Churches* [London: Hodder and Stoughton, 1878, The Spurgeon Library], 57).

56. Cf. Matt 13:50; 25:46; Rev 21:8.

57. Cf. Jer 2:13.

58. Cf. Matt 21:21; 1 Cor 16:13; 2 Cor 5:7; Heb 11:1–39.

59. Second Corinthians 12:10, "Therefore I take pleasure in infirmities, in reproaches, in necessities, in persecutions, in distresses for Christ's sake: for when I am weak, then am I strong."

60. Philippians 4:13, "I can do all things through Christ which strengtheneth me."

SERMON 109

Mal 3. 10.   Prove me now herewith.

God had many ends to be answered by his servants the prophets to foretell future events, both as a warning to sinners & a comfort to the faithful — as also to express his displeasure at any sin then raging — Both the designs were answered by Malachi — We shall

I. Explain the text.
II. Apply the text to the parties for whom now intended.

I. In explaining it, it may be well to notice the 2 parts.

1. Here is an exhortation to improve their conduct. In Malachi's time, which was probably the time when Nehemiah was governor, the people were unwilling to pay the tithes. The priests had sinned in marrying strange wives, and therefore had not courage enough to reprove the people, when they themselves were notoriously wrong: the people took still further advantage and even prevailed on them, to offer not as they were wont unblemished beasts — but the refuse of the cattle. There was profligacy among the priests & niggard worldliness among the people. Sorrow, famine and disasters came & then Malachi points out the one cause of their trouble and directs them to improve "Bring ye all the tithes". Tithes were a quit rent to the great owner of the soil — the tenth was an acknowledgment that all came from him. The payment of tithes ceased when the Mosaic economy was extinguished. It is nonsense to plead for them now — since neither Jesus, nor Peter, nor Paul even hint a word about them. And above all it is preposterous to imagine that Church Clergymen are successors of the Levites — they are not

109

PROVE ME NOW HEREWITH
Malachi 3:10[1]

"Bring ye all the tithes into the storehouse, that there may be meat in mine house, and prove me now herewith, saith the Lord of hosts, if I will not open you the windows of heaven, and pour you out a blessing, that there shall not be room enough to receive it."

God had many ends to be answered by his servants, the prophets, to foretell future events, both as a warning to sinners and a comfort to the faithful, as also to express his displeasure at[2] any sin then raging. Both [of] the designs were answered by Malachi. We shall:

I. Explain the text.

II. Apply the text to the parties for whom [it is] now intended.[3]

I. IN EXPLAINING IT, IT MAY BE WELL TO NOTICE THE 2 PARTS.

1. Here is an exhortation to <u>improve</u> their conduct.

    In Malachi's time, which was probably the time when Nehemiah was governor, the people were unwilling to pay the tithes. The priests had sinned in marrying strange wives, and therefore had not courage enough to reprove the people when they themselves were notoriously wrong. The people took still further advantage and even prevailed on them, to offer not as they were wont—unblemished beasts—but the refuse of the cattle.

    There was profligacy among the priests and niggard[4] worldliness among the people. Sorrow, famine, and disasters came, and then Malachi points out the one cause of their trouble and directs them to improve. "Bring ye all the tithes." Tithes were a quit rent[5] to the great owner of the soil. The tenth was an acknowledgment that all came from him. The payment of tithes ceased when the Mosaic economy was extinguished.

    It is nonsense to plead for them now since neither Jesus, nor Peter, nor Paul even hint a word about them. And above all, it is preposterous to imagine that Church Clergymen are successors of the Levites. They are not even successors of the Apostles — if they were they would not advance so stupid a claim. The Church of Christ does not demand tithes of money — the Church of England in that as well as in a multitude of other things errs from the truth. But still God does demand tithes. Such as a broken and contrite heart. a thankful spirit, and constant recognition of his hand. Of his children he requires not tithe but all — A contribution to the cause according to our power. fervent prayer on the behalf of the Church, labour in its behalf according to ability — faith & gratitude. Give him his tythe of your time. Sabbath day &c — Tithes of tongues, of thoughts, all your love, your heart "all the tithes". Some of the Jews paid a part just to quiet conscience — so do some now, but this is wrong bring in all. all or else none. no half-pay — "into the storehouse" the proper place of payment. so let the Christian pay his tribute in the place God has appointed him. He intimates that so much was due that if all were paid, there would be need to store it up — ah! if our shortcomings could be made up we should want a vast granary, and even now though all say they cannot do much, there would be enough and to spare if all did what they ought. "that there may be meat in mine house." for the Levites had not enough to support them. God's table ought to have the choicest dish on it. No wonder they had to go without meat at their own table, when their even successors of the Apostles. If they were, they would not advance so stupid a claim. The Church of Christ does not demand tithes of money. The Church of England in that, as well as in a multitude[6] of other things, errs from the truth.[7] But still, God does demand tithes.

Such as a broken and contrite heart, a thankful spirit, and constant recognition of his hand. Of his children he requires not tithe, but all: a contribution to the cause according to our power, fervent prayer on the behalf of the Church, labour in its behalf according to ability, faith, and gratitude.

Give him his tythe[8] of your time. Sabbath day, etc. Tithes of tongues, of thoughts, all your love, your heart. "All the tithes." Some of the Jews paid a part just to quiet conscience. So do some now, but this is wrong. Bring in all. All, or else none. No half-pay.

"Into the storehouse," the proper place of payment. So let the Christian pay his tribute in the place God has appointed him. He intimates that so much was due that if all were paid, there would be need to store it up. Ah! if our shortcomings[9] could be made up we should want a vast granary. And even now, though all say they cannot do much, there would be enough and to spare if all did what they ought.

"That there may be meat in mine house," for the Levites had not enough to support them. God's table ought to have the choicest dish on it. No wonder they had to go without meat at their own table when their sins robbed God's table of meat.   God needs no meat but surely if he giveth all their meat he has a right to require us to return a portion. —   Well my friends if you have not paid your tithes lately – I advise you to cash up for

2. Here is an exhortation to <u>prove</u> God, by serving him
"You are depressed – well then pay up your tithes and just see if I will not get you out of your trouble". So he said to Israel of old and so to Israel now.
"prove me <u>now</u>" not in a years time "now is the accepted time
"<u>herewith</u>" in this manner. I promise on a condition fulfil that condition – and thus prove me.
"saith the Lord of Hosts" this is no word of man. God the Eternal mentions his name to shew his omnipotence.
"open you the windows of heaven" Heaven has windows for God to look at the world and for him to send blessing down. Mark! all good comes through the windows of heaven – nothing good is traceable to any other quarter Jesus is the window of heaven, its light, the way whereby God pours blessings down. —   "<u>Open</u>" they want opening for sometimes God closes them - never entirely but often partly —   "open <u>you</u>" we want it for ourselves. God opens to others we want him to open to us. —   Man thinks God cannot draw the bolts but God says prove me and see.
"pour you out a blessing" not throw you out a penny but pour out a copious shower. <u>empty</u> out the margin says. i.e. you shall not miss one real blessing.
"not be room enough to receive it"   "your worldly business shall wondrously prosper" says God "if you pay my dues"
Faith make room for a blessing when prayer has sought it but faith seldom makes room enough.

sins robbed God's table of meat. God needs no meat, but surely if he giveth all their meat he has a right to require us to return a portion. Well my friends, if you have not paid your tithes lately, I advise you to cash up, for

2. Here is an exhortation to prove God, by serving him.

"You are depressed? Well then pay up your tithes and just see if I will not get you out of your trouble." So he said to Israel of old and so to Israel now.

"Prove me now." Not in a year's time. "Now["] is the accepted time." "Herewith" in this manner. I promise on a condition. Fulfil that condition and thus prove me.

"Saith the Lord of Hosts." This is no word of man. God the Eternal mentions his name to shew his omnipotence.

"Open you the windows of heaven." Heaven has windows for God to look at the world and for him to send blessings down. Mark! All good comes through the windows of heaven. Nothing good is traceable to any other quarter. Jesus is the window of heaven, its light [is] the way whereby God pours blessings down.

"Open." They want opening, for sometimes God closes them. Never entirely, but often partly. "Open you." We want it for ourselves. God opens to others; we want him to open to us. Man thinks God cannot draw the bolts,[10] but God says, prove me and see.

"Pour you out a blessing." Not throw you out a penny, but pour out a copious shower. Empty out, the margin says,[11] i.e., you shall not miss one real blessing. "Not be room[12] enough to receive it." "Your worldly business shall wondrously prosper, 'says God,'[13] if you pay my dues."

Faith make[s] room for a blessing when prayer has sought it, but faith seldom makes room enough.

In the words is intended. that God will vastly surpass all our expectations, and even do so much that faith shall hardly believe it can be real. She cannot take all in. There may not be room enough for us to take it in but our neighbours barns are often empty and we shall spread God's grace around to others.
This is not all the promise but enough. see verses 11 & 12.

II. I come now to apply the text.
1. To the Ungodly. — you say what profit is there if we serve God — now come and see. give yourself to God.
2. To the young Christian — do your duty and then expect great things. "you shall not have room &c"
3. To the backslider — thou art not prospering but now I tell thee, do thy first works and then thou too shalt be blessed. But if thou robbest God — thou shalt be robbed.
4. To the growing Christian — Brother there is a "yet beyond", which thou dost not now conceive of — on. on. and thou shalt see lands unrecked of.
5. To the Church. If the windows are shut pull the bolts, pay the tithes and open them. Are the windows open — remember they are yet capable of being opened wider — do it — build great barns, strive for greater things. — Pray till the windows are wide open. Let thy word be. The past shall blush, when the future smiles.
14 & 19 G

PROVE ME NOW HEREWITH—*Malachi 3:10*

In the words is intended that God will vastly surpass all our expectations, and even do so much that[14] faith shall hardly believe it can be real. She cannot take all in.

There may not be room enough for us to take it in, but our neighbour[']s[15] barns are often empty, and we shall spread God's grace around to others.

This is not all the promise, but enough.[16] See verses 11 and 12.[17]

II. I COME NOW TO APPLY THE TEXT.

1. To the Ungodly. You say, what profit is there if we serve God? Now come and see. Give yourself to God.

2. To the young Christian. Do your duty and then expect great things.[18] "You shall not have room, etc."

3. To the backslider. Thou art not prospering, but now I tell thee, do thy first works and then thou too shalt be blessed. But if thou robbest God, thou shalt be robbed.

4. To the growing Christian. Brother, there is a "yet beyond" which thou dost not now conceive of.[19] On, on,[20] and thou shalt see lands unrecke[ne]d[21] of.

5. To the Church. If the windows are shut, pull the bolts, pay the tithes, and open them.[22] Are the windows open? Remember, they are yet capable of being opened wider. Do it. Build great barns. Strive for greater things. Pray till the windows are wide open. Let thy word be:

> The[23] past shall blush when the future smiles.[24]

148. 196

SERMON 109

1. On the morning of the Surrey Gardens Music Hall disaster on October 19, 1856, Charles preached a sermon on Mal 3:10 entitled "Proving God" (*MTP* 53, Sermon 3036). The sermon was included in the *MTP* series on April 18, 1907, fifty-one years after he preached it. In Charles's autobiography he reflected, "In the Preface to Vol. II. of *The Pulpit Library*, I wrote:—'The first sermon in this volume—"Prove Me now," Malachi iii:10,—was preached at New Park Street Chapel in the morning of that Lord's-day on which the fatal accident occurred at the Surrey Gardens Music Hall. By many readers it will now be perused with curiosity, but the preacher himself reviews each sentence with thrilling emotion. Its subject was entirely suggested by the enlarged sphere of labour he was about to occupy, and the *then* unprecedented number of souls he was expecting ere nightfall to address. If any passage seems to forestall the calamity, he can only say it is genuine'" (*Autobiography* 2:199, italics in the original). There is not enough overlapping content or structural similarity to suggest Charles had in mind the above sermon when writing his later one.

2. The word "at" was smeared toward the bottom of the page. The letter "t" likely provided the source for the smear.

3. This is the first time Charles deductively listed his sermon divisions before the first Roman numeral. Later in his ministry, this became a common habit.

4. From Icelandic *ninggr*, the adjectival form of the word "niggard" is defined as "sordid; avaricious; parsimonious" (Johnson's *Dictionary*, s.v. "niggard"). Charles's use of the word differed from the racial prejudice conveyed in the modern derivative of the word.

5. The term "quit rent" was common in Spurgeon's day and referred to the amount of money required to close a real estate deal. Approximately six years after Charles preached the sermon above, an advertisement appeared in the *Cambridge Chronicle* for the auctioning of land "*quit rent*" at Littleport ("Old-Licensed Public House and Land, at Littleport. To Be Sold by Auction, by John Cross & Son," *Cambridge Chronicle and University Journal, Isle of Ely Herald, and Huntingdonshire Gazette*, April 10, 1858, italics in the original).

6. The letter "t" appears beneath the "m" in the word "multitude." Charles likely

wrote the first letter of the word "truth" prematurely as he did seven words later in the line below.

7. Charles may have been referring to the State Church Tax, a forced tithe by the Church of England. Several months prior to the preaching of this sermon, *The Cambridge Independent Press* published the minutes of a meeting at Willingham Baptist Chapel. In the meeting Josiah Smith said, "We hold that freedom of thought and liberty of conscience are sacred rights.... [W]e strive for the abolition of tithes and State Churches" ("Willingham.–Church and State," *The Cambridge Independent Press, and Huntingdon, Bedford, & Peterborough Gazette*, January 11, 1851).

8. Charles departed from the modern spelling of the word "tithe" here and instead used the older English form, "tythe."

9. A series of stipples appears above and below the "ings" in the word "shortcomings."

10. Charles refers here to the bolts on windows, not of lightning. On the next page he used the word "bolts" again in his fifth point under his second primary division.

11. The phrase "Empty out" likely appeared in the margin of Charles's Bible. Oxford Hebrew scholar Edward Pocock also noted the marginal notation in his seventeenth-century commentary on Malachi: "Instead of what is in the Text of our Bibles, is put in the Margin, *empty out*, which either must be understood, as that in the Text, or else will not be so clear an expression" (Edward Pocock, *A Commentary on the Prophecy of Malachi* [Oxford: printed at the Theater, 1677], 73, italics in the original).

12. Charles originally placed a period after the word "room." The ink of that period is smeared toward the bottom of the page.

13. Charles placed double quotation marks around "says God" because he was quoting Mal 3:10. Single quotation marks have been inserted to show this is a quotation inside a quotation.

14. An ink blot appears above the letter "t" in the word "that."

15. The absence of the apostrophe at the end of the word "neighbours" makes uncertain whether Charles intended the word to be in the singular or plural possessive.

16. The letter "g" appears beneath "o" in the word "enough."

17. The handwriting of the phrase "see verses 11 & 12" differs from that in the body of the sermon. Charles likely inserted it into the margin afterward.

18. Charles may have had in mind an expression used by William Carey on May 31, 1792, in a sermon on Isa 54:2–3: "First, *Expect great things from God*; Second, *Attempt great things for God*" (James Culross, *William Carey* [New York: A. C. Armstrong and Son, 1882], 44, italics in the original).

19. Charles originally wrote the word "off." However, the context suggests the correct word is "of," and the addition of the final letter "f" was unintentional.

20. The words "On, on" may be an example of dittography. More likely, however, is the modern reading "[Go] on, [go] on" or "On[ward], on[ward]." See also Charles's use of the expression "Go on" in his sermon "Envy Forbidden, Piety Commanded" (Sermon 112).

21. Charles originally wrote the word "unrecked." However, the context suggests he intended to write "unreckoned." A modern reading of this line is "You will see lands not thought of."

22. In early nineteenth-century Britain, windows were often taxed, and many citizens boarded them up to avoid having to pay this fee. The attic in Charles's grandfather's study in Stambourne is an example of one such window. Charles referred to it as the "light-excluding tax" (*Autobiography* 1:22). Efforts were undertaken to abolish this tax (See "The Window Tax," *The Lincolnshire Chronicle and Northampton, Rutland, and Nottingham Advertiser*, March 3, 1848).

23. The letter "T" in the word "The" is heavily smeared toward the lower left. The entire sentence is written with noticeably greater pressure and is distinctly darker than the preceding text.

24. "Oh, for more conversions! more hearts for Jesus! Would that the dews of heaven would fall in sevenfold abundance upon us, and our fellow Christians, and the past be put to blush by the future!" (*MTP* 20:14).

Matthew XXVIII. 19. 20. The minister's commission.

We expect that men professing to be ambassadors should shew their warrant from court, and on such important business as soul affairs we should do wrong to trust without good grounds — Where does the Mormonite find his commission to take all men to the Salt Lake? and where is the navy to carry us over.   Well. Here's my commission.

I. Gospel ministers are to "go and teach all nations".
*(Jesus was speaking to poor fishermen and tells them to go and teach) — we shall notice.

1. The teachers. (Supply) poor fishermen, yet they are to go — no curates — no waiting for a fine education.

2. Their duty — "Ye" do not wait for people to come "go" at all hazards, in the midst of dangers go — not send tracts and Bibles but "go ye" — for preaching is the great means of men's conversion. — "teach" you seem to be ignorant but I tell you ye shall be wise enough to teach. not fight, not force, not entice they were to "disciple" all nations as the original has it, not that this is possible for man to do alone but we are to preach as if it were — yea even more confidently remembering the promise appended. teach men, their sin, the punishment of sin, the death and atonement of Jesus and justification by faith alone. These are things which men knew not except as the gospel revealed it unto them. Another form of this commission says "preach" which means "cry out" to shew that it should be done in right earnest style. we teach but not as Irene, nor as schoolmasters.

THE MINISTER'S COMMISSION—*Matthew 28:19–20*

110

The MINISTER'S COMMISSION
Matthew[1] 28:19–20[2]

"Go ye therefore, and teach all nations, baptizing them in the name of the Father, and of the Son, and of the Holy Ghost; teaching them to observe all things whatsoever I have commanded you: and, lo, I am with you always even unto the end of the world. Amen."

We expect that men professing to be ambassadors should shew their warrant from court, and on such important business as soul affairs we should do wrong to trust without good grounds. Where does the Mormonite find his commission to take all men to the Salt Lake?[3] And where is the navy to carry us over? Well, here's my commission:

I. GOSPEL MINISTERS ARE TO "GO AND TEACH ALL NATIONS."

★(Jesus was speaking to poor fishermen and tells them to go and teach)

We shall notice:

1. The teachers. (^Supply^)[4] [They are] poor fisherman, yet they are to go. No curates. No waiting for a fine education.[5]

2. Their duty. "Go." Do not wait for people to come. "Go." At all hazards, in the midst of dangers, go. Not send tracts[6] and Bibles, but "go ye," for preaching is the great means of men's conversion. "Teach." You seem to be ignorant, but I tell you ye shall be wise enough to teach. Not fight, not force, not entice. They were to "disciple" all nations, as the original has it.[7] Not that this is possible for man to do alone, but we are to preach as if it were. Yea, even more confidently remembering the promise appended. Teach men their sin, the punishment of sin,[8] the death and atonement of Jesus,[9] and justification by faith alone.[10]

These are things which men knew not except as the gospel revealed it unto them. Another form of this commission says "preach," which means "cry out," to shew that it should be done in right, earnest style. We teach, but not as some, nor as schoolmasters.

3. The persons to be taught or made disciples of "all nations" not Jews alone but gentiles. Not the unlearned but the wise also. Not the rich alone but all — not good men but all. However they may fancy they do not want it all nations.

II. Having discipled men we are next to "baptize". Teaching is first because it is most important & also because it comes first in order. Baptize means to dip in water, to bury in water — to shew that now the man professes to die to sin & hopes that his sins are washed away. Teaching is made one of God's means in order to curb man's vanity, and Baptism is made the initiatory ceremony in order to see whether he is made really like a child. It shews too that before man can enter into communion with God he must be washed. Infants cannot be taught and ought not to be baptized. No man has any right to reverse God's order. Do not think we are wrong in wanting to have men baptized for here is our grand warrant.

III. They are to baptize men in the name of the Trinity. Since all three approve of the ordinance, witness the Baptism of Jesus. Since the candidate is under obligations to all and in this ordinance solemnly consecrates himself to all. He is baptized in their name & shall if a true saint be one day baptized in their holy nature. It says

THE MINISTER'S COMMISSION—*Matthew 28:19–20*

3. The persons to be taught or made disciples of "all nations." Not Jews alone, but Gentiles.[11] Not the unlearned, but the wise also. Not the rich alone, but all. Not good men, but all. However they may fancy[12] they do not want it,[13] all "nations."

II. HAVING DISCIPLED MEN, WE ARE NEXT TO "BAPTIZE."

Teaching is first because it is most important, and also because it comes first in order. Baptize means to dip in water, to bury in water, to shew that now the man professes to die to sin and hopes that his sins are washed away.

Teaching is made one of God's means in order to curb man's vanity, and Baptism[14] is made the initiatory ceremony in order to see whether he is made really like a child. It shows, too, that before man can enter into communion with God he must be washed.

Infants cannot be taught and ought not to be baptized.[15] No man has any right to reverse God's order. Do not think we are wrong in wanting to have men baptized, for here is our grand warrant.

III. THEY ARE TO BAPTIZE MEN IN THE NAME OF THE TRINITY SINCE ALL THREE APPROVE OF THE ORDINANCE.

Witness the Baptism of Jesus.[16] Since the candidate is under obligations to all, and in this ordinance solemnly consecrates himself to all, he is baptized in their name and shall, if a true saint, be one day baptized in their holy nature. It says name, to shew the Unity of the Trinity – each verily God but still only <u>one</u>. Socinian shut thy silly mouth.

<u>IV</u>. He mentions teaching again to shew its importance. "all things". all the ordinances. Baptism & the Supper. all doctrines, keeping back no one on any pretence. all duties, moral, civil, relative or religious. teach them no traditions but "whatsoever I have commanded"

<u>V</u>. A sweet promise concludes the commission. "I am now leaving in person but I will be with you by the Holy Spirit". As indeed he was with the apostles always, if he were once away – Ah then! Ah then! for ever, to the end. of the Gospel dispensation, he is with all his ministers. He is with us to protect. He tells us what to speak. He helps us in speaking. He applies the truth when spoken – well is it said <u>Amen</u>. this is Christ's amen to certify it It is the amen of the Church. It is the evangelist's amen. It is mine. Is it yours?

Now may God help me to teach once more. yea to preach, and cry out with burning soul. The Lord grant I may be guiltless of the dear people's blood – <u>Amen. Amen, Amen</u>

149.

THE MINISTER'S COMMISSION—*Matthew 28:19-20*

name to shew the Unity of the Trinity. Each verily God, but still only <u>one</u>. Socinian, shut thy silly mouth.[17]

IV. HE MENTIONS TEACHING AGAIN TO SHEW ITS IMPORTANCE.

"<u>All things</u>." All the ordinances.[18] Baptism and the Supper. All doctrines. Keeping back no one on any pretence. All duties: moral, civil, relative, or religious. Teach them no traditions, but "<u>whatsoever I have commanded</u>."

V. A SWEET PROMISE CONCLUDES THE COMMISSION.

"I am now leaving in person, but I will be with you by the Holy Spirit."[19] As indeed he was with the apostles <u>always</u>, if he were once away—Ah then! Ah then! For ever, to the end of the Gospel dispensation he is with all his ministers.[20] He is with us to protect. He tells us what to speak. He helps us in speaking. He applies the truth when spoken. Well is it said <u>Amen</u>.

This is Christ's amen to certify it. It is the amen of the Church. It is the evangelist's amen. It is mine. Is it yours?

Now may God help me to teach once[21] more. Yea, to preach and cry out with burning soul.

The Lord grant I may be guiltless of the dear people's blood. <u>Amen. Amen. Amen.</u>

149.

SERMON 110

1. A purple ink blot appears beneath the letter "a" in the word "Matthew." A similar blot can be found on the previous page above the word "that" in the second line. Charles may have begun revising the sermons in this notebook for publication in 1857. Many of his later sermon redactions were written in purple ink as well. See also the purple stain in "The Noble Bereans" (Sermon 114).

2. Charles preached two additional sermons on Matt 28:19–20: "The Missionaries' Charge and Charts" (*MTP* 7, Sermon 383) and "The Power of the Risen Saviour" (*MTP* 20, Sermon 1200). There is not enough overlapping content or structural similarity to suggest Charles had in mind the above sermon when writing his later ones.

3. Joseph Smith published the Book of Mormon in 1830, four years before Charles was born. In June 1844, Smith was murdered in a prison in Carthage, Illinois, by a mob of 200 men. Brigham Young was elected as the prophet of the burgeoning religion; in 1847, only five years before Charles preached the sermon above, Mormonism took root in Salt Lake City, Utah, when Young first arrived there with his pioneers (see "Mormonism," *Reading Mercury, Oxford Gazette, Newbury Herald, and Berks County Paper; General Advertiser for Berks, Bucks, Hants, Oxon, Somerset, Surrey, Sussex, Middlesex, and Wilts*, March 25, 1854). By 1850, Mormonism had succeeded in popularity and organization in Utah. Some equated the movement with the formation of a nation (see "The Mormons," *The Stirling Observer*, September 12, 1850). Charles referenced the growth of Mormonism in his earliest Waterbeach sermons (see "What Think Ye of Christ?" [Notebook 1, Sermon 70]), and also after he moved to London. In 1854, Charles called Mormonism "the haggard superstition of the West" (*MTP* 50:535). The following year he labeled it "the accursed imposture of the West that has lately arisen" and denounced its practice of polygamy (*NPSP* 1:207). In his personal library Charles owned the following two books: Joseph Smith, trans., *The Book of Mormon: An Account Written by the Hand of Mormon, upon Plates Taken from the Plates of Nephi, Fifth European Edition. Stereotyped* (Liverpool: F. D. Richards; London: sold at the L. D. Saints' Book Depot, 1854, The Spurgeon Library) and *The Mormons; or, Latter-Day Saints with Memoirs of the Life and Death of Joseph Smith the "American Mahomet." Third Edition, Illustrated with Forty Engravings* (London: published at 227 Strand, 1852, The Spurgeon Library). Charles may have possessed the latter book when he wrote the sermon above. For additional references to Joseph Smith and Mormonism in this notebook, see "Justification by Imputed Righteousness" (Sermon 117).

4. As also demonstrated in his sermons "The Wise Men's Offerings" (Notebook 1, Sermon 58) and "Christ's Constant Intercession" (Sermon 126), Charles inserted an asterisk in his sermon to indicate the location of a footnote. In this instance Charles inserted the asterisk immediately following his first point, "The teachers," to indicate the location of the sentence he wrote in the line above, "(Jesus was speaking to poor fishermen and tells them to go and teach)." When the two sentences are combined, they read, "Jesus was speaking to poor fishermen and tells them to go and teach. [They are] poor fisherman, yet *they* are to go" (emphasis added). Charles wrote the word "Supply" in superscript above the asterisk.

5. Charles may have had in mind his decision not to pursue formal academic education at Stepney College. Cf. "The Dog and Swine" (Sermon 85).

6. Before moving to Cambridge and immediately after his conversion in January 1850, Charles distributed tracts at Newmarket. In a letter to his mother on February 19, 1850, Charles wrote, "I have 33 houses at present where I leave tracts.... Oh, how I wish that I could do something for Christ! Tract-distribution is so pleasant and easy that it is a nothing—nothing in itself, much less when it is compared with the amazing debt of gratitude I owe" (Angus Library and Archive, Regent's Park College, Oxford University, D/SPU 1, Letter 1).

7. Charles likely consulted John Gill's *Exposition of the New Testament*, which noted, "[T]he antecedent to the relative *them*, cannot be *all nations*; since παντα τα εθνη, the words for *all nations*, are of the neuter gender, whereas αυτους, *them*, is of the masculine: nor can it be thought that it should be the mind of Christ, that all the individuals of all nations should be baptized, as heathens, *Turks*, and *Jews*; but μαθευτας, *disciples*, supposed and contained in the word μαθετευσατε, *teach*, or *make disciples*; such as are taught, and made disciples by teaching, or under the ministry of the word by the spirit of God" (Gill, *Exposition of the New Testament*, 1:337, italics in the original).

8. Cf. Rom 6:23.

9. Cf. 1 John 2:2.

10. Cf. Rom 4:5; 5:1; Gal 2:16.

11. Cf. Isa 65:1; Rom 3:29; 9:24.

12. Cf. "fancy" in "Inventory and Title of Our Treasures" (Sermon 92).

13. An alternative reading of this line is "However they may fancy, they do not want it."

SERMON 110

14. An ink residue caused by the asterisk and parenthesis on the back side of the page appears between the letters "B" and "a" in the word "Baptism."

15. Charles was baptized as an infant by his paternal grandfather, James Spurgeon, on August 3, 1834, in Stambourne.

16. Cf. Matt 3:13–17.

17. Cf. "Pleasures in the Stones of Zion" (Notebook 1, Sermon 53).

18. Cf. "God's Estimation of Men" (Notebook 1, Sermon 41).

19. This is a paraphrase of John 16:7, "Nevertheless I tell you the truth; It is expedient for you that I go away: for if I go not away, the Comforter will not come unto you; but if I depart, I will send him unto you." For additional examples of Charles's use of paraphrase, see "The Physician and His Patients" (Notebook 1, Sermon 74).

20. Matthew 28:20, "Teaching them to observe all things whatsoever I have commanded you: and, lo, I am with you always, even unto the end of the world. Amen."

21. The letter "e" appears beneath the "c" in the word "once." Charles originally wrote the word "one" before changing it to "once."

111. Prov. III. 35.   Wise men and fools.

Many believe the Scriptures who yet give little heed to it, and many will speak well of Solomon who yet despise his advice and will not listen to his counsel. But now if Solomon deserve it just attend to him.

I. The true Christian is the "wise" man here meant. The learned and knowing will many of them perish. But a man may be a wise man and yet know very little. Yea, a truly wise man, and yet have but little judgment. — Such for the most part are Christians. Unlearned wise men. Ignorant yet wondrously wise. Wisdom is the right use of knowledge and knowledge is only useful when it is turned into practical wisdom. Wisdom is founded on knowledge.   Now the Christian

1. Knows there is a God — knows that he is almighty &c — and turns this into wisdom by making God his friend.
2. He knows the bible is true — he reads it, studies it, obeys its precepts, believes the doctrines.
3. He knows he is a sinner — he acts wisely, he repents, he grasps Jesus as his Saviour.
4. He knows there is a future state — He lives in preparation for it, he lays up treasures in it.
5. He knows that Jesus is all in all — He therefore puts his own works in the fire and trusts for all.

The Christian's wisdom lies not in the extent of his knowledge, but in a judicious use of what he has.   The Christian is wise only by grace. he has been put to school with a good teacher

111

WISE MEN *and* FOOLS
Proverbs 3:35[1]

"The wise shall inherit glory: but shame shall be the promotion of fools."

Many believe the Scriptures who yet give little heed to it, and many will speak well of Solomon who yet despise his advice[2] and will not listen to his counsel.

But now, if Solomon deserve[s] it, just attend to him.

I. THE TRUE CHRISTIAN IS THE "WISE" MAN HERE MEANT.

The learned and knowing will, many of them, perish. But a man may be a wise man and yet know very little. Yea, [he may be] a truly wise man and yet have but little judgment.[3] Such, for the most part, are Christia[ns]. Unlearned wise men.[4] Ignorant, yet wondrously wise. Wisdom is the right use of knowledge,[5] and knowledge is only useful when it is turned into practical wisdom. Wisdom is founded on knowledge. Now, the Christian:

1. Knows there is a God, knows that he is almighty, etc., and turns this into wisdom by making God[6] his friend.

2. He knows the [B]ible is true. He reads it, studies it, obeys its precepts, believes the doctrines.

3. He knows he is a sinner. He acts wisely, he repents, he grasps Jesus as his Saviour.

4. He knows there is a future state. He lives in preparation for it. He lays up treasures in it.[7]

5. He knows that Jesus is all in all.[8] He therefore puts his own works in the fire and trusts for all. The Christian's wisdom lies not in the extent of his knowledge, but in a judicious use of what he has.

The Christian is wise only by grace. He has been put to school with a good teacher.[9]

SERMON 111

<u>II</u>. The ungodly are the "fools" here meant.

Fools because they put their heads into the Devil's mouth. Fools because knowing there is a God & believing the Bible they yet live practical infidels. Fools to have sin though they know well that hell is the consequence. Fools because they lose the solid pleasures of religion — and heaven at last.

The hypocrite is a fool, since he cannot deceive God.

The Sunday-man is a fool — God will have the week too.

The Gambler is a fool. he will gamble his soul away too.

The Card-player is a fool, to worship papers.

The Loose & Giddy are fools, thus to dance on hell's mouth.

The Drunkard is a great fool — not a beast would do it, — what foolish things some men do in drink & for it.

The Swearer — is a fool to make God his enemy.

Old Sinners are old fools — Young Sinners have the fool's cap on their heads. Crowds of fools.

<u>III</u>. The truly wise shall inherit glory.

Sometimes they have respect on earth, but oftener they are the song of the drunkard — hated for Christ. They shall "inherit" not purchase — it is all of grace. Now how right it is that the sons of God should live with their Father & that his servants should have wages.

Glory — aye — Eternal Glory —

<u>IV</u>. The Fool shall be exalted by shame.

No higher promotion for him — the depths of hell will be his highest rise. Shame when they die — when in judgment — when with the Lost. You will all be ashamed if now you are ashamed of Jesus.

150.

II. THE UNGODLY ARE THE "FOOLS" HERE MEANT.

Fools because they put their heads into the Devil's mouth. Fools because, knowing there is a God and believing the Bible, they yet live [as] practical infidels. Fools to have sin, though they know well that hell is the consequence. Fools because they lose the solid pleasures of religion and heaven at last.

> The hypocrite is a fool since he cannot deceive God.[10]
>
> The Sunday-man is a fool. God will have the week, too.
>
> The Gambler is a fool. He will gamble his soul away, too.
>
> The Card-player is a fool to worship papers.
>
> The Loose and Giddy are fools thus to dance on hell's mouth.
>
> The Drunkard is a great fool. Not a beast would do it. What foolish things some men do in drink and for it.
>
> The Swearer is a fool to make God his enemy.
>
> Old Sinners are old fools.
>
> Young Sinners have the fool's cap[11] on their heads. Crowds of fools.

III. THE TRULY WISE SHALL INHERIT GLORY.

Sometimes they have respect on earth, but oftener they are the song of the drunkard, hated for Christ. They shall "inherit," not purchase. It is all of grace.[12] Now, how right it is that the sons of God should live with their Father and that[13] his servants should have wages.

> Glory, aye, Eternal Glory.

IV. THE FOOL SHALL BE EXALTED BY SHAME.

No higher promotion for him. The depths of hell will be his highest rise. Shame when they die, when in judgment, when with the Lost. You will all be ashamed if now you are ashamed of Jesus.[14]

150.

SERMON 111

1. This is the only time Charles preached a sermon on Prov 3:35.

2. Charles originally wrote the letter "s" beneath the "c" in the word "advice."

3. An alternative reading of this line is "Yea, [he can be] a truly wise man, and yet have but little judgment."

4. An alternative reading of this line is "Such, for the most part, are Christia[ns], unlearned wise men."

5. Charles bolded the letters "kn" in the word "knowledge," likely by accident.

6. Charles originally did not capitalize the word "god." He inserted the capital "G" afterward.

7. Matthew 6:20, "But lay up for yourselves treasures in heaven, where neither moth nor rust doth corrupt, and where thieves do not break through nor steal."

8. Colossians 3:11, "Where there is neither Greek nor Jew, circumcision nor uncircumcision, Barbarian, Scythian, bond nor free: but Christ is all, and in all."

9. The handwriting in the two sentences "The Christian is wise only by grace" and "He has been put to school with a good teacher" differs both in size and pressure. Either Charles intended these two sentences to be emphasized, or he wrote them at different times.

10. Galatians 6:7, "Be not deceived; God is not mocked: for whatsoever a man soweth, that shall he also reap."

11. Johnson does not offer a definition for the words "fool's cap." According to Worcester's 1859 *Dictionary*, it is "the cap of a fool" (Joseph Worcester, *A Dictionary of the English Language* [London: Sampson Low, Son & Co., 1859, The Spurgeon Library], s.v. "Fool's-Cap"). Another name for fool's-cap was "dunce cap." Worcester defined the word "dunce" as "a foolish person; a thickskull; a dolt; a simpleton; a blockhead" (Worcester's *Dictionary*). According to an article published approximately two years before Charles preached the sermon above, a "dunce's cap" was placed on the head of six-year-old Edward Hyde as a method of punishment ("Cruelty to a Child," *The Kilkenny Journal, and Leinster Commercial, and Literary Advertiser*, March 9, 1850).

12. In his diary entry for May 12, 1850, Charles wrote, "'Tis all of grace. I can do nothing, I am less than nothing; yet what a difference,—once a slave of hell, now the son of the God of Heaven! Help me to walk worthy of my lofty and exalted vocation!" (*Autobiography* 1:137). Charles used the phrase "all of grace" on numerous occasions throughout his ministry, including in the title of his 1886 publication *All of Grace. An Earnest Word with Those Who Are Seeking Salvation by the Lord Jesus Christ* (New York: Robert Carter & Brothers, 1886, The Spurgeon Library). This book had "the double distinction of having been translated into more foreign languages and of having been blessed to the salvation of more souls than any other of Mr. Spurgeon's works" (*Autobiography* 4:308). Thomas wrote a poem about his father's book: "'All of grace'—from base to summit, / Grace on every course and stone; / Grace in planning, rearing, crowning, / Sovereign grace, and grace alone!" (W. Y. Fullerton, *Thomas Spurgeon: A Biography* [London, New York, Toronto: Hodder and Stoughton, 1919], 124). Charles quoted his son's poem in his sermon "A Testimony to Free and Sovereign Grace" (*MTP* 33:162). For two sermons containing the phrase "all of grace" in their titles, see "Salvation All of Grace" (*MTP* 19, Sermon 1064) and "All of Grace" (*MTP* 61, Sermon 3479). See also *NPSP* 3:370; *MTP* 9:preface; 12:432; 13:447; 15:128; 19:334; 26:421; 32:262; 41:531; 47:324; *ST* January 1887:3–10; *Lectures* 1:147–48. On January 16, 1859, Charles summarized the entirety of his ministry with the phrase "all of grace." "If any of you want to know what I preach every day, and any stranger should say, 'Give me a summary of his doctrine,' say this, 'He preaches salvation all of grace, and damnation all of sin'" (*NPSP* 5:119).

13. Charles originally wrote the word "this" before changing it to "that."

14. Cf. Mark 8:38; Luke 9:26.

O.3.52. 112 Prov. 23.17.18 – Envy forbidden, piety commanded.

The Bible infinitely above all other books, gives a faithful description of the human heart, the most admirable rules for holy living, and the most useful helps thereto. Solomon speaks wisdom – Some of the Rabbi's think that the words "his leaf also shall not wither" means than even the trifling observations of good men shall be treasured – Surely then inspired fragments demand peculiar attention. Here is

I. A disease spoken of "Envy of sinners."
All sinners are not envied, some are objects of quite a contrary emotion See the wretch enfeebled by debauchery or drunkenness – the thief in chains – the murderer hung. but some are very much envied – for their riches, their merriment, the applause they enjoy. but we are not to do so but to lay aside all envy.

1. Envy is at all times wrong – It is an importation from hell. it is the parent of the foulest crimes – Joseph & Jesus. it is forbidden by law – it hurts ourselves

2. Envy of sinners. is treasonable. It looks like being tired of God, careless of heaven. it is rebellion to our great king – It shows great unbelief & carnality

3. Envy of sinners is abominably foolish. how are they really more happy? When Conscience frowns and God abhors why envy? God gives them all now – The Husks should go to the swine. –

II. The cure for this disease. "Be in the fear of the Lord. not go and have a little of those pleasure but

ENVY FORBIDDEN, PIETY COMMANDED—*Proverbs 23:17–18*

V3.52.[1]

112

ENVY FORBIDDEN, PIETY COMMANDED
Proverbs 23:17–18[2]

"Let not thine heart envy sinners: but be thou in the fear of the Lord *all the day long. For surely there is an end; and thine expectation shall not be cut off."*

The Bible, infinitely above all other books, gives a faithful description of the human heart, the most admirable rules for holy living,[3] and the most useful helps thereto. Solomon speaks wisdom. Some of the Rabbis[4] think that the words "his leaf also shall not wither"[5] means tha[t][6] even the trifling observations of good men shall be treasured. Surely, then, inspired fragments demand peculiar attention. Here is:

I. A DISEASE SPOKEN OF. *"Envy of[7] sinners."*

All sinners are not envied. Some are objects of quite a contrary emotion. See the wretch enfeebled by debauchery or drunkenness, the thief in chains, the murderer hung. But some are very much envied for their riches, their merriment, the applause they enjoy. But we are not to do so, but to lay aside all envy.

1. Envy is at all times wrong. It is an[8] importation from hell.[9] It is the parent of the foulest crimes. Joseph[10] and Jesus.[11] It is forbidden by law.[12] It hurts ourselves.[13]

2. Envy of sinners is treasonable.[14] It looks like being tired of God, careless of heaven. It is rebellion to our great king. It shows great unbelief and carnality.

3. Envy of sinners is abominably foolish.[15] How are they really more happy? When Conscience frowns and God abhors, why envy?[16] God gives them all now. The Husks should go to the swine.[17]

II. THE CURE FOR THIS DISEASE. *"Be in the fear of the Lord.*[*"*]

Not, go and have a little of those pleasure[s], but

get more religion. Fear of God means all true religion.
1. Live always believing there is a God.
2. Live remembering "thou God seest me"
3. Live thinking of his divine character.
4. Live in love to him.

"All the day" begin, go on, and end with God. Go no where without God, take him with you. Go to nothing upon which you dare not ask his blessing. Get so much religion that you shall be happy with it. Never go one inch from the line

III. A further remedy in a solemn consideration.
1. Death is coming on and awful judgment.
2. The joys of the wicked shall soon end.
3. Thy troubles shall soon end.
4. Thou shalt soon have thine expectation satisfied.

1 Sinner, see thy danger. — the end surely comes.
2. Saint, behold thy duty — pray, pity the sinner
3. Let all men see the instability of mortal things.

152.

get more religion. Fear of God means all true religion.

1. Live always believing there is a God.
2. Live remembering "thou God seest me."[18]
3. Live thinking of his divine character.[19]
4. Live in love to him.[20]

"All the day." Begin, go on,[21] and end with God. Go no where without God. Take him with you. Go to nothing upon which you dare not ask his blessing. Get so much religion that you[22] shall be happy with it. Never go one inch from the line.[23]

III. A FURTHER REMEDY IN A SOLEMN CONSIDERATION.

1. Death[24] is coming on and awful judgment.
2. The joys of the wicked[25] shall soon end.[26]
3. Thy troubles shall soon end.[27]
4. Thou shalt soon have thine expectation satisfied.

1. Sinner, see thy danger. The end surely comes.[28]
2. Saint, behold thy duty. Pray, pity the sinner.[29]
3. Let all men see the instability of mortal things.[30]

152.

SERMON 112

1. This is the final of the four sermons in Notebook 2 in which Charles cited the publication *Sketches of Sermons* (see also "Inventory and Title of Our Treasures" [Sermon 92]; "The Tranquillity, Security, and Supplies Afforded to the Gospel Church" [Sermon 97]; and "Justification, Conversion, Sanctification, Glory" [Sermon 102]). The inscription V3.52—volume 3, sermon 52—is incorrect. The accurate reference is actually V3.62 since the sermon Charles cited, "A Caution Against Envy, and a Call to Piety" (*Sketches of Sermons* 3:250–54), is sermon 62 instead of 52. Overlapping content is noted below.

2. On June 22, 1890, Charles preached an additional sermon on Prov 23:17–18 entitled "All the Day Long" (*MTP* 36, Sermon 2150). There is not enough overlapping content or structural similarity to suggest Charles had the above sermon in mind when writing his later one.

3. "The Proverbs of Solomon contain some of the finest maxims of morality, and the most admirable rules of holy living with which the world has ever been favoured" (*Sketches of Sermons* 3:250). Charles departed from the sermon outline by originating the remainder of the introduction.

4. Charles likely consulted John Gill's *Exposition of the Old Testament*, which cited Rabbi Yitzchak Arama's commentary on Ps 1:3 (Gill, *An Exposition of the Old Testament* 3:493). Charles originally inserted an apostrophe before the letter "s" in the word "Rabbis." The context suggests, however, he intended this word to be plural, not possessive.

5. Psalm 1:3, "And he shall be like a tree planted by the rivers of water, that bringeth forth his fruit in his season; his leaf also shall not wither; and whatsoever he doeth shall prosper."

6. Charles originally wrote the word "than." However, the context suggests a better reading is the word "that."

7. Charles originally misspelled the word "envy." He reinforced the letter "v" and also added an additional letter beneath the "o" in the word "of."

8. Charles originally wrote the word "am" before striking through the arc and arm of the letter "m" to construct the letter "n."

9. "When God made man, it formed no part of his character, it had no existence in his mind. It was then the sole property of the devil; this moved him to meditate the ruin of mankind: hence envy is the basest, most degrading, and most fiendlike disposition that can possibly find dominion in a human spirit; and nothing can be more mischievous" (*Sketches of Sermons* 3:251).

10. Cf. Gen 37:11.

11. "Some of the foulest crimes that have been ever perpetrated upon the earth have been the offspring of envy. 'The Patriarchs, moved with envy, sold Joseph into Egypt,' Acts vii. 9. How cruel to sell a brother so innocent and so unoffending! What a deep and lasting affliction to an aged parent! The murder of the Prince of Life resulted from this principle; for when the Jews delivered him to Pilate, he knew that for envy they delivered him" (*Sketches of Sermons* 3:251). Cf. Matt 27:18.

12. Exodus 20:17, "Thou shalt not covet thy neighbour's house, thou shalt not covet thy neighbour's wife, nor his manservant, nor his maidservant, nor his ox, nor his ass, nor any thing that is thy neighbour's."

13. "But envy is not less injurious to ourselves than others" (*Sketches of Sermons* 3:251).

14. Charles departed from *Sketches of Sermons* by writing the word "treasonable" instead of "absurd" (cf. *Sketches of Sermons* 3:251). He may have been inspired by the phrase "To envy sinners is unjust" (3:252).

15. "It is foolish to envy sinners: even now their circumstances are most pitiable" (*Sketches of Sermons* 3:251).

16. "Conscience condemns them; heaven frowns upon them; hell is moved from beneath to meet them: and oh! their end will be destruction" (*Sketches of Sermons* 3:251).

17. The expression "The Husks should go to the swine" was common to the Victorians. In the same year Charles preached the sermon above, *The Waterford News* published an article condemning the treatment of tenants, or "laboring serfs," by their landlords: "Are there no filthy dens on their estates where their human fellow-creatures are degraded to the social level of the meanest and most

disgusting brute?—where men, women, and children, who are heirs of eternity, through whose eyes an immortal soul looks out, associate with swine, and feed on the husks of swine?" ("The Portlaw Agricultural Show," *The Waterford News and General Weekly Advertiser*, October 22, 1852).

18. "Often say to yourself, 'thou God seest me,' and remember, in all the labour of your hands, 'that for these things God will bring you into judgment'" (*Sketches of Sermons* 3:253).

19. "*1. To be in possession of correct and spiritual ideas of his holy and exalted character.* How erroneous are the notions men entertain of God! . . . Some think God is altogether such a one as themselves" (*Sketches of Sermons* 3:252, italics in the original).

20. "*To cultivate suitable dispositions of heart towards him.* Not only to think of God as he really is, but to feel towards him all those affectionate, reverential, and devout dispositions which his nature and character are calculated to inspire. . . . Let your voice be heard every morning, in the sacred and hallowed exercises of prayer and praise. What gratitude is due to God for the mercies of the night, to have laid down in peace, and arose in safety; what reason for prayer, that God may defend and provide for us!" (*Sketches of Sermons* 3:252, italics in the original). Cf. John 15:9.

21. See also Charles's use of the expression "On, on" in the sermon "Prove Me Now Herewith" (Sermon 109).

22. The letter "e" appears beneath the "o" in the word "you." Charles likely wrote the word "ye" before updating it.

23. The expression "Never go one inch from the line" is similar to "I'll not budge an inch" in William Shakespeare's *The Taming of the Shrew* (Stephen Greenblatt, eds., et al, *The Norton Shakespeare: Based on the Oxford Edition, Second Edition, with an Essay on the Shakespearean Stage by Andrew Gurr* [New York and London: W. W. Norton, 2008], 170, lines 5–6). For Charles's personal copy of Shakespeare's poems, see George Gilfillan, *The Poetical Works of William Shakespeare and the Earl of Surrey. with Memoirs, Critical Dissertations, and Explanatory Notes* (Edinburgh: James Nichol, 1856, The Spurgeon Library). See also footnotes for "Abraham Justified by Faith" (Notebook 1, Sermon 3).

24. Charles reinforced the letters "ath" in the word "Death," likely by accident. A similar pressure in the writing instrument is found in Roman numeral III in the line above.

25. Charles may have originally added the letter "s" to the end of the word "wicked" before striking through it.

26. "*There is an end to that prosperity with which the efforts of sinners are crowned.* Have they riches? they will either escape through their instability, or sinners will soon be constrained to leave them. Have they honours? these will soon be torn from them. Have they pleasures? these must shortly end. There is an end, this is certain, Ps. xxxvii. 35.36. This end may come suddenly, 1 Thess. v.3; Ps. lxxiii. 17–19. Who then can envy sinners?" (*Sketches of Sermons* 3:253, italics in the original).

27. "*There is an end to the tribulations of the saints.* Their afflictions are light and momentary. From all temptations they will soon obtain an eternal deliverance. The storm of persecution will ere long blow over. Want and pain will soon end, 'For they shall hunger no more,' &c. Rev. vii. 16" (*Sketches of Sermons* 3:253, italics in the original).

28. "From the text—Sinners may learn their awful situation; they may prosper in this world, but their prosperity will soon end" (*Sketches of Sermons* 3:254).

29. "Saints may learn their duty; instead of envying sinners, they should pity them, pray for them, set them good examples, and try to save them" (*Sketches of Sermons* 3:254).

30. "And all may learn that the present state is preparatory to a fixed, final, and endless life" (*Sketches of Sermons* 3:254).

SERMON 113

113. S.97 Hos. XIV. 5.7 —   God's visits and the effects thereof.

No poetry equal to the poetry of the Bible — its imagery is matchless, sublime, yet simple.   As employed to set forth the most important truths — they are doubly precious. Now in these verses are both poetry and importance.

I. God's favour to his people. "I will be as the dew to Israel" Dew at the creation supplied the place of rain and in tropical countries it falls in most copious abundance. All men are naturally barren and need dew to fall on them — but on none does it fall save on Israel, on God's elect, on the Godly — Dew never falls on places destitute of vegetation. —   God's Israel ever need the dew and particularly after a drought of backsliding. —   Hypocrites and Pharisees can water with their watering pots — but the true Israel want dew. This God has promised and under this figure gives

1. A plentiful supply — the dews on Israel are very heavy
2. Often an imperceptible supply — there is no noise about it.
3. An effectual supply — the silent dew does its work, it insinuates itself into the soil
4. A constant supply — no perishing if God manages the clouds.

The dew falls in the night — so do God's blessings often come to us in trouble.   Well this dew is soon seen producing

II. The effects produced on God's people by the dew. These are visible in the plant and are

1. A beautiful upgrowing in divine love and spirituality like the lily. — The daffodil lily springs up quickly on the first fall of dew — here is a fine emblem of a Christian full of his first love — green and beautiful — but with this is
2. A strong secret downgrowing — in knowledge of divine

S. 97[1]

GOD'S VISITS *and the* EFFECTS THEREOF
Hosea 14:5–7[2]

"I will be as the dew unto Israel: he shall grow as the lily, and cast forth his roots as Lebanon. His branches shall spread, and his beauty shall be as the olive tree, and his smell as Lebanon. They that dwell under his shadow shall return; they shall revive as the corn, and grow as the vine: the scent thereof shall be as the wine of Lebanon."

No poetry [is] equal to the poetry of the Bible.[3] Its imagery is matchless,[4] sublime yet simple.[5] As employed to set forth the most important truths, they are doubly precious. Now, in these verses are both poetry and importance.

I. **GOD'S FAVOUR TO HIS PEOPLE,** *"I will be as the dew to Israel."*[6]

Dew at the creation supplied the place of rain, and in tropical countries it falls in most copious abundance.[7] All men are naturally barren and need dew to fall on them, but on none does it fall, save on Israel, on God's elect, on the Godly. Dew never falls on places destitute of vegetation. God's Israel ever need the dew, and particularly after a drought of backsliding.

Hypocrites[8] and Pharisees can water with their watering pots,[9] but the true Israel want[s] dew.

This God has promised, and under this figure gives:

1. A plentiful supply. The dews on Israel are very heavy.
2. Often an imperceptible supply. There is no noise about it.
3. An effectual supply. The silent dew does its work. It insinuates itself into the soil.[10]
4. A constant supply. No perishing if God manages the clouds.[11] The dew falls in the night. So do God's blessings often come to us in trouble. Well, this dew is soon seen producing.

II. **THE EFFECTS PRODUCED ON GOD'S PEOPLE BY THE DEW.**

These are visible in the plant and are:

1. A beautiful upgrowing in divine love and spirituality like the lily.[12] The daffodil lily[13] springs up quickly on the first fall of dew. Here is a fine emblem of a Christian full of his first love,[14] green and beautiful. But with this is:
2. A strong secret downgrowing[15] in knowledge of divine

truth - in feeling sense of weakness, in humility and all true graces - firm he sets his roots like a cedar or like the foot of the mighty mountain Lebanon.

3. A more clear profession of Jesus. leaves are generally put for profession here the branches spread - he is more known to be a Christian, more distinguished from the world.

4. An heavenly beauty of character. - good men are beautiful Moses' face shone. how religion adorns a man. even God admires his own plant — nor is his beauty subject to decay it is like the "olive" evergreen. Always fair. -

5. His beauty consists in his fruitfulness - as does the beauty of the olive - get plenty of dew then we shall be useful. The most beautiful Christian is he who is most useful.

6. Fragrancy - shall succeed a plentiful bedewing - see the Christian in the morning how sweet his breath, attend him how blessed his conversation, he has been in bed of spices and he smells of them - God & Jesus love it —

III. The good others receive - No man can revive himself without at the same time becoming a means of good to others. The sun's rays must be dispersed. "They that dwell under his shadow" if a father, his children — if a master, the servants — if one of a household his relation — if a minister, his people.

"shall return" they often wander far enough off. It is a source of grief - let us look to it that our own barrenness has not caused their departure - let us amend and then they shall also return.

1. They shall be fruitful. and so shall support him his example shall make the corn grow. There is often blight but if a Christian be strong, others too shall be freed from this - Ah! we want to see men revive as corn.

GOD VISITS AND THE EFFECTS THEREOF—*Hosea 14:5–7*

truth, in feeling [a] sense of weakness, in humility, and all true graces.[16] Firm he sets his roots like a cedar or like the foot of the mighty mountain Lebanon.[17]

3. A more clear profession of Jesus. Leaves are generally put for profession. Here, the branches spread. He is more known to be a Christian, more distinguished from the world.[18]

4. An heavenly beauty of character. Good men are beautiful. Moses'[s] face shone.[19] How religion adorns a man. Even God admires his own plant. Nor is his beauty subject to decay. It is like the "olive," evergreen. Always fair.[20]

5. His beauty consists in his fruitfulness,[21] as does the beauty of the olive. Get plenty of dew, then we shall be useful. The most beautiful Christian is he who is most useful.

6. Fragrancy shall succeed a plentiful bedewing. See the Christian in the morning. How sweet his[22] breath. Attend him. How blessed his conversation.[23] He has been in beds of spices and he smells of them. God and Jesus love it.[24]

III. THE GOOD OTHERS RECEIVE.

No man can revive himself without at the same time becoming a means of good to others. The sun's rays must be dispersed. "They that dwell under his shadow."[25] If a father, his children.[26] If a master, the servants. If one of a household, his relation. If a minister, his people.

"Shall return." They often wander far enough off.[27] It is a source of grief. Let us look to it that our own barrenness has not caused their departure. Let us amend, and then they shall also return.

1. They shall be fruitful, and so shall support[28] him. His example shall make the corn grow. There is often blight,[29] but if a Christian be strong, others too shall be freed from this. Ah![30] we want to see men revive as corn.

2. Others shall grow by his help as the vine on the wall. The oak helps the ivy — so the Christian supported by God supports others too ——. whilst the vine he allows to train itself around him shall yield him much sweet wine of comfort.

3. Even when a Christian is gone, he leaves his scent behind him — in his life he smells as a cask of the fine old wine of Lebanon — and when poured out he leaves his scent in the cask. Yes and like the wine of Lebanon if only put in a vessel for a little while, it can be seen that it was there once. The Son of God shall leave traces behind him indelible — the scent shall endure for ever.

1. How blessed is a Christian — Scarce can the whole of natures fair flowers furnish a figure to set out his excellence — his is the dew and all its effects.

2. How necessary that a Christian should be in a flourishing state — since others lose by his losses gain by his gains — let us think of those under our shadow

3. Let us wait on God — be always uncovered for his dew and desiring earnestly to be Israelites so that we may enjoy all the sweet promises.

Lord revive both me & the people. Amen
154. 157. 160. 165. 191. 295. 467

GOD VISITS AND THE EFFECTS THEREOF—*Hosea 14:5-7*

2. Others shall grow by his help as the vine on the wall. The oak helps the ivy.³¹ So the Christian, supported by God, supports others too whilst the vine he allows to train itself around him shall yield him much sweet wine of comfort.

3. Even when a Christian is gone, he leaves his scent behind him. In his life he smells as a cask of the fine old wine of Lebanon, and when poured out he leaves his scent in the cask. Yes, and like the wine of Lebanon if only put in a vessel for a little while, it can be seen that it was there once. The Son of God shall leave traces behind him.³² Indelible—the scent shall endure forever.

1. How blessed is a Christian. Scarce can the whole of nature[']s fair flowers furnish³³ a figure to set out his excellence. His is the dew and all its effects.

2. How necessary that a Christian should be in a flourishing state since others lose by his losses, gain by his gains. Let us think of those under our shadow.³⁴

3. Let us wait on God.³⁵ Be always uncovered for his dew and desiring earnestly to be Israelites so that we may enjoy all the sweet promises.

Lord, revive both me and the people.³⁶

Amen

154. 157. 160. 165. 191. 295. 467³⁷

SERMON 113

1. The inscription S.97, or skeleton 97, corresponds to Charles Simeon's sermon outline on Hos 14:5–7 entitled "The Fruits of God's Favour" (Simeon, *Helps to Composition* 1:532–35). For additional sermons in which Spurgeon borrowed from Simeon's works, see "The Son's Love to Us Compared with God's Love to Him (Notebook 1, Sermon 38); "Regeneration, Its Causes and Effects" (Notebook 1, Sermon 46); "The Treasure in Earthen Vessels" (Sermon 80); and "The Invitation of Moses to Hobab" (Sermon 98). Overlapping content is noted below.

2. Charles's sermon on Hos 14:5–7, "Grace Reviving Israel" (*NPSP* 6, Sermon 342), follows closely the sermon above, which was surely used in its composition. On April 17, 1879, Charles preached a sermon on Hos 14:6 entitled "The Beauty of the Olive Tree" (*MTP* 55, Sermon 3176). However, there is not enough overlapping content to suggest Charles had the above sermon in mind.

3. "There are instances of beautiful imagery in the Scriptures equal to any that can be found in the works of the most renowned authors. They are enhanced too by the importance of the subjects they contain" (Simeon, *Helps to Composition* 1:532). An alternative reading of this line is "No poetry equal[s] the poetry of the Bible." "We had rather, for poetry's sake, lose all the books that have ever been written by all the poets that ever lived, than lose the sacred Scriptures.... [I]t is the book of God: yea, as Herbert says, 'The god of books'" (*NPSP* 6:445).

4. "Imagination cannot conceive a richer display of divine blessings than God here vouchsafes to his church and people" (Simeon, *Helps to Composition* 1:532).

5. The phrase "sublime yet simple" may have been inspired by Simeon's line "The metaphor of 'dew' is at once simple and sublime" (Simeon, *Helps to Composition* 1:532).

6. "I. The favour which God will shew his people" (Simeon, *Helps to Composition* 1:532).

7. "For some time after the creation, dew supplied the place of rain" (Simeon, *Helps to Composition* 1:532). In footnote "a" at the bottom of the page Simeon wrote, "Where the rains are periodical, and the climate hot, the dews are more abundant." Evidently, Charles supplied his own examples of this environment, namely the "tropical countries." Lectures and publications about tropical

climates were not uncommon in Charles's day. Notices of lectures were occasionally published in newspapers. For instance, in his lecture "On Some Points of Physical Geography," Dr. Bell Salter "continued the subject of the physical agency of heat. Having already treated of its effects on the earth and sea, he proceeded to treat of its relation with the atmosphere, first in reference to its expansive power, and secondly, in its relation with aqueous vapour" ("Ryde Literary Institute," *Isle of Wight Observer*, April 30, 1853).

8. Charles originally wrote the letter "i" beneath the "y" in the word "Hypocrites."

9. See "Gardening for Ladies," *The Sussex Advertiser, Surrey Gazette, & West Kent Courier*, July 18, 1854.

10. "The communications of God to his people are fitly compared to it. It distils silently and almost imperceptibly on the ground. Yet it insinuates itself into the plants on which it falls. And thus maintains their vegetative powers. In the same manner God's visits to his people are secret. But he gains access to their inmost souls. He cheers and revives their fainting spirits. And thus he fulfils to them his own most gracious promise" (Simeon, *Helps to Composition* 1:533).

11. Cf. Job 5:10; 26:8–9.

12. "II. Its fruit and effects. The effects of the dew are seen by the progress of vegetation. The descent of God's Spirit on the soul produces Growth. The 'lily' springs up speedily, but is of short duration" (Simeon, *Helps to Composition* 1:533). "This refers to the daffodil lily, which on a sudden, in a night, will spring up.... Mark, that is what grace does in a man's soul. Wherever grace comes, its first operation is to make us grow up" (*NPSP* 6:447).

13. The daffodil lily, also called "Golden daffodil (*narcissus pseudo-narcissus*), though common, is a beautiful flower, 'tossing its head in sprightly dance'" ("April Garden Flowers," *The Fife Herald. Kinross, Strathearn, and Clackmannan Advertiser*, April 17, 1851).

14. Cf. Jer 2:2; Rev 2:4.

15. "After having grown up, the Christian grows down" (*NPSP* 6:448).

16. "His inward dispositions of humility and love are ornaments" (Simeon, *Helps to Composition* 1:534).

17. "The cedars of 'Lebanon cast forth their roots' to a great extent" (Simeon, *Helps to Composition* 1:533).

18. "The effects of the dew are seen by the progress of vegetation" (Simeon, *Helps to Composition* 1:533) and "His outward conduct is rendered amiable in every part. . . . He is transformed into the very image of God" (Simeon, *Helps to Composition* 1:534).

19. Cf. Exod 34:29–35.

20. "There is peculiar grace and 'beauty in the olive-tree.' And such is there in the soul that communes much with God" (Simeon, *Helps to Composition* 1:533).

21. "Fruitfulness. The 'corn and the vine' are just emblems of a Christian's fruitfulness. They often wear the most unpromising appearance" (Simeon, *Helps to Composition* 1:534). Cf. Matt 7:16; 12:33; Gal 5:22.

22. The letter "e" appears beneath the "i" in the word "his." Charles originally wrote the word "he."

23. "I know some dear saints of the Lord who, if they come to my house for five minutes, leave a refreshing savour behind them for five weeks. They come and talk to me of the things of the kingdom, and I have not forgotten their sweet influence on my spirit for a long time after they have gone" (*NPSP* 6:451).

24. "Fragrancy. Lebanon was no less famous for its odoriferous vines than for its lofty cedars. And does not the Christian diffuse a savour all around him? How animated his discourse when God is with him! How refreshing and delightful to those who enjoy his conversation. How pleasing is it also to his God and Saviour!" (Simeon, *Helps to Composition* 1:534). For clarity, by using the words "God and Jesus," Charles (and Simeon) did not draw ontological distinctions between the *nature* of God the Father and his Son. Instead, the distinction is found between the *person* of God the Father and the Son.

25. Cf. Ps 91:1.

26. Cf. Matt 7:11.

27. Cf. Matt 18:12; Luke 15:11–32.

28. A dark yellow stain, likely the result of the aging process of the manuscript, envelops the words "support" and "There" in the line below.

29. For additional references to blights and the failure of agriculture in Notebook 2, see "The Harvest of Souls" (Sermon 89) and "Man's Weakness and God's Strength" (Sermon 108).

30. The letter "A" in the word "Ah" is smeared to the right side of the page.

31. Charles owned a copy of Charlotte Elizabeth's *Chapters on Flowers* in his personal library. In it she wrote, "The ivy, as I have formerly observed, is to me a lively representation of the work and power of faith. Its strength consists in the tenacity with which it clings to something foreign to its own substance, identifying itself, by a wonderful process, with what it adheres to. Alone, it cannot stand: if you tear it from its prop, down must fall every branch, at the mercy of any trampling foot of man or beast" (Charlotte Elizabeth, *Chapters on Flowers. Third Edition* [London: printed for R. B. Seeley & W. Burnside, 1839, The Spurgeon Library], 303).

32. Charles may be thinking of John 14:27, "Peace I leave with you, my peace I give unto you: not as the world giveth, give I unto you." It is unlikely he is making a pneumatological reference here.

33. Charles originally wrote the word "figure" before changing it to "furnish." This is an example of dittography.

34. Charles later revisited the topic of ministerial integrity in a lecture to the students at the Pastors' College entitled "The Minister's Self-Watch": "It is with us and our hearers as it is with watches and the public clock; if our watch be wrong, very few will be misled by it but ourselves; but if the Horse Guards or Greenwich Observatory should go amiss, half London would lose its reckoning. So it is with the minister; he is the parish-clock, many take their time from him, and if he be incorrect, they all go wrongly" (*Lectures* 1:10).

35. Cf. Ps 27:14; Hos 12:6; 1 Cor 1:7; Heb 9:28.

36. Charles concluded his later sermon with the words, "O God! save souls! O God! save souls! Amen! Amen!" (*NPSP* 6:452).

37. The number 6 is smeared to the left side of the page.

Acts XVII. 11.12.   The noble Bereans.

If all men were ready to receive the Gospel the preaching of it would be easy indeed and its growth rapid. But just notice the treatment it has received at the hands of men for whom it was designed — some despised it so much as to give it no attention — others swelled in rage against — some by philosophy and some by barbarism were prejudiced — and the most heard but with carelessness. — Nevertheless it has won its way, it has prevailed because God has prepared the minds of a happy few for its ready reception. Among this remnant stand the Bereans.

I. Let us notice their conduct.

Paul with great success had preached in Thessalonica. They there used nothing but Scripture as there argument, in proof of the doctrine, worthy of all acceptation, that Christ must needs have suffered or else redemption could not be procured — and that Jesus was that Christ. — Here was solid truth and sound argument, which by God's grace soon prevailed. But where Christ has a church, the Devil will soon be a growling — so the Jews are vexed at the Gentiles being converted — what they counted worth nothing they yet would not let the Gentiles have. — They had recourse to brute force — formed a mob — attacked the apostle's lodging and missing him drew Jason out — They charged him with turning the world upside down — well the devil turned it wrong and we want to put it right. — Paul then runs to Berea — persecution fanned the flame of religion. Paul goes at his work again, he preaches in the synagogue on the Sabbath, they hear him with candour

114

The NOBLE BEREANS
Acts 17:11–12[1]

"These were more noble than those in Thessalonica, in that they received the word with all readiness of mind, and searched the scriptures daily, whether those things were so. Therefore many of them believed; also of honourable women which were Greeks, and of men, not a few."

If all men were ready to receive the Gospel, the preaching of it would be easy indeed and its growth rapid. But just notice the treatment it has received at the hands of men for whom it was designed. Some despised it so much as to give it no attention. Others swelled in rage against. Some by philosophy and some by barbarism were prejudiced and the most heard, but with carelessness. Nevertheless, it has won its way. It has prevailed because God has prepared the minds of a happy few for its ready reception. Among this remnant stand the Bereans.

I. LET US NOTICE THEIR CONDUCT.

Paul, with great success, had preached in Thessalonica.[2] They there used nothing but Scripture as their[3] argument in proof of the doctrine worthy of all acceptation,[4] that Christ must needs have suffered or else redemption could not be procured, and that Jesus was that Christ. Here was solid truth and sound argument which, by God's grace, soon prevailed.

But where Christ has a church, the Devil will soon be a growling.[5] So the Jews are vexed at the Gentiles being converted. What they counted worth nothing they yet would not let the Gentiles have. They had recourse to brute force, formed a mob,[6] attacked[7] the apostle's lodging and, missing him, drew Jason out.[8]

They charged him with turning the world upside down. Well, the devil turned it wrong and we want to put[9] it right. Paul then runs to Berea.[10] Persecution fanned the flame of religion. Paul goes at his work again. He preaches in the synagogue on the Sabbath. They hear him with candour, and on returning home, take down the Scriptures and investigate the doctrines propounded. The Thessalonians drove away the preachers these heard what they had to say — they did not forget — but studied them. Would God our congregations would all do so. They <u>searched the Scriptures</u>. They went to the fountain head of truth — they left reason or rather kept it in subordination to faith — they received the Bible as the only rule of faith and practise. —

They <u>searched</u>. The truth like gold is not always on the <u>surface</u> — it is often in grains often down deep in the earth — They read diligently, just as a student works at any point propounded Jesus gospel has nothing to fear from the most minute examination — though critical readers have much to fear for themselves. The consequence was many believed, of all classes, & both sexes. But the Jews soon followed. "When they persecute you in one city flee unto another" Off went the apostle again preaching Christ with zeal. The Bereans heard.
1. With devout and respectful attention.
2. With impartial candour.
3. With careful investigation. —
II The commendation bestowed on them.
They were "noble" — wherein did this consist.
1. They were above all ignorant apathy. The ignoble care only for their bellies these cared for their mind

THE NOBLE BEREANS—*Acts 17:11-12*

and on returning home, take down the Scriptures and investigate the doctrines propounded.

The Thessalonians drove away the preachers. These heard what they had to say. They did not forget, but studied them. Would God[11] our congregations would all do so.

They searched the Scriptures. They went to the fountain head of truth. They left reason, or rather kept it in subordination to faith. They received the Bible as the only rule of faith and practices.

They searched. The truth, like gold, is not always on the surface. It is often in grains, often down deep in the earth. They read diligently, just as a student works at any point propounded.[12]

Jesus['s] gospel has nothing to fear from the most minute examination, though critical readers have much to fear for themselves.[13] The consequence was many believed of all classes and both sexes.[14]

But the Jews soon followed. "When they persecute you in one city, flee unto another."[15] Off went the apostle again preaching Christ with zeal.

The Bereans heard:

1. With devout and respectful attentions.
2. With impartial candour.
3. With careful investigation.

II. THE COMMENDATION BESTOWED ON THEM.

They were "noble." Wherein did this consist?

1. They were above all ignorant apathy. The ignoble care only for their bellies. These cared for their minds.

some men do not care which is right or which is wrong so long as bredd is cheap – these are the true rabble.

2. They were above all childish credulity. – Some believe every thing just like schoolboys – they are not yet men but no these would not believe till they had weighed the matter – Believe nothing without good testimony

3. They did not rashly conclude by mere appearance this is another mean vice – judge no man by his Thi. Poor Paul who is he? He is a scamp who has run away from Thessalonica – No No. let us just hear

4. They were not such fools as to be infidels. men like to be infidels just to be remarkable, just as some boys smoke to seem men. These men were above such abominable littleness.

5. They were free from Bigotry – Though they would not throw away the religion of their fathers without just reason yet they were open to conviction. The thing was new and strange but for all that just let me examine – It is contrary to my former views but just let me see.

Bible searchers are the peers of heaven. Noble in their aims, noble in their spirit, noble in their conduct, noble in thought and principles. God demands that you search the Scriptures All Christians demand it. The Baptist denomination demands it – your minister demands it But to stimulate you to this duty consider,

III. The benefits received thereby.

"Many of them believed" God bestowed on them

Some men do not care which is right or which is wrong so long as bread is cheap. These are the true rabble.[16]

2. They were above all childish credulity. Some believe every thing just like schoolboys. They are not yet men. But no, these would not believe till they had weighed the matter. Believe nothing without good testimony.

3. They did not rashly conclude by mere appearance. This is[17] another mean vice. Judge no man by his skin.[18] Poor Paul, who is he? He is a scamp[19] who has run away from Thessalonica. No, No. Let us just hear.[20]

4. They were not such fools as to be infidels. Men like to be infidels just to be remarkable, just as some boys smoke to seem men.[21] These men were above such abominable littleness.

5. They were free from Bigotry. Though they would not throw away the religion of their fathers' without just reason, yet they were open to conviction. The thing[22] was new and strange, but for all that, just let me examine. It is contrary to my former views,[23] but just let me see.

Bible searchers are[24] the peers of heaven. Noble in their[25] aims, noble in their spirit, noble in their conduct, noble[26] in thought and principles. God demands that you search the Scriptures.[27] All Christians demand it. The Baptist denomination[28] demands it. Your minister demands it.

But to stimulate you to this duty, consider:

III. THE BENEFITS RECEIVED THEREBY.

"Many of them believed." God bestowed on them

SERMON 114

the precious grace of faith — which now has lifted them up to glory — Those hearts are prepared for the reception of Jesus which are open to his word. The searching of the Scriptures is used by the Spirit.
1. For the conviction of the ungodly of their sin.
2. For dispelling all ignorance as to the way.
3. For encouraging the growth of the seed.
4. For so bright a display of Jesus as to ravish the soul
In all these ways it produces faith —
Many — doubtless all true searchers, of all conditions

1. To the Christian wouldest thou increase thy faith? Search the Scriptures daily.
2. Sinner. Dost thou desire salvation? 'Tis by faith, and that comes by God's word.
3. How dreadful the sin of neglecting the Bible. Repent of this — Amend your ways — pull out your dusty Bibles — Read or be damned. Read, mark, learn, digest and may God's grace make the word of profit to you
155. Amen

the precious grace of faith which now has lifted them up to glory. Those hearts are prepared for the reception of Jesus which are open to his [W]ord.

The searching of the Scriptures is used by the Spirit:

1. For the conviction of the ungodly of their sin.

2.[29] For dispelling all ignorance as to the way.

3. For encouraging the growth of the seed.

4. For so bright a display of Jesus as to ravish the soul. In all these ways it produces faith.

"Many."[30] Doubtless all true searchers of all conditions.

1. To the Christian, wouldest thou increase thy faith? Search the [S]criptures daily.

2. Sinner, dost thou desire salvation? 'Tis by faith, and that comes by God's [W]ord.[31]

3. How dreadful the sin of neglecting the Bible. Repent of this. Amend your ways. Pull out your dusty Bibles. Read or be damned. Read, mark, learn, digest, and may God's grace make the word of profit to you.

155.
Amen

SERMON 114

1. This is the only time Charles preached a sermon on Acts 17:11–12.

2. Cf. Acts 17:1.

3. Charles originally wrote the word "there." However, the context suggests he intended to write the word "their."

4. See Andrew Fuller, *The Gospel Worthy of All Acceptation; or, the Duty of Sinners to Believe in Jesus Christ. Third Edition, with Corrections and Additions: To Which Is Added an Appendix, on the Question, Whether the Existence of Any Holy Disposition of Heart Be Necessary in Order to Believing in Christ* (Philadelphia: printed by Charles Cist, 1805).

5. Cf. 1 Pet 5:8.   6. Cf. Acts 17:5.

7. The stem of the letter "t" appears beneath the "a" in the word "attacked." Charles likely prematurely began to write the word "the."

8. Cf. Acts 17:9.

9. Charles originally wrote the letter "t" beneath the "p" in the word "put." He may have intended to write the word "turn."

10. Cf. Acts 17:10.

11. The expression "Would God" or "Would to God" was a common translation for ὄφελον in the KJV. First Corinthians 4:8b, "I would to God ye did reign, that we also might reign with you." A modernized reading of this line might be "May God grant that our congregations would all do so."

12. An alternative reading of this line is "They read diligently, and just as a student works, at any point propounded."

13. "The Word of God can take care of itself, and will do so if we preach it, and cease defending it. See you that lion. They have caged him for his preservation; shut him up behind iron bars to secure him from his foes! See how a band of armed men have gathered together to protect the lion. What a clatter they make with their swords and spears! These mighty men are intent upon defending a lion. O fools, and slow of heart! Open that door! Let the lord of the forest come forth free. Who will dare to encounter him? What does he want with your

guardian care? Let the pure gospel go forth in all its lion-like majesty, and it will soon clear its own way and ease itself of its adversaries" (*MTP* 34:42).

14. Cf. Acts 17:12.

15. Matthew 10:23, "But when they persecute you in this city, flee ye into another: for verily I say unto you, Ye shall not have gone over the cities of Israel, till the Son of man be come."

16. "A tumultuous crowd; an assembly of low people" (Johnson's *Dictionary*, s.v. "rabble").

17. An illegible letter, likely "a," appears beneath the "i" in the word "is." Charles likely began writing the word "another."

18. In a letter likely to his father, Charles took inventory of the expenses he incurred in Cambridge. In addition to "Hair Cuttings," "Piece of Riband for my Watch," and "Tincture of Iodine for my chillblains," he also wrote, "Gave to a poor Black man" (Angus Library and Archive, Regent's Park College, Oxford University, D/SPU 1). See also Charles's loss of reputation in America for his abolitionist sentiment in the years leading to the U.S. Civil War (Notebook 1, editor's preface).

19. Johnson did not define the word "scamp." However, according to Worcester's *Dictionary*, a scamp is "a cheat; a knave; a swindler; a worthless fellow; a rascal" (Worcester's *Dictionary*).

20. Charles originally wrote the word "here." He reinforced the letters "ar" to construct the word "hear."

21. Charles later smoked cigars and pipes. In a letter to the *Daily Telegraph*, Charles wrote, "No Christian should do anything in which he cannot glorify God—and this may be done, according to Scripture, in eating and drinking and the common actions of life. When I have found intense pain relieved, a weary brain soothed, and calm, refreshing sleep obtained by a cigar, I have felt grateful to God and have blessed His name; this is what I meant, and by no means did I use sacred words triflingly. If through smoking I had wasted an hour of my time—if I had stinted my gifts to the poor—if I had rendered my mind less vigorous—I trust I should see my fault and turn from it, but he who charges me with these things

SERMON 114

shall have no answer but my forgiveness. I am told that my open avowal will lessen my influence, and my reply is that if I have gained any influence through being thought different from what I am, I have no wish to retain it" ("Mr. Spurgeon on Smoking," *Daily Telegraph*, quoted in *The Manchester Courier, and Lancashire General Advertiser*, September 28, 1874). To see Charles's pipe and also one of the last cigars found on his body after his death, see The Spurgeon Library display case at Midwestern Baptist Theological Seminary in Kansas City, Missouri.

22. The stem of an illegible letter—likely "t," "l," or "k"—appears beneath the "g" in the word "thing."

23. Charles did not intend the sentence "It is contrary to my former views" to be autobiographical. Instead, he assumed the perspective of the Bereans.

24. An illegible letter, likely "i" or "s," appears beneath the "r" in the word "are." Charles may have originally written the word "as." More likely, though, he wrote the word "aim" prematurely (see "aim" in the line below).

25. Charles likely wrote the word "the" before changing it to "their."

26. A diagonal line, likely accidental, begins above the letter "e" in the word "noble" and concludes above the letter "n" in the word "in."

27. John 5:39, "Search the scriptures; for in them ye think ye have eternal life: and they are they which testify of me."

28. Charles originally spelled this word "denominatin" before adding the letter "o" to construct the correct spelling, "denomination."

29. A purple ink stain, similar to the one in "The Minister's Commission" (Sermon 110), appears over the number 2. The color of the stain suggests Charles may have redacted this sermon in London as he prepared his early sermons for publication.

30. Charles did not originally insert quotation marks around the word "Many." The punctuation is added for consistency with other scripture quotations.

31. Cf. Rom 10:17.

2 Pet. 3.12. The day of God.

There is a future state - for even the heathen imagine the soul to be immortal. If we believe in a God as the Deist we must then conclude that he is just — and must therefore punish the wicked and reward the good - but notoriously it is not so in this life - therefore. There is another state.
But the Christian system soon decides all doubt on this subject. it clearly reveals what nature can only guess at.
Since then there is a future state, anything about that must be highly important and it becomes us to seek to be well prepared for all its grandeurs & terrors.
The Christian will always find matter for holy joy and the sinner may well shake for terror. —
I. The solemn event — "the day of the Lord, wherein"
Death is solemn but it derives its solemnity from this one day — we die, we sleep not, but our spirits go at once to judgment, are condemned or acquitted then & there.
The wicked go to hell at once and saints leap to glory.
But after time shall have spun out her thread, eternity shall demand her account — and then all both saints and sinners shall leave their places & come upon the earth again and there shall stand in mortal flesh again — To the saint this will be no hardship since he carries heaven about him.
To the sinner this absence for a time from hell will be no relief but the worm shall go with them —
The whole race is there - all - all - good, bad, all nations - there they stand, mixed in one great assembly.
The herald angels blow their trumpets the oath

115

The DAY *of* GOD
2 Peter 3:12[1]

"Looking for and hasting unto the coming of the day of God, wherein the heavens being on fire shall be dissolved, and the elements shall melt with fervent heat."

There is a future state, for even the heathen[2] imagine the soul to be immortal. If we believe in a God as the Deist, we must then conclude that he is just, and must, therefore, punish the wicked and reward the good. But notoriously, it is not so in this life. Therefore, there is another state.

But the Christian system soon decides all doubt on this[3] subject. It clearly reveals what nature can only guess at. Since, then, there is a future state, anything about that must be highly important, and it becomes us to seek to be well prepared for all its grandeurs and terrors. The Christian will always find matter for holy joy and the sinner may well shake for terror.

I. **THE SOLEMN EVENT.** *"The day of the Lord, wherein."*

Death is solemn, but it derives its solemnity from this one day. We die.[4] We sleep not, but our spirits go at once to judgment,[5] are condemned or acquitted then and there. The wicked go to hell at once and saints leap to glory. But after time shall have spun out her thread, eternity shall demand her account, and then all, both saints and sinners, shall leave their places and come upon the earth again and there shall stand in mortal flesh again.

To the saint this will be no hardship since he carries heaven about him.

To the sinner this absence for a time from hell will be no relief, but the worm shall go with them.[6]

The whole race is there. All. All. Good, bad, all nations. There they stand, mixed in one great assembly. The herald angels blow their trumpets, the vast[7] hosts of angels stand in marshalled legions, the great white throne is set upon the clouds — all is breathless suspense — the judge comes. The triune J——l— whose awful name one dares not write. Conspicuous is the Son — all glorious — The Lion of Judah. Ah — those fiery eyes — Ah — sweet, lovely, glorious eyes — yet how awful — hark a nation shrieks at once. This is the day of God. ——

1. The Day of his glory — the sinner's day of honour is gone — the pomp and pride of kings are gone — 'tis God's turn now — What a throne, what attendants what a judgment hall — what prisoners — conceive ye angels its grandeur man cannot — Time has some of God's glory — but it sees more contempt but now 'tis all glory in radiant effulgence —

2. The day of Gods power. He doth now as it were hold himself in — the giant only moves his finger but then — he will upturn the earth — the dead shall rise his stoutest foes shall quail — his saints shall be taken away & then — ah — then — the air shall turn itself to blazing gas — the comets and meteors shall make the earth their common centre — the secret fires shall burst — unrestrained the fire shall consume all — it licks up all the oceans as a drop — it burns not only the garnishing of earth but the solid world itself. Now the storm & tempest shew & their fury — The day of power.

hosts of angels stand in marshalled legions, the great white throne is set upon the clouds.[8] All is breathless suspense.

The judge comes, the triune J——[9], whose awful name one dares not write. Conspicuous is the <u>Son</u>. All glorious. The Lion of Judah.[10] Ah, those fiery eyes. Ah, sweet, lovely, glorious eyes. Yet how awful.[11] Hark, a nation shrieks at once.[12]

This is the day[13] of God.

1. The Day of his glory. The sinner's day of honour is gone. The pomp and pride of kings are gone. 'Tis God's turn now. What a throne. What attendants. What a judgment hall. What prisoners.[14] Conceive, ye angels, its grandeur. Man cannot. Time has some of God's glory, but it sees more contempt. But now, 'tis all glory in radiant effulgence.

2. The day of God's power. He doth now, as it were, hold himself in. The giant only moves his finger, but then he will upturn the earth. The dead shall rise.[15] His stoutest foes shall quail. His saints shall be taken away, and then, ah then, the air shall turn itself to blazing gas. The comets and meteors shall make the earth their common centre.[16] The secret fires shall burst unrestrained. The fire shall consume all.[17] It licks up all the oceans as a drop.[18] It burns not only the garnishing of earth but the solid world itself. Now the storm and tempest shows[19] their fury, the day of power.

3. The Day of his wrath – Now 'tis mercy – now forbearance. the devil is saucy and man is impudent – but then his turn shall come, forbearance shall have now no place. mercy shall drop its golden sceptre – and fierce justice shall draw forth the iron rod, the glittering sword – the fire –

4. The Day of God's triumph – as one by one the saints shall rise from 'mid the throng none can hold them down – and as with smiling face they shall return to their own mansions – their foes shall be ashamed. The boasting-vaunting foe – shall shut his mouth. Jesus shall have a public triumph – crush the serpent's head

II. The conduct of the saints – in prospect of this – Do they wring their hands – do they fear – no. they look for it

1. Their minds are exercised upon it – they believe and therefore look for it & moreover ardently expect it.

2. Their lives are influenced by it – they make themselves ready for it. they try to <u>hasten</u> it, & they hasten for it – no time for sleep – "look"! no time for loitering haste!

III. The reflections it should suggest. Even those who look not for it shall see it – let us then just try to learn at a distance lessons, which it will be too late to learn when the great reality flashes on our view

1. How awful sin is – even the earth the scene of sin must come down. –

2. The emptiness & vanity of the world – seeing it must all pass away.

3. The necessity of being saved through Jesus –

Tell them the only way and God save many for Jesus Christ's sake. amen. amen. amen.

158.

THE DAY OF GOD—2 Peter 3:12

3. The Day of his wrath. Now 'tis mercy. Now forbearance. The devil is saucy and man is impudent. But then his turn shall come. Forbearance shall have now no place. Mercy shall drop its golden sceptre and fierce justice shall draw forth the iron rod, the glittering sword,[20] the fire.

4. The Day of God's triumph. As one by one the saint[s] shall rise from 'mid[21] the throng, none can hold them down. And as with smiling face[s] they shall return to their own mansions.[22] Their foes shall be ashamed. The boasting, vaunting foe shall shut his mouth. Jesus shall have a public triumph, crush the serpent's head.[23]

II. THE CONDUCT OF THE SAINTS IN PROSPECT OF THIS.

Do they wring their hands? Do they fear? No, they look for it.[24]

1.[25] Their minds are exercised upon it. They believe and therefore look for it, and moreover, ardently expect it.

2. Their lives are influenced by it. They make themselves ready for it. They try to <u>hasten</u> it,[26] and they hasten for it.

No time for sleep.[27] "Look!" No time for loitering. "Haste!"

III. THE REFLECTIONS IT SHOULD SUGGEST.

Even those who look not for it shall see it. Let us then just try to learn at a distance lessons which it will be too late to learn when the great reality flashes on our view:

1. How awful sin is. Even the earth, the scene of sin, must come down.

2. The emptiness and vanity of the world,[28] seeing it must all pass away.[29]

3. The necessity of being saved through Jesus.

Tell them the only way,[30] and God, save many
for Jesus Christ's sake.[31]

158. <u>Amen. Amen. Amen.</u>

SERMON 115

1. This is the only time Charles preached on 2 Pet 3:12 (see also "The World on Fire" [*MTP* 19, Sermon 1125]).

2. The diagonal ink stroke beneath the letters "e" and "n" in the word "heathen" is similar in color to the purple spot after the word "this" five lines below. Additional strokes are found over the letter "t" in the word "notoriously" three lines below and over the letter "r" in the word "another" four lines below.

3. A purple ink spot appears over the letter "s" in the word "this." This is likely evidence Charles had begun redacting this sermon for publication in London.

4. Cf. 1 Cor 15:22.

5. Cf. Heb 9:27.

6. Cf. Mark 9:48.

7. The words "their trumpets, the vast" are smeared significantly to the lower right of the page. The stem of the letter "d" in the line above is also smeared. The directionality suggests these words were smeared by the same swift motion.

8. Cf. Rev 20:11–15.

9. Charles refrained from writing the name "Jehovah" in this line. His rationale for only penning the capital letter "J" is found in the next phrase: "whose awful name one dares not write." Charles may have consulted Edward Robinson's *Lexicon of the Old Testament*: "The Jews, who superstitiously avoided to pronounce the name יהוה, were accustomed wherever this latter occurs in the sacred text, to substitute for it אֲדֹנָי in reading. Hence the vowels of אֲדֹנָי are usually written in יְהֹוָה; and in later writers the former word is often used instead of the latter" (Edward Robinson, trans., *Hebrew and English Lexicon of the Old Testament, Including the Biblical Chaldee. Translated from the Latin of William Gesenius, Doct. and Prof. of Theology in the University of Halle-Wittenberg* [Boston: Crocker and Brewster; New York: Leavitt, Lord & Co., 1836, The Spurgeon Library], 15).

10. Cf. Hos 5:14; Rev 5:5.

11. An incomplete letter "f" was written over the "w" in the word "awful."

THE DAY OF GOD—2 Peter 3:12

12. The words "at once" are written in a noticeably tighter handwriting and may have been added later.

13. An ink dot appears between the words "of" and "God." It is smeared toward the upper left of the page.

14. Charles originally inserted a dot between the letters "r" and "s" in the word "prisoners." It is likely he intended this dot to serve as an apostrophe. However, the context suggests plurality, not possession; thus, an apostrophe is not included.

15. Cf. 1 Cor 15:20, 22; 1 Thess 4:16; Rev 20:5.

16. By the mid-nineteenth century, advances in astronomy were frequent. Through mathematical calculations, the trajectories of comets, meteors, and other heavenly bodies could be predicted (see "Comets and Cometic Meteors," *The Manchester Courier, and Lancashire General Advertiser*, June 15, 1850). Cf. Rev 12:4.

17. An alternative reading of this line is "The secret fires shall burst. Unrestrained, the fire shall consume all."

18. Cf. Rev 8:8.

19. Charles originally wrote the words "shows its." To construct subject and verb agreement in this sentence, he struck through the final "s" in the word "shows" and converted the word "its" to "their."

20. Cf. Rev 1:16; 19:15.

21. Abbr. "amid."

22. Cf. John 14:2.

23. Charles exaggerated the stem of the letter "d" in the word "head" so that it encompassed the top of the x-height and ascender line of the letters "pents" in the word "serpents." An alternative reading of this line is "Jesus shall have a public triumph [and] crush the serpent's head." Cf. Gen 3:15; 2 Cor 2:14.

24. A faint line is detected after the word "it" and above the first point. Charles may have originally intended to conclude his sermon here.

25. Charles originally wrote a dash before adding the number "1."

26. Cf. Rev 22:20.

27. Cf. 1 Thess 5:2; 2 Pet 3:10; Rev 16:15.

28. Cf. Eccl 1:1–2.

29. Cf. 1 John 2:17.

30. Cf. John 14:6; Acts 4:12; 1 Tim 2:5.

31. An alternative reading of this sentence is "God [shall] save many for Jesus Christ's sake." Interpreting the sentence in the declarative mood alters the meaning dynamically. Instead of a prayer for God to "save many for Jesus Christ's sake," the sentence becomes an observation or prediction of what God shall/will do when the condition, "Tell them the only way," is met. For consistency with the additional prayers in this notebook such as "God, help men to come through Jesus" ("David in the Cave of Adullam" [Sermon 116]), the imperative mood is the preferred reading of this line.

SERMON 116

116   1. Sam. XXII. 2.   David in the cave of Adullam.
David was in many things a type of Jesus. — in being chosen from his brethren so Christ was God's first elect. he was both a shepherd and a King — he fought the foes of Israel singly — though much hated yet he came off conqueror at length. — So here in Adullam he was eminently a type of Jesus in his church, the captain of our salvation — enlisting vile sinners in his cause. As a recruiting officer it becomes me

I. To describe, the Prince, Lord Jesus, our Captain. He is descended of a noble family, he is no impostor. he is the son of the King of Kings. He has a fine person and is the most gallant general soldiers ever had. He has seen hard service and has now many deep scars, he has gained many victories in fact he has never lost one in his life: He is exceedingly affable he is accustomed to live in the same tents as the privates. He gives you a crown with his own hand. He will cure all wounds gained in battle, indeed if men would but keep close to his rules they would never be wounded. He is sure to be in the hottest of the battle, helping the weak and enabling them to put the foes to flight. He is a good paymaster — he makes all his soldiers as rich as kings & gives them a Kingdom apiece. His soldiers never die. They only wade a river and then they are all right — he is at war with the Black Prince. The Dragon — He wants to win back the world, he wants to deliver poor sinners

DAVID IN THE CAVE OF ADULLAM—*1 Samuel 22:2*

116

DAVID *in the* CAVE *of* ADULLAM
1 Samuel 22:2[1]

"David therefore departed thence, and escaped to the cave Adullam: and when his brethren and all his father's house heard it, they went down thither to him."

David was, in many things, a type of Jesus. In being chosen from his brethren, so Christ was God's first elect. He was both a shepherd and a king. He fought the foes of Israel singly.[2] Though much hated, yet he came off conqueror at length. So here in Adullam he was eminently a type of Jesus in his church, the captain of our salvation,[3] enlisting vile sinners in his cause.

As a recruiting officer, it becomes me:

I. TO DESCRIBE[4] THE PRINCE, LORD JESUS, OUR CAPTAIN.

He is descended of a noble family.[5] He is no impostor. He is the son of the King of Kings. He has a fine person and is the most gallant general soldiers ever had. He has seen hard service and has now many deep scars.[6] He has gained many victories. In fact, he has[7] never lost one in his life.[8] He is exceedingly affable. He is accustomed to live in the same tents as the privates.[9] He gives you a crown with his own hand.[10] He will cure all wounds gained in battle. Indeed, if men would but keep close to his rules, they would never be wounded.

He is sure to be in the hottest of the battle, helping the weak and enabling them to put the foes to flight. He is a good paymaster. He makes all his soldiers as rich as kings and gives them a kingdom apiece. His soldiers never die. They only wade a river[11] and then they are all right. He is at war with the Black Prince, The Dragon.[12] He wants to win back the world. He wants to deliver poor sinners.

SERMON 116

He will gain nothing. He has come to set the captive free merely because he is abundantly gracious.

Now I want to enlist some men, and here I come

II. To describe the soldiers required. —

Surely so first-rate a captain deserves good soldiers but the finer sort reject him — the gentry will not have him. he now therefore will not have *them* but he invites the motley herd of villains to come, and with such an army he declares that he will rout — the Devil and all his golden men. — Come on then.

1 "Every one in distress" — are you sure you are vile and do you weep, does your heart tell you, you are lost and that hope is clean gone. Are you beaten out of all your creature powers — come on — right-welcome comrade

2. "Every one in debt." Unable to pay the load of sin and fearing the cruel creditor — He'll settle that for thee — only come and every farthing shall be paid.

3. "Every one that is discontented." With his present state, his old master, his horrid wages — with himself because he is vile indeed — come on mutineers. I am not content with inviting the mutineers. I will even stir you up to rise and mutiny.

What fools to serve the old Devil — and all for nothing. What fruit have you? what joy? what solid confidence. He is a scoundrel. He is enticing you to hell. To arms. To arms. Down with the tyrant. Do not lose so fine an opportunity. Why will you yet love sin? — why are you content to be lost? well he is mad who would work hard to be burned for ever —

He will gain nothing.

He has come to set the captive free[13] merely because he is abundantly gracious. Now, I want to enlist some men, and here I come:

II. TO DESCRIBE THE SOLDIERS REQUIRED.

Surely so firstrate a captain deserves good soldiers, but the finer sort reject him. The gentry will not have him. He now, therefore, will not have <u>them</u>, but he invites the motley[14] herd of villains to come,[15] and with such an army he declares that he will rout the Devil and all his golden men. Come on then:

1. "Every one in distress." Are you sure you are vile and do you weep? Does your heart tell you, you are lost and that hope is clean gone? Are you beaten out of all your creature powers? Come on, right-welcome[16] comrade.

2. "Every one in debt." Unable to pay the load of sin and fearing the cruel creditor? He'll settle that for thee. Only come and every farthing[17] shall be paid.

3. "Every one that is discontented" with his present state, his old master, his horrid wages, with himself because he is vile indeed. Come on, mutineers. I am not content with inviting the mutineers. I will even stir you up to rise and mutiny.

What fools to serve the old Devil, and all for nothing.

What fruit have you? What joy? What solid confidence? He is a scoundrel. He is enticing you to hell.

To arms. To arms. Down with the tyrant. Do not lose so fine an opportunity. Why will you yet love sin? Why are you content to be lost? Well, he is mad who would work hard to be burned for ever.

SERMON 116

Come, who will enlist? But stop let me
III Give you a hint or two as to the service,
For I would have none come without counting the cost.
Jesus will be Captain and we know no one else is
at all fit for it but him. As captain he requires
submission to his code of Rules which are these –

1. All soldiers of whatsoever class, condition, age, or country
are required to strip themselves of every rag of that
apparel which they have been accustomed to wear,
neither are they to retain so much as one thread.
These rags are at once to be burned in the fire.

2. After this stripping, it is moreover enacted that
the person do at once wash himself in the bath,
Purging both the filth of his former life and
taking away the disease of his skin. For be
it known unto all that this bath is medicinal
as well as cleansing. – Thus thoroughly washed

3. It is further required that the soldier put
on the inner garment of needle-work – called
the seamless robe of the righteousness of Jesus and
moreover the outer livery suit of sanctification
or the Spirit's embroidered cloak. –

4. That from this time, henceforth, and for
ever, the soldier is and is to be considered
as the property of Jesus. He is by solemn
covenant to make over all goods and chattels,
ally, and several his estates and property to
the Captain – yea and likewise shall be
as to his own person actually the bona fide

DAVID IN THE CAVE OF ADULLAM—*1 Samuel 22:2*

Come. Who will enlist? But stop, let me:

III. GIVE YOU A HINT OR TWO AS TO THE SERVICE.

For I would have none come without counting the cost.[18] Jesus will be Captain, and we know no one else is at all fit for it but him. As captain he requires submission to his code of Rules, which are these:

1. [19] All soldiers of whatsoever class, condition, age, or country are required to strip themselves of every rag of that apparel which they have been accustomed to wear.[20] Neither are they to retain so much as one thread. These rags are at once to be burned in the fire.

2. After this stripping, it is moreover enacted that the person do at once wash himself in the bath, Purging both the filth of his former life and taking away the disease of his skin. For be it known unto all that this bath is medicinal[21] as well as cleansing. Thus, thoroughly washed,

3. It is further required that the soldier put on the inner garment of needle-work called the seamless robe of the[22] righteousness of Jesus,[23] and moreover, the outer livery suit of sanctification, or the Spirit's embroidered cloak.

4. That from this time henceforth and for ever, the soldier is and is to be considered as the property of Jesus.[24] He is by solemn covenant to make over all goods and chattels,[25] alls, and several[26] his estates and property to the Captain. Yea, and likewise shall be as to his own person actually the bona fide

property of the captain – It is requested that this should be done in the gate of the city, in the public place of concourse – by dipping in water.

5. No man is to be admitted as a soldier in any legion of the army who will not manifest a love to all the other legions, howsoever distinguished by colours differing in minor points. Howbeit it is required that each recruit do ~~watch~~ examine the old original standard, & stand in that file which comes nearest in its colours to the said standard.

6. It is specially enacted that all men enlisting under his royal highness – the Prince Emanuel are to submit to the discipline required by his laws martial – which are.

   I. No communication, nor unity with the enemy.
   II. No wandering from the line of march. Keep in step.
   III. No quarter either to be asked or taken.
   IV. No guns, swords, spears or other ammunition belonging to the enemy are to be used, but to be burned with fire.
   V. That no weapon be allowed to rust.
   VI. No fear, cowardice, or trembling to be tolerated
   VII. No sleep, rest, ease, or surrender.

7. It is moreover required that all soldiers practise the following postures of drill.

   Pos. I. On both knees, hands uplifted, heart heavenward.
   " II. Feet fast. position of patience. Stand still.
   " III. Quick march. continued progression.
   " IV. Double quick – resisting temptation by running away.
   " V. Eyes shut, ears close, tongue tied, heart bound, when in vanity fair.
   " VI. Eyes open, ears open, sword drawn, step firm in close conflict.
   " VII. Hands open, eyes joyful, heart glad when helping brethren.

Now here are some of the rules and I dare not alter

property of the captain. It is requested that this should be done in the gate of the city, in the public place of concourse, by dipping in water.

5. No man is to be admitted as a soldier in any legion of the army who will not manifest a love to all the other legions, howsoever distinguished by[27] colours differing in minor points.[28] Howbeit, it is required that each recruit do ~~search~~ examine[29] the old original standard and stand in that file which comes nearest in its colours to the said standard.

6. It is specially enacted that all men enlisting under his royal highness, the Prince Emanuel,[30] are to submit to the discipline required by his laws martial, which are:

    I. No communication nor unity with the enemy.[31]

    II. No wandering from the line[32] of march. Keep in step.

    III. No quarter[33] either to be asked or taken.

    IV. No guns, swords, spears or other ammunition belonging to the enemy are to be used, but to be burned with fire.

    V. That no weapon be allowed to rust.

    VI. No fear, cowardice, or trembling to be tolerated.

    VII. No sleep,[34] rest, ease, or surrender.

7. It is moreover required that all soldiers practise the following postures of drill[s]:

    Pos.[35]   I. On both knees, hands uplifted, heart heavenward.

    "[36]   II. Feet fast, position of patience, stand still.

    "   III. Quick march, continued progression.

    "   IV. Double quick, resisting temptation by running away.[37]

    "   V. Eyes shut, ears close[d], tongue tied, heart bound when in vanity fair.[38]

    "   VI. Eyes o[p]en,[39] ears open, sword drawn, step firm in close conflict.

    "   VII. Hands open, eyes joyful, heart glad when helping brethren.

Now, here are some of the rules, and I dare not alter

so much as one of the least — Yet if the service be hard the devil's service is harder — and remember the difference in the pay each master gives —
God help men to come through Jesus.
Amen
159

117.   Job. 25.4 — Justification by imputed Righteousness.
Job though a patient man was not perfect. His great fault was selfrighteousness — perhaps engendered by the perpetual sunshine of his early life — and much aggravated by the unjust charges of his friends. Job's affliction was a clear gain to him, even if he only learned the one lesson "I am in need of a better righteousness than my own." —
I. The importance of this question.
1. It is one that must be answered since man must be justified somehow. Man must keep all the law in some way or other or he is under its curse and in all justice cannot receive its blessing. It can in nowise be dispensed with — it must be answered.
2. It must be answered rightly. for a mistake here would be a mortal wound to the soul — it would affect all our views on other doctrines — it will if misunderstood wonderfully weaken our faith, and so spoil our confidence and comfort

so much as one of the least. Yet if this service be hard, the devil's service is harder. And remember the difference in the pay each master gives.

God, help men to come through Jesus.

<u>Amen</u>

159

117

JUSTIFICATION *by* IMPUTED RIGHTEOUSNESS[1]
Job 25:4[2]

"How then can man be justified with God? Or how can he be clean that is born of a woman?"

Job, though a patient man, was not perfect. His great fault was self-righteousness,[3] perhaps engendered by the perpetual sunshine of his early life and much aggravated by the unjust charges of his friends. Job's affliction was a clear gain to him, even if he only learned the one lesson, "I am in need of a better righteousness than my own."[4]

I. THE IMPORTANCE OF THIS QUESTION.

1. It is one that must be answered since man must be justified somehow. Man must keep all the law in some way or other, or he is under its curse, and in all justice cannot receive its blessing. It can in nowise be dispensed with. It must be answered.

2. It must be answered rightly, for a mistake here would be a mortal wound to the soul. It would affect all our views on other doctrines. It will, if misunderstood, wonderfully weaken our faith and so spoil our confidence and comfort.

This is no curious question but a serious one & the more so when we consider

II. The difficulties in the way of man's justification.
1. Man himself — in him there are many serious difficulties.
   He has fallen federally in Adam who was our representative.
   He is born with depravity innate within him.
   He universally disobeys from the first moment of his rational being to the very last, growing viler still.
   Not one of all the race is perfect — the best have native sin.
2. The Law — in its stringency punishing even one offence demanding nothing less than universal obedience.
   — in its spirituality touching the thoughts, words, desires.
   — in its extent punishing acts of omission as well as commission
   — in its eternity — enduring without change 'till time ceases and punishing sin for ever and ever in hell.
3. God — in his very dignity there is an awful barrier, even angels deserve nothing but live on his benevolence his omniscience beholds such sin as to stop man's mouth. his justice and holiness must be magnified
   His faithfulness — yea — all his attributes are so many glorious swords guarding the avenues of Paradise.
   Yet man has ventured to push in. Let us look at —

III. The vain schemes of man.
1. The Purgatorial scheme — which offers by fires & various other refining agencies so to refine man, as that the vile sinner may get to heaven even if he dies in his sin. He suffers tortures, his friends pay, and the priest prays, and thus he gets out of hell and into heaven.
   But where is the Scripture for this.
Is not hell a place of eternal torment, is not the gulf fixed, is not faith in Jesus the only way, does not

This is no curious question but a serious one, and the more so when we consider:

II. THE DIFFICULTIES IN THE WAY OF MAN'S JUSTIFICATION.

1. Man himself. In him there are many serious difficulties:

    He has fallen federally in Adam who was our representative.[5]

    He is born with depravity innate within him.[6]

    He universally disobeys from the first moment of his rational being to the very last, growing viler still.[7] Not one of all the race is perfect.[8] The best have native sin.

2. The Law. In its stringency, punishing even one offence, demanding nothing less than universal obedience.

    —In its spirituality, touching the thoughts, words, desires.

    —In its extent,[9] punishing acts of omission as well as commission.

    —In its eternity, enduring without change 'till time ceases, and punishing sin for ever and ever in hell.

3. God. In his very dignity there is an awful barrier. Even angels deserve nothing but live on his benevolence. His omniscience beholds such sin as to stop man's mouth.[10] His justice and holiness must be magnified. His faithfulness, yea, all his attributes[11] are so many glorious swords guarding the avenues of Paradise.

Yet man has ventured to push in. Let us look at:

III. THE VAIN SCHEMES OF MAN.

1. The Purgatorial scheme,[12] which offers by fires and various other refining agencies so to refine man as that the vile sinner may get to heaven even if he dies in his sin. He suffers tortures, his friends pay, and the priest prays, and thus he gets out of hell and into heaven.

    But where is the Scripture for this?

    Is not hell a place of eternal torment?[13] Is not the gulf fixed? Is not faith in Jesus the only way?[14] Does not

SERMON 117

the tree lie for ever just where it falls? are not the old antediluvians still in hell? what is the use of preaching? If so we may live as we list. 'Tis a mere money getting lie, 'tis a bastard of the whore of Babylon, a whelp of the old Dragon —

2. The ceremonial scheme — concocted, devised and extolled by Messrs Pharisees, Pope, Pusey & Mormon. A noble firm; its real signature is Beelzebub & Co. These gentry propose either by ceremonies of their own invention or by those of the Church borrowed for the occasion so to lift man up that he shall be right. They fetched anciently the old forms from the sanctuary but when these were laid aside — they took the two new ones. Baptism — considered to be saving both by Pope, Pusey & Joe Smith. The Lord's supper turned into a devil's dinner — a priest's drunkenness and pride — and a poor sinner's ticket to heav no-no Seeing these suffice not the Pope puts them on salt & spittle the seven abominable farces &c &c — Mr Pusey invents Confi-mation, God-fathering &c — Joe Smith sends them all to the S.L.ake

But where does Scripture allow this —
Paul was not saved so. Why did Jesus die? What on earth connection is there between the Salt Lake and sin. Just as much as between Sodom & sin. The one is the sink of the other. The modern sea of Sodom.

What connection is there between a mere form and the pardon of sin — What nonsense. How foolish is man.

the tree lie for ever just where it falls?[15] Are not the old antediluvians[16] still in hell? What is the use of preaching? If so, we may live as we list. Tis a mere money getting lie. 'Tis a bastard of the whore of Babylon,[17] a whelp[18] of the old Dragon.[19]

2. The ceremonial scheme. Concocted, devised, and extolled by Messrs[20] Pharisees,[21] Pope, Pusey, and Mormon.[22] A noble firm, its real signature is Beelzebub and C°. These gentry[23] propose, either by ceremonies of their own invention or by those of the Church borrowed for the occasion so to lift man up that he shall be right. They fetched anciently the old forms from the sanctuary, but when these were laid aside they took the two new ones: Baptism, considered to be saving both by Pope, Pusey and Joe[24] Smith. The Lord's supper, turned into a devil's dinner, a priest's drunkenness and pride, and a poor sinner's ticket to heav[en]. **No. No.**[25]

Seeing these suffice not, the Pope puts them on salt and spittle.[26] The seven abominable farces,[27] etc., etc. Mr. Pusey invents Confirmation,[28] God-fathering,[29] etc. Joe Smith sends them all to S[alt] Lake.[30]

But where does Scripture allow this?

Paul was not saved so. Why did Jesus die? What on earth connection is there between the Salt Lake and sin?[31] Just as much as between Sodom and sin. The one is the sink of the other. The modern sea of Sodom.

What connection is there between a mere form and the pardon of sin? What nonsense. How foolish is man.

3. The commutation scheme — which stipulates that through Jesus' merits our sincere obedience shall be accepted just as if it were perfect, and so we shall be saved — Here is a mongrel monster. Neither Law nor gospel will own it. It is the foe of both the one & the other. What saith the Scriptures? Either all grace or all works — Men like this, it flatters them so much. But though a devil in the garb of an angel of light, it is a devil nevertheless — Why then men may do as little as they like, — but no the scheme is horrible.

4. The mercy scheme — which makes men hope that God will be kind to them even though Jesus be rejected. But is Justice dead. Pray where is he buried. For this would be a pleasant piece of news for Lucifer's Chronicle. Is the Law changed. Does yes mean no. Does the Bible say so — Ah, where is your scheme.

5. The last one I would not pass over it is The Sanctification scheme. Many good men hold that the works done by the help of Divine grace do constitute the righteousness of the saints. But let us look in the Bible — Men are justified by faith not by works in any sense. They are justified as soon as ever they believe, even before they are sanctified — and therefore sanctification does not justify. Again is sanctif.ⁿ perfect? — and when so can that atone for past sin? Then the thief was not justified. Is not this our own righteousness and is not that filthy rags? Here is somewhat of the Galatian Spirit though often unintentionally. A pure, perfect, spotless, divine robe is wanted.

3. The commutation[32] scheme, which stipulates that through Jesus'[s] merits our sincere obedience shall be accepted just as if it were perfect, and so we shall be saved. Here is a mongrel monster. Neither Law nor gospel will own it. It is the foe of both the one and the other. What saith the Scriptures? Either all grace or all works. Men like this. It flatters them so much. But though a devil in the garb of an angel of light,[33] it is a devil nevertheless. Why then, men may do as little as they like. But no, the scheme is horrible.

4. The mercy scheme, which makes men hope that God will be kind to them even though Jesus be rejected. But is Justice dead? Pray, where is he buried? For this would be a pleasant piece of news for Lucifer's Chronicle. Is the Law changed? Does yes mean no? Does the Bible say so? Ah, where is your scheme?

5. The last one I would not pass over: it is The Sanctification scheme. Many good men hold that the works done by the help of Divine grace do constitute the righteousness of the saints. But let us look in the Bible. Men are justified by faith, not by works in any sense.[34] They are justified as soon as ever they believe, even before they are sanctified. And therefore, sanctification does not justify.

Again, is sanctif[n35] perfect? And when so, can that atone for past sin? Then the thief was not justified.[36] Is not this our own righteousness, and is not that filthy rags?[37] Here is somewhat of the Galatian Spirit,[38] though often unintentionally. A pure, perfect, spotless, divine[39] robe is wanted.

__IV__. The only way is by the righteousness of Jesus imputed by God to every believing man. Men are counted and treated as holy for the sake of Jesus. This is a plan whereby the Law fulfils its own oath that none shall enter Heaven except they can show a perfect righteousness. Justice herein abates not a mite.

But let us come to Scripture it is well illustrated by Zech III, & the wedding garment — and is abundantly sustained by. Rom. IV. 6. Rom. V. 15. Phil. 8. 9. Is. 54. 17. & by numerous places in which occur the phrases "righteousness of God", "of the Lord", "of Jesus Christ"   Deut. 9. 4 —

Obj. Does the robe of Xt's righteousness cover over man's sin and hide it only.

By no means — pardon cleanses, sanctification heals, or else the man shall never be covered. It is not a napkin to hide filth but a robe to adorn purity.—

Imputed Righteousness is not absurd.—

1. Poor Penitent thou mayest be justified.
2. Brother Believer look off self, on to Jesus.
3. Sinner beware, thou art not found naked.
4. Moral Man — look to it — cobwebs will not serve thy turn —   God cloathes us all.
   <u>Amen</u>.—

161.

IV. THE ONLY WAY IS BY THE RIGHTEOUSNESS OF JESUS, IMPUTED BY GOD TO[40] EVERY BELIEVING MAN.

Men are counted and treated as holy for the sake of Jesus. This is a plan whereby the Law fulfils[41] its own oath that none shall enter Heaven except they can show a perfect righteousness. Justice herein abates not a mite.[42]

But let us come to Scripture. It is well illustrated by Zech. III,[43] and the wedding garment,[44] and is abundantly sustained by Rom. IV.6,[45] Rom. V.15,[46] Phil. 8.9,[47] Is. 54.17,[48] and by numerous places in which occur the phrases "righteousness of God," "of the Lord," "of Jesus Christ." Deut. 9.4.[49]

Obj.[50] Does the robe of Xn[51] righ[ns][52] cover over man's sin and hide it only?

> By no means. Pardon cleanses, sanctification heals, or else the man shall never be covered. It is not a napkin[53] to hide the filth, but a robe to adorn purity.

Imputed Righteousness is not absurd.

1. Poor Penitent, thou mayest be justified.
2. Brother Believer, look off self on to Jesus.[54]
3. Sinner, beware thou art not found naked.[55]
4. Moral Man, look to it. Cobwebs will not serve thy turn. God cloathes[56] us all.

Amen.

161.

SERMON 116

1. Charles preached an additional sermon on 1 Sam 22:1–2 entitled "Recruits for the King," later published on October 12, 1916 (*MTP* 62, Sermon 3533). There is not enough overlapping content or structural similarity to suggest Charles had in mind this early sermon when writing his later one.

2. "Individually; particularly" (Johnson's *Dictionary*, s.v. "singly").

3. Cf. "Christ About His Father's Business" (Notebook 1, Sermon 15).

4. Charles reinforced the stem of the letter "b" in the word "describe" and inserted a caret to indicate its location. He might have prematurely written the letter "e."

5. Cf. Matt 1:1–17.

6. Cf. John 20:27.

7. Charles wrote the word "has" above and between the words "he" and "never." He indicated its location with a caret beneath the line.

8. Cf. John 6:39.

9. Cf. John 1:14; Phil 2:5–8.

10. Cf. 2 Tim 4:8; Jas 1:12.

11. See Christian's crossing of the River Jordan before entering the Celestial City in John Bunyan, *The Pilgrim's Progress*, 188–95. For a retelling of this narrative, see "The Beloved of the Lord in Safety" (Sermon 100).

12. Cf. Rev 12:3; 20:2, 10.

13. Cf. Isa 61:1; Luke 4:18.

14. The letter "b" appears beneath the "t" in the word "motley." Charles likely wrote the word "mob" before changing it to "motley."

15. Cf. Matt 22:1–10; Luke 14:15–24.

16. An alternative reading of this line is "Come on, right[ly] welcome[d] comrade."

17. A "farthing" was a British coin worth one-fourth of a penny. Samuel Johnson called it "the smallest English coin" (Johnson's *Dictionary*, s.v. "farthing"). The farthing was officially phased out as legal tender on December 31, 1960. For additional references to this coin, see "King of Righteousness and Peace" (Notebook 1, Sermon 42); "Inventory and Title of Our Treasures" (Sermon 92); "David in the Cave of Adullum" (Sermon 116); *NPSP* 3:154; 5:203; *MTP* 18:198; 28:198; 29:504; 41:593; and 63:112.

18. Cf. Luke 14:28.

19. The size and placement of the number 1 in the margin suggest Charles did not originally intend to begin a list and added it after he wrote the paragraph. Also, the handwriting in this section is significantly different from that seen in Roman numeral III. Charles likely began using a different writing instrument.

20. Charles may have had in mind Isa 64:6, Zech 3:4, or Heb 12:1.

21. Cf. "The Physician and His Patients" (Notebook 1, Sermon 74).

22. Charles wrote the word "the" between and above the words "of" and "righteousness." He indicated its location with a caret.

23. Cf. Ps 132:9; Isa 61:10.

24. Cf. 1 Cor 6:19–20.

25. "Any movable possession: a term now scarce used but in form of law" (Johnson's *Dictionary*, s.v. "chattel").

26. Samuel Johnson defined the word "several" as "1. a state of separation, or partition" and "2. each particular singly taken" (Johnson's *Dictionary*, s.v. "several"). Charles used the word "several" as a verb in this sentence to mean "to separate" or "to partition."

27. The letter "i" appears beneath the "b" in the word "by." Charles originally wrote the word "in" before reinforcing the letter "b" to construct the word "by."

28. For Charles's ecumenism, see "Can Two Walk Together Unless They Are Agreed?" (Notebook 1, Sermon 76).

29. Charles struck through the word "search" and wrote "examine" in superscript above the word.

30. Cf. Isa 7:14; Matt 1:23.

31. Cf. Rom 14:4; 1 John 2:15.

32. Cf. "Never go one inch from the line" ("Envy Forbidden, Piety Commanded" [Sermon 112]).

33. "Treatment shown by an enemy" (Johnson's *Dictionary*, s.v. "quarter").

SERMON 116

34. Cf. "No time for sleep" ("The Day of God" [Sermon 115]).

35. Abbr. "Posture." Charles may have also intended the abbreviation to represent the word "Position."

36. Charles inserted six ditto marks in this column to signify the repetition of the word "Posture" (or "Position") in the line above. For additional uses of ditto marks, see "Adoption" (Notebook 1, Sermon 1) and "Future Judgment" (Notebook 1, Sermon 96).

37. Charles may have had in mind Joseph's escape from Potiphar's wife in Gen 39:12, "He left his garment in her hand, and fled, and got him out."

38. See Vanity Fair in John Bunyan's *The Pilgrim's Progress*, 102–16.

39. Charles originally wrote the word "oben" instead of "open."

JUSTIFICATION BY IMPUTED RIGHTEOUSNESS—*Job 25:4*

1. For additional sermons on justification, see "The Saints' Justification and Glory" (Notebook 1, Sermon 68) and "Justification, Conversion, Sanctification, Glory" (Sermon 102).

2. This is the only time Charles preached a sermon on Job 25:4.

3. Charles originally combined the two words "self" and "righteousness." For consistency, the word is hyphenated.

4. Cf. Job 35:2; Phil 3:9.

5. "Man's being sinful, is in the logic of justice, a reason for punishment; man's being sinful from his youth by inheritance from his federal head, becomes through mercy a reason why sovereign grace should light upon men while fallen angels are left to perish for ever" (*MTP* 11:106). "How great is the goodness of God, *which he laid up in the covenant of grace!* He determined to bless us in a way of covenant relationship, into which he entered on our behalf with our federal head, the Lord Jesus. To attempt, my dear brethren, to read to you the treasures, which God has made over to us in the covenant of grace, were to attempt an impossibility. The catalogue is far too comprehensive. Behold, he has given all things to you in the covenant of his eternal love, for all things are yours, whether things present or things to come—life and death, time and eternity; nay, more, God himself is yours!" (*MTP* 13:543, italics in the original). "The first man has ruined us; but we have the second Man now, who heads up his people, having become their federal Representative; and in him they are saved beyond all fear of falling" (*MTP* 46:509). See also "God in the Covenant" (*NPSP* 2, Sermon 93); "Christ in the Covenant" (*NPSP* 2, Sermon 103); "The Blood of the Covenant" (*MTP* 20, Sermon 1186); "The Covenant Pleaded" (*MTP* 25, Sermon 1451); "The Covenant Promise of the Spirit" (*MTP* 37, Sermon 2200); and "The Wondrous Covenant" (*MTP* 58, Sermon 3326).

6. Cf. Rom 7:18.

7. Cf. Ps 51:5.

8. Cf. Rom 3:10.

9. An illegible letter, likely "c," appears beneath the "x" in the word "extent." Charles might have originally misspelled the word.

10. Cf. Job 40:4.

11. Cf. "Faith Precious" (Notebook 1, Sermon 23).

12. In 1844, the Roman Catholic Church earned £300,000 in annual confessions in Ireland with an additional £100,000 earned for prayers dedicated to those in purgatory ("Political Intelligence," *The Lancaster Gazette, and General Advertiser for Lancashire, Westmoreland &c*, March 9, 1844). See also "Purgatory and Indulgences," *The Belfast Protestant Journal*, May 25, 1850. "They are all swept away in one solitary instant; the crimes of many years; extortions, adulteries, or even murder, wiped away in an instant; for you will notice the absolution was instantaneously given. God did not say to the man—'Now you must go and perform some good works, and then I will give you absolution.' He did not say as the Pope does, 'Now you must swelter awhile in the fires of Purgatory, and then I will let you out.' No, he justified him there and then; the pardon was given as soon as the sin was confessed" (*NPSP* 4:415). "To the righteous soul there is no sleeping in the grave, no delay in purgatory before he enters into heaven. 'To-day shalt thou be with me in paradise,' is the portion of all who trust in Jesus" (*MTP* 13:223).

13. Matthew 25:46, "And these shall go away into everlasting punishment: but the righteous into life eternal."

14. Cf. John 14:6; Acts 4:12; 1 Tim 2:5.

15. Ecclesiastes 11:3, "If the clouds be full of rain, they empty themselves upon the earth: and if the tree fall toward the south, or toward the north, in the place where the tree falleth, there it shall be."

16. Charles is likely referring to the fallen angels mentioned in Gen 6:1–7 and Jude 6.

17. Cf. Rev 17:5.

18. "The young of any beast of prey" (Johnson's *Dictionary*, s.v. "whelp").

19. Cf. Revelation 12.

20. Abbr. "Messieurs."

JUSTIFICATION BY IMPUTED RIGHTEOUSNESS—*Job 25:4*

21. Charles originally wrote the word "Pharisees" before striking through the letter "s" to construct the singular.

22. Cf. "Salvation in God Only" (Notebook 1, Sermon 24) and "The Minister's Commission" (Sermon 110).

23. In his previous sermon, "David in the Cave of Adullam" (Sermon 116), Charles spoke disparagingly about the gentry class who rejected Christ: "Surely, so first rate a captain deserves good soldiers, but the finer sort reject him. The gentry will not have him."

24. Abbr. "Joseph."

25. Charles wrote the bolded and underscored words "**No. No.**" in superscript above the line.

26. The words "salt and spittle" were derogatory references to Roman Catholicism. Six years prior to the preaching of the sermon above, Robert Herrick published a poem entitled "The Fairie Temple" in which he mocked the "*Fasting-Spittle*" and "*sacred Salt*" in the Roman Catholic tradition: "They have their *Cups* and *Chalices*; / Their *Pardons* and *Indulgences*: / Their *Beads* of *Nits*, *Bels*, *Books*, & *Wax* / *Candles*, forsooth, and other knacks: / Their *Holy Oyle*, their *Fasting-Spittle*; / Their *sacred Salt* here, not a little" (Robert Herrick, *Hesperides: Or the Works Both Humane and Divine of Robert Herrick Esq. Vol. I* [London: William Pickering, 1846], 123, italics in the original).

27. The "seven abominable farces" were likely the seven sacraments in Roman Catholicism: baptism, confirmation, the Holy Eucharist, penance, extreme unction, holy orders, and holy matrimony.

28. Edward Bouverie Pusey (1800–1882) was a prominent Anglican who gave leadership to the Oxford Movement, which was a resurgence of conservative Anglicanism at Oxford University sparked by John Keble's 1883 sermon "National Apostasy" (see R. W. Church, *The Oxford Movement: Twelve Years 1833–1845*, vol. 6 [London: MacMillan, 1897]). Pusey championed the doctrine of baptismal regeneration, as seen in his *Tract for the Times by Members of the University of Oxford*, no. 67: *Scriptural Views of Holy Baptism*, part I (2nd ed.: J. G. F. & J. Rivington; Oxford: J. H. Parker, 1840), 4. Charles's opposition to this doctrine resulted in his highly

controversial sermon in 1864, "Baptismal Regeneration" (*MTP* 10, Sermon 573). For a recent work on Pusey, see Rowan Strong and Carol Engelhardt Herringer, eds., *Edward Bouverie Pusey and the Oxford Movement* (Anthem Nineteenth-Century Series; London: Anthem Press, 2012). On one occasion, Charles remembered hearing "Mr. Jay, of Bath" preach sermons against Puseyism, saying, "You do need a Mediator between yourselves and God, but you do not need a Mediator between yourselves and Christ" (*Autobiography* 1:208). Mr. Jay also said, "Puseyism is a lie" (*MTP* 26:386–87). See also "Salvation in God Only" (Notebook 1, Sermon 24).

29. "The sponsor at the font" (Johnson's *Dictionary*, s.v. "godfather"). "See yonder priest pointing to *the wall of ceremonies*, behind which many rest so contentedly. Were you not christened? Oh! the blessedness of that christening—a thing which is as gross a piece of superstition as ever was practiced by Mahomet, which has no more warrant in the word of God than the baptism of bells or the burning of Hindoo widows, and yet this idle farce, this wicked mockery, this god-fathering and godmothering, no ordinance of God's, but an invention of the Pope of Rome" (*MTP* 14:339–40, italics in the original) [Cf. "Jesus's Dead Body Whilst on the Cross" (Sermon 107)].

30. See "The Minister's Commission" (Sermon 110).

31. In his mind, Charles may have connected Mormonism in Salt Lake City with Lot's wife, who turned into salt when looking back at Sodom (cf. Gen 19:26).

32. "To exchange; to put one thing in the place of another; to give or receive one thing for another. . . . To buy off, or ransom one obligation for another. . . . To atone; to bargain for exemption" (Johnson's *Dictionary*, s.v. "commute").

33. Second Corinthians 11:14, "And no marvel; for Satan himself is transformed into an angel of light." In the fourth century St. Martin, bishop of Tours, was in his cell when "the devil came to him environed with light, clothed in royal robes, and with a crown of gold and precious stones upon his head, and, with a gracious and pleasant countenance, told him twice that he was Christ. . . . By this the saint, after some pause, discerned the evident marks of the angel of darkness, and said to him: 'The Lord Jesus said not that he was to come clothed with purple, and crowned and adorned with a diadem. Nor will I ever believe him to be Christ who shall not come in the habit and figure in which

Christ suffered, and who shall not bear the marks of the cross in his body.' At these words the fiend vanished, and left the cell filled with an intolerable stench" (Alban Butler, *The Lives of the Primitive Fathers, Martyrs, and Other Principal Saints: Compiled from Original Monuments, and Other Authentic Records: Illustrated with the Remarks of Judicious Modern Critics and Historians, The Third Edition. In Twelve Volumes. Vol. XI* [Edinburgh: printed by J. Moir for J. P. Coghlan, P. Keating, E. Booker, and F. Coates, 1799], 214). Charles may have had this episode in mind since John Gill referenced it in his exposition of Gal 3:1–3, which Charles likely consulted for his "Galatian Spirit" remark below (Gill, *Expositions of the New Testament*, 3:13).

34. Romans 3:28, "Therefore we conclude that a man is justified by faith without the deeds of the law."

35. Abbr. "sanctification." See also Charles's abbreviation in "The Best Feast" (Sermon 125).

36. Charles wrote the sentence "Then the thief was not justified" in superscript above "Is not this our own righteousness?" The context suggests Charles intended to place this sentence after the previous question, "And when so, can that atone for past sin?"

37. Isaiah 64:6, "But we are all as an unclean thing, and all our righteousnesses are as filthy rags; and we all do fade as a leaf; and our iniquities, like the wind, have taken us away."

38. Charles likely consulted Gill's *Exposition of the New Testament* in which he noted the Galatians were "in opposition to the Spirit of God, by which they endeavored to perform obedience to the law" (Gill, *Exposition of the New Testament*, 3:14).

39. Charles originally spelled the word "divene." He did not insert a tittle over the letter "e"; however, he did reinforce the stem of the letter "i" to construct the correct spelling of the word "divine."

40. Charles originally wrote the word "the" before converting it to "to."

41. A dark amber spot appears over the letter "u" in the word "fulfils." Its cause is the aging process of the manuscript.

42. "The twentieth part of a grain. . . . Anything proverbially small; the third part of a farthing" (Johnson's *Dictionary*, s.v. "mite").

43. Zechariah 3:3–5, "Now Joshua was clothed with filthy garments, and stood before the angel. And he answered and spake unto those that stood before him, saying, Take away the filthy garments from him. And unto him he said, Behold, I have caused thine iniquity to pass from thee, and I will clothe thee with change of raiment. And I said, Let them set a fair mitre upon his head. So they set a fair mitre upon his head, and clothed him with garments."

44. Matthew 22:11–12, "And when the king came in to see the guests, he saw there a man which had not on a wedding garment: And he saith unto him, Friend, how camest thou in hither not having a wedding garment? And he was speechless."

45. Romans 4:6, "Even as David also describeth the blessedness of the man, unto whom God imputeth righteousness without works."

46. Romans 5:15, "But not as the offence, so also *is* the free gift. For if through the offence of one many be dead, much more the grace of God, and the gift by grace, which is by one man, Jesus Christ, hath abounded unto many."

47. Instead of "Phil. 8.9," Charles likely intended to write Phil 3:9, "And be found in him, not having mine own righteousness, which is of the law, but that which is through the faith of Christ, the righteousness which is of God by faith."

48. Isaiah 54:17, "No weapon that is formed against thee shall prosper; and every tongue that shall rise against thee in judgment thou shalt condemn. This is the heritage of the servants of the Lord, and their righteousness is of me, saith the Lord."

49. Deuteronomy 9:4, "Speak not thou in thine heart, after that the Lord thy God hath cast them out from before thee, saying, For my righteousness the Lord hath brought me in to possess this land: but for the wickedness of these nations the Lord doth drive them out from before thee."

50. Abbr. "Objection."

51. Abbr. "Christian."

52. Abbr. "righteousness."

53. Charles originally wrote the word "hapkin" before striking through the stem of the letter "h" to construct the word, "napkin." Charles may have originally begun writing the word "hide," as he did two words to the right.

54. Charles was converted in a Primitive Methodist Chapel in Colchester in January 1850 when an anonymous layman preached a sermon on Isa 45:22, "Look unto me, and be ye saved, all the ends of the earth" (*Autobiography* 1:102–4).

55. Revelation 16:15, "Behold, I come as a thief. Blessed is he that watcheth, and keepeth his garments, lest he walk naked, and they see his shame."

56. Charles originally pluralized the word "cloathes" before striking through the letter "s." The change significantly shifts the meaning of this sentence. With the letter "s," the phrase is in the declarative mood. Without the letter "s," the phrase becomes a prayer. See also the prayer at the conclusion of "The Day of God" (Sermon 115).

Luke XV. 18. 19. *The prodigal's resolution.*

The Pharisees were a pest to Jesus and he was continually declaiming against them — Christ's system of Salvation ever will be opposed by the self righteous. How foolish this conduct is for if they like it not, they should suffer poor sinners to hear it — This Parable well sets out the experience of men plucked as brands from the burning and this resolution must be formed by every penitent. In order to set it out clearly let us look at

I. The prodigal's vile conduct.

Here we notice, 1. Pride — he thought he would be master. 2. Ingratitude — he turns his father's gifts so as to grieve him. He gained his request and but a little after went far away from his kind parent — 3. His rioting — drunkenness — extravagance — debauchery — 4. The extreme lengths, he spent all, he went as far as possible.

II. The prodigal in distress —

1. Sin wasted his substance, his health, hopes & all.
2. Sin makes a famine in a country — it has no good fruit. there was a mighty famine, what a mercy his money was all spent, or else he would not have gone home, and then he would have perished in the great destruction. Well what does he — he asks the devil for help but no he gives him a mean employment — he asks his old companions but they do not care for him, he asks the legalists but he gives him hard work and only a few husks — but he is too proud to come

THE PRODIGAL'S RESOLUTION—*Luke 15:18–19*

118

The PRODIGAL'S RESOLUTION
Luke 15:18–19[1]

"I will arise and go to my father, and will say unto him, Father, I have sinned against heaven, and before thee, and am no more worthy to be called thy son: make me as one of thy hired servants."

The Pharisees were a pest to Jesus, and he was continually declaiming against them.[2] Christ's system of salvation ever will be opposed by the self righteous. How foolish this conduct is, for if <u>they</u> like it not, they should suffer poor sinners to hear it. This Parable well sets out the experience of men plucked as brands from the burning,[3] and this resolution must be formed by every penitent.

In order to set it out clearly, let us look at:

I.[4] THE PRODIGAL'S VILE CONDUCT.

Here we notice:

1. Pride. He thought he would be master.

2. Ingratitude. He turns his father's gifts so as to grieve him.[5] He[6] gained his request, and but a little after went far away from his kind parent.[7]

3. His rioting, drunkenness, extravagance, debauchery.

4. The extreme lengths. He spent all.[8] He went as far as possible.

II. THE PRODIGAL IN DISTRESS.

1. Sin wasted his substance, his health, hopes and all.

2. Sin makes a famine in a country. It has no good fruit. There was a mighty famine. What a mercy his money was all spent or else he would <u>not have gone home</u>, and then he would have perished in the great destruction. Well, what does he? He asks the devil for help. But no, he gives him a mean employment. He asks his old companions, but they do not care for him. He asks the legalists, but he gives him hard work and only a few husks. But he is too[9] proud to come.

perhaps too he is afraid that he will not be received.

III. The prodigal reflecting "he came to himself."
He had been mad, giddy, intoxicated now he comes to
1. He sees sin to be a servile state. "pig feeding"
2. He feels it to be an unsatisfactory state "husks".
3. He finds no help in creature "no man gave"
4. He remembers that there is one who can help.
5. He thinks of the many, who are feasting to their full, even though as to worldly affairs servants as well as he. he thinks how some have been received
6. He remembers the sad alternative, go or famish.

IV. The prodigal's ~~reply~~ resolution "I will arise"–
1. He shakes off carelessness and apathy and bestirs.
2. He makes up his mind to go to head quarters "father"
3. He confesses his own sinfulness – & aggravates it by God's omniscience which sees & notes all.
4. He lays aside all worthiness "no more worthy"
5. He humbly requests the meanest place

V. The prodigal's reception – He would not let him end the tale, he is as willing to receive as ever sinner can be to return –
Poor sinner God sees thee a great way off. He is willing to take thee in though a drunkard or an harlot. I tell thee Come — Jesus draw them
162. 172. 460. amen

THE PRODIGAL'S RESOLUTION—*Luke 15:18–19*

Perhaps, too, he is afraid that he will not be received.

III. THE PRODIGAL REFLECTING, *"he came to himself."*

He had been mad, giddy, intoxicated. Now he comes to.[10]

1. He sees sin to be a servile state, "pig feeding."[11]
2. He feels it to be an unsatisfactory state, "husks."[12]
3. He finds no help in creature, "no man gave."[13]
4. He remembers that there is one who can help.
5. He thinks of the <u>many</u> who are feasting to their full,[14] even though as to worldly affairs, servants as well as he.[15] He thinks how some have been received.
6. He remembers the sad alternative, go or famish.

IV. THE PRODIGAL'S ~~REfOL~~[16] RESOLUTION, *"I will arise."*

1. He shakes off carelessness and apathy and bestirs.
2. He makes up his mind to go to head quarters, "father."
3. He confesses his own sinfulness, and aggravates it by God's omniscience, which sees and notes all.
4. He lays aside all worthiness, "no more worthy."
5. He humbly requests the meanest place.

V. THE PRODIGAL'S RECEPTION.

He would not let him end the tale. He is as willing to receive as ever [a] sinner can be to return.

Poor sinner, God sees thee a great way off.[17] He is willing to take thee in, though a drunkard or an harlot. I tell thee, Come.

Jesus, draw them.

<u>Amen</u>

162. 172. 460.

SERMON 118

1. This is the only time Charles preached on Luke 15:18–19. Additional sermons on the parable of the Prodigal Son include "The Prodigal's Return" (*NPSP* 4, Sermon 89); "The Prodigal's Reception" (*MTP* 10, Sermon 588); "Prodigal Love for the Prodigal Son" (*MTP* 37, Sermon 2236); "The Prodigal's Climax" (*MTP* 41, Sermon 2414); and "The Old Testament 'Prodigal'" (*MTP* 59, Sermon 3354).

2. Charles originally wrote the word "him." He inserted the letter "t" and converted the "i" to "e" to construct the word "them."

3. Charles's reference to the "men plucked as brands from the burning" may have been inspired by his consultation with Zech 3:2 in the previous sermon: "And the Lord said unto Satan, The Lord rebuke thee, O Satan; even the Lord that hath chosen Jerusalem rebuke thee: is not this a brand plucked out of the fire?" See also "Brand Plucked from the Fire" (Notebook 5, Sermon 242) and "God's Firebrands" (*MTP* 57, Sermon 3233). Charles may have also had in mind Joseph Alleine's *A Sure Guide to Heaven,* which his mother read to him as a child (*Autobiography* 1:68). In his section "An Earnest Invitation to Sinners to Turn to God, in Order to Their Eternal Salvation," Alleine wrote, "If I were to quiet a crying infant, I might sing him to a pleasant mood, and rock him asleep. But when the Child is fallen into the Fire, the Parent takes another course; he will not go to still him with a song or trifle" (Joseph Alleine, *A Sure Guide to Heaven; or, an Earnest Invitation to Sinners to Turn to God, in Order to Their Eternal Salvation. Shewing the Thoughtful Sinner What He Must Do to Be Saved* [London: printed for Tho. Parkhurst at the Bible and Three Crowns, at the lower end of Cheapside near Mercers Chappel, 1700, The Spurgeon Library], 4).

4. A notable discoloration of the page appears above and to the left of Roman numeral I due to residue stains from the piece of string used in the central binding of the notebook's pages.

5. Cf. Luke 15:12.

6. An ink blot, likely unintentional, covers the word "He." There is no evidence to suggest Charles intended to strike through the word.

7. Cf. Luke 15:13.   8. Cf. Luke 15:14.

9. The final letter "o" in the word "too" is smeared toward the bottom of the page.

THE PRODIGAL'S RESOLUTION—*Luke 15:18–19*

10. Charles wrote the word "to" with greater pressure than the words in the body of this sermon. Its location in the margin suggests he added the word afterward.

11. Luke 15:15, "And he went and joined himself to a citizen of that country; and he sent him into his fields to feed swine."

12. Luke 15:16a, "And he would fain have filled his belly with the husks that the swine did eat."

13. Luke 15:16b, "[A]nd no man gave unto him."

14. Cf. Luke 15:17.

15. An alternative reading of this line is "He thinks of the many who are feasting to their full, even though, as to worldly affairs, [they are] servants as well as he."

16. Charles struck through the letters "reſol" likely because he originally spelled the word with the long Puritan "s," as he did in the word "carelessness" in the line below. This may explain why he wrote the word "resolution" without the long "s" immediately afterwards.

17. Cf. Luke 15:20.

SERMON 119

2 Cor. 6 – 17. 18. Come ye out from among them. –

Paul before giving this exhortation is careful to declare the relation in which he stood to them as one longing to do them service and more ready to communicate than they were to receive. Let us remark that it is highly necessary that pastor & people should stand on a footing of mutual love. Since without this the one is unfitted to reprove and the other to harken. We hear best those whom we love most and who love us most. –

Let these words of the apostle be received as those of a true friend. and in improving them

I. Let us notice their scope, meaning, and extent.

The Christians were then surrounded by Jews and heathens and the apostle bids them neither to form intimate relations with them nor to become conformed to their likeness but to be distinct. Not that they were to go out of the world as hermits or monks *Quaker's distinctions are unnecessary. but yet let our clothing be becoming.* we must be in the world, it is essential to its very existence, it is necessary for its renovation & only there can we exercise many of the graces by which we glorify God. yet we are told to come out. Perhaps the modern Jew is one of the best types of Christian separation — He is in the world buying & selling, he mixes with all society and notwithstanding he remains a Jew, distinguished by the secret mark of the covenant, his very contour, manners speech and religion — There should be an actual separation "Come ye out". This implies that we were once in & so we were, alike given to sin with others. — We first heard these words with power at the moment of effectual calling – and still doth it ring in our ears – when we find ourselves overtaken by evil habits or in evil society. –

"be ye separate". when we obeyed the heavenly mandate. then our separation began. may it for ever continue. We were by God's decree separated by election & the eternal

COME YE OUT *from* AMONG THEM
2 Corinthians 6:17–18[1]

*"Wherefore come out from among them, and be ye separate, saith the L*ORD*, and touch not the unclean thing; and I will receive you. And will be a Father unto you, and ye shall be my sons and daughters, saith the Lord Almighty."*

Paul, before giving this exhortation, is careful to declare the relation in which he stood to them as one longing to do them service and more ready to communicate than they were to receive.[2] Let us remark that it is highly necessary that pastor and people should stand on a footing of mutual love, since without this, the one is unfitted to reprove and the others to harken. We hear best those whom we love most and who love us most.

Let these words of the apostles[3] be received as those of a true friend, and in improving them:

I. LET US NOTICE THEIR SCOPE, MEANING, AND EXTENT.

The Christians were then surrounded by Jews and heathens, and the apostle bids them neither to[4] form intimate relations with them nor to become[5] conformed to their likeness,[6] but to be distinct.[7] Not that they were to go out of the world as hermits or monks.[8] Quakers['] distinctions are unnecessary. But yet, let our clothing be becoming.[9] We <u>must</u> be in the world.[10] It is essential to its very existence. It is necessary for its renovation, and only there can we exercise many of the graces by which we glorify God. Yet, we are told to come out.

Perhaps the modern Jew is one of the best types of Christian separation. He is in the world buying and selling. He mixes with all society, and notwithstanding, he remains a Jew distinguished by the secret mark of the covenant, his very contour, manners, speech, and religion. There should be an actual separation.

"<u>Come ye out</u>." This implies that we were once in, and so we were alike given to sin with others. We first heard these words with power at the moment of effectual calling, and still doth it ring in our ears when we find ourselves overtaken by evil habits or in evil society.

"Be ye separate." When we obeyed the heavenly mandate, then our separation began. May it for ever continue. We were by God's decree separated by election[11] and the eternal covenant, we are actually separated the first moment we believe, but we are openly so when we confess his name among men, and continue so by a consistent walk & conversation. "touch not the unclean thing," have nothing whatever to do with sin. Spare no lust even though it be a little one. avoid the appearance of evil — "touch not" for the world will magnify it, touch not for that leads to worse — He who does not begin cannot go to excess. "touch not".

In all ages this has been a standing ordinance "be ye separate." & it was obeyed alike in Jewish, heathen & Catholic times — our forefathers would by no means conform to the Anglican society for 'tis no church. Nor should we have any union either with Popery or its rouged sister Puseyism. Rev XVIII. 4 — Come out —

II. I will endeavour to send home the exhortation by a few arguments showing its necessity —

1. Remember that it augurs ill when the church lies in the arms of the world — giants shall then be born — giants in sin — and then judgments are frequent and awful — witness the flood, the day of plague, when 24,000 died in the wilderness because they companied with the Moabites — the incursions of enemies into Canaan, — the Captivity — the sparing of but one Agag destroyed Saul therefore. No union on pain of the anger of the Lord, the Jealous one.

2. It is not consistent with the character of the regenerate that he should mingle with the world. Is he a soldier let him not sit in his enemies tent. Is he a pilgrim let him never take his portion here. Is he a sheep let him not be found devouring garbage as the dog. Is he a prince let him not live like the Irishman with pigs. Is he alive why should he live in the tomb or dwell in the coffin. Is he washed and are his garments beauteous — let him have

covenant. We are actually separated the first moment we believe, but we are openly so when we confess his name among men, and continue so by a consistent walk and conversation.

"Touch not the unclean thing." Have nothing whatever to do with sin.[12] Spare no lust, even though it be a little one. Avoid the appearance of evil.[13] "Touch not," for the world will magnify it. Touch not, for that leads to worse. He who does not begin cannot go to excess.[14] "Touch not."

In all ages this has been a standing ordinance: "Be ye separate." And it was obeyed alike in Jewish, heathen, and Catholic times. Our forefathers would by no means conform to the Anglican society, for 'tis no church. Nor should we have any union either with Popery or its rouged[15] sister, Puseyism.[16] Rev. XVIII. 4.[17] Come out.

II. I WILL ENDEAVOUR TO SEND HOME THE EXHORTATION BY A FEW ARGUMENTS SHOWING ITS NECESSITY.

1. Remember that it augurs ill[18] when the church lies in the arms of the world. Giants shall then be born.[19] Giants in sin. And then judgments are frequent and awful. Witness the flood,[20] the day of plague when 24,000 died in the wilderness because they companied with the Moabites,[21] the incursions of enemies into Canaan, the captivity.[22] The sparing of but one Agag destroyed Saul.[23] Therefore, no union on pain of the anger of the Lord, the Jealous one.[24]

2. It is not consistent with the character of the regenerate that he should mingle with the world. Is he a soldier? Let him not sit in his enem[y's][25] tent. Is he a pilgrim? Let him never take his portion here. Is he a sheep? Let him not be found devouring garbage as the dog. Is he a prince? Let him not live like the Irishman with pigs.[26] Is he alive? Why should he live in the tomb[27] or dwell in the coffin? Is he washed[28] and are his garments beauteous? Let him have

a care of the Kennel — However we are spoken of separation is implied
3. Consider the harm a good man receives in bad company. It is a poke to the fire of his lust — grace pours water on it and the world turns bellows to it. — if not burned by the ash he will be blackened — Sin is infectious have a care of leprous men. They are our enemies though they speak fair — may a saint has been robbed by them. and may have to bless sovereign grace that they were not murdered & picked to the bone — A christian gets broken bones though his neck is safe — How long bad things stick by you — how often do they come up unwanted — Come out —
4. Let gratitude, the very root of evangelical obedience have great weight with us — Consider we are.
Elect — when others are passed over — Chosen others are rejected. Redeemed and that too at an immense cost even the precious heart's blood and life of Jesus. Sought out by the Holy Spirit and found when wandering far. Pardoned notwithstanding the vast number of our sins. We have been supported in the hour of trial, we have had much enjoyment, innumerable mercies — We have been loved above others — let us love God more than others.
5. Remember his glorious promises, a golden mine. He promises final perseverance — perfection in glory. a glorious death, an acquittal at judgment, a glorious resurrection and eternal bliss — come then — do this one little thing out of pure love — Thou wilt be separate in heaven be separate now — but I back it up with —

III The gracious promise. of reception & adoption.
Not for the sake of our good coming out — no, no — that is bestowed from mere grace — Adoption cannot be purchased. "I will receive you" — as the father did the returning prodigal "I will be a Father unto you" this is the extreme of love. The topmost point of grace's towering mountains. —

COME YE OUT FROM AMONG THEM—2 Corinthians 6:17-18

a care of the kennel. However we are spoken of, separation is implied.

3. Consider the harm a good man receives in bad company. It is a poke to the fire of his lust. Grace pours water on it and the world turns bellows to it. If not burned by the ash, he will be blackened.

   Sin is infectious. Have a care of leprous men. They are our enemies. Though they speak fair, many a saint has been robbed by them, and many have to bless sovereign grace that they were not murdered and picked to the bone. A Christian gets broken bones though his neck is safe. How long bad things stick by you. How often do they come up unwanted. Come out.

4. Let gratitude, the very root of evangelical obedience, have great weight with us. Consider, we are: Elect, when others are passed over. Chosen. Others are rejected. Redeemed, and that, too, at an immense cost,[29] even the precious heart's blood and life of Jesus.[30] Sought out by the Holy Spirit and found when wandering far. Pardoned, notwithstanding the vast number of our sins. We have been supported in the hour of trial. We have had much enjoyment, innumerable mercies. We have been loved above others. Let us love God more than others.

5. Remember his glorious promises, a golden mine.[31] He promises final perseverance,[32] perfection in glory, a glorious death, an acquital at judgment, a glorious resurrection, and eternal bliss. Come then, do this one little thing out of pure love. Thou wilt be separate in heaven,[33] be separate now. But I back it up with:[34]

III. THE GRACIOUS PROMISE OF RECEPTION AND ADOPTION.[35]

Not for the sake of our good coming out. No, no. That is bestowed from mere grace. Adoption cannot be purchased. "I will receive you" as the father did the returning prodigal.[36] "I will be a Father unto you." This is the extreme of love, the topmost point of grace's towering[37] mountains.

SERMON 119

1. Separation and Adoption go together — when God adopts one of the children of wrath — he takes him away from the other family. — It is absurd for a man to say that he is born again and yet live just like those who are dead in sin.

2. In proportion as our conduct becomes more & more marked, and the difference between us and the world more evident, so shall we be able to read our titles and adoption with a more steady eye. — These precious promises are such great givers, they ask so little of us and that little is so much for our benefit that surely we should "Come out" "be separate" & "touch not".——

1. Convinced sinner — if thou dost believe, thou shalt come out — but you cannot be saved where you are. Go not now with old companions lest convictions die.

2. Young convert — Let not presumption allow thee to touch — thou hast just come out and dost thou dare go back. If so thou art no Christian thou art a washed swine; for Jesus' sake keep out —

3. Old Christian — thou oughtest to have a more outward difference. thy beard should be longer. Say hast thou ever got good by evil company — Warn the young look to thine own feet — God keep us.
Amen

166.

1. Separation and Adoption go together. When God adopts one of the children of wrath, he takes him away from the other family.[38] It is absurd for a man to say that he is born again and yet live just like those who are dead in sin.

2. In proportion. As our conduct becomes more and more marked and the difference between us[39] and the world more evident, so shall we be able to read our titles and adoption with a more steady eye.

These precious promises are such great givers. They ask so little of us. And that little is so much for our benefit that surely we should "come out,["] "be separate," and "touch not." — — — — —

1. Convinced sinner, if thou dost believe, thou shalt come out. But you cannot be saved where you are. Go not now with old companions lest convictions die.

2. Young convert, Let not presumption allow thee to touch. Thou hast just come out and dost thou dare go back? If so, thou art no Christian. Thou art a washed swine. For Jesus'[s] sake, keep out.

3. Old Christian, though ough[t]est[40] to have a more outward difference. Thy beard should be longer.[41] Say, hast thou ever got good by evil company?

Warn the young. Look to thine own feet.[42] God keep us.

<u>Amen</u>

166.

1. This is the only time Charles preached a sermon on 2 Cor 6:17–18.

2. Cf. 2 Cor 6:4–11.

3. Charles originally wrote the word "apostles." However, he intended the word to be singular and struck through the letter "s."

4. Charles wrote the word "to" in superscript between and above the words "neither" and "form."

5. This is the first time Charles hyphenated the word "be-come" in his early sermon notebooks.

6. An illegible letter, possibly "l" or "d," was written beneath the "n" in the word "likeness."

7. Cf. 2 Cor 6:14–16.

8. Charles was referring to the early church anchorites, hermits, and monks like St. Anthony who withdrew into the Egyptian wilderness. Philip Schaff noted, "Anchorites, properly speaking, were persons who retired from the world, and practised their devotional exercises in solitude in order to fight out the spiritual battle with so much the more prospect of success" (Philip Schaff, et al, eds., *A Religious Encyclopaedia: Or Dictionary of Biblical, Historical, Doctrinal, and Practical Theology. Based on the Real-Encyklopädie of Herzog, Plitt, and Hauck. Together with an Encyclopaedia of Living Divines and Christian Workers of All Denominations in Europe and America. Third Edition, Revised and Enlarged. Vol. 1* [New York, Toronto, London: Funk & Wagnalls Company, 1891], 80).

9. Charles wrote the words "Quakers['] distinctions are unnecessary. But yet, let our clothing be becoming" in superscript above the words "the world, it is essential to its very existence." Charles's contemporary John Cunningham described the attire of Quakers as follows: "From the first they had a fondness for drab, or otherwise dingy-coloured garments, for splendour of apparel they thought, did not become men who clothed themselves simply to cover their nakedness, and protect themselves from the cold, and not to pamper a sinful pride." He added in a footnote, "The Quakers were frequently twitted about their buttons. [George] Fox was charged with ostentation in wearing silver ones" (John

COME YE OUT FROM AMONG THEM—2 Corinthians 6:17–18

Cunningham, *The Quakers from Their Origin till the Present Time: An International History* [Edinburgh: John Menzies & Co.; London: Hamilton, Adams & Co.; Crieff: George M'culloch, 1868, The Spurgeon Library], 103).

10. Cf. Mark 16:15.

11. Cf. "Election" (Notebook 1, Sermon 10). It is unclear what Charles intended by writing the oval between the words "election" and "&."

12. Cf. Eph 5:11.

13. First Thessalonians 5:22, "Abstain from all appearance of evil."

14. "Beware of beginnings; he who does not take the first wrong step will not take the second" (C. H. Spurgeon, *John Ploughman's Talk and Pictures, or Plain Advice for Plain People. In One Volume* [New York: Robert Carter & Brothers, 1884, The Spurgeon Library], 137).

15. Johnson defined the word "rouge" as "red paint" (Johnson's *Dictionary*). Worcester offered a more applicable definition for the verbal form of the word: "to paint the face or cheeks with rouge" and "to paint or color with rouge" (Worcester's *Dictionary*).

16. Cf. "Salvation in God Only" (Notebook 1, Sermon 24).

17. Revelation 18:4, "And I heard another voice from heaven, saying, Come out of her, my people, that ye be not partakers of her sins, and that ye receive not of her plagues."

18. "One who pretends to predict by omens, as by the flight of birds" (Johnson's *Dictionary*, s.v. "augur"). The phrase "It augurs ill" was a common Victorian expression. In the same year Charles preached from the above sermon, *The Southern Reporter and Cork Commercial Courier* stated, "However, we do think it augurs ill of the commercial spirits of this part of Ireland, that with all that has been said and written about the profitableness and the suitableness of the flax industry . . ." (*The Southern Reporter and Cork Commercial Courier*, April 22, 1852).

19. Charles may have had Gen 6:1–5 in mind.

SERMON 119

20. Cf. Genesis 7.

21. Cf. Num 25:8–9.

22. Cf. 2 Kgs 24:15; 2 Chron 36:10; Esth 2:6; Jer 22:25.

23. Cf. 1 Samuel 15.

24. Cf. Exod 34:14.

25. Charles originally wrote the word "enemies." However, the context suggests he intended the word to be possessive, "enemy's," instead of plural.

26. In the 1850s, many Irish immigrants came to England due to crop failure caused by the water-born fungus *phytophthora infestans* (Susan Campbell Bartoletti, *Black Potatoes: The Story of the Great Irish Famine, 1845–1850* [Boston: Houghton Mifflin Co., 2001], 36). England's economy struggled to accommodate the surge of immigrants. One year prior to the preaching of the sermon above, *The Era* published the following words: "Amongst the numerous visitors crowding to the metropolis we find a class arriving in shoals, with whose presence we could in every sense dispense, seeing that their company, so far from being of the slightest possible honour, credit, or benefit to the land, is in every respect precisely the reverse. We allude to the swarms of Irish paupers to be seen traversing our streets in rags and squalor. These undesirable imports . . . [are] in no better condition than the swine" ("The Great Irish Pauper Nuisance," *The Era*, March 30, 1851). Charles adopted a sympathetic posture toward Irish immigration after he moved to London in 1854. He first preached in Ireland in 1858 and returned on numerous occasions (see *Autobiography* 2:339–42).

27. Cf. Mark 5:3.

28. The letters "shed" in the word "washed" were smeared toward the bottom of the page. In the line above, the letters "ld" in the word "should" were smeared in the same direction, likely from the same motion.

29. Cf. 1 Cor 6:20.

30. An alternative reading of this line is "even [at the cost of] the precious heart's blood and life of Jesus."

31. For an additional reference to gold, see "Condescending Love of Jesus" (Notebook 1, Sermon 5).

32. Cf. "Final Perseverance" (Notebook 1, Sermon 8); "Final Perseverance Certain" (Sermon 82).

33. Cf. Matt 25:32.

34. Charles wrote the word "with" above the line due to a lack of space in the margin.

35. Cf. "Adoption" (Notebook 1, Sermon 1).

36. Cf. Luke 15:20.

37. The ink in the letters "tow" of "towering" is smeared toward the bottom right of the page, resulting in Charles's partial fingerprint.

38. Orphans in Victorian England had few rights because "he can *inherit* nothing, being looked upon as the son of nobody" (William Blackstone, *Commentaries on the Laws of England, in Four Books. The Fourteenth Edition, with the Last Corrections of the Author, and with Notes and Addition by Edward Christian* [London: printed by A. Strahan for T. Cadell and W. Davies, in the Strand, 1803], 458, italics in the original). For a further discussion of adoption in the context of Charles's orphan ministry in London, see "Offending God's Little Ones" (Notebook 1, Sermon 67).

39. Charles originally wrote the word "me" before inserting the letter "u" over the "m" to construct the word "us."

40. Charles intended to write the words "thou oughtest" in this line. A modern reading of this sentence is "Old Christian, you should have a more outward difference."

41. In 1853, approximately one year after Charles preached the sermon above, he addressed the Cambridge Sunday School Union along with two other ministers. He later recalled this address, saying, "I do not now recollect anything that I said on that occasion, but I have no doubt that I spoke in my usual straightforward fashion. I do not think there was anything in my remarks to cause the other speakers to turn upon me so savagely as they did when it came to their turn to address the large gathering. One of them, in particular, was very personal and also most insulting in his observations, specially referring to my youth, and then, in what he seemed to regard as a climax, saying that it was a pity that boys did not adopt the Scriptural practice of tarrying at Jericho till their beards were grown

SERMON 119

before they tried to instruct their seniors. Having obtained the chairman's permission, I reminded the audience that those who were bidden to tarry at Jericho were not boys, but full-grown men, whose beards had been shaved off by their enemies as the greatest indignity they could be made to suffer, and who were, therefore, ashamed to return home until their beards had grown again. I added that, the true parallel to their case could be found in a minister who, through falling into open sin, had disgraced his sacred calling, and so needed to go into seclusion for a while until his character had been to some extent restored. As it happened, I had given an exact description of the man who had attacked me so unjustly, and for that reason all who were present, and knew the circumstances, would be the more likely to remember the incident" (*Autobiography* 1:298). A man named George Gould was in attendance that evening. He was so impressed with Charles's handling of the situation that he told Thomas Olney, a deacon at New Park Street Chapel in London, about Charles. Olney then invited Charles to preach there. The event, Charles reflected, "became, in the hand of God, the means of my transference from Cambridgeshire to the metropolis" (298). Cf. 2 Sam 10:5.

42. An alternative reading of this line is "Warn the young [to] look to thine own feet." Without the word "[to]," it appears Charles is speaking to himself, which is likely.

Ezek. 3. 17.18.19 — The watchman, his work, warning & promise
Ezekiel was called into the rank of prophets by a singular vision sent with a roll of lamentation redundantly full & commanded to speak it all in the ears of the children of Israel.
The words before us are equally applicable to the Christian minister — Let us notice

I. The minister's commission.
"Son of Man" this was said to humble him least the greatness of his vision & the honour should puff him up — remember you are only the son of man. Jesus as a preacher bore this name he was made in all things like unto his brethren. —
"I have made thee". It is God's work to give a man talents and to direct his mind to the use of his talents in the ministry. Let none rush in uncalled, nor let them do it in their own name
"a watchman, unto the house of Israel" his commission was limited ours is unbounded — blessed be the great God.
"hear the word at my mouth" of old by dream, vision, voice, or impression — now by the Bible and the gracious Spirit not what clever, great men say or like, but at my mouth
"give them warning" of their ruined state, of hell, judgment of any sins in particular rife among them, or of any danger to which they may be exposed — "give them warning"
"from me" — God is the master, we are mouth for him and if the truth is spoken, it is God who is speaking
The minister is a watchman even in a civil view he is, if a true one, the best policeman to be found.
But he is called a watchman to shew —
1. The vigilance he will have to exercise; he must have his eyes about him and must not sleep — he must look to discover hypocrites, reprove sin, help the feeble.

THE WATCHMAN, HIS WORK, WARNING, . . .—*Ezekiel 3:17–19*

120

The WATCHMAN, HIS WORK, WARNING, *and* PROMISE
Ezekiel 3:17–19[1]

"Son of man, I have made thee a watchman unto the house of Israel: therefore hear the word at my mouth, and give them warning from me. When I say unto the wicked, Thou shalt surely die; and thou givest him not warning, nor speakest to warn the wicked from his wicked way, to save his life; the same wicked man shall die in his iniquity; but his blood will I require at thine hand. Yet if thou warn the wicked, and he turn not from his wickedness, nor from his wicked way, he shall die in his iniquity; but thou hast delivered thy soul."

Ezekiel was called into the rank of prophets by a singular vision sent with a roll of lamentation redundantly full, and commanded to speak it all in the ears of the children of Israel.

The words before us are equally applicable to the Christian minister. Let us notice:

I. THE MINISTER'S COMMISSION.[2]

"Son of Man." This was said to humble him lest[3] the greatness of his vision and the honour should puff him up. Remember, you are only the son of man. Jesus as a preacher bore this name.[4] He was made in all things like unto his brethren.[5]

"I have made thee." It is God's work to give a man talents and to direct his mind to the use of his talents in the ministry. Let none rush in uncalled, nor let them do it in their own name.[6]

"A watchman unto the house of Israel." His commission was limited. Ours is unbounded. Blessed be the great God.

"Hear the word at my mouth." Of old by dream, vision, voice, or impression. Now by the Bible and the gracious Spirit. Not what clever, great men say or like, but at my mouth.

"Give them warning" of their ruined state, of hell, judgment, of any sins in particular rife among them, or of any danger to which they may be exposed. "Give them warning."

"From me." God is the master. We are mouth[s] for him, and if the truth is spoken, it is God who is speaking.[7]

The minister is a watchman, even in a civil view. He is, if a true one, the best policeman to be found.

But he is called a watchman to shew:

  1. The vigilance he will have to exercise. He must have his eyes about him and must not sleep. He must look to discover hypocrites, reprove sin,[8] help the feeble,

SERMON 120

fight with the feeble against the robber Satan — he sits like the Shepherd in the wilderness — like the eagle on the rock in watch for prey — like the sentinel listening to the smallest sound.

2. To shew the weariness of the duty — few think of the poor watchman when safe in bed, but it is weary work sad work to see deserters sliding down the wall, to witness covert attacks others know not, to call a hundred times & yet never wake one. Often in the cold night, biting frost, driving sleet, midnight scuffles — whilst others are locked in sweet repose.

3. To shew how we ought to preach. just as the watchman shouts out loudly so we earnestly — as he plainly so we — as he constantly & so we — as he entirely free from fear of disturbing people so we — Shout, cry out, plain, blunt, home truths —

II. The minister's responsibility —

An awful judgment hangs on him if he be unfaithful and this is just since if the watchman cry not the city may be taken — he who puts an immortal soul in jeopardy deserves double wrath — this was the old law — the guard dies if the prisoner be not secured — — We are to declare all Gods judgments though compassion falsely fired might bid us keep back such truths — We are to admonish him to turn & give the assurance that through Jesus the penitent shall find mercy — our intention is ever to be not to alarm merely for its own sake but that men may thereby turn to God. if this is not done — the sinner shall die justly as a punishment for his own sin,

THE WATCHMAN, HIS WORK, WARNING, . . .—*Ezekiel 3:17–19*

fight with the feeble against the robber, Satan. He sits like the shepherd in the wilderness, like the eagle on the rock in watch for prey, like the sentinel listening to the smallest sound.

2. To shew the weariness of the duty. Few think of the poor watchman when safe in bed, but it is weary work, sad work, to see deserters sliding down the wall, to witness covert attacks others know not, to call a hundred times and yet never wake one. Often in the cold night, biting frost, driving sleet, midnight scuffles, whilst others are locked in sweet repose.

3. To shew how we ought to preach. Just as the watchman shouts out loudly, so we, earnestly. As he plainly, so we. As he constantly, so we. As he entirely free from fear of disturbing people, so we. Shout, cry out, plain, blunt, home truths.[9]

II. THE MINISTER'S RESPONSIBILITY.

An awful judgment hangs on him if he be unfaithful. And this is just since if the watchman cry not, the city may be taken. He who puts an immortal soul in jeopardy deserves double wrath.[10] This was the old law. The guard dies if the prisoner be not secured.[11]

We are to declare all God[']s judgments, though compassion falsely fired might bid us keep back such truths. We are to admonish him to turn and give the assurance that through Jesus the penitent shall find mercy. Our intention is ever to be not to alarm merely for its own sake, but that men may thereby turn to God. If this is not done, the sinner shall die justly as a punishment for his own sin, and the unfaithful minister will be called to give an account and shall be condemned for his own sin of unfaithfulness. See here the reason why we talk so much of hell fire. And here I will by God's grace fall to warning them again of sin, the law, judgment, hell, mercy by Jesus through faith specially reminding them of the temptation of this horrible feast. Speaking also to the professedly righteous that they be not found liars and that they slide not into sin —

III. The minister's comfort — Many will turn and as to those who do not, having delivered his message he has delivered his own soul. The wicked who turn not shall perish doubtless with double damnation — Many never will turn notwithstanding all that shall be said but we are free —

1. Let not men think so lightly of preaching or hearing as some are wont to do, both are awful, solemn, work.
2. Let the prayers of the saints always ascend up to God's throne on the behalf of your unworthy brother, the watchman, seeing his labour, responsibility and danger.
3. You sinners who sin notwithstanding all I say, I shall meet you face to face one day — I tell you now not to mix with sinners at the feast. If you do then you shall bear it all yourself yea more I shall be a witness against you —

Oh God, Eternal, help me to clear my head of the blood of all men and then I shall be the greatest debtor in thy dominion. I ask it through Jesus.
<u>Amen</u>

167

and the unfaithful minister will be called to give an account and shall be condemned for his own sin of unfaithfulness.

See here the reason why we talk[12] so much of hell fire. And here I will by God's grace fall to warning them again of sin, the law, judgment, hell, mercy by Jesus through faith. Specially reminding them of the temptation of this horrible feast. Speaking also to the professedly righteous that they be not found liars and that they slide not into sin.

III. THE MINISTER'S COMFORT.

Many will turn, and as to those who do not, having delivered his message he has delivered his own soul. The wicked who turn not shall perish doubtless with double damnation. Many never will turn notwithstanding all that shall be said. But we are free.

1. Let not men think so lightly of preaching or hearing as some are wont to do. Both are awful, solemn work.

2. Let the prayers of the saints always ascend up to God's throne[13] on the behalf of your unworthy brother, the watchman, seeing his labour, responsibility, and danger.

3. You sinners who sin notwithstanding all I say, I shall meet you face to face one day. I tell you now not to mix with sinners at the feast. If you do, then you shall bear it all yourself. Yea more, I shall be a witness against you.

Oh God, Eternal, help me to clear my head of the blood of all men, and then I shall be the greatest debtor in thy dominion. I ask it through Jesus.

Amen

167

SERMON 120

1. Charles preached an expanded, eight-page version of this sermon entitled "The Minister" in Notebook 8 (Sermon 367). On September 1, 1878, he preached an additional sermon on Ezek 3:17 entitled "The Message from the Lord's Mouth" (*MTP* 24, Sermon 1431). There is not enough overlapping content or structural similarity in the 1878 sermon to suggest Charles had in mind his early outline.

2. Cf. "The Minister's Commission" (Sermon 110).

3. Charles originally wrote the word "least." The context suggests, however, he intended to write "lest." For additional examples, see "The Church Needs the Spirit" (Sermon 131) and "By Faith Jericho Fell" (Sermon 133).

4. Cf. Mark 14:62; Luke 19:10.

5. Cf. Phil 2:7.

6. For references to the denomination ("Spurgeonism") Charles almost inadvertently founded, see "Spurgeonism Again" (*ST* June 1866:281–84); "Spurgeonism," *The Nation* (Dublin), June 13, 1857; and "Spurgeonism," *Dundee, Perth, and Cupar Advertiser*, April 2, 1861.

7. Smeared stippling surrounds the words "truth is spoken, it is God who is speaking."

8. The letter "e" in the word "reprove," the letters "si" in the word "sin," and also the letter "t" in the word "not" in the line above are all smeared to the right side of the page, likely from the same motion.

9. An alternative reading of this line is "As he [is] entirely free from fear of disturbing people, so we shout, cry out, plain, blunt, home truths."

10. Cf. Mark 9:42.

11. Cf. Acts 16:27.

12. An illegible letter, likely "k," was written beneath the "l" in the word "talk." Charles likely wrote the letter "k" prematurely before converting it into an "l."

13. Cf. Rev 8:4.

121. Luke XIX. 41 — The Redeemer's tears over sinners.

Jesus had a triumphant entrance into Jerusalem; he rode not on the forbidden horse of Egypt, but on the noble ass of Palestine; all around were shouting, palm branches were waving, clothes spread on the ass and on the ground, while the whole city was stirred. 'Tis a man riding on the ass, and in triumph, too, and yet this triumphant man weeps;— he is looking on a fair & beautiful city, and yet he weeps — There were pleasing associations connected with it; there, Abraham offered Isaac; there, David danced before the ark, & dwelt in solemn state. Through its streets Solomon once rode in regal splendour;— there, Josiah held his great passover. — Once, happy feet ransomed from Babylon had trod its stones;— thither the tribes went up every year in joyful procession; but these are not in his mind, for see he weeps. ——— He wept at the grave of Lazarus, but then he lost a friend; but now 'tis for a city flourishing, blooming, gorgeous with a temple surpassing all edifices on earth. — —

I. He wept at the remembrance of what she had been.
1. A city abounding with privileges, but having not at all improved them.
2. A city to whom prophets had been sent, but she had spilt their blood, and disregarded all.
3. A city of the highest order & degree about to be brought down to the lowest depths.

II. What she then was —
1. A city filled with those whom he had benefitted,

THE REDEEMER'S TEARS OVER SINNERS—*Luke 19:41*

121

The REDEEMER'S TEARS *over* SINNERS
Luke 19:41[1]

"And when he was come near, he beheld the city, and wept over it."

Jesus had a triumphant entrance into Jerusalem; he rode not on the forbidden horse of Egypt[2] but on the noble ass of Palestine. ~~yet~~ All around were shouting. Palm branches were waving.[3] Clothes spread on the ass and on the ground[4] while the whole city was stirred. 'Tis a man riding on the ass, and in triumph, too. And yet this triumphant man weeps. He is looking on a fair and beautiful city, and yet he weeps.

There were pleasing associations connected with it. There, Abraham offered Isaac.[5] There, David danced before the ark[6] and dwelt in solemn state. Through its streets Solomon once rode in regal splendour.[7] There, Josiah held his great passover.[8] Once, happy feet ransomed from Babylon had trod its stones.[9] Thither the tribes went up every year in joyful procession.[10] But these are not in his mind, for see, he weeps.

He wept at the grave of Lazarus,[11] but then, he lost a friend. But now 'tis for[12] a city flourishing, blooming, gorgeous with a temple surpassing all edifices on earth.

I. HE WEPT AT THE REMEMBRANCE OF WHAT SHE HAD BEEN.

1. A city abounding[13] with privileges but having not at all improved them.
2. A city to whom prophets had been sent, but she had spilt their blood and disregarded all.
3. A city of the highest order and degree about to be brought down to the lowest depths.[14]

II. WHAT SHE THEN WAS.

1. A city filled with those whom he had benefitted,

and those same persons remaining most ungrateful.
2. He knew her state of sinfulness, & wept at the remembrance that she was a sink of sin, — cruel, bloody, vile, hypocrites there.
3. A city he had lived and preached in.
4. A city given over — condemned —
III. What she would be —
1. She was to be stript of all her privileges.
2. Utterly ruined and destroyed —

Now let Jesus stand up, and weep over Waterbeach, & over this congregation —
You have been distinguished for sin; yes, many here; and your sin is aggravated by your many privileges.
You are now many, yes, most of you, dead in trespasses and sins, and some especially vile —
You have long resisted divine calls, — you will yet go on in sin, and many of you will be damned.
Weep, oh preacher! Weep. Weep. Weep, — men, women!
Now let Jesus stand up, & weep over you one by one.
1. Over the open reprobate, despisers, drunkards.
2. Over the unconverted many-year hearer.
3. Over the hopeful young, who yet will go aside.
4. Over convinced sinners wiping their tears away.
5. Over many feast-goers, who go despite warnings.
6. Over old men, on the brink of hell.
7. Over hypocrites, deceiving their own souls.
8. Over those who are given up & let alone.
9. Over careless, laughing, critical, &c hearers —
   Weep one by one — Oh, that mine eyes were fountains of tears!
   Bless. Bless.

THE REDEEMER'S TEARS OVER SINNERS—*Luke 19:41*

    and those same persons remaining most ungrateful.

2. He knew her state of sinfulness and wept at the remembrance that she was a sink of sin.[15] Cruel, bloody, vile, hypocrites there.

3. A city he had lived and preached in.

4. A city given over, condemned.[16]

III. WHAT SHE WOULD BE.

1. She was to be stript[17] of all her privileges.

2. Utterly ruined and destroyed.

Now let Jesus stand up and weep over Waterbeach and over this congregation.[18]

You have been distinguished for sin. Yes, many here. And your sin is aggravated by your many privileges. You are now many, yea, most of you, dead in trespasses and sins, and some especially vile.

You have long resisted divine calls. You will yet go on in sin, and many of you will be damned.

Weep, oh preacher! Weep.[19] Weep. Weep. Men, women!

Now let Jesus stand up and weep over you, one by one:

1. Over the open reprobate, despisers,[20] drunkards.

2. Over the unconverted, many-year hearer.

3. Over the hopeful young who yet will go aside.

4. Over convinced sinners, wiping their tears away.

5. Over many feast-goers, who go despite warnings.

6. Over old men on the brink of hell.

7. Over hypocrites, deceiving their own souls.

8. Over those who are given up and let alone.

9. Over careless, laughing, critical, etc., hearers.

    Weep, one by one. Oh,[21] that mine eyes were fountains of <u>tears</u>!

    Bless. Bless.[22]

168.

SERMON 121

1. Charles preached an additional sermon on Luke 19:41 entitled "The Lamentations of Jesus" (*MTP* 26, Sermon 1570). There is not enough overlapping content or structural similarity to suggest Charles had his early outline in mind when writing his later sermon. See also Charles's 1889 sermon on John 11:35 entitled "Jesus Wept" (*MTP* 35, Sermon 2091).

2. Deuteronomy 17:16, "But he shall not multiply horses to himself, nor cause the people to return to Egypt, to the end that he should multiply horses: forasmuch as the LORD hath said unto you, Ye shall henceforth return no more that way."

3. Luke did not mention the waving of palm branches. It is found instead in Matt 21:8, Mark 11:8, and John 12:13.

4. Cf. Luke 19:35–36.

5. Cf. Gen 22:1–19.

6. Cf. 2 Sam 6:14.

7. Cf. 1 Kgs 1:33, 38.

8. Cf. 2 Kgs 23:23; 2 Chron 35:1.

9. Cf. Ezra 2:1.

10. Cf. 2 Chron 30:1; Zech 14:16; Luke 2:41; John 5:1.

11. Cf. John 11:35.

12. A smear appears across the letters "fo" in the word "for." The source of the smear is the ink from the dot above the word "surpassing" in the line below.

13. To construct the letter "o," Charles extended the height of the ligature on the bowl of the letter "a."

14. Charles may have had in mind the sacking of Jerusalem by the Roman armies of Titus in AD 70. Cf. Matt 24:2; Mark 13:2; Luke 21:6.

15. Charles likely consulted John Bunyan's sermon on Luke 24:47, "Good News for the Vilest of Men; or, a Help for Despairing Souls," in *The Jerusalem Sinner Saved; or, Good News for the Vilest of Men: Being a Help for Despairing Souls, Showing, That Jesus Christ Would Have Mercy in the First Place Offered to the Biggest Sinners*: "Jerusalem was therefore now greatly backslidden, and become the place where truth and true religion were much defaced. It was also now become the very sink of sin and seat of hypocrisy, and gulf where true religion was drowned" (George Offor, ed., *The*

Works of John Bunyan. With an Introduction to Each Treatise, Notes, and a Sketch of His Life, Times, and Contemporaries. Volume First. Experimental, Doctrinal, and Practical [Glasgow: Blackie and Son, 1856, The Spurgeon Library], 69). See also Charles's reference to the "sink of sin" in "Beginning at Jerusalem" (Notebook 1, Sermon 29).

16. Charles indented the fourth point likely because he added it after writing the line below.

17. Abbr. "stripped."

18. In 1889, Charles described London similarly: "I confess I can never go through this huge city without feeling unhappy. I never pass from end to end of London without feeling a black and dark cloud, hanging like a pall over my spirit. How my heart breaks for thee, O sinful city of London! Is it not so with you, my brethren? Think of its slums, its sins, its poverty, its ungodliness, its drunkenness, its vice! These may well go through a man's heart like sharp swords. How Jesus would have wept in London!" (*MTP* 35:342).

19. Charles reinforced the letter "p" in the word "weep," likely because he originally wrote a third letter "e."

20. Charles originally spelled the word "desps" before adding the letters "isers" to construct the correct spelling, "despisers."

21. The letter "h" in the word "Oh" is either struck through or smudged. The latter interpretation is preferred.

22. For a stroke similar to the one after the word "Bless," see "Justification by Imputed Righteousness" (Sermon 117).

SERMON 122

122.   II Cor. 2...11.   Satan and his devices.

An individual in the Church of Corinth had committed incest with his father's wife: he was not expelled until Paul wrote his first epistle, and then reversing their conduct, though before too lenient they became too harsh and would not re-admit him even though he expressed extreme penitence — Paul therefore felt grieved lest their harshness should drive him to despair and give them world reason to speak ill. For Satan makes use of anything he can lay hold of.

I. Let us look at our enemy "Satan" i.e "adversary". He was once an angel but sinning he fell and with him a host of lesser angels. He was condemned to eternal punishment — and at once became filled with malice against God & rage against all his creatures specially men. We find him in the garden of Eden, we find him tempting Job. setting on David to number the people — Tempting Jesus — endeavouring to sift Peter — grievously afflicting poor demoniacs — driving the swine down into the sea. He hates all truth and goodness because those are the offspring of God. He has great power as appears by his bearing Jesus body up to the temple — shewing him all the kingdoms of the world — But his subtilty is greater than his power — he lies in wait. He his angelic intellect & long experience

He loves nothing — he is a hater of all and moreover an universal tempter — He tempted angels, he tempted Adam & the Second Adam. He tempts good men, not because he thinks he can destroy them but thereby to grieve them & help his own cause. He tempts the wicked to sin — not because he loves to see them happy, but because he longs for their

122

SATAN *and* HIS DEVICES
2 Corinthians 2:11[1]

"Lest Satan should get an advantage of us: for we are not ignorant of his devices."

An individual in the Church of Corinth had committed incest with his father's wife.[2] He was not expelled until Paul wrote his first epistle. And then, reversing their conduct, though before too lenient, they became too harsh and would not re-admit him even though he expressed extreme penitence. Paul, therefore, felt grieved lest their harshness should drive him[3] to despair and give the~~m~~ world reason to speak ill. For Satan makes use of anything he can lay hold of.

I. LET US LOOK AT OUR ENEMY "SATAN," I.E., "ADVERSARY."

He was once an angel,[4] but sinning he fell,[5] and with him a host of lesser angels. He was condemned to eternal punishment and at once became filled with malice against God and rage against all his creatures, specially man. We find him in the garden of Eden.[6] We find him tempting Job,[7] setting on David to number the people,[8] Tempting Jesus,[9] endeavouring to sift Peter,[10] grievously afflicting poor demoniacs,[11] driving the swine down into the sea.[12]

He hates all truth and goodness because those are the offspring of God. He has great power as appears by his bearing Jesus['s] body up to the temple,[13] shewing him all the kingdoms of the world.[14] But his subtilty[15] is greater than his power. He has angelic intellect and long experience.[16] He lies in wait.

He loves nothing. He is a hater of all, and moreover, an universal tempter. He tempted angels, he tempted Adam and the Second Adam. He tempts good men, not because he thinks he can destroy them, but sherely[17] to grieve them and help his own cause. He tempts the wicked to sin, not because he loves to see them happy but because he longs for their destruction — We must all be tempted 'tis useless to try to escape the trial but let us learn his subtilty & so escape.

II. Some of Satan's devices.
 1. Against the Church as a whole.
  a. He stirs up persecution against it.
  B. He slanders the ministers and people.
  ϒ. He prompts his own to play the hypocrite & get in.
  δ. He splits the church by Bigotry & bitterness.
  E. He encourages latitudinarian Charity.
 2. Against the wicked.
  a. He keeps them away from the means of grace.
  b. He hides the punishment & publishes the pleasure of sin.
  c. He forbids thought and calls religion gloomy.
  d. He tempts to infidelity
  e. He tells them that there is time enough.
 3. Against the converted.
  a. He prompts them to despair.
  b. He puffs them up with too good an opinion of themselves.
  c. He encourages hard thoughts.
  d. He injects blasphemous, profane, unbelieving thoughts.
  c. He sets our relations on us.
  d. He leaves off tempting & that's the worst temptation.

III. Let us learn.
 1. Never to run into Satan's way.
 2. Ever to be looking out for him.

Remember the crown — remember the loss if you are overcome — give battle in Jesus strength

169. 170. 193. 307. ~~467~~. 523

destruction. We must all be tempted. 'Tis useless to try to escape the trial,[18] but let us learn his subtilty and so escape.

II. SOME OF SATAN'S DEVICES.

1. Against the Church as a whole.

    α.[19] He stirs up persecution against it.

    β. He slanders the ministers and people.

    γ. He prompts his own to play the hypocrite and get in.

    δ. He splits the church by Bigotry and bitterness.

    ε. He encourages latitudinarian[20] Charity.

2. Against the wicked.

    a.[21] He keeps them away from the means of grace.[22]

    b. He hides the punishment and publishes the pleasure of sin.

    c. He forbids thought and calls religion gloomy.

    d. He tempts to infidelity.

    e. He tells them that there[23] is time enough.

3. Against the converted.

    a. He prompts them to despair.

    b. He puffs them up with too good an opinion of themselves.

    c. He encourages hard thoughts.

    d. He injects blasphemous, profane, unbelieving thoughts.

    e. He sets our relations on us.

    [f].[24] He leaves off tempting, and that's the worst temptation.

III. LET US LEARN.

1. Never tor[25] run into Satan's way.

2. Ever to be looking out for him.

Remember the crown. Remember the loss if you are overcome. Give battle in Jesus['s] strength.

169. 170. 193. 307. ~~469~~.[26] 523

SERMON 122

1. This is the only time Charles preached a sermon on 2 Cor 2:11. For additional sermons about Satan, see "Satan's Banquet" (*NPSP* 5, Sermon 225); "Satanic Hindrances" (*MTP* 11, Sermon 657); "Satan's Punctuality, Power, and Purpose" (*MTP* 25, Sermon 1459a); "Satan in a Rage" (*MTP* 25, Sermon 1502); "Blinded by Satan" (*MTP* 39, Sermon 2304); "An Antidote to Satan's Devices" (*MTP* 46, Sermon 2707); and "Satan's Arrows and God's" (*MTP* 57, Sermon 3262).

2. Cf. 1 Cor 5:1–5.

3. An illegible word, possibly "a," appears beneath the word "him."

4. Cf. 2 Cor 11:14.

5. Cf. Isa 14:12–15; Luke 10:18.

6. Cf. Gen 3:1–7.

7. Cf. Job 1:1–2:7.

8. Cf. 1 Chron 21:1.

9. Cf. Matt 4:1–11; Mark 1:12–13; Luke 4:1–13.

10. Cf. Luke 22:31.

11. Cf. Matt 12:43–45; Mark 9:25; Luke 11:14; Acts 16:16–18.

12. Cf. Matt 8:28–34; Mark 5:12–13; Luke 8:33.

13. Cf. Luke 4:9.

14. Cf. Luke 4:5.

15. A modern spelling of the word "subtilty" is "subtlety."

16. Charles wrote the sentence "He has angelic intellect and long experience" in superscript above the words "power. He lies."

17. Either the word "sherely" is an archaic spelling or Charles intended to spell the word "surely."

18. The sentence "'Tis useless to try to escape the trial" is similar to one Charles wrote in the following sermon: "It is useless to avoid affliction" ("Enduring Temptation" [Sermon 123]).

19. Charles used three types of numbering techniques in this sermon: English letters, Arabic numbers, and Greek letters (alpha, beta, gamma, delta, and epsilon). The reason for his inconsistency is not apparent. For additional examples,

see "Condescending Love of Jesus" (Notebook 1, Sermon 5) and "Christian Prosperity and Its Causes" (Notebook 1, Sermon 51).

20. "Not refrained; not confined; thinking or acting at large" and "one who departs from orthodoxy" (Johnson's *Dictionary*, s.v. "latitudinarian").

21. Charles might have originally written the Greek letter alpha before writing the letter "a."

22. For an additional instance in which Charles referenced "means of grace," see "God's Grace Given to Us" (Notebook 1, Sermon 14).

23. Charles originally wrote the word "their." The context suggests, however, he intended to write the word "there."

24. Charles originally wrote the letter "d" instead of an "f."

25. Charles added the letter "r" to the word "to" before striking through it. He likely began writing the word "run" without inserting a space after the word "to."

26. Charles struck through the number 469 because he had already preached a sermon on the 469th occasion ("God's Care of the Stars" [Notebook 4, Sermon 189]).

James. 1. 12 — Enduring temptation —

There is no subject that requires more to be studied than that of temptation or trial since these are our constant companions.

I. The persons pronounced to be blessed "endurers of temptation". This word is often used in a bad sense as meaning temptation to sin but it does not necessarily imply that but often simply means any "trial" or "affliction". — These we are continually meeting with either in our outward circumstances, the world, Satan or our own hearts — it is useless to avoid affliction but here those are pronounced happy who do so endure. Not those who suffer — nor who fall — nor those who run into sin but those who endure and come off conquerors. The world thinks the rich, the prosperous are happy but God says they who are just the reverse are blessed.
　1. For no trouble can touch a Christian's joy.
　2. Sometimes affliction increases it.
But let us have care that we do endure and again let us be careful that it be for Christ's sake.

II. The main reason of their blessedness. They know that trial must precede crowning and in their trials they read a title to that crown. Notice what Christians are to receive
"life" as opposed to the second death & its horrors
"life" as being the thing most desired by creatures
"crown of life" not a square but a circle, an endless life — and notice 'tis the best of life — the cream the crown of life —. we are to have
"a crown" one would think a poor man's garb were enough but no we are raised to dignity

123

ENDURING TEMPTATION
James 1:12[1]

"Blessed is the man that endureth temptation: for when he is tried, he shall receive the crown of life, which the Lord hath promised to them that love him."

There is no subject that requires more to be studied than that of temptation or trial since these are our constant companions.

I. THE PERSONS PRONOUNCED TO BE BLESSED, *"endurers of temptation."*

This word is often used in a bad sense[2] as meaning temptation to sin, but it does not necessarily imply that. But often [it] simply means any "trial" or "affliction."[3] These we are continually meeting with, either in our outward circumstances, the world, Satan, or our own hearts.[4] It is useless to avoid affliction.[5] But here those are pronounced happy who do so endure.

Not those who suffer, nor who fall, nor those who run into sin, but those who endure and come off conquerors. The world thinks the rich, the prosperous, are happy, but God says they who are just the reverse are blessed.

  1. For no trouble can touch a Christian's joy.
  2. Sometimes affliction increases it.[6]

But let us have care that we do endure. And again, let us be careful that it be for Christ's sake.[7]

II. THE MAIN REASON OF THEIR BLESSEDNESS.

They know that[8] trial must precede crowning, and in their trials they read a title to that crown.

Notice what Christians are to receive:

"Life," as opposed to the second death and its horrors.
"Life," as being the thing most desired by creatures.
"Crown of life." Not a square but a circle, an endless life. And notice, 'tis the best of life, the cream, the crown of life. We are to have "a crown." One would think a poor man's garb were enough. But no, we are raised to dignity[9]

As an expression of God's love to us and an open testimony of triumph over Satan — Now it is this crown that is the great comfort — for this immortal crown we run. The gamesters ran for parsley or laurel crowns we for an eternal "crown of life" — After we are tried "No cross no crown"

<u>III</u>. The only ground of their hope.

God has promised — not we have earned it — The Promise is our great prop — our main pillar "Love to God" is the one great evidence. Not love to a minister — nor love to a sect — nor is it promised to fear for slavish fear is no evidence of sonship nor to strong confidence for that may be presumption but to love because —

    1. Love is unnatural — it shows divine power.
    2. Love is the daughter of faith & love is the parent of all
    3. Because love alone can make us endure.

1. Trials are not against us but on our side.
2. Let us set present suffering in the balance with future glory.
3. Let us doubt our love, if we are not laughed at.
4. Let us increase in love & so in endurance

171 . 321.

as an expression of God's love[10] to us and an open testimony of triumph over Satan.

Now it is this crown that is the great comfort. For this immortal crown we run. The gamesters ran for parsley or laurel crowns.[11] We, for an eternal "crown of life."[12] After we are tried. "No cross, no crown."[13]

III. THE ONLY GROUND OF THEIR HOPE.

God has promised. Not, we have earned it. The Promise is our great prop.,[14] our main pillar. "Love to God" is the one great evidence.

Not love to a minister, nor love to a sect, nor is it promised to fear, for slavish fear is no evidence of sonship. Nor to strong confidence, for that may be presumption.

But to love, because:

1. Love is unnatural. It shows divine power.
2. Love is the daughter of faith, and love is the parent of all.
3. Because love alone can make us endure.

1. Trials are not against us but on our side.
2. Let us set present suffering in the balance with future glory.[15]
3. Let us doubt our love if we are not laughed at.[16]
4. Let us increase in love, and so in endurance.

171. 321.

SERMON 123

1. On December 13, 1885, Charles preached a sermon on Jas 1:12 entitled "A Discourse upon True Blessedness Here and Hereafter" (*MTP* 31, Sermon 1874). There is not enough structural similarity to suggest Charles had this early outline in mind when writing his 1885 sermon.

2. Charles originally spelled this word "senses." However, the context suggests he intended the word to be 'sense.'

3. Charles likely consulted John Gill: "Not the temptations of Satan, or temptations to sin; for these cannot be a matter of joy, but grief; these are fiery darts, and give a great deal of uneasiness and trouble; but afflictions and persecutions for the sake of the Gospel, which are so called here and elsewhere, because they are the trials of the faith of God's people" (John Gill, *An Exposition of the New Testament*, 3:464–65).

4. "God by these tempts his people, as he did *Abraham*, when he called him to sacrifice his son; he thereby tried his faith, fear, love, and obedience" (Gill, *An Exposition of the New Testament*, 3:465, italics in the original).

5. The sentence "It is useless to avoid affliction" is similar to one Charles wrote in the preceding sermon: "'Tis useless to try to escape the trial" ("Satan and His Devices" [Sermon 122]). Cf. John 16:33.

6. "I bear my witness that the worst days I have ever had have turned out to be my best days. And when God has seemed most cruel to me, he has then been most kind. If there is anything in this world for which I would bless him more than for anything else, it is for pain and affliction. I am sure that in these things the richest, tenderest love has been manifested to me. Our Father's wagons rumble most heavily when they are bringing us the richest freight of the bullion of his grace. Love letters from heaven are often sent in black-edged envelopes. The cloud that is black with horror is big with mercy. Fear not the storm. It brings healing in its wings, and when Jesus is with you in the vessel, the tempest only hastens the ship to its desired haven" (*MTP* 27:373).

7. Cf. 1 Pet 2:20.

8. An illegible letter, likely "a," appears beneath the "h" in the word "that." Charles likely forgot to insert the letter "h" and wrote the "a" prematurely.

9. Cf. Eph 2:6; Col 3:1.

10. An illegible letter, possibly "p," was written beneath the "v" in the word "love." An alternative interpretation is that Charles originally began writing the word "loss" using the long "s."

11. "When God has tried what is in his heart . . . and has purged away his dross and sin, and has refined and purified him, as gold and silver are refined and purified in the furnace . . . *he shall receive the crown of life*; eternal happiness called a *crown*, because of the glory of it, which will be both upon the bodies and souls of believers to all eternity; and as suitable to their character, they being kings, and having a kingdom and thrones prepared for them; and in allusion to the crown that was given to the conquerors in the *Olympic* games" (Gill, *An Exposition of the New Testament*, 3:467, italics in the original).

12. An alternative reading of this line is "We [run] for an eternal 'crown of life.'"

13. See William Penn, *No Cross, No Crown. Part the First. Containing a Discourse, Shewing the Nature and Discipline of the Holy Cross of Christ, and that the Denyal of Self, and Daily Bearing of Christ's Cross, is the Alone Way to the Rest and Kingdom of God. The Eighth Edition, Corrected* (Leeds: printed by James Lister, 1743).

14. Abbr. "proposition." Charles also abbreviated "Inference" (Cf. "Future Judgment" [Notebook 1, Sermon 6]).

15. Romans 8:18, "For I reckon that the sufferings of this present time are not worthy to be compared with the glory which shall be revealed in us."

16. Cf. Matt 10:22, Mark 13:13; Luke 21:17; John 15:19.

124.   1 Sam. V. 2.3.4. —   The Downfall of Dagon.

Doubtless every incident recorded in Scripture is intended to teach some important lesson. & though we ought not to strain and allegorize the word of God — yet let us go as far as we may and see what truth we can gather. — God on account of the sin of the Israelites allowed the ark to be taken — the Philistines thought to honour the ark and perhaps to associate it with Dagon — but God will not have it & Dagon falls. See the folly of idolaters — God avenges Sampson's death.

I. The entrance of the ark into Dagon's temple well sets out the entrance of grace into man's heart. — Dagon was an image having the lower parts of a fish and the upper part human like the fabled mermaids. But — man worships a God equally as vile and his unrenewed heart is an idols temple — yea there are many Dagon's in one heart. Think of the Lord. there are many false arks in the world. This temple will never be disturbed till the ark comes in. — That is the doctrines, laws and actings of God in grace. — In this case the Philistines fetched the ark in but 'tis never so in a gracious soul. The ark is too heavy for mortal powers to carry — but see it comes — the ark is in. — So is there a time when grace enters into God's elect, it is not there naturally. Dagon is not turned out all at once but at the first entrance of grace he is still firm. — The ark is set by Dagon. Oh mercy that ever God should come into a place so defiled but yet he does. Well we leave the man with Dagon yet firm & grace newly introduced — but let us go by and by and notice

124

The DOWNFALL of DAGON
1 Samuel 5:2–4[1]

"When the Philistines took the ark of God, they brought it into the house of Dagon, and set it by Dagon. And when they of Ashdod arose early on the morrow, behold, Dagon was fallen upon his face to the earth before the ark of the Lord. *And they took Dagon, and set him in his place again. And when they arose early on the morrow morning, behold, Dagon was fallen upon his face to the ground before the ark of the* Lord; *and the head of Dagon and both the palms of his hands were cut off upon the threshold; only the stump of Dagon was left to him."*

Doubtless every incident[2] recorded in Scripture is intended to teach some important lesson, and though we ought not to strain and allegorize the [W]ord of God,[3] yet let us go as far as we may and see what truth we can gather. God, on account of the sin of the Israelites, allowed the ark to be taken.[4] The Philistines thought to honour the ark and perhaps to associate it with Dagon. But God will not have it and Dagon falls.

See the folly of idolaters. God avenges Sampson's death.[5]

I. THE ENTRANCE OF THE ARK INTO DAGON'S TEMPLE WELL SETS OUT THE ENTRANCE OF GRACE INTO MAN'S HEART.

Dagon was an image having the lower parts of a fish and the upper part human like the fabled mermaids. But man worships a God equally as vile[6] and his unrenewed heart is an idol[']s temple.[7] Yea, there are many Dagons[8] in one heart. <u>The ark of the Lord.</u> There are many false[9] arks in the world. This temple will never be disturbed till the ark comes in. That is the doctrines, laws, and actings of God in grace.

In this case, the Philistines fetched the ark in, but 'tis never so in a gracious soul.[10] The ark is too heavy for mortal powers to carry—but see, it comes. The ark is in. So is there a time when grace enters into God's elect. It is not there naturally. Dagon is not turned out all at once, but at the first entrance of grace he is still firm. The ark is set by Dagon. Oh mercy that ever God should come into a place so defiled, but yet he does. Well we leave the man with Dagon yet firm and grace newly introduced.[11] But let us go by and by and notice:

II. The downfall of Dagon in a short time — notably shews the dethronement of sin when grace comes in. —

Well the two principles will not be long at peace — fire & water cannot agree — so they are not long easy: but then surely old Dagon sits the firmest and he will conquer.. No. no. not by might or power belt yet down comes Dagon on his face _to the earth_ _not halfway_. Whatever our antigod is — whether sin or our own righteousness it shall come down — and that "on its face" not on its knee a little — Where grace rules sin must die & that too early in the morning — very early in Christian experience Dagon falls — yes at the very earliest period. Tis of no use our trying to have God and devil too — one must down for though Satan does not mind a partner — God will not have one. — He made us all, and altogether — he does all in redemption — in conversion all in all — he ought then to have all the glory. — See then grace pulls sin down but the Philistines try to put it up — the devil, the flesh the world hoist it on its seat again but only to see it fall with a double overthrow — This time the ark makes it come down — cuts off its head and hands, even on the very threshold that is openly — So shall grace cut off the head the reigning power of sin — the hands the greedy following sin — "both the palms" one sin as well as another, & this is done openly so that all may see on "the threshold" on the morrow morning early — very soon — grace delays not — sin stays only a day in a Christian's heart. Dagon did not sit longer that that — as soon as the Philistines were gone and the temple shut out from the world the stupid god falls down — So shall sin. —

III. The remaining of Dagon's stump shows how sin remains even in the hearts of the regenerate. —

Though the head & hands are gone yet the stump remains so in all true Christians the sovereign power and activity of sin is gone but still there's the stump. —

THE DOWNFALL OF DAGON—*1 Samuel 5:2–4*

II. THE DOWNFALL OF DAGON IN A SHORT TIME NOTABLY SHEWS THE DETHRONEMENT OF SIN WHEN GRACE COMES IN.

Well the two principles will not be long at peace. Fire and water cannot agree,[12] so they are not long easy. But then, surely, old Dagons sits the firmest and he will conquer. No. No. Not by might or power, but yet <u>down comes Dagon on his face to the earth</u>.[13] <u>Not half way</u>. Whatever our antigod is, whether sin or our own righteousness,[14] it shall come down, and that, "<u>on its face</u>." Not on its knee a little. Where grace rules sin must die, and that, too, <u>early in the morning</u>. Very early in [the][15] Christian experience, Dagon falls. Yes, at the very earliest period.[16]

Tis of no use our trying to have God and devil too. One must [come] down, for though Satan does not mind a partner, God will not have one. He made us <u>all</u>, and <u>altogether</u>. He does <u>all</u> in redemption—in conversion <u>all in all</u>. He ought then to have all the glory.

See, then, grace pulls sin down, but the Philistines try to put it up. The devil, the flesh, the world hoist it on its seat again[17] but only to see it fall with a double overthrow. This time the ark makes it come down—cuts off its head and hands,[18] even on the very threshold, that is, openly. So shall grace cut off the head, the reigning power of sin. The hands, the greedy, following sin. "Both the palms." One sin as well as another, and this is done openly so that all may see on "the threshold," on the morrow morning, early, very soon. Grace delays not. Sin stays only a day in a Christian[']s heart.[19] Dagon did not sit longer tha[n][20] that. As soon as the Philistines were gone and the temple shut out from the world the stupid god falls down. So shall sin.

III. THE REMAINING OF DAGON'S STUMP SHOWS HOW SIN REMAINS EVEN IN THE HEARTS OF THE REGENERATE.

Though the head and hands are gone, yet the stump remains. So in all true Christians the sovereign power and activity of sin is gone. But still there's the stump.

SERMON 124

Even Paul complained of this — he was no perfectionist but let us take care 'tis only the stump — Some men make this a pretext for deceiving themselves — But still every child of God finds by daily experience that though sin is broken on the threshold, the stump is still remaining within — This stump is like the stump of a tooth, it causes very much pain — And like the old stumps of trees you must look after them or they will shoot — Blessed be God the stump will be uprooted one day — when we die — Now Brethren as it is in an individuals heart so is it in the world — The ark of our holy religion has already laid Dagon on his face and let Heathens, Popes, Priests or Devils put it up again it must & shall fall and be broken to powder — So in this place though the feast has set the Devil up, we have pulled him down once and the Lord will smash him down again — let us expect ten times as great a triumph as we yet have seen —

1. Those have no grace in whom Dagon is entire.
2. If Dagon is never knocked down then he and his temple shall be burned in the fire of hell.
3. Christian thou seest here thy weapon wherewith to resist Satan "the ark of the Lord." —

173

THE DOWNFALL OF DAGON—*1 Samuel 5:2–4*

Even Paul complained of this.[21] He was no perfectionist. But let us take care 'tis only the stump.[22] Some men make this a pretext for deceiving themselves. But still, every child of God finds by daily experience that though sin is broken on the threshold, the stump is still remaining within.

This stump is like the stump of a tooth. It causes very much pain.[23] And like the old stumps of trees, you must look after them or they will shoot.[24] Blessed be God, the stump will be uprooted one day when we die.[25]

Now Brethren, as it is in an individual[']s heart, so is it in the world. The ark of our holy religion has[26] already laid Dagon on his face,[27] and let Heathens, Popes, Priests, or Devils put it up again.[28] It must and shall fall and be broken to powder.

So in this place.[29] Though the feast has set the Devil up, we have pulled him down once and the Lord will smash him down again. Let us expect ten times as great a triumph as we yet have see[n].

1. Those have no grace in whom Dagon is entire.
2. If Dagon is never knocked down, then he[30] and his temple shall be burned in the fire of hell.[31]
3. Christian, thou seest here thy weapon where with to resist Satan, "the ark of the Lord."

173

SERMON 124

1. In 1877 Charles preached a sermon on 1 Sam 5:2–4 entitled "Dagon's Ups and Downs" (*MTP* 23, Sermon 1342). The structure is identical in places and suggests Charles used this sermon when composing his later one.

2. The letters "re" appear beneath "in" in the word "incident." Charles likely began writing the word "recorded," which immediately follows. Charles may have originally intended the line to read "Doubtless, every recorded incident."

3. Charles was aware of the dangers of over-allegorizing and later discussed it in his lecture "On Spiritualizing" (see *Lectures* 1:102–16). He criticized his predecessor Benjamin Keach who, in his "laborious treatise" on metaphors (*Tropologia*), ran "not only on all-fours, but on as many legs as a centipede" (*Commenting and Commentaries*, 61). Charles also criticized another predecessor, John Gill, for his interpretation of the fatted calf in Luke 15:23 (*Lectures* 1:112). It should be noted that in Charles's own handling of the text in "The Reception of Sinners" (*MTP* 20, Sermon 1204), he too interpreted the fatted calf as being Jesus Christ (*MTP* 20:652–53). See also "The Prodigal's Climax" (*MTP* 41:249); cf. *MTP* 37:658. In his 1877 sermon on 1 Sam 5:2–4, Charles justified his use of allegory: "And now, though it would be very wrong to make out the word of God to be a mere set of allegories, and so to deny that it records facts—and this, I trust, we shall never do—yet, as the Apostle Paul has shown us that many of the events in the Old Testament are an allegory, and as, indeed, these things are evidently types, and must be regarded as emblems and patterns of things that still occur—we shall use this passage in a spiritual way, and make it the channel of experimental teachings" (*MTP* 23:135).

4. Cf. 1 Sam 5:1.

5. Charles wrote the line "See the folly of idolaters. God avenges Sampson's death" in superscript above the first sentence of Roman numeral I. Charles's spelling of the name Samson is consistent with the spelling in the KJV. Cf. Judg 16:30.

6. In his 1877 sermon, Charles drew a sharper comparison between Dagon and Roman Catholicism: "He was a carved image, like that which the papists worship and call the Blessed Virgin, or Saint Peter, or Saint Remy" (*MTP* 23:135).

7. "The human mind is, so to speak, a perpetual forge of idols" (Henry Beveridge, trans., *Institutes of the Christian Religion by John Calvin, Volume 1* [London: James Clarke

& Co., Limited, n.d.], 97). Charles later acquired Benjamin Beddome's copy of Calvin's *Institutes* in which is found, "Wherby we may gather that the wit of man is, as I may so call it, a continuall worship of idols" (*The Institution of Christian Religion, Written in Latine by Master John Calvine, and Translated into English Accordyng to the Authors Last Edition, by T N. Wherunto Is Added a Table, to Fynde the Principall Matters Entreated of in Thy Boke, Conteyning by Order of Common Places, the Summe of the Whole Doctrine Taught in the Same, Seen and Allowed According to the Order Appointed in the Queenes Maiesties Iniunctions* [imprinted at London in White Crosse Strete by Richard Harrison, 1562, The Spurgeon Library], 25). The Latin reads, "*Unde colligere licit hominis ingenium perpetuam, ut its loquar, esse idolorum fabricam*" (A. Tholuck, trans., *Ioannis Calvini, Institutio Christianae Religionis: Cum Brevi Annotatione Atque Indicibus Locupletissimis ad Editionem Amstelodamensem Accuratissime Excribi Curavit, Pars Prior* [Berolini: Apud Gustanum Eichler, 1834], 79).

8. Charles originally inserted an apostrophe between the letters "n" and "s" in the word "Dagons." However, the context suggests he intended this word to be plural, not possessive.

9. Charles wrote the line "<u>The ark of the Lord</u>. There are many false" beneath the words "This temple will." The remainder of the sentence, "arks in the world," he wrote beneath the words "never be disturbed." Charles might have intended this line to be located before the words "This temple will never be disturbed." However, the line fits more naturally after the phrase "doctrines, laws, and actings of God in grace."

10. "The Philistines brought in the ark of the Lord, but only an act of divine power can bring the grace of God into the soul" (*MTP* 23:136).

11. An alternative reading of this sentence is "Well, we leave the man with Dagon, [though he is] firm and grace [is] newly introduced."

12. "The two great principles of sin and grace will not abide in peace with each other, they are as opposite as fire and water" (*MTP* 23:136).

13. Charles wrote the phrases "to the earth" and "not half way" above and below the word "face." An alternative reading of this line is "down comes Dagon on his face, not half way, to the earth."

14. See *MTP* 23:137.

15. Charles may have also intended the line to read "very early in Christian[']s experience."

16. An alternative reading of these sentences is "Where grace rules, sin must die, and that, too, early in the morning, very early in [the] Christian experience, Dagon falls. Yes, at the very earliest period."

17. Cf. 1 Sam 5:3.

18. See *MTP* 23:140; cf. 1 Sam 5:4.

19. "It does not take grace long, when it is once in the soul, to overturn the reigning power and the active energy of sin, when these for a while appear to get the upper hand" (*MTP* 23:140).

20. Charles originally wrote the word "that" twice. This is an example of dittography.

21. Cf. Rom 7:14–25.

22. A modernized translation of this line is "But let us take care [that it is] only the stump."

23. In the late 1880s, Charles fell down a flight of marble stairs in Mentone, France. After completing a double somersault, he chipped his tooth. The whole event, he quipped, was "a painless dentistry" (*Autobiography* 4:222).

24. "Alas, the stump of sin within us is not a slab of stone, but full of vitality, like the tree cut down, or which Job said, 'At the scent of water it will bud'" (*MTP* 23:142).

25. Charles may have had in mind Rom 7:24–25: "O wretched man that I am! who shall deliver me from the body of this death? I thank God through Jesus Christ our Lord. So then with the mind I myself serve the law of God; but with the flesh

the law of sin." See *MTP* 23:141–44. The morning Scripture reading for this sermon was Rom 7:1–14; 8:1–14 (*MTP* 23:144). "The day is coming, brother, sister, in which there will be no more inclination in you to sin than there is in an angel" (*MTP* 23:143).

26. It is unclear why Charles wrote the two dots above the word "has."

27. Charles originally wrote the word "feet." He wrote the letters "ace" over the word to construct the word "face."

28. "We carry a bomb-shell heart about with us, and we had better keep clear of all the devil's candles lest there should be an explosion of actual sin" (*MTP* 23:143).

29. By using the phrase "this place," Charles was referencing Waterbeach. Nine sermons later he wrote, "Dagon stands fast here. But the ark is come" ("By Faith Jericho Fell," Sermon 133).

30. The words "he" and also "hell" in the line below were smeared toward the right side of the page, likely by the same motion.

31. Cf. Rev 20:10.

Isa. XXV. 6. 7. 8 — The best feast. —

The ungodly in their feasts speak contemptuously of religion, of God's church and the pleasures enjoyed therein — they have their portion now, we wait for ours till another world shall dawn, but still let us boast of what we now enjoy —

I. The Church under the figure of a mountain.

By this mountain is intended God's believing people. The Church — is called "the mount of the Lord" "thy holy hill" "my holy mountain" "Mount Zion" — Because Jerusalem stood on mountains and also because

1. A mountain is conspicuous so are all who stand on Mount Zion — angels behold with joy — devils with rage men with wonder. — See how great a distance we are seen.

2. A mountain is much exposed to storms. when the valleys escape these receive all — so here the storms of persecution & Satan's temptations spend themselves.

3. A mountain is extensively beneficial — as a shelter to the world from God's immediate wrath — as drawing down the clouds — as giving water to the lower grounds.

4. A mountain is immovable and secure. God's promise and oath keep every particle of the mountain — though the goats on it, the hypocrites shall perish. — It is in this mountain a feast is provided.

5. A mountain is one of the mightiest works of God and is opposed to all mounds of man's upcasting — the church is as much a display of God's power as a mountain & like a mountain she is God's own work alone.

125

The BEST FEAST
Isaiah 25:6–8[1]

> *"And in this mountain shall the* Lord *of hosts make unto all people a feast of fat things, a feast of wines on the lees, of fat things full of marrow, of wines on the lees well refined. And he will destroy in this mountain the face of the covering cast over all people, and the vial that is spread over all nations. He will swallow up death in victory and the Lord* God *will wipe away tears from off all faces; and the rebuke of his people shall he take away from off all the earth: for the* Lord *hath spoken it."*

The ungodly in their feasts speak contemptuously of religion, of God's church and the pleasures enjoyed therein. They have their portion now. We wait for ours till another world shall dawn. But still, let us boast of what we now enjoy.

I. THE CHURCH, UNDER THE FIGURE OF A MOUNTAIN.

By this mountain is intended God's believing people. The Church is called "the mount of the Lord,"[2] "thy holy hill,"[3] "my holy mountain,"[4] "Mount Zion."[5] Because Jerusalem stood on mountains and also because:

1. A mountain is conspicuous. So are all who stand on Mount Zion. Angels behold with joy, devils with rage, men with wonder. See how great a distance we are seen.

2. A mountain is much exposed to storms. When the valleys escape, this[6] receive[s] all. So here, the storms of persecution and Satan's temptations spend[7] themselves.

3. A mountain is extensively beneficial as a shelter to the world from God's immediate wrath, as drawing down the clouds, as giving water to the lower grounds.

4. A mountain is immovable and secure. God's promise and oath keep every particle of the mountain. Though the goats [are] on it, the hypocrites shall perish. It is in this mountain a feast is provided.

5.[8] A mountain is one of the mightiest works of God and is opposed to all mounds of man's upcasting. The church is as much a display of God's power as a mountain, and like a mountain[9] she is God's own work alone.

II. True religion under the figure of a feast
1. The Lord of hosts - provides the feast - who but he could bear the infinite expense? He suggested it & makes it
2. All men must eat his provisions or starve. None are allowed to bring their own provisions - all people of all conditions or countries - the vilest of the vile.
3. The food is the daintiest to be found.
  (1) Carefully selected. wisdom, righteousness, sanc'n & redemption
  (2) Dearly purchased by the blood & agonies of Jesus.
  (3) Supremely excellent - as all know who taste them
  (4) Highly gratifying - where can pleasure like this be found
"fat things" - "wines on the lees" i.e. good old wines.
"fat things full of marrow" - "wines on the lees well refined" by settling -   here are the richest figures of language.

III. The Benefits accrueing to the feasters.
 In other feasts there is weariness, redness of eyes, sin, sorrow, discontent, but this leaves blessings behind it.
1. The removal of darkness for like Jonathan's honey it enlightens the eyes - spiritual darkness & the blindness of sin is only removed by this feasting
 The Christian dispensation lifted the vail of mystery with which Mosaic ceremonies surrounded truth and also gave light to the Gentiles.
2. Conquest over death. (Death shall be but a homœopathic grain mixed in an ocean of victory
 By supporting a Christian so that dying is forgotten amid the raptures of Jesus' presence
 By saving from the second death through Jesus great conquest over sin death & hell.

THE BEST FEAST—*Isaiah 25:6–8*

II. TRUE RELIGION UNDER THE FIGURE OF A FEAST.

1. The Lord of hosts provides the feast. Who but he could bear the infinite expense? He suggested it and makes it.

2. All men must eat his provisions or starve. None are allowed to bring their own provisions. All people of all conditions or countries, the vilest of the vile.

3. The food is the daintiest to be found.

    (1) Carefully selected. Wisdom, righteousness, sancⁿ,[10] and redemption.

    (2) Dearly purchased by the blood and agonies of Jesus.[11]

    (3) Supremely excellent as all know who taste them.

    (4) Highly gratifying. Where can pleasure like this be found? "Fat things," "wines on the lees," i.e., good old wines, "fat things full of marrow," "wines on the lees[12] well refined" by settling.[13] Here are the richest figures of language.

III. THE BENEFITS ACCRUEING[14] TO THE FEASTERS.

In other feasts there is weariness, redness of eyes, sin, sorrow, discontent. But this leaves blessings behind it.

1. The removal of darkness. For like Jonathan's honey[15] it enlightens the eyes. Spiritual darkness and the blindness of sin is only removed by this feasting. The Christian dispensation lifted the vail of mystery with which Mosaic ceremonies surrounded truth and also gave light to the Gentiles.[16]

2. Conquest over death. Death shall be but a homeopathic[17] grain mixed in an ocean of victory.

    By supporting a Christian so that dying is forgotten amid the raptures of Jesus'[s] presence.

    By saving from the second death[18] through Jesus['s] great conquest over sin, death, and hell.

By lifting the soul by death to glory — thus making sorrow joy and punishment — reward —: death — victory —
3. Deliverance from sorrow — Here is the cure for all ills all tears even for sin — God shall wipe away from all faces. In glory — tears cannot fall — God has so decreed.
4. Removal of reproach — we are now rebuked and despised but no despising then when we shall feast our full of sacred, eternal joy. —

1. Well brethren — let us have an antepast of heaven now, lift up your heads — get on the mountain get a good meal — rejoice, rejoice.
2. Sinners you cannot have two feasts. God will not find bread and Satan beer — Drink Gods' wine but mind — none of the devils homebrewed therewith.
3. Oh that all would come seeing all things are ready — of the best kind — and affording such great benefits long after they are eaten.
God feed us for Jesus Christ's sake. Amen
174.

THE BEST FEAST—*Isaiah 25:6-8*

By lifting the soul by death to glory, thus making sorrow, joy; and punishment, reward; death, victory.

3. Deliverance from sorrow. Here is the cure for all ills, all tears, even for sin. <u>God</u> shall wipe away from all faces. In glory, tears cannot fall. Gods[19] has so decreed.

4. Removal of reproach. We are now rebuked and despised, but no despising then when we shall feast our full of sacred, eternal joy.

1. Well, brethren, let us have an antepast[20] of heaven now. Lift up your heads.[21] Get on the mountain. Get a good meal. Rejoice, rejoice.

2. Sinners, you cannot have two feasts.[22] God will not find bread and Satan['s] beer. Drink God's wine, but mind none of the devil[']s homebrewed therewith.

3. Oh that all would come, seeing all things are ready of the best kind, and affording such great benefits long after they are eaten.

God, feed us for Jesus Christ's sake.

<u>Amen</u>

174.

1. On December 20, 1868, Charles preached a sermon on Isa 25:6 entitled "Good Cheer for Christmas" (*MTP* 14, Sermon 846). There is not enough overlapping content or structural similarity to suggest Charles had the above sermon in mind when writing his 1868 sermon.

2. Genesis 22:14, "And Abraham called the name of that place Jehovahjireh: as it is said to this day, In the mount of the LORD it shall be seen."

3. Psalm 15:1, "LORD, who shall abide in thy tabernacle? who shall dwell in thy holy hill?" See also Ps 43:3.

4. Ezekiel 20:40, "For in mine holy mountain, in the mountain of the height of Israel, saith the Lord God, there shall all the house of Israel, all of them in the land, serve me: there will I accept them, and there will I require your offerings, and the firstfruits of your oblations, with all your holy things." See also Ps 2:6; Isa 11:9; 56:7; Obad 1:16.

5. Obadiah 1:17, "But upon mount Zion shall be deliverance, and there shall be holiness; and the house of Jacob shall possess their possessions." See also Ps 125:1; Heb 12:22.

6. The letter "e" appears beneath the "i" in the word "this." Charles originally wrote the word "the."

7. It is unclear why Charles reinforced the letters "sp" in the word "spend."

8. Charles struck through Roman numeral II because he sought to continue his numerical list as demonstrated in the Arabic number 5 immediately following.

9. The word "mountain" is smeared toward the right side of the page.

10. Abbr. "sanctification." For an additional abbreviation of this word, see "Justification by Imputed Righteousness" (Sermon 117).

11. Cf. Acts 20:28; 1 Cor 6:20; 1 Pet 1:19.

12. "Dregs; sediment" (Johnson's *Dictionary*, s.v. "lees").

13. "To subside; to sink to the bottom and repose there," and "To lose motion or fermentation" (Johnson's *Dictionary*, s.v. "settle").

14. Charles mispelled the word "accruing."

15. Cf. 1 Sam 14:28–29.

16. An alternative reading of this line is "The Christian dispensation lifted the vail of mystery with which Mosaic ceremonies surrounded truth, and also gave light to the Gentiles."

17. In a letter to his ill mother on January 10, 1866, Charles wrote, "Homeopathy for ever, I say, because there is no physic at all and you need no doctor if you take the trouble to read for yourself" (Letter to his mother, Angus Library and Archive, Regent's Park College, Oxford University, D/SPU 1, Letter 25). By the mid-nineteenth century, homeopathic medicine had come under severe scrutiny. In 1851, the year before Charles preached the sermon above, *Trewman's Exeter Flying Post* published an article in which "Dr. Cormack" reported at the Provincial Medical and Surgical Association at Brighton: "We have thought it best to direct your attention solely to what is called homeopathy, as, along with it, is almost invariably associated the practice of other systems of charlatanry. . . . It is not necessary in this assembly to prove that homeopathy is a mere chimera—a system opposed to reason, common sense, and all medical experience" ("The Provincial Medical and Surgical Association versus Homeopathy," *Trewman's Exeter Flying Post; Devon, Cornwall, Somerset, Dorset, Wilts, and Gloucester Advertiser*, September 4, 1851). See also "Homeopathic Medicines and Handbook," *The Cork Examiner*, August 30, 1870.

18. The letter "p" is written beneath the "a" in the word "death." It is possible Charles originally wrote the word "depth."

19. By adding the letter "s" to the end of the word "God," Charles may have originally intended to make this word possessive, i.e., "God's decree."

20. "A foretaste; something taken before the proper time" (Johnson's *Dictionary*, s.v. "antepast"). See also "Inventory and Title of Our Treasures" (Sermon 92) and "Bring My Soul Out of Prison" (Notebook 3, Sermon 164).

21. An alternative reading of this line is "Well, brethren, let us have an antepast of heaven. Now, lift up your heads." Cf. Ps 24:9.

22. Cf. Jas 3:11.

126. Isa. 62. 1. Christ's constant intercession.

Much that passes in the world of spirits is unknown to us; and of the little which is known how great a portion is forgotten or buried in thoughtlessness.

The devil's activity, angelic succours, the divine presence Satan's accusings, and Jesus' pleadings we too oft forget amid the flurry and worry of this mortal life but now retiring from the seen let us think on the unseen.

I. Christ is not inactive, but is still engaged either in intercession, overruling, or sending the Spirit.

1. He is always correcting, revising, adding to, and offering up our poor prayers, here is a vast business.

2. He is perpetually pleading the covenant, he looks on the church's enemies and straight he asks for succour — he sees one tried & he prays for him even before he prays for himself — he is always requesting the fulfilment of the covenant — the destruction of sin

3. He holds the reins of government, restrains the evil ones, overrules the sinfulness of man, dispenses the Holy Spirit and makes all work for good.

4. He answers the malicious accusations of Satan who is ever urging charges against God's people

II. The constancy of Christ's work.

He never rests or stays for a moment, he is

*. 'Tis wrong to suppose that Jesus' work was confined to what he did when incarnate, He worked before that in election and the covenant, and ever since he labours still

CHRIST'S CONSTANT INTERCESSION
Isaiah 62:1[1]

"For Zion's sake will I not hold my peace, and for Jerusalem's sake I will not rest, until the righteousness thereof go forth as brightness, and the salvation thereof as a lamp that burneth."

Much that passes in the world of spirits is unknown to us, and of the little which is known, how great a portion is forgotten or buried in thoughtlessness.

The devil's activity, angelic succours, the divine presence, Satan's accusings, and Jesus'[s] pleadings we too oft forget amid the flurry and worry of this mortal life. But now, retiring from the seen, let us think on the unseen.

I. CHRIST IS NOT INACTIVE[2] BUT IS STILL ENGAGED EITHER IN INTERCESSION, OVERRULING, OR SENDING THE SPIRIT.[3]

*[4]

1. He is always correcting, revising, adding to, and offering up our poor prayers. Here is a vast business.

2. He is perpetually pleading the covenant. He looks on the church's[5] enemies and straight he asks for succour. He sees one tried and he prays for him even before he prays for himself. He is always requesting the fulfilment of the covenant, the destruction of sin.

3. He holds the reins of government,[6] restrains the evil ones, overrules the sinfulness of man, dispenses the Holy Spirit, and makes all work for good.[7]

4. He answers the malicious accusations of Satan, who is ever urging charges against God's people.

II. THE CONSTANCY OF CHRIST'S WORK.

He never rests or stays for a moment. He is

---

* Tis wrong to suppose that Jesus'[s] work was confined to what he did when incarnate. He worked before that in election and the covenant,[8] and ever since he labours still.[9]

not hindered by our ingratitude, by the multitude of our suits — It is one of our own ways of expressing a constant perseverance "I will not rest." "I will not hold my peace" — alas! we do too often give up, he never does: He stays not for a single moment.

III. He does this for his people's sake.
He prays for them not for the world. These being the persons chosen in election, specially redeemed, for them he intensely agonized — these he has fetched out from their low estate and to these he is married

IV. He will not rest until his desires are consummated. —
1. In every one of the redeemed receiving the knowledge of his justification and salvation.
2. In the holy walk and conversation of every one of his saints shining like a burning lamp.
3. In the universal spread of his kingdom so that it shall be known all under heaven.
4. In the final glory of the whole of the elect.

V. There is one duty arising from this.
That since he for our sake takes no rest, neither should we rest, nor give God rest, till in our own soul, our own life, and in the world in general — his righteousness go forth as brightness. God bless us with his help. Amen

176.

not hindered by our ingratitude, by the multitude[10] of our suits. It is one of our own ways of expressing a constant perseverance. "I will not rest." "I will not hold my peace." Alas! we do too often give up. He never does. He stays not for a single moment.

III. HE DOES THIS FOR HIS PEOPLE'S SAKE.

He prays for them, not for the world.[11] These, being the persons chosen in election,[12] specially redeemed. For them he intensely agonized. These he has fetched out from their low estate, and to these he is married.[13]

IV. HE WILL NOT REST UNTIL HIS DESIRES ARE CONSUMMATED.

1. In every one of the redeemed receiving the knowledge of his justification and salvation.

2. In the holy walk and conversation of every one of his saints shining like a burning lamp.[14]

3. In the universal spread of his kingdom so that it shall be known [to][15] all under heaven.

4. In the final glory of the whole of the elect.[16]

V. THERE IS ONE DUTY ARISING FROM THIS.

That since he, for our sake, takes no rest, neither should we rest, nor give God rest, till in our[17] own soul, our own life, and in the world in general, his righteousness go[es] forth as brightness.

God bless us with his help.[18]

Amen

176.

SERMON 126

1. This is the only time Charles preached a sermon on Isa 62:1. Additional sermons on Christ's intercession include "Christ's Prayer for His People" (*NPSP* 1, Sermon 47); "The Holy Spirit's Intercession" (*MTP* 26, Sermon 1532); and "Intercession and Supplication" (*MTP* 47, Sermon 2745).

2. Charles originally wrote the words "no inactive." He inserted the letter "t" at the end of the word "no" to construct the phrase "not inactive."

3. Cf. John 15:26; Acts 1:4.

4. Charles inserted an asterisk here to signal the inclusion of the content in his footnote at the bottom of the page beneath the line. For additional examples, see "The Wise Men's Offerings" (Notebook 1, Sermon 58) and "The Minister's Commission" (Sermon 110).

5. Charles originally spelled the word "churche's." There is no evidence to suggest he intended to strike through the letter "e" to form the correct spelling of the word, "church's."

6. Cf. John 19:11; Rom 13:1.

7. Cf. Gen 50:20; Rom 8:28.

8. "With the telescope of his prescience, [Christ] foresaw our existence, and he loved us when we had no being. Then he struck hands with the great Father, and entered into covenant on our behalf, and engaged that he would stand sponsor for us, and redeem us from the ruin of our sin" (*MTP* 39:65).

9. Cf. Rom 8:34; Heb 7:25.

10. The letter "d" in the word "multitude" is smeared toward the top of the page.

11. John 17:9, "I pray for them: I pray not for the world, but for them which thou hast given me; for they are thine."

12. See "Election" (Notebook 1, Sermon 10).

13. Cf. Isa 54:5; Eph 5:25–27; Rev 19:7–9; 21:2.

14. Cf. Matt 5:14.

15. The preposition "by" may also be substituted here: "In the universal spread of his kingdom so that it shall be known [by] all under heaven."

16. See "The Glory, Unity, and Triumph of the Church" (*MTP* 25, Sermon 1472) and "Glory!" (*MTP* 29, Sermon 1721).

17. The letter "f" appears beneath the "o" in the word "our." Charles may have originally begun writing the word "life," as he did in the line below.

18. An alternative reading of this line is "[May] God bless us with his help."

127. (Deut. 32.31 — The most excellent Rock.

There is nothing which a Christian finds in the Bible which he needs to be ashamed of — The Bible itself is his boast. Its laws are the very epitome of justice. Its doctrines are the foundations of holiness. Its spirit is heavenly love — Its effects are unparalleled. Its promises most cheering — Its truth indisputable. But the God of the Bible is the greatest glory of the Bible — Let us notice

I. God is called a rock. —————

1. As the great foundation of all, the rock that begat us. The earth rests on the rocks. God is the origin, first cause.

2. As the firm and solid one, able to bear the most immense loads — All his saints, their burdens, sins &c.

3. As the immovable and Eternal. The rock stirs not. God moves not from his purposes, he is eternal.

4. As the source of blessing — as of old water came from the flinty rock so now from our God.

5. As a place of protection — the clefts of our rock are inaccessible by all our foes — here let us sleep.

II. The rocks of the wicked are not like our Rock. As applied to the Gods of the heathen this is true at once. But let us put our enemies in the witness box & ask.

1. Do you find any real happiness from any created thing. Does the water ever gush out.

2. Can you in the hour of trial feel resigned or does your spirit sink? Have you any place to run to for certain safety.

The MOST EXCELLENT ROCK
Deuteronomy 32:31[1]

"For their rock is not as our Rock, even our enemies themselves being judges."

There is nothing which a Christian finds in the Bible which he needs to be ashamed of.[2] The Bible[3] itself is his boast. Its laws are the very epitome of justice. Its doctrines are the foundations of holiness. Its spirit is heavenly love. Its effects are unparalleled. Its promises, most cheering. Its truth, indisputable. But the God of the Bible is the greatest glory of the Bible. Let us notice:

I. GOD IS CALLED A ROCK.

1. As the great foundation of all, the rock that begat us.[4] The earth rests on the rocks. God is the origin, first cause.

2. As the firm and solid one, able to bear the most immense loads. All his saints, their burdens, sins, etc.

3. As the immovable and Eternal. The rock stirs not. God moves not from his purposes.[5] He is eternal.

4. As the source of blessing. As of old, water came from the flinty rock,[6] so now from our God.

5. As a place of protection. The clefts of our rock are inaccessible by all our foes. Here, let us sleep.

II. THE ROCKS OF THE WICKED ARE NOT LIKE OUR ROCK.

As applied to the Gods[7] of the heathen, this is true at once.

But let us put our enemies in the witness box[8] and ask:

1. Do you find any real happiness[9] from any created thing? Does the water ever gush out?

2. Can you, in the hour of trial, feel resigned? or does your spirit sink? Have you any place to run to for certain safety?

3. Do you feel a solid security, a confident hope, or a glorious expectation or are you gloomy and fearing.
4. Do you think your rock will bear you when you die? do you ever long for death or do you dread it?

To all these things all our foes must answer "No". But we can say "Yes". Here we surpass them even they themselves being judges. Infidels, Despisers even great men have declared the same thing.

III. What do we infer from this?
1. That no Christian man ought for a moment to turn away from this rock, to one confessedly inferior.
2. That if a Christian has a rock to rest on, he ought to rest firmly on it and have great faith.
3. That seeing we have the best rock we ought to be the best people on earth.
4. Knowing the insecurity of other rocks let us try to teach men where to build; pulling them as it were by force from their old rocks.

May God pull us all off the sand on to the rock. Jesus Christ.
Amen

178. 258. 259. 282.

3. Do you feel a solid security, a confident hope, or a glorious expectation? Or are you gloomy and fearing?

4. Do you think your rock will bear you when you die? Do you ever long for death, or do you dread it?

To all these things all our foes must answer "No." But we can say "Yes." Here we surpass them, even they themselves being judges.[10] Infidels. Despisers. Even great men have declared the same thing.

III. WHAT DO WE INFER FROM THIS?

1. That no Christian man ought for a moment to turn away from this rock to one confessedly inferior.

2. That if a Christian has a rock to rest on, he ought to rest firmly on it and have great faith.

3. That seeing we have the best rock, we ought to be the best people on earth.

4. Knowing the insecurity of other rocks, let us try to teach men where to build, pulling them, as it were, by force from their old rocks.

May God pull us all off the sand[11]
on to the rock, Jesus Christ.

Amen

178. 258. 259. 282.

SERMON 127

1. This is the only time Charles preached a sermon on Deut 32:31.

2. Cf. Luke 9:26; Rom 1:16.

3. Charles embellished the letter "B" in the word "Bible" here and throughout the sermon.

4. Cf. Gen 1:1; Col 1:16.

5. Cf. Ps 33:11; Isa 46:10; Mal 3:6.

6. Cf. Num 20:11; Ps 105:41.

7. Though rare when referencing pagan deities, Charles capitalized the word "Gods."

8. A "witness box" was similar to today's courtroom witness stand. See also "Law Intelligence," *Brighton Gazette, Lewes Observer, Chichester Arundel, Worthing, Horsham, Eastbourne, Hastings, St. Leonards, Rye, and Tunbridge Wells Journal; Fashionable Chronicle, Sussex and General Advertiser* (July 25, 1850).

9. Stippling can be seen above the word "happiness."

10. An alternative reading of this line is "Here, we surpass them even [though] they themselves [are] judges."

11. Cf. Matt 7:26–27.

128. — CXVIII Psalm. 22 verse. — The Corner stone.

The whole of this psalm admits of a double application both to David and to Jesus Christ. —

In the 1 – 4 David & Jesus give thanks & praise
From the 5 – 18 He encourages himself & others by rehearsing God's acts.
From the 19 – 23. Is a tribute of praise to God for exalting him

To the end — is a chorus of people &c blessing God for the exaltation of their king. —

So in this verse David could tell how Samuel passed him by and how his brethren mocked, how Saul persecuted, how the men of Israel rebelled against him & yet though refused, he did become the very top-stone in the building of the Jewish state.

I. How did the builders refuse Jesus?
1. The Jewish scribes & Pharisees denied his Mission.
2. The Socinian builders deny his divinity
3. Some builders deny or lessen his atonement.
4. Some builders reject salvation by faith.
5. Some builders deny his efficacious grace in the soul.
6. They do — who hope to reform the world without him.

II. Why do the builders refuse Jesus?
1. Because he will not lay on their wood, hay & stubble.
2. Because he says he will be at the top.
3. Because he is too firm to yield to their cutting.
4. And is not of the right shape & size for their building, they want only a little pebble to help.
5. Because he does not come out of any earthly

THE CORNER STONE—*Psalm 118:22*

128

The CORNER STONE
Psalm 118:22[1]

"The stone which the builders refused is become the head stone of the corner."

The whole of this psalm admits of a double application, both to David and to Jesus Christ.[2]

In the 1–4, David and Jesus give thanks and praise.

From the 5–18, he encourages himself and others by rehearsing God's acts.[3]

From the 19–23,[4] is a tribute of praise to God for exalting him.[5]

To the end[6] is a chorus of people, etc., blessing God for the exaltation of their king.

So in this verse, David could tell how Samuel passed him by,[7] and[8] how his brethren mocked,[9] how Saul persecuted,[10] how the men of Israel rebelled[11] against him,[12] and yet, though refused, he did become the very top-stone in the building of the Jewish state.[13]

I. HOW DID THE BUILDERS REFUSE JESUS?

1. The Jewish scribes and Pharisees denied his Mission.
2. The Socinian builders deny his divinity.[14]
3. Some builders deny or lessen his atonement.[15]
4. Some builders reject salvation by faith.
5. Some builders deny his efficacious grace in the soul.
6. They do who hope to reform the world without him.[16]

II. WHY DO THE BUILDERS REFUSE JESUS?

1. Because he will not lay on their wood, hay, and stubble.[17]
2. Because he says he will be at the top.[18]
3. Because he is too firm to yield to their cutting.
4. And is not of the right shape and size for their building. They want only a little pebble to help.
5. Because he does not come out of any earthly

quarry but is a stone of God's cutting, not by hands.

III. How is he the headstone of the corner?
1. The whole scheme, acting out, and perfection of the gospel depends upon him.
2. The whole plan is intended to glorify him.
3. In the great building of gospel doctrines all run to him — election, justification, perseverance.
4. In the living temple of the saints on earth he is the precious head-stone.
5. In the glorious temple of heaven he is the head stone, the only glorious & glorified.

———————————————

1. Let us take care lest we reject this stone.
2. Let us rejoice that though rejected of man he is chosen of God and precious.
3. Let us build on him and have him built on us, or rather may we beneath him try to exalt him —

   <u>Precious Corner-stone.</u>
   <u>Bless me</u>

179, 197, 218
Cottenham Wythe Zeventh aug 2/52

Three joined the Church at Cottenham
through the sermons on Sabbath 179.

THE CORNER STONE—*Psalm 118:22*

quarry but is a stone of God's cutting, not by hands.

III. HOW IS HE[19] THE HEADSTONE OF THE CORNER?

1. The whole scheme, acting out, and perfection of the gospel depends upon him.

2. The whole plan is intended to glorify him.[20]

3. In the great building of gospel doctrines, all run to him: election,[21] justification,[22] perseverance.[23]

4. In the living temple of the saints on earth, he is the precious head-stone.[24]

5. In the glorious temple of heaven, he is the head stone, the only glorious and glorified.[25]

---

1. Let us take care lest we reject this stone.

2. Let us rejoice that, though rejected of man, he is chosen of God and precious.

3. Let us build on him and have him built on us. Or rather, may we beneath him try to exalt him.

Precious Corner-stone,

Bless me

179.[26] 197.[27] 218[28]

    Three joined the Church at Cottenham
    through the sermons on Sabbath. 179.

SERMON 128

1. Charles originally wrote the Scripture reference in Roman numerals as follows: "CXVIII Psalm. 22 Verse." He uses Roman numerals for scripture references in the remainder of the sermons in this notebook with the exception of "God, the Father of a Family" (Sermon 129). He continues this practice in Notebook 3. On June 23, 1878, Charles preached a sermon on Ps 118:22–25 entitled "The Head Stone of the Corner" (*MTP* 24, Sermon 1420). There is not enough overlapping content or structural similarity to suggest Charles had in mind his early sermon when writing his later one. See also "Faith's Sure Foundation" (*MTP* 24, Sermon 1429) and Charles Spurgeon, *The Treasury of David: Containing an Original Exposition of the Book of Psalms; A Collection of Illustrative Extracts from the Whole Range of Literature; A Series of Homiletical Hints upon Almost Every Verse; and Lists of Writers upon Each Psalm. Vol. V. Psalm CIV. to CXVIII* (London: Passmore & Alabaster, 1878, The Spurgeon Library), 330–33.

2. Charles continued his allegorical/typological treatment here as in the previous four sermons. In "The Most Excellent Rock" (Sermon 127), Charles compared God to a mountain. In this sermon he emphasized God as the cornerstone.

3. The words "God's acts" are written above the word "rehearsing."

4. Charles might have intended to include verse 24 in this section: "This is the day which the Lord hath made; we will rejoice and be glad in it."

5. An alternative reading of this line is "[Verses] 19–23 [are] tribute[s] of praise to God for exalting him."

6. If Charles intended verse 24 to be included in the section "of praise to God for exalting him" in the line above, then the remaining verses would be 25–29.

7. Cf. 1 Samuel 16.

8. The word "and" suggests Charles originally intended to conclude this sentence with the words "Samuel passed him by."

9. Cf. 1 Sam 17:33.

10. Cf. 1 Samuel 19.

11. Charles originally wrote the word "rebl" before changing the letter "l" to an "e" to construct the word "rebelled."

12. Cf. 2 Samuel 15; 1 Kgs 12:19.

13. Charles used the words "corner stone" synonymously with "top-stone" throughout this sermon. However, the two stones served different engineering functions. In biblical times, a cornerstone was laid before the others in order to set correctly the angle of the walls ("corner-stone," in W. R. F. Browning, ed., *A Dictionary of the Bible, Oxford Biblical Studies Online*). In contrast, a top-stone, or "key stone," was placed at the summit of an arch (Walter A. Elwell, ed., *Baker's Evangelical Dictionary of the Bible* [Grand Rapids: Baker Books, 1996]). Cf. Zech 4:7 and Ps 118:22.

14. For references to Socinianism, see "What Think Ye of Christ?" (Notebook 1, Sermon 71).

15. "The Atonement is scouted, the inspiration of Scripture is derided, the Holy Spirit is degraded into an influence, the punishment of sin is turned into fiction, and the resurrection into a myth, and yet these enemies of our faith expect us to call them brethren, and maintain a confederacy with them!" (original handwritten draft, eventually published as "Another Word concerning the Down-Grade" [*ST*, August 1887], from the personal collection of Jason K. Allen).

16. Charles may have been referring to social activist groups such as Chartism, a group named after the 1838 People's Charter drafted by William Lovett. Chartism advocated six primary reforms in society: "Universal manhood suffrage, equal electoral districts, vote by ballot, annually elected Parliaments, payment of members of Parliament, and abolition of the property qualifications for membership" ("Chartism," in *Encyclopædia Britannica Online*). On November 1, 1848, the *Dundee Courier* labeled the movement a "quackery." Feargus O'Conner, a leading figure in Chartism, was described as being "big in promises and absolutely nothing in performances" ("Chartism," *Dundee Courier* [November 1, 1848]).

17. Cf. 1 Cor 3:11–13. A dark yellow stain, likely the result of the aging process of the manuscript, appears after the word "stubble." Its imprint is also found on the opposite page.

18. Cf. Eph 1:20–22.

SERMON 128

19. Two diagonal pencil strokes, likely in the hand of Charles, appear above the words "he" and "scheme" in the line below.

20. Cf. Rom 11:36; 1 Pet 4:11.

21. See "Election" (Notebook 1, Sermon 10).

22. See "The Saints' Justification and Glory" (Notebook 1, Sermon 68) and "Justification, Conversion, Sanctification, Glory" (Sermon 102).

23. See "Final Perseverance Certain" (Sermon 82).

24. First Peter 2:4–5, "To whom coming, as unto a living stone, disallowed indeed of men, but chosen of God, and precious, Ye also, as lively stones, are built up a spiritual house, an holy priesthood, to offer up spiritual sacrifices, acceptable to God by Jesus Christ." Cf. 1 Cor 3:16.

25. An alternative reading of this line is "In the glorious temple of heaven he is the head stone, the only [one] glorious and glorified."

26. Beneath these numbers Charles wrote in pencil the dates and villages corresponding to the preaching of this sermon. The notations are in the handwriting of Charles, though the date of their writing is unknown. These inscriptions suggest Charles, though serving as pastor of Waterbeach Chapel, also ministered itinerantly in the villages surrounding Cambridge. Beneath the number 179 are the notations "June 13" and "Cottenham." See also the conversion of a young man in Cottenham in "Hew Down the Tree" (Notebook 4, Sermon 215). The above sermon resulted in the joining of three people into membership, indicated in pen beneath the pencil notations: "Three joined the Church at Cottenham through the sermons on Sabbath. 179."

27. Beneath the number 197 are the notations "July 7" and "Hythe." According to his Notebook 1 notations, Charles preached the following three sermons in the village of Hythe: "Adoption" (Notebook 1, Sermon 1); "God's Grace Given to Us" (Notebook 1, Sermon 14); and "Christ About His Father's Business" (Notebook 1, Sermon 15). All three sermons were preached during the month of July 1851.

28. Beneath the number 218 is the date "Aug 2/52" and the word "Teversham." The "church at Teversham" likely referred to the cottage where Charles preached his first sermon (*Autobiography* 1:199–202). The handwriting of this sentence is

noticeably different in size and characteristic. For similar disparities in handwriting, see "Sinners Must Be Punished" (Notebook 1, Sermon 9); "Hew Down the Tree" (Notebook 4, Sermon 215); and "I Have Found a Ransom" (Notebook 4, Sermon 224).

SERMON 129

129 —   Jer. 31 – 9 ——   God, the father of a family.
Israel the two tribes and Ephraim the ten are here
in the first place alluded to, but no doubt the
words principally intend the chosen of God on earth.
Miracle of love Israel the idolatrous and rebellious
shall come forth from captivity and Ephraim
viler still, the greatest transgressor shall be Gods
firstborn — both together God shall own them as children.
  God has a large family — let us enquire.
I. How men become God's children.
  Not by nature, nor by baby-baptism but by
1. Adoption whereby God takes Satan's blackamoors
and makes them his own sons.
2. Regeneration whereby the blacks are made anew
their image and colour being made like God.
II. How God feeds his children.
  At first they will not eat his food, they love the breasts
of earth too much so he weans them by putting
bitters with the milk — Then they often are not
hungry but he soon finds them an appetite a little
bitter sets them right — or confinement in the prison.
He give different foods according to their wants.
To some milk, others bread, some meat. Gods children
never eat too much — their fault is not eating enough.
He give them solid, substantial meats — dainties

GOD, THE FATHER OF A FAMILY—*Jeremiah 31:9*

129

GOD, *the* FATHER *of a* FAMILY
Jeremiah 31:9[1]

"They shall come with weeping, and with supplications will I lead them: I will cause them to walk by the rivers of waters in a straight way, wherein they shall not stumble: for I am a father to Israel, and Ephraim is my firstborn."

Israel, the two tribes, and Ephraim,[2] the ten, are here in the first place alluded to. But no doubt the words principally intend the chosen of God on earth. Miracle of love. Israel, the idolatrous and rebellious, shall come forth from captivity,[3] and Ephraim, viler still, the greatest transgressor, shall be God[']s firstborn. Both together, God shall own them as children.

God has a large family. Let us enquire:

I. HOW MEN BECOME GOD'S CHILDREN.

Not by nature,[4] nor by baby-baptism,[5] but by:

1. Adoption, whereby God takes Satan's blackamoors[6] and makes them his own sons.

2. Regeneration, whereby the blacks are made anew, their image and colour being made like God.

II. HOW GOD FEEDS HIS CHILDREN.

At first they will not eat his food. They love the breasts of earth too much, so he weans them by putting bitters[7] with the milk. Then they often are not hungry, but he soon finds them an appetite. A little bitter sets them right—or confinement in the prison.

He give[s] different foods according to their wants. To some, milk;[8] others, bread; some, meat. God's children never eat too much—their fault is not eating enough. He give[s] them solid, substantial meats, dainties and sweets too and some wine to cheer their hearts.

III. How God clothes his children. —
Their every day dress is good and strong it has two principal parts —
1. The inner garment of imputed righteousness.
2. The outer garment of inwrought righteousness.
No linsey-woolsey garments. This they wear till they die and then they have a Sabbath suit yet more glorious though made of the same materials.

IV. How God rules his children.
1. With love — he tells them he loves them & bids them obey.
2. With filial fear and reverence he is still the awful God.
3. With wonderful patience & longsuffering.
4. With unalterable firmness. He must have obedience, even if the rod must be used.
He has the most unruly family under heaven. Sometimes they even take to fighting each other.

V. How God educates his children.
They are sent to the day school as well as Sunday School. — Mr Law is one hard schoolmaster. He must have them educated before they come home — we are out at boarding school now
God's plans are
1. He gives easy lessons first.
2. He says the same thing over & over again.
3. He speaks in the simplest language.
4. He teaches us by experiment.
5. He uses emulation or at least stimulation

GOD, THE FATHER OF A FAMILY—*Jeremiah 31:9*

and sweets, too, and some wine to cheer their hearts.[9]

III. HOW GOD CLOTHES HIS CHILDREN.

Their every day dress is good and strong. It has two principal parts:

1. The inner garment of imputed righteousness.[10]
2. The outer garment of inwrought righteousness.

No linsey-woolsey[11] garments. This they wear till they die, and then they have a Sabbath suit yet more glorious, though made of the same materials.[12]

IV. HOW GOD RULES HIS CHILDREN.

1. With love. He tells them he loves them[13] and bids them obey.
2. With filial fear[14] and reverence. He is still the awful <u>one</u>.
3. With wonderful patience and longsuffering.[15]
4. With unalterable firmness. He must have obedience, even if the rod must be used.[16]

He has the most unruly family under heaven. Sometimes they even take to fighting each other.

V. HOW GOD EDUCATES HIS CHILDREN.

They are sent to the day school as well as Sunday School. Mr. Law is one hard school master. He must have them educated before they come home. We are out at boarding school now.

God's plans are:

1. He gives easy lessons first.
2. He says the same thing over and over again.
3. He speaks in the simplest language.[17]
4. He teaches us by experiment.
5. He uses emulation,[18] or at least stimulation.[19]

VI. What prospects God keeps before his children.
He bids them neither seek riches nor fame on earth.
He bids them seek only to please God and to live
in anticipation of heaven, their own inheritance.

  1. Have I been born, been weaned, chastened &c —
  2. Let us learn several lessons as to training children
  3. Let us behave as sons of God, redeemed.
180. 182. 278.

---

130.   Isa III. 10   Well with the righteous.
  "What cheering words are these
  "Their sweetness who can tell
  "In time and through eternal days
  "Tis with the righteous well.
Well in youth — since religion keeps us from temptation
Well in middle age — to keep us from worldly associations
Well in old age — to cheer and prepare for death.
Well in prosperity & well in adversity.
Well in death — well in heaven.
Because his heart is well. God is on his side
Men in the lifeboat — Men insured from fire
  But say ye to the wicked 'tis ill with him
181

GOD, THE FATHER OF A FAMILY *and* WELL WITH THE RIGHTEOUS

VI. WHAT PROSPECTS GOD KEEPS BEFORE HIS CHILDREN.

He bids them neither seek riches[20] nor fame[21] on earth.

He bids them seek only to please God and to live in anticipation of heaven, their own inheritance.

1. Have I been born, been weaned, chastened, etc.?
2. Let us learn several lessons as to training children.
3. Let us behave as sons of God, redeemed.

180. 182. 378.[22]

130

WELL *with the* RIGHTEOUS
Isaiah 3:10[1]

"Say ye to the righteous, that it shall be well with him: for they shall eat the fruit of their doings."

> "What cheering words are these![2]
> "Their sweetness who can tell?
> "In time, and through[3] eternal days,
> "Tis with the righteous well.

Well in youth since religion keeps us from temptation.
Well in middle age to keep us from worldly associations.
Well in old age to cheer and prepare for death.
Well in prosperity and well in adversity.
Well in death. Well in heaven.

Because his heart is well.[4] God is on his side.
Men in the lifeboat.[5] Men insured from fire.

But say ye to the wicked, 'tis ill with him.

181[6]

SERMON 129

1. On April 29, 1866, Charles preached an additional sermon on Jer 31:8–9 entitled "Gathering in the Chosen." There is not enough overlapping content or structural similarity to suggest Charles had in mind his early sermon when writing his later one.

2. Cf. Gen 41:52; 1 Chron 7:20–27.

3. Cf. Ezra 2:1–2; Neh 7:6–7.

4. Cf. Rom 7:5, 18; Gal 5:17; Eph 2:3.

5. See "God's Estimation of Men" (Notebook 1, Sermon 41) and "Faith before Baptism" (Notebook 9, Sermon 396).

6. "A man by nature of a black complexion; a negro" (Johnson's *Dictionary*, s.v. "blackamoor"). Two years before Charles preached the sermon above, the *Newry Examiner & Louth Advertiser* published an article entitled "Daily News—Washing the Blackamoor White," which recounted Lord Broughman's efforts at restoring George Hudson's reputation, or, "trying to wash a blackamoor white" ("Daily News—Washing the Blackamoor White," *Newry Examiner & Louth Advertiser* [October 9, 1850]. Charles's use of "blackamoor" here and "blacks" in the line below were not racially motivated derogatory descriptions about skin color but instead the spiritualizing of human depravity. Charles held firmly to his abolitionist convictions and instructed his congregation, "Judge no man by his skin" ("The Noble Bereans" [Sermon 114]). Five years after Charles preached this sermon, he sacrificed his reputation in America's Southern states for opposing slavery (see Notebook 1, editor's preface). Had Charles visited America he may have been executed, as articulated in a Virginia newspaper: "Pity that that cord from the South is not applied to his eloquent throat!" ("Review of a Letter from Rev. Jas. B. Taylor, of Richmond, Va.," *The Liberator*, July 6, 1860).

7. "A very bitter liquor, which drains off in making of common salt, and used in the preparation of Epsom salt" (Johnson's *Dictionary*, s.v. "bittern"). In Charles's day, bitters were often mixed with other ingredients such as in G. Oldham's "Aperient Family Pills," which offered "an efficacious and valuable remedy for Bilious derangement, Indigestion, Habitual Costiveness, or Nervous Affections.—They contain no mercurial preparation, being composed of vegetable aperients and

bitters" ("Established Medicines, Prepared and Sold by G. Oldham and Co.," *The Weekly Freeman's Journal*, April 10, 1852). See also "The Physician and His Patients" (Notebook 1, Sermon 74).

8. Cf. 1 Cor 3:2; Heb 5:12; 1 Pet 2:2.

9. Cf. Ps 104:15.

10. "Imputed" and "inwrought" righteousness (see line below) describe the doctrines of justification (the immediate right standing of the sinner before God on behalf of the work of Jesus Christ) and sanctification (the gradual process by which the sinner becomes like Jesus Christ). To impute is "to charge upon; attribute to" and "to reckon to one what does not properly belong to him" (Johnson's *Dictionary*, s.v. "impute"). Johnson defined the word "inwrought" as "adorned with work" (Johnson's *Dictionary*). A helpful summary of these two doctrines is found in Charles's personal copy of *Confessions of Faith*, chapter 11, "Of Justification": "Those whom God effectually calleth, he also freely (Rom. iii. 24; viii. 30) justifieth, not by infusing righteousness into them, but by (Rom. iv. 5, 6, 7, 8; Eph. i. 7) pardoning their sins, and by accounting and accepting their persons as (1 Cor. i. 30, 31; Rom. v. 17, 18, 19) righteous; not for anything wrought in them, or done by them, but for Christ's sake alone, not by imputing faith itself, the act of believing, or any other (Phil. iii. 8, 9; Eph. ii. 8, 9, 10) evangelical obedience to them, as their righteousness; but by imputing Christ's active obedience unto the whole law, and passive obedience in his death, for their whole and sole righteousness, they (John i. 12; Rom. v. 17) receiving, and resting on him, and his righteousness, by faith; which faith they have not of themselves, it is the gift of God" (Edward Bean Underhill, ed., *Confessions of Faith, and Other Public Documents, Illustrative of the History of the Baptist Churches of England in the 17th Century* [London: printed for the Hanserd Knollys Society by Haddon, Brothers, and Co., 1854, The Spurgeon Library], 198). See also "By Faith Jericho Fell" (Sermon 133); "Abraham Justified by Faith" (Notebook 1, Sermon 3); and "The Lord Our Righteousness (*MTP* 7, Sermon 395).

11. "Made of linen and wool mixed. Vile; mean; of different and unsuitable parts" (Johnson's *Dictionary*, s.v. "linseywoolsey"). Charles later devoted an entire sermon to this word (see "Linsey-Woolsey Forbidden" [Notebook 4, Sermon 210]).

SERMON 129

12. Charles is speaking here of the physical resurrection of the body. Cf. 1 Cor 15:42, 51.

13. Cf. Ps 86:15; John 3:16; Rom 5:8; Eph 2:4–5; 1 John 3:1; 4:9–11.

14. Cf. Prov 9:10.

15. Cf. Exod 34:6; Num 14:18; Pss 103:8; 145:8; Nah 1:3.

16. Cf. Prov 22:15; Heb 12:6.

17. See "The Eloquence of Jesus" (Notebook 1, Sermon 49).

18. Cf. 1 Cor 4:16; 11:1.

19. The letters "lati" in the word "stimulation" are smeared toward the right of the page.

20. Cf. Matt 6:19–21; Mark 10:25; 1 Tim 6:7–10; Heb 13:5.

21. Cf. Matt 6:1–7.

22. Charles originally wrote the number 278. He added an additional loop at the top of the number 2 to construct the number 3.

WELL WITH THE RIGHTEOUS—*Isaiah 3:10*

1. On January 13, 1867, Charles preached an additional sermon on Isa 3:10–11 entitled "Cheering Words and Solemn Warnings" (*MTP* 13, Sermon 729). There is some overlapping content between this sermon and his later one, particularly in his use of John Kent's hymn. However, Charles quoted only the first stanza of the hymn in this sermon. In his 1867 sermon, he also quoted the third and seventh stanzas (*MTP* 13:16). Charles may have had the sermon above in mind when writing his later one.

2. This excerpt is the first stanza of the hymn "Say Ye to the Righteous, It Shall Go Well with Him," first published in 1803 in *A Collection of Original Gospel Hymns* by Calvinism hymnist John Kent (1766–1843). The entire hymn reads: "1. What cheering words are these! / Their sweetness who can tell? / In time, and to eternal days, / 'Tis with the righteous well. / 2. In ev'ry state secure, / Kept as Jehovah's eye, / 'Tis well with them while life endure, / And well when call'd to die. / 3. Well when they see his face, / Or sink amidst the flood; / Well in affliction's thorny maze, / Or on the mount with God. / 4. 'Tis well when Zion's breasts / No consolations give; / But better far by faith to rest, / And on the promise live. / 5. Well when the gospel yields / Her honey, milk, and wine; / Well when thy soul her leanness feels, / And all her joys decline. / 6. Well when the promise speaks / Sweet words of peace to thee; / Well when thy soul with sorrow breaks, / And thou no Christ canst see. / 7. 'Tis well when joys arise, / 'Tis well when sorrows flow, / 'Tis well when darkness veils the skies, / And strong temptations blow. / 8. 'Tis well when at his throne / They wrestle, weep, and pray; / 'Tis well when at his feet they groan, / Yet bring their wants away. / 9. 'Tis well when they can sing / As sinners bought with blood, / And when they touch the mournful string, / And mourn an absent God. / 10. 'Tis well when on the mount / They feast on dying love, / And 'tis as well, in God's account, / When they the furnace prove. / 11. 'Tis well when grace abounds / To heal sin's rankling sores, / When Zion's trumpet sweetly sounds, / Or Sinai's thunder roars. / 12. 'Tis well when Jesus calls, / 'From earth and sin arise,' / 'Join with the host of virgin souls,' / 'Made to salvation wise'" (John Kent, *A Collection of Original Gospel Hymns, The Sixth Edition, with Additional Hymns* [London: printed for W. Simpkin and R. Marshall, 1826], Hymn CLXII, 148–50). In addition to the hymn above, Charles included nine other hymns by Kent in *Our Own Hymn-Book*, the hymnal he compiled and published for worship at the Metropolitan Tabernacle. They include "Everlasting Love," "The Covenant," "Love before Atonement," "All Mercies Traced to Electing Love," "Eternal Love

Exalted," "Sin Removed by the Cross," "Grace Exalted," "The Reign of Grace," and "He Is Precious" (C. H. Spurgeon, *Our Own Hymn-Book. A Collection of Psalms and Hymns for Public, Social, and Private Worship* [London: Passmore & Alabaster, 1885, The Spurgeon Library]). For additional references to Kent's hymns in Charles's later sermons, see *NPSP* 3:118; *NPSP* 6:77; and *MTP* 57:259.

3. Kent's original line reads "In time, and to eternal days." It is unclear why Charles changed the word "to" to "through."

4. An alternative reading of this line is "[He is] well in heaven because his heart is well."

5. For a reference to "boatsmen," see "An Answer Required" (Notebook 1, Sermon 19, footnote 6).

6. The number 181 is smeared toward the upper right side of the page.

Isa. XXXII. 13.14.15. The Church needs the Spirit

In the first instance this is a description of Palestine when her inhabitants were carried away - as well as of Judea at the present time — and God had decreed that she should flourish again by the grace of the Spirit.

I. What the Church must be without the Spirit.
 1. A land of briars & thorns - contention and war - and consequently she has sorrow instead of joy.
 2. A church having no increase — the palaces forsaken i.e - none joining in her fellowship.
 3. A church backsliding - ceasing to pray, leaving the city - falling away.
 4. A church perverted to evil purposes — her towers or pulpits turned into strongholds of sin, wild asses feasting on her - she is perverted.

II. But see the Church blessed by the Holy Ghost.
 1. The briars & thorns all die - peace is restored.
 2. She becomes a growing & fertile church.
 3. Her already somewhat fertile ones are outstripped.
 4. She becomes the glory of the land.

III. ~~By what means~~ How the Spirit comes.
 1. It must come copiously "pour"
 2. It must come personally "on us"
 3. It must be really divine "from above"

The CHURCH NEEDS the SPIRIT
Isaiah 32:13–15[1]

"Upon the land of my people shall come up thorns and briers; yea, upon all the houses of joy in the joyous city: because the palaces shall be forsaken; the multitude of the city shall be left; the forts and towers shall be for dens for ever, a joy of wild asses, a pasture of flocks; until the sprit be poured upon us from on high, and the wilderness be a fruitful field, and the fruitful field be contoured for a forest."

In the first instance, this is a description of Palestine when her inhabitants were carried away,[2] as well as of Judea at the present time. And God had decreed that she should flourish again by the grace of the Spirit.

I. WHAT THE CHURCH MUST BE WITHOUT THE SPIRIT.

1. A land of briars and thorns, contention and war. And consequently, she has sorrow instead of joy.
2. A church having no increase. The palaces forsaken, i.e., none joining in her fellowship.
3. A church backsliding, ceasing[3] to pray, leaving the city, falling away.
4. A church perverted to evil purposes. Her towers, or pulpits, turned into strongholds of sin. Wild asses feasting on her. She is perverted.

II. BUT SEE THE CHURCH BLESSED BY THE HOLY GHOST.

1. The briars and thorns all die. Peace is restored.
2. She becomes a growing and fertile church.
3. Her already somewhat fertile ones are outstripped.
4. She becomes the glory of the land.

III. ~~BY WHAT MEANS~~ HOW THE SPIRIT COMES.

1. It must come copiously, "pour."
2. It must come personally, "on us."
3. It must be really divine, "from above."

1. Let us learn our entire dependance on the Spirit.
2. Let us look and see if our hearts are barren and learn here the only fertilizer.
3. Take heed you do not despise this Spirit least he swear in wrath, never to work in you.

183. 202.

---

132.   John X. 28. 29.   Christ's sheep.
Here is another beautiful discourse forced out of Jesus by his enemies. He walked in Solomon's porch and these men came to entrap him. He told them he was the Messiah & told them they did not believe because they were not his elect — nor his sheep.

I. The persons spoken of "my sheep". —
"Sheep" because poor defenceless creatures. ever apt to wander, needing the greatest care — associating together, and often slaughtered but yet useful creatures, meek, cleanly, inoffensive in their lives. "my" sheep" — They are Christ's by election & God's gift, by actual purchase and by their consecration vow.

II. The evidences of this character.
"They hear my voice". they love to hear him in the outward means and they hear moreover with the heart while others are spiritually deaf. They hear providence, they hear conscience & so Christ

1. Let us learn our entire dependance on the Spirit.[4]
2. Let us[5] look and see if our hearts are barren and learn here [of] the only fertilizer.
3. Take heed you do not despise this Spirit lest[6] he swear in wrath never to work in you.[7]

183. 202.

132

CHRIST'S[1] SHEEP
John 10:28–29[2]

> "And I give unto them eternal life; and they shall never perish, neither shall any man pluck them out of my hand. My Father, which gave them me, is greater than all; and no man is able to pluck them out of my Father's hand."

Here is another beautiful discourse forced out of Jesus by his enemies. He walked in Solomon's porch[3] and these men came to entrap him. He told them he was the Messiah,[4] and told them they did not believe because they were not his elect, nor his sheep.[5]

I. THE PERSONS SPOKEN OF, *"my sheep."*

"Sheep" because [they are] poor, defenseless creatures, ever apt to wander, needing the greatest care, associating together, and often slaughtered. But yet useful creatures: meek, cleanly, inoffensive in their lives. "My sheep." They are Christ's by election[6] and God's gift by actual purchase[7] and by their consecration vow.

II. THE EVIDENCES OF THIS CHARACTER, *"They hear my voice."*[8]

They love to hear him in the outward means and they hear moreover with the heart, while others are spiritually deaf.

They hear providence. They hear conscience, and so, Christ.[9]

SERMON 132

"I know them" if so then he will come & see us here is another clear evidence for then we shall know him "they follow me" — here is the grand evidence — do I love his word & run to his house. Do I participate in his sufferings & shame. Do I go in duty's path & labour to serve God. Sheep must follow y^r Shepherd.

III. The precious promise made to the sheep. "I give unto them eternal life" so he does by covenant by foretaste, by faith's assurance, by pledge of the Spirit. So will he by actual fruition

"and they shall never perish" though lost in Adam, trembling fearing — even falling into sin — yet never - never "neither shall any pluck them out of my hand, no! no! nor can they slip between his fingers — for how then could the former promise of not perishing be realized. no — we are immutably safe. all the power of the Mediator & the Triune God are sworn to accomplish our Salvation.

1. Take no comfort, till you can give evidence
2. Rejoice true Sheep — for thou art secure.
3. Sinner where are thy senses — that thou dost lose such glorious security for nought
        Help Jesus Amen. Amen

185. 392.

"I know them."[10] If so, then he will come and see us. Here is another clear evidence, for then we shall know him.

"They follow me."[11] Here is the grand evidence. Do I love his [W]ord and run to his house? Do I participate in his sufferings and shame?[12] Do I go in duty's path and labour to serve God? Sheep must follow [your][13] Shepherd.[14]

III. THE PRECIOUS PROMISE MADE TO THE SHEEP.

"I give unto them eternal life." So he does by covenant, by foretaste, by faith's assurance, by pledge of the Spirit.[15] So will he by actual fruition.

"And they shall never perish." Though lost in Adam,[16] trembling, fearing, even falling into sin. Yet never, never.

"Neither shall any pluck them out of my hand. No! No! Nor can they slip between his fingers.[17] For how, then, could the former promise of not perishing be realized? No, we are immutably safe. All the power of the Mediator and the Triune[18] God are sworn to accomplish our Salvation.

1. Take no comfort till you can give evidence.
2. Rejoice, true sheep, for thou art secure.[19]
3. Sinner, where are thy senses, that thou dost lose such glorious security for nought?

Help, Jesus. Amen. Amen.

185. 392.

SERMON 131

1. This is the only time Charles preached a sermon on Isa 32:13–15. For additional sermons on the Holy Spirit, see "The Personality of the Holy Ghost" (*NPSP* 1, Sermon 4); "The Work of the Holy Ghost" (*NPSP* 4, Sermon 178); "The Outpouring of the Holy Spirit" (*NPSP* 4, Sermon 201); and "Grieving the Holy Spirit" (*NPSP* 5, Sermon 278).

2. Cf. 2 Kgs 15:29.

3. It is unclear why Charles reinforced the letter "c" in the word "ceasing."

4. On the title page of Notebook 1 beneath the words "Skeletons I to LXXVII" Charles wrote, "And only skeletons without the Holy Ghost."

5. The smudge beneath the word "us" originated from a dot of ink that was smeared toward the upper left of the page. The uniqueness of this smudge is found in the diagonal lines beneath the dot. These lines are likely Charles's partial fingerprint. An additional example of his fingerprint is found in "The Lost Saved" (Sermon 94).

6. Charles likely intended to write the word "lest" here instead of "least." For additional examples of this error, see "The Watchman, His Work, Warning, and Promise" (Sermon 120) and "By Faith Jericho Fell" (Sermon 133).

7. Cf. Matt 12:31; Mark 3:29; Luke 12:10; Heb 10:26–29.

CHRIST'S SHEEP—*John 10:28–29*

1. The letter "G" appears beneath the "C" in the word "Christ's." Charles may have intended the sermon title to be "God's Sheep."

2. Charles preached two additional sermons on John 10:28–29: "Life Eternal" (*MTP* 12, Sermon 726) and "Perseverance without Presumption" (*MTP* 18, Sermon 1056). There is not enough overlapping content or structural similarity to suggest he had the sermon above in mind when writing his later ones.

3. Cf. John 10:23. Charles originally wrote the letters "poc" before converting the "c" into an "r" to construct the correct spelling of the word "porch."

4. Cf. John 10:7, 9, 11, 14.   5. Cf. John 10:26.

6. Cf. "Election" (Notebook 1, Sermon 10).

7. Cf. Acts 20:28; 1 Cor 6:20; 1 Pet 2:9.

8. John 10:27a, "My sheep hear my voice."

9. An alternative reading of this line is "They hear conscience, and so, [they hear] Christ."

10. John 10:27b, "[A]nd I know them." An alternative reading of this line is "They hear conscience and so Christ [says], 'I know them.'"

11. John 10:27c, "[A]nd they follow me."

12. Cf. 2 Cor 1:5; Phil 3:10; 1 Pet 4:13.

13. Charles abbreviated the word "your."

14. Charles originally spelled this word "Spepherd" before striking through the base of the stem of the letter "p" to construct the letter "h." An alternative reading of this line is "Sheep must follow [after their] Shepherd."

15. Two illegible letters are found beneath "ri" in the word "Spirit." Charles likely misspelled the word before correcting it.

16. Cf. 1 Cor 15:22.

17. "We are *called* the children of God, and *we are* the children of God, and this cannot be undone. How greatly do I rejoice in the final perseverance of the saints! As I have often said, I would not go across the street to pick up the other kind of salvation, which only saves me for a while, and afterwards lets me slip through. Grace brings me into the family of God, and keeps me there. . . . There! I do not feel as if I wanted to preach about it. I long to sit down, and cry over it for a very joy of heart. That ever God should have put *me* among his children shall be my everlasting wonderment" (*MTP* 32:677–78, 679, italics in the original).

18. Charles originally wrote the word "Triun." He added the final letter "e" to construct the correct spelling of the word "Triune."

19. In his diary entry for May 25, 1850, Charles wrote, "Free grace, sovereign love, eternal security are my safeguards" (*Autobiography* 1:140).

133 ... Heb XI. 30. By faith Jericho fell.—

Faith is the one grand essential in salvation. It must be inwrought or else there will be no spiritual life at first.— It is necessary ever after in numberless ways.— We cannot have knowledge of gospel doctrines without faith — nor can we lay hold on the promises without it.— The graces are all dependant on faith.— He loves most who believes most. He will have most zeal who has much of this. Humility is produced and hope breathes faith.— In doing good to others & particularly in combats let us have faith.—

I. Faith is the grace to which victory is given.
1. The other graces are not decked with laurel least man should steal the crowns, but faith is too tall, man cannot touch his head — faith has less to do with man & more with God than any of the others. For faith is looking away from self and trusting the eternal.—
2. Faith has victory because she engages the arm of the Almighty — She has power with him.
3. That man is most able to bear the joy of victory with humility who endured its conflict by faith — he will give glory to God.
4. Other graces do wonders but she does impossi-
-bilities because she is the only grace that will

133

By FAITH JERICHO FELL
Hebrews 11:30[1]

"By faith the walls of Jericho fell down, after they were compassed about seven days."

Faith is the one grand essential in salvation. It must be inwrought[2] or else there will be no spiritual life at first. It is necessary ever after in numberless ways. We cannot have knowledge of gospel doctrines without faith, nor can we lay hold on the promises without it. The graces are all dependent on faith. He loves most who believes most. He will have most zeal who has much of this. Humility is produced and hope breathes faith.

In doing good to others, and particularly in combats, let us have faith.

I. FAITH IS THE GRACE TO WHICH VICTORY IS GIVEN.

1. The other graces are not decked with laurel[3] lest[4] man should steal the crowns. But faith is too tall. Man cannot touch his head. Faith has less to do with man and more with God than any of the others. For faith is looking away from self and trusting the eternal.

2. Faith has victory because she engages the arm of the Almighty. She has power with him.

3. That is[5] man is most able to bear the joy of victory with humility who endured its conflict by faith. He will give glory to God.

4. Other graces do wonders, but she does impossibilities because she is the only grace that will

do, in such a place — She is intended for this very purpose.

II. Faith wins her victories in God's appointed way.
She uses no means of her own contrivance — She waits on God. She neglects not his appointments, She is not presumptuous When she uses. She does not despise — She ungirds the sword — She follows the ark — She hears the ram's horns. She is laughed at for seeming folly but that she smiles at in her turn — She does her maker's will. She expects the blessing but all in an orderly way.

That is no faith at all which believes & does nothing. We may not expect to be saved by faith, unless faith pushes us on running in God's way.

Whether we seek salvation, the good of our friends, the stopping of evil, the destruction of our corruptions let us do it in the true appointed way. —

III. Faith wins her victories in God's time.
She goes her thirteen times — She expects it will come down at last, so round and round she goes. She expects that on her last day her sins will all fall & she thinks her work well paid when she knows it will fall one day — She is persevering.

Now let us apply these thoughts.

1. To the pulling down of Jericho in our hearts, we want to slay all the old inhabitants — but the lofty wall stands strong. Let us have faith. Let us follow the ark. Let us hear the trumpets even though only ram's horns. Let us go round

do in such a place. She is intended for this very purpose.

II. FAITH WINS HER VICTORIES IN GOD'S APPOINTED WAY.

She uses no means of her own contrivance.[6] She waits on God. She neglects not his appointments. She is not presumptuous. When she uses, she does not despise. She ungirds the sword. She follows the ark. She hears the ram's horns. She is laughed at[7] for seeming folly, but that she smiles at in her turn. She does her maker's will. She expects the blessing but all in an orderly way.

That is no faith at all which believes and does nothing.[8] We may not expect to be saved by faith unless faith pushes us on running in God's way. Whether we seek salvation, the good of our friends, the stopping of evil, the destruction of our corruptions, let us do it in the true, appointed way.

III. FAITH WINS HER VICTORIES IN GOD'S TIME.

She goes her thirteen times. She expects it will come down at last, so round and round she goes. She expects that on her last day, her sins will all fall and she thinks her work well paid when she knows it will fall one day. She is persevering.[9]

Now, let us apply these thoughts:

1. To the pulling down of Jericho in our hearts, we want to slay all the old inhabitants, but the lofty wall stands strong. Let us have faith. Let us follow the ark. Let us hear the trumpets, even though [they are] only ram's horns.[10] Let us go round

SERMON 133

all the seven days – that is all the week and all the days of our life. Let us groan inwardly but not grumble with our lips and soon when the last allotted day appears – the walls will tumble we shall shout and our enemies will begone.

2. To the pulling down of Jericho in the world. Sin has strong & lofty towers. The tower of Babel or Babylonish Rome, idolatry &c – let us yet believe these will tumble – let us keep on our rounds as minister, sunday school teachers, christians, keep the poor ramshorn going – do your duty and one day Jesus shall reign universally.

3. To the pulling down Jericho in this village. Dagon stands fast here. But the ark is come. The trumpeters of God have blowed the trumpet long, the ram's horns are sounding now loud and with rough blast. Many are following the ark but the time is not just come. Keep on brethren, and Oh give a unanimous shout, all at once – by faith – down will the mighty walls come rolling over. The Lord help us to believe and then fulfil his promises Amen through Jesus.

186.

BY FAITH JERICHO FELL—*Hebrews 11:30*

    all the seven days. That is, all the week and all the days of our life. Let us groan inwardly,[11] but not grumble with our lips.[12] And soon, when the last allotted day appears, the walls will tumble, we shall shout, and our enemies will be gone.

2. To[13] the pulling down of Jericho in the world. Sin has strong and lofty towers: the tower of Babel[14] or Babylonish Rome,[15] idolatry, etc. Let us yet believe these will tumble. Let us keep on our rounds. As minister, sunday school teachers, Christians,[16] keep the poor ram[']s horn going. Do your duty and one day Jesus shall reign universally.

3. To the pulling down [of] Jericho in this village.[17] Dagon stands fast here.[18] But the ark is come. The trumpeters of God have blowed[19] the trumpet long. The ram's horns are sounding now loud and with rough blast. Many are following the ark, but the time is not just come.

Keep on, brethren, and Oh, give a unanimous shout all at once. By faith, down will the mighty walls come rolling over.

The Lord[20] help us to believe and then fulfil his promises. <u>Amen</u> through <u>Jesus</u>.

186.

1. Charles originally wrote X before adding the I to construct Roman numeral XI. This is the only time Charles preached a sermon on Heb 11:30. Additional sermons on Jericho include "The Blind Beggar" (*NPSP* 5, Sermon 266) and "Joshua's Vision" (*MTP* 14, Sermon 795).

2. See "inwrought righteousness" in "Man's Weakness and God's Strength" (Sermon 108).

3. "A tree, called also the cherry bay" (Johnson's *Dictionary*, s.v., "laurel"). Johnson's adjectival form of the word is more applicable to the above sermon: "Crowned or decorated with laurel; laureate" (s.v., "laureled"). For an additional reference to laurel in this notebook, see "Enduring Temptation" (Sermon 123).

4. Charles originally wrote the word "least." The context suggests, however, he intended to write the word "lest." For additional examples of this mistake, see "The Watchman, His Work, Warning, and Promise" (Sermon 120) and "The Church Needs the Spirit" (Sermon 131).

5. Charles struck through the word "is," likely because he wrote it prematurely before writing the word "man."

6. Cf. Eph 2:8–9.

7. "Let us doubt our love if we are not laughed at" ("Enduring Temptation" [Sermon 123]).

8. Cf. Jas 2:17, 20.

9. See "Final Perseverance Certain" (Sermon 82).

10. "Serve God with such education as you have, and thank him for blowing through you if you are a ram's horn, but if there is a possibility of your becoming a silver trumpet, choose it rather" (*Lectures* 3:25).

11. Cf. Rom 8:22–23.

12. Cf. Phil 2:14.

13. The letter "f" appears over the bowl of the "o" in the word "To." Charles may have originally written the word "If."

14. Cf. Genesis 11.

15. The early church often compared the city of Rome to the city of Babylon in the book of Revelation. Tertullian wrote, "So, again, Babylon, in our own John, is a figure of the city Rome, as being equally great and proud of her sway, and triumphant over the saints" (Tertullian, "An Answer to the Jews," in Alexander Roberts and James Donaldson, eds., *The Ante-Nicene Fathers. Translations of the Writings of the Fathers Down to A.D. 325. American Reprint of the Edinburgh Edition. Revised and Chronologically Arranged, with Brief Prefaces and Occasional Notes, by A. Cleveland Coxe. Volume III. Latin Christianity: Its Founder, Tertullian. I. Apologetic; II. Anti-Marcion; III. Ethical* [New York, Charles Scribner's Sons, 1903, reprint], 162). During Charles's lifetime Roman Catholicism was often equated with Babylon. See "The Church of Rome, Foredoomed Babylon of the Apocalypse," *The Blackburn Standard*, March 31, 1852.

16. Charles did not capitalize the word "christians." It has been capitalized for consistency.

17. Charles was referencing the village of Waterbeach.

18. See "The Downfall of Dagon" (Sermon 124).

19. Charles originally wrote the word "blowed." The letters "ed" were struck through in pencil and replaced with "n" to construct the word "blown."

20. A dark yellow stain, likely the result of the aging process of the manuscript, appears above the word "Lord." The stain bled through the back of the page and can be seen above the final letter "t" in the word "inhabitants." The source of the stain is found over the letter "h" in the word "change" in "Set Thine House in Order" (Sermon 134).

Is. XXXVIII. 1   Set thine house in order.

Gracious God help me to write & preach this sermon just as if it were my last; if indeed it be not.

This advice if only applying to temporals is highly proper for men should take care to arrange all family matters, lest death come on a sudden & their children be losers by their delay. But how much more in spirituals.

Man's house is out of order, the affections, will and intellect are not in their proper place. Sin has upset all, and since God sees & knows all things how loudly are we called on to make the crooked straight. If we were to live here for ever we had better have the house in order, we shall be the happier for it. But since we must soon die — the call is stronger prepare to meet thy God.

If the house be awry when our Lord comes woe unto us, and let us remember he searches the corners and crannies, so ye moral men beware.

This is our only chance — there is no change in a future world — Life is the only candle. —

1. To myself the voice comes. Thou art one year older, search thy heart and see that you are

134

SET THINE HOUSE *in* ORDER
Isaiah[1] 38:1[2]

> "In those days was Hezekiah sick unto death. And Isaiah the prophet the son of Amoz came unto him, and said unto him, Thus saith the Lord, Set thine house in order: for thou shalt die, and not live."

Gracious God, help me to write and preach this sermon just as if it were my last, if indeed it be not.[3]

This advice, if only applying to temporals, is highly proper, for men should take care to arrange all family matters lest death come on a sudden and their children be losers by their delay. But how much more in spirituals?

Man's house is out of order. The affections, will, and intellect are not in their proper place. Sin has upset all. And since God[4] sees and knows all things,[5] how loudly are we called on to make the crooked straight. If we were to live here for ever,[6] we had better have the house in order. We shall be the happier for it. But since we must soon die, the call is stronger: prepare to meet thy God.

If the house be awry when our Lord comes, woe unto us. And let us remember he searches the corners and crannies, so ye moral men beware. This is our only chance. There is no change[7] in a future world. Life is the only candle.

1. To myself the voice comes: Thou art one year older.[8] Search thy heart and see that you are

right. Thou hast a large house entrusted to thee. Do all thou can'st and preach with all thy might for thou shalt soon die and then thy hour is gone.

2. To my fellow members and to all true Christians see to the firm foundation, try your own selves.— You each have some housework to do — set it in order. Have the books right for the head overseer — set your houses in order.

3. To parents. Your children are a sacred trust — do not neglect the solemn charge. Soon you must leave them. Act so that you may not fear to leave them & may not fear to see them before the judgment seat.

4. Old people — tottering — you must die but you are unprepared — well death will not wait for you for a moment.

5. Moral but yet unconverted — your house is well whitewashed out side but ah! remember God will walk in — and what a muddle is there. None but the power of God can set thy filthy soul right.—

6. Open sinner — Confessedly you are wrong. Thief — restore the stolen goods — Go and confess to God and ask his help.

right. Thou hast a large house[9] entrusted to thee. Do all thou cans't[10] and preach with all thy might, for thou shalt[11] soon die and then thy hour is gone.

2. To my fellow members and to all true Christians, see to the firm foundation.[12] Try your own selves. You each have some housework to do. Set it in order. Have the books right for the head overseer. Set your houses in order.

3. To parents, your children are a sacred trust.[13] Do not neglect the solemn charge. Soon you must leave them. Act so that you may not fear to leave them, and may not fear to see them before the judgment seat.

4. Old people, tottering, you <u>must</u> die,[14] but you are unprepared. Well, death will not wait for you for a moment.

5. Moral but yet unconverted, your house is well whitewashed outside.[15] But ah! Remember, God will walk in, and what a muddle is there. None but the power of God can set thy filthy soul right.

6. Open sinner, confessedly you are wrong. Thief, restore the stolen goods. Go and confess to God and ask his help.

SERMON 134

Fighter — God says turn thy boxing gloves out.
Swearer — wash thy foul mouth with blood divine
Unclean Fornicator. turn thy lust out.
Sabbath Breaker. How wilt thou restore thy lost Sabbaths
Drunkard — turn thy glass bottom upwards
Haters. there must not be one hating spider in heaven

    We must die and not live!
What tells us this is true? Why reason blind as she is — The aches and pains we feel. — The tolling bell — God's word — Every day deaths and our friends' burials especially. —

    We must die sooner or later!
    We come nearer death every day!
    We may die <u>directly</u>! —

The rules we should remember are.
    Learn to die every day!
    Reckon each day your last!
    Place your actions in the glare of eternity!
    Do a days work in a day!
Set thine house in order for thou shalt die and not live!! —

187. 189.   Lord see to my house
                       amen —

SET THINE HOUSE IN ORDER—*Isaiah 38:1*

Fighter, God says, turn thy boxing gloves out.[16]

Swearer, wash thy foul mouth with blood divine.

Unclean Fornicator, turn thy lust out.

Sabbath Breaker, how wilt thou restore thy lost Sabbaths?[17]

Drunkard, turn thy glass bottom upwards.

Haters, there must not be one hating spider in heaven.[18]

    We must die and not live!

What tells us this is true? Why, reason, blind as she is, [does]. The aches and pains we feel. The tolling bell.[19] God's [W]ord. Everyday deaths.[20] And our friends' burials especially.

    We must die sooner or later![21]

    We come nearer [to] death every day!

    We may die <u>directly</u>!

The rules we should remember are:

    Learn to die every day![22]

    Reckon each day your last!

    Place your actions in the glare of eternity!

    Do a day[']s work in a day!

Set thine house in order, for thou shalt die and not live!!

                            Lord, see to my house.

                                      Amen

187. 189.

SERMON 134

1. Charles is not consistent in his abbreviation of the word "Isaiah" (see "The Tranquillity, Security, and Supplies Afforded to the Gospel Church" [Sermon 97]; "The Best Feast" [Sermon 125]; "Christ's Constant Intercession" [Sermon 126]; "Well with the Righteous" [Sermon 130]; and "The Church Needs the Spirit" [Sermon 131].

2. Charles preached an additional sermon on Isa 38:1 entitled "Landlord and Tenant" (*MTP* 53, Sermon 3021). There is not enough overlapping content or structural similarity to suggest Charles had in mind the sermon above when writing his later one.

3. This is the first time in his early sermon notebooks that Charles penned a prayer at the beginning of his sermon.

4. The smudged letter "s" appears after the word "God." Charles may have originally intended to write the word "God's."

5. Cf. Ps 33:13; Prov 15:3; Heb 4:13.

6. Charles originally wrote the words "forever."

7. A dark yellow stain appears over the stem of the letter "h" in the word "change." The imprint of this stain is found in the previous sermon "By Faith Jericho Fell" (Sermon 133) above the letter "t" in the word "inhabitants" on the second page and also above the letter "r" in the word "Lord" on the third page.

8. Charles disclosed his age on the front flap of this notebook: "[Fi]nis. June 19. My 18th." The word "[Fi]nis" suggests Charles wrote this inscription after writing this final sermon.

9. Waterbeach Chapel was the "house" Charles referenced.

10. A modern translation of this sentence is "Do all [you can] and preach with all [your] might, for [you will] soon die, and then [your] hour is gone." For additional uses of "cans't," see "The Golden Crown of Holiness" (Notebook 3, Sermon 149); "Boast Not Thyself of Tomorrow" (Notebook 3, Sermon 150); "Absolute Sovereignty" (Notebook 3, Sermon 177); and "Mary and Jesus in the Garden" (Notebook 3, Sermon 175).

11. Charles originally wrote the word "shall" before inserting a crossbar over the final letter "l" to construct the letter "t," which changed the word to "shalt."

12. See "The Corner Stone" (Sermon 128).

13. Cf. Ps 127:3. Charles became a parent approximately four years after the sermons in this notebook were preached. On September 20, 1856, Susannah bore twin sons who they named Charles and Thomas.

14. "Young men may die soon. Old men *must* die" (NPSP 2:223, italics in the original).

15. Cf. Matt 23:27.

16. The phrase "turn out" was a popular expression in Charles's day. It could mean "give up" or "walk out," as seen in an 1852 police report: "Thomas Harper, another brogue maker, of Little George's-street, charged his son, of the same trade, with combination, and inciting his journeymen to revolt and turn out for higher wages" ("Police Office Cases: Broguemakers," *Waterford Mail*, November 24, 1852).

17. Charles wrote the word "Sabbaths" above the line due to a lack of space in the margin.

18. "Few people like spiders. No doubt these insects must have their merits and their uses, since none of God's creatures are made in vain; all living things are endowed with instincts more or less admirable; but the spider's plotting, creeping ways, and a sort of wicked expression about him, lead one to dislike him as a near neighbour" ("Antipathy to Spiders," *Bell's Weekly Messenger*, September 2, 1850).

19. The phrase "tolling bell" was associated with funerals when the "knell" or "knel," defined by Johnson as "the sound of a bell rung at a funeral," rang out (Johnson's *Dictionary*, s.v. "knel"). In his famous poem "No Man Is an Island ... For Whom the Bell Tolls," John Donne (1572–1631) wrote, "No Man is an *Island*, entire of itself, every man is a piece of the *Continent*, a part of the *main*; if a clod be washed away by the *sea*, *Europe* is the less, as well as if a *Promontory* were, as well as if a *Manor* of thy *friends*, or of *thine own* were; Any Man's *death* diminishes *me*, because I am involved in Mankind; And therefore never send to know for whom the bell

tolls; It tolls for thee" (John E. Booty, ed., *John Donne: Selections from Divine Poems, Sermons, Devotions, and Prayers* [New York: Paulist Press, 1990], 58, italics in the original). The phrase "tolling bell" gained tremendous popularity in the twentieth century and became one of "the most widely quoted bits of non-biblical prose in the English language" after Ernest Hemmingway borrowed the final line of Donne's poem for use in the title of his 1940 publication *For Whom the Bell Tolls* (Achsah Guibbory, ed., *The Cambridge Companion to John Donne* [Cambridge: Cambridge University Press, 2006], 241). For additional uses of the phrase, see "Boast Not Thyself of Tomorrow" (Notebook 3, Sermon 150); *NPSP* 1:179; 3:313; *MTP* 11:78; 12:455.

20. Cf. Luke 9:23.

21. Charles died at the age of fifty-seven in Menton, France, on January 31, 1892, after falling into a coma at the Hotel Beau-Rivage. On the title page of Notebook 4, Charles wrote, "I hope to die singing."

22. Cf. Matt 16:24; Luke 9:23; 1 Cor 15:31.

NOTEBOOK INDEX

Self deception 78

NOTEBOOK INDEX

Self deception .... 78[1]

---

[1] The entry "Self Deception" (Sermon 78) represented Charles's attempt to create an index to Notebook 2 as he did at the conclusion of Notebook 1. The three vertical pencil lines on this page represent three columns in which Charles would have written the sermon titles and numbers of this notebook. It is not clear why Charles discontinued his indexing after writing only one entry. He may have realized the lack of space on this page would prevent the inclusion of all fifty-six sermons. More likely, however, the busyness of his schedule took precedence over the inventorying of his sermons. His index at the conclusion of Notebook 1 is also incomplete. A dark ink spot appears on the left edge of the page.

DOXOLOGY

Better is the end of life than the beginning.
Better the end of labour than the starting.

These sketches are so many proofs of the power of faith — By faith I got them. —

They are evidences of God's love — for oft have they come just at the moment when had they tarried, I had been undone.

Blessed be God — for making men so much his darlings as to let them speak his word.

May it be my topmost desire to live as much to God's glory as possible — and

 When I shall die
 Receive me I'll cry.
 For Jesus has lov'd me
 I cannot tell why...

In health, contentment and peace. June 19/52
Only feeling the thorns of sin & sin's effects. —

DOXOLOGY

Better is the end of life than the beginning.

Better the end of labour than the starting.

These sketches are so many proofs of the power of faith. By faith I got them.

They are evidences of God's love, for oft have they come just at the moment when, had they tarried, I had been undone.[1]

Blessed be God for making men so much his darlings as to let them speak his word.

May it be my topmost desire to live as much to God's glory as possible, and,

> When I shall die,
>
> Receive me, I'll cry.
>
> For Jesus has lov'd me,
>
> I cannot tell why.[2]

In health,[3] contentment, and peace. June 19/52.[4]

Only feeling the thorns of sin and sin's effects.[5]

DOXOLOGY

1. A modern translation of this sentence is "They are evidences of God's love, for oft[en] have they come just at the moment when, [if they] had tarried, I [would have] been undone." Spurgeon confessed his selection of Scripture texts was "quite an embarrassment" (*Autobiography* 1:207). His general method involved "sit[ting] hour after hour praying and waiting for a subject" (*Autobiography* 1:207). In his lecture "On the Choice of a Text," he told his students at the Pastors' College, "I believe that almost any Saturday in my life I make enough outlines of sermons, if I felt liberty to preach them, to last me for a month. . . . When the text gets a hold of us, we may be sure that we have a hold of it, and may safely deliver our souls upon it. To use another simile: you get a number of texts in your hand, and try to break them up; you hammer at them with might and main, but your labour is lost; at last you find one which crumbles at the first blow, and sparkles as it falls in pieces, and you perceive jewels of the rarest radiance flashing from within. . . . It charms and fascinates you, or it weighs you to your knees and loads you with the burden of the Lord. . . . Wait for that elect word, even if you wait till within an hour of the service" (*Lectures* 1:88–89). He summarized his method for selecting Scripture references by saying, "Cry to God for it!" (*Lectures* 1:90). Charles and Susannah often entertained guests on Saturday evenings. However, at 6:00 PM Charles told them, "Now, dear friends, I must bid you 'Good-bye,' and turn you out of this study; you know what a number of chickens I have to scratch for, and I want to give them a good meal to-morrow" (*Autobiography* 4:64). The process of text selection could be agonizing for Charles. He sometimes called to Susannah, saying, "Wifey, what shall I do? . . . God has not given me my text yet" (*Autobiography* 4:65). Susannah reflected, "Sometimes, when I left him on Saturday evening, he did not know either of his texts for Sunday. But he had a well-stored mind; and when he saw his lines of thought, a few catchwords on a half-sheet of notepaper sufficed. Before we parted, he used to offer up a short prayer which was an inspiration to both of us" (*Autobiography* 4:274).

2. This stanza is part of a hymn entitled "A Farewell to the World" written by Rowland Hill (1744–1833) and published in *Psalms & Hymns*. The hymn reads, "O tell me no more / Of earthly vain store; / The time for such trifles through mercy is o'er. / A Canaan I've found, / Where true joys abound, / 'Tis heav'nly dwelling on that happy ground. / The souls that believe / In Paradise live, / And me in that number may Jesus receive. / No mortal doth know / What he can bestow, /

What life, love, and comfort—go after—him, go. / Ah! do not delay, / Christ calls thee away: / Rise, follow thy Saviour, and bless the—glad day. / And when I shall die, / 'Receive me,' I'll cry; / For Jesus hath lov'd me, I cannot say why. / But this I do find, / We two are so join'd, / He'll not live in glory, and leave me—behind" (Rowland Hill, *Psalms & Hymns, Chiefly Intended for Public Worship, Collected, Corrected, and Composed, Eighth Edition* [London: printed and published by Page and Son, 1830], 134–35). For additional references to Hill's hymns in Charles's later sermons, see *NPSP* 1:74; *NPSP* 1:87; *NPSP* 1:131–32; and *NPSP* 3:77.

3. Charles's health began to deteriorate after he moved to London. His son Charles once remarked that his father's handwritten letters "look[ed] almost like hieroglyphics, because they were hurriedly scribbled, when his poor hands were swollen with gout" (*Autobiography* 3:294).

4. Charles wrote a similar inscription on the front flap of this notebook. According to Susannah, Charles wrote, "Finis. June 19. My 18th birthday. With my staff I crossed this Jordan, and now I am become two bands. Lovingkindness runs faster than time; it outstrips me, and then waits to be gracious" (*Autobiography* 1:222).

5. Susannah recorded the contents of this page in *Autobiography* 1:222. Whereas Charles used "broken lines" to separate his sentences, Susannah inserted four-dot ellipses between the words "faith" and "By faith." Her inconsistency with ellipses implies missing content between these two words. For instance, the punctuation Charles placed after the word "love" is the same as that following the word "faith." Susannah's insertion of an em dash before the word "for" is not warranted in the original text. Susannah also altered the capitalization of "his" and "word" in the sentence, "His darlings as to let them speak His Word!" At the end of this sentence, Susannah exchanged Charles's period for an exclamation mark. In the next-to-last sentence on the page, Susannah placed a comma after the number 52 in the absence of Charles's punctuation.

BACK COVER OF NOTEBOOK 2

ABOUT THE EDITOR

CHRISTIAN T. GEORGE

(Ph.D., University of St. Andrews, Scotland) serves as curator of The Spurgeon Library and assistant professor of historical theology at Midwestern Baptist Theological Seminary in Kansas City, Missouri. For more information, visit *www.spurgeon.org*.

SCRIPTURE INDEX

GENESIS
1:1 *277, 450*
1:16 *277*
1:28 *125*
3 *37, 181*
3:1–7 *414*
3:15 *264, 345*
6:1–5 *392*
6:1–7 *370*
7 *277, 392*
11 *489*
15:6 *207*
19 *268*
19:26 *372*
19:30 *261*
22:1–19 *408*
22:14 *438*
32:10 *28*
37:11 *313*
39:12 *368*
41:41–46 *278*
41:52 *466*
45:4–7 *278*
47:31 *188*
50:20 *88, 444*

EXODUS
2:5–6 *113*
10:20 *181*
10:21–23 *230*
13:17–18 *278*
13:21 *189*
14:21 *278*
15:23 *268*
16 *30*
16:2–3 *188*
17:1–7; 16 *278*
19:12 *137*
19:21 *160*
20:17 *313*
26:31–33 *153, 158*
34:6 *241, 468*
34:7 *181*
34:14 *56, 392*
34:29–35 *324*
39:38–39 *160*

LEVITICUS
7:15 *241*
14:13 *136*
16:2 *153, 159*
21:11 *264*
22:29 *241*

NUMBERS
10:29 *165, 173*
11:1–15 *188*
14:2 *188*
14:18 *468*
19:11 *264*
19:14 *264*
20:11 *450*
25:8–9 *392*

DEUTERONOMY
4:24 *56*
7:7 *240*
9:4 *365, 374*
17:16 *408*
29:29 *160*
32:31 *447, 450*
33 *188*
33:12 *185, 188*

509

SCRIPTURE INDEX

JOSHUA
3:5   *67, 127*
20   *261*
24:15   *67, 183*

JUDGES
1   *278*
6   *278*
13–16   *278*
16:15–21   *217*
16:30   *428*

1 SAMUEL
5:1   *428*
5:2–4   *423, 428*
5:3   *430*
5:4   *430*
14:28–29   *439*
15   *392*
16   *456*
17   *278*
17:33   *456*
19   *456*
22:1–2   *366*
22:2   *349*

2 SAMUEL
6:14   *408*
10:5   *394*
15   *457*

1 KINGS
1:33   *408*
1:38   *408*
8:11   *74*
12:19   *457*

2 KINGS
15:29   *478*
23:23   *408*
24:15   *392*

1 CHRONICLES
7:20–27   *466*
16:11   *128, 241*

21:1   *414*

2 CHRONICLES
3:14   *153, 159*
29:31   *241*
30:1   *408*
35:1   *408*
36:10   *392*

EZRA
1   *278*
2:1   *408*
2:1–2   *466*

NEHEMIAH
7:6–7   *466*
9:6   *277*

ESTHER
2:6   *392*
2:12   *126*

JOB
1:1–2:7   *414*
5:10   *323*
17:9   *60*
23:12   *56*
25:4   *357, 369*
26:8–9   *323*
28:18   *30*
28:25–27   *278*
29:14   *229*
35:2   *369*
40:4   *370*
40:15–24; 41   *239*

PSALMS
1:3   *312*
2   *191, 196*
2:1   *196*
2:1–3   *191*
2:2   *196*
2:3   *197*
2:4   *198*
2:4–5   *191*

SCRIPTURE INDEX

2:5a *197*
2:5b *198*
2:6 *198, 438*
2:6–7 *191, 198*
2:7 *198*
2:8 *198*
2:8–9 *193*
2:9a *199*
2:9b *199*
2:10–12 *193*
2:11 *199*
2:12a *199*
8:3 *239*
8:5 *238*
15:1 *438*
18:1 *67*
19:10 *30*
20:4 *182*
20:7–8 *128, 241*
22:7 *99*
23:1 *240*
24:9 *439*
27:1 *128, 182, 241, 277*
27:14 *325*
28:7 *208*
33:11 *450*
33:13 *496*
34:10 *30*
34:20 *264*
37:4 *182*
37:35–36 *315*
37:39 *277*
43:3 *438*
46:1 *208*
46:1–3 *261*
48:2 *198*
51:5 *82, 140, 369*
55:22 *182*
72:11 *279*
73:17–19 *315*
86:15 *468*
91:1 *324*
91:2 *261*
91:5 *189*
95:8–9 *181*

97:4 *199*
99:1 *199*
103:8 *468*
103:19 *182*
103:20 *242*
104:15 *467*
105:41 *450*
107:8 *233, 238*
107:21–22 *241*
114:7 *199*
118:1–4 *453*
118:5–18 *453*
118:19–23 *453, 456*
118:22 *453, 456, 457*
118:22–25 *456*
118:24 *456*
118:25–29 *456*
119:9 *42*
119:11 *43, 57*
119:16 *43*
119:28 *208*
119:120 *199*
125:1 *438*
125:1–2 *60*
127:1 *181*
127:3 *497*
128:3 *183*
132:9 *229, 367*
135:7 *278*
139:13 *238*
145:8 *468*
145:19 *182*
147:8 *278*
148:2 *242*
148:3–6 *277*

PROVERBS

1:7 *199*
3:5 *12, 13, 177, 180*
3:35 *303, 306*
9:10 *468*
11:2 *66*
14:26 *245, 260*
15:3 *496*
17:3 *126*

SCRIPTURE INDEX

22:15 *468*
23:17–18 *309, 312*
27:1 *277*
28:13 *66*

ECCLESIASTES
1:1–2 *346*
11:3 *370*

SONG OF SOLOMON
2:1 *29*
4:7 *29*
6:1–3 *189*

ISAIAH
1:18 *207*
3:10 *465*
3:10–11 *469*
7:14 *367*
8:22 *199*
11:9 *438*
14:12–15 *414*
25:6 *438*
25:6–8 *433*
25:8 *182*
30:19 *230*
32:13–15 *473, 478*
33:19 *168*
33:20–21 *163*
33:20–23 *168*
34:7 *266*
35:1 *267*
38:1 *491, 496*
40:26 *277*
40:29 *100, 208*
41:10 *128, 241*
42:1 *88*
45:12 *277*
45:22 *199, 375*
46:4a *208*
46:10 *450*
49:14 *55, 61*
54 *60*
54:2 *170*
54:2–3 *290*

54:5 *127, 444*
54:10 *55, 61*
54:17 *365, 374*
55:2 *30*
55:7 *100, 101*
56:7 *438*
61:1 *366*
61:10 *189, 229, 367*
62:1 *441, 444*
64:2 *199*
64:6 *367, 373*
65:1 *300*

JEREMIAH
2:2 *323*
2:13 *279*
10:7 *85, 88*
15:16 *56*
16:19 *261*
22:25 *392, 478*
31:3 *261*
31:8–9 *466*
31:9 *461*
31:35 *55, 61*
32:39 *55, 60*
33:11 *241*
45:5 *5*

EZEKIEL
3:17 *402*
3:17–19 *397*
18:23 *175*
20:40 *438*
22:19–22 *126*

DANIEL
3 *278*
5:4 *108*
5:6 *108*
5:17 *108*
5:22 *108*
5:24–28 *108*
5:26 *108*
5:27 *105, 108*
6 *278*

SCRIPTURE INDEX

9:2 *108*
12:2 *127*

HOSEA
5:14 *344*
12:6 *325*
14:5–7 *317, 322*
14:6 *322*

JOEL
2:31 *199*
3:16 *199*

AMOS
3:6 *199*

OBADIAH
1:16 *438*

JONAH
1:17 *438*
2:1 *113*
3:6–9 *278*

NAHUM
1:3 *468*

HABAKKUK
3:19 *208*

ZEPHANIAH
1:15 *199*

ZECHARIAH
3 *365*
3:2 *380*
3:3–5 *374*
3:4 *229, 367*
4:7 *457*
12:10 *255, 265*
13:9 *126*
14:9 *88*
14:16 *408*

MALACHI
1:8 *136*
3:2–3 *126*
3:6 *450*
3:10 *281, 288, 289*
3:11–12 *287, 290*

MATTHEW
1:1–17 *366*
1:18–20 *198*
1:23 *367*
3:8 *66*
3:13–17 *300*
3:17 *198*
4:1–11 *42, 414*
4:4 *29*
5:13 *137*
5:14 *444*
5:16 *57*
5:33–37 *109*
6:1–5 *102*
6:1–7 *468*
6:19–21 *468*
6:20 *306*
6:21 *128*
6:31–32 *208*
7:6 *79, 82*
7:11 *147, 324*
7:16 *324*
7:23 *109*
7:26–27 *450*
8:11–12 *221, 228*
8:26–27 *278*
8:28–34 *414*
9:9–13 *230*
9:38 *102*
10:22 *189, 421*
10:23 *335*
10:28 *189, 230, 260*
10:34 *42*
11:19 *182*
11:24 *268*
12:31 *478*
12:33 *324*
12:36 *108*

SCRIPTURE INDEX

12:43–45   *414*
12:48–49   *127*
13:1–23   *57*
13:41   *260*
13:42   *75*
13:50   *230, 279*
16:24   *136, 498*
18:12   *324*
21:8   *408*
21:11   *127*
21:21   *279*
21:22   *56*
22:1–10   *366*
22:11–12   *374*
22:37   *67*
23:12   *128*
23:27   *497*
24:1–2   *161*
24:2   *408*
24:44   *75*
25:32   *393*
25:40   *109*
25:46   *279, 370*
26:28   *266*
26:57–58   *160*
27:18   *313*
27:25   *268*
27:31   *30*
27:45   *264*
27:50–51   *158*
27:50–54   *264*
27:51   *159*
28:2   *278*
28:6   *74*
28:18–19   *88*
28:19–20   *293, 298*
28:20   *72, 300*

MARK

1:12–13   *414*
3:17   *124*
3:29   *478*
5:3   *392*
5:12–13   *414*
8:38   *307*
9:25   *414*
9:42   *402*
9:48   *344*
10:9   *267*
10:23   *102, 276*
10:24   *276*
10:25   *276, 468*
10:26   *277*
10:27   *271, 276*
10:35–45   *98*
11:8   *408*
12:30   *208*
13:1–2   *161*
13:2   *408*
13:13   *189, 421*
14:50   *98*
14:62   *402*
15:38   *153, 159*
16:15   *391*
16:19   *74, 75*

LUKE

2:41   *408*
3:22   *59*
4:1–13   *414*
4:5   *414*
4:9   *414*
4:18   *366*
5:31–32   *66*
8:18   *51, 56*
8:33   *414*
9:23   *268, 498*
9:26   *307, 450*
9:54   *124*
10:18   *414*
11:14   *414*
11:28   *67, 89*
12:5   *230*
12:10   *478*
12:32   *167, 174*
12:34   *128*
13:28   *75*
14:15–24   *366*
14:28   *65, 181, 366*
14:29–30   *66*

15:10   *59*
15:11–32   *324*
15:12   *380*
15:13   *380*
15:14   *380*
15:15   *381*
15:16a   *381*
15:16b   *381*
15:17   *381*
15:18–19   *377, 380*
15:20   *381, 393*
15:23   *428*
16:19–31   *230*
16:22   *153, 159*
17:5   *262*
18:1   *57*
18:13   *230*
19:1–10   *230*
19:10   *139, 140, 402*
19:35–36   *408*
19:41   *5, 405, 408*
21:6   *408*
21:17   *189, 421*
22:31   *414*
22:54   *160*
22:63   *98*
23:33   *98*
23:34   *99*
23:40–41   *98*
23:42   *91, 98*
23:43   *98*
23:45   *159*
24:5–6   *74*
24:47   *408*

JOHN

1:3   *277*
1:5   *100*
1:12   *112, 467*
1:14   *100, 127, 366*
1:16   *93, 100*
1:29   *74*
3:3   *240*
3:16   *59, 102, 198, 468*
4:14   *55, 61, 266*

4:21   *160*
4:28   *102*
4:30   *102*
4:35   *95, 102*
5:1   *408*
5:24   *55, 61*
5:39   *336*
5:41   *102*
6:37   *55, 61, 182*
6:39   *366*
7:38   *266*
8:12   *100*
8:28   *99*
10:7   *479*
10:9   *479*
10:11   *479*
10:14   *479*
10:23   *479*
10:26   *479*
10:27a   *479*
10:27b   *479*
10:27c   *479*
10:28   *55, 60, 61, 182*
10:28–29   *475, 479*
11:35   *408*
12:13   *408*
12:15   *127*
12:33   *99*
12:43   *102*
13:23   *125*
14:2   *345*
14:6   *88, 346, 370*
14:15   *67*
14:15–17   *240*
14:27   *325*
15:5   *128, 277*
15:9   *314*
15:15   *182*
15:16   *240*
15:18   *189*
15:19   *421*
15:26   *444*
16:7   *300*
16:33   *66, 420*
17   *53*

17:9   444
17:12   55, 62, 88
18:10   98
18:37   127
19:11   264, 444
19:26   263
19:30   75, 263, 264
19:33–34   251
19:35   263
19:36   264
19:39   126
20:4   263
20:27   264, 366
21:20   125

ACTS

1:4   444
1:6   98
1:9   74
2:38   56
3:19   56
4:12   346, 370
4:36   124
5:31   198
5:34   159
7:9   313
8:9–24   268
9:1–9   278
9:27   124
10:14–15   229
10:28   229
11:22–24   124
12:7   278
13:10   125
13:33   240
16:16–18   414
16:25–26   279
16:26   278
16:27   402
17:1   334
17:5   334
17:9   334
17:10   334
17:11–12   327, 334
17:12   335

17:31   58
20:21   66
20:28   102, 266, 438, 479

ROMANS

1:7   189
1:16   228, 450
1:20   183
2:1   183
2:4   241
3:10   369
3:20   218
3:22   99, 160
3:23   82, 109, 265
3:24   29, 30, 59, 228, 240, 467
3:25   189
3:28   101, 373
3:29   228, 300
4:5   207, 300
4:5–8   467
4:6   365, 374
5:1   30, 59, 99, 100, 112, 137, 210, 240, 260, 300
5:8   468
5:12   82
5:15   365, 374
5:17   467
5:17–19   467
5:18   74, 218
6:22   201, 206
6:23   300
7:5   466
7:14–25   430
7:18   369, 466
7:24–25   430
8:2   137
8:3   160
8:15   113
8:17   199
8:18   421
8:22–23   488
8:28   444
8:28–30   30, 136, 228, 260
8:30   467
8:34   59, 75, 444
8:35   55, 61

SCRIPTURE INDEX

8:38–39   *161*
9:24   *300*
9:25   *189*
10:12   *160, 228*
10:13   *66*
10:14   *56*
10:17   *336*
11:5   *30, 136, 228, 260*
11:25   *137*
11:29   *60*
11:36   *458*
12:1   *131, 136*
12:2   *207, 210, 367*
12:4–5   *265*
13:1   *444*
14:11   *75*
16:20   *264*

1 CORINTHIANS

1:7   *325*
1:24   *100, 228*
1:27   *230*
1:30   *88, 100, 240*
1:30–31   *467*
1:31   *277*
2:2   *76*
2:4   *124*
2:16   *100*
3:2   *467*
3:6   *124*
3:11–13   *457*
3:16   *458*
3:21–23   *115, 123*
4:7   *147, 218*
4:8b   *334*
4:16   *468*
5:1–5   *414*
6:10   *109*
6:19–20   *127, 367*
6:20   *261, 266, 392, 438, 479*
7:23   *261, 266*
10:31   *67*
11:1   *468*
12:9–10   *241*
12:27   *59, 265*

13:13   *260*
15   *127*
15:9   *109*
15:10   *112*
15:15   *182*
15:20   *74, 345*
15:22   *109, 265, 344, 345, 479*
15:25   *75*
15:31   *498*
15:33   *66*
15:35–58   *279*
15:42   *468*
15:51   *468*
15:54   *182*
16:10   *109*
16:13   *279*

2 CORINTHIANS

1:5   *479*
1:10   *279*
1:22   *59, 182*
2:11   *411, 414*
2:14   *345*
4:4   *37*
4:7   *47, 48, 58*
5:7   *279*
5:17   *112*
5:20   *231*
5:21   *66, 73*
6:4–11   *390*
6:14   *260*
6:14–16   *390*
6:17–18   *383, 390*
11   *48*
11:6   *124*
11:14   *372, 414*
11:30   *218*
12:5–10   *277*
12:10   *279*
13:14   *100*

GALATIANS

2:13   *124*
2:16   *59, 99, 101, 219, 300*
2:19   *136*

SCRIPTURE INDEX

2:20 *209, 268*
3:13 *101*
3:23 *213, 216, 218*
3:23–24 *218*
3:26 *261*
3:28 *160*
4:4 *127*
4:6 *111, 112*
5:17 *466*
5:22 *324*
6:3 *35, 37*
6:3a *37*
6:3b *38*
6:7 *37, 306*
6:8 *125*

EPHESIANS

1:4 *30, 101, 137, 228, 260*
1:5 *59, 112, 126, 137, 240*
1:7 *101, 127, 207, 240, 467*
1:13 *59*
1:20–22 *457*
2:3 *197, 466*
2:4–5 *468*
2:5 *210*
2:6 *420*
2:8 *174*
2:8–9 *218, 488*
2:8–10 *467*
2:10 *137, 238*
3:1–13 *160*
3:12 *160*
3:17 *189*
4:2 *66*
4:4 *265*
4:18 *181*
5:2 *242*
5:11 *391*
5:25–27 *444*
5:27 *127*
6:10 *208*
6:16 *189*
6:17 *41, 42, 43*
6:18 *57*
6:20 *231*

PHILIPPIANS

1:6 *53, 58*
2:3 *66, 128, 136*
2:5–8 *366*
2:7 *127, 402*
2:9 *198*
2:10 *75*
2:14 *128, 488*
3:8 *67*
3:8–9 *467*
3:9 *66, 369, 374*
3:10 *479*
3:20 *206*
4:6 *57*
4:13 *88, 100, 128, 241, 277, 279*
4:19 *240*

COLOSSIANS

1:16 *450*
1:18 *59, 265*
1:26 *160*
2:10 *109*
2:15 *75*
3:1 *420*
3:2 *56*
3:3–4 *209*
3:10 *160*
3:11 *306*
3:12 *189*
4:6 *209*

1 THESSALONIANS

4:3 *210*
4:16 *345*
5:2 *346*
5:3 *315*
5:22 *391*

2 THESSALONIANS

2:13 *30, 101, 137, 228, 260*

1 TIMOTHY

1:12 *277*
2:5 *346, 370*
6:7–10 *468*

SCRIPTURE INDEX

6:15 *127, 242*
6:16 *149*

2 TIMOTHY
4:8 *366*
4:18 *167, 174, 279*

TITUS
3:5 *112*

HEBREWS
1:3 *88*
2:7 *238*
3:7–9 *181*
4:12 *42*
4:13 *496*
4:14–15 *74*
4:14–16 *127*
4:16 *160*
4:17 *41*
5:5 *198*
5:12 *467*
6:4–8 *55, 61*
6:9–10 *60*
6:13 *240*
6:17 *55, 61*
7:25 *59, 444*
8:10 *188*
8:13 *100*
9:7 *161*
9:22 *266*
9:27 *344*
9:28 *73, 74, 325*
10:1 *160*
10:11 *74*
10:12–13 *69, 72, 75*
10:14 *88*
10:14–20 *158*
10:19–20 *158*
10:20 *160*
10:26–29 *478*
11:1–39 *279*
11:10 *206*
11:21 *188*
11:30 *483, 488*

12:1 *367*
12:6 *468*
12:18 *137*
12:22 *438*
12:26 *278*
12:28 *199*
13:5 *468*
13:14 *206*
13:15 *102*

JAMES
1:12 *366, 417, 420*
1:17 *143, 146*
1:18 *74*
2:17 *488*
2:17–18 *137*
2:20 *488*
2:23 *182*
3:11 *440*
4:7 *67, 207*
4:10 *66, 128*
5:9 *128*
5:12 *109*

1 PETER
1:5 *60*
1:7 *126*
1:19 *266, 438*
2:2 *56, 467*
2:4–5 *458*
2:9 *161, 189, 479*
2:20 *420*
3:7 *125*
3:18 *74*
4:5 *279*
4:11 *458*
4:13 *479*
4:17 *161*
5:6 *128, 207*
5:7 *182*
5:8 *66, 334*

2 PETER
2:4 *230*
2:5 *56*

SCRIPTURE INDEX

2:22   *79*
3:9   *175*
3:10   *125, 279, 346*
3:12   *339, 344*
3:18   *100*

1 JOHN

1:5   *148*
1:7   *127*
1:9   *100, 101*
2:2   *300*
2:15   *189, 367*
2:17   *346*
2:19   *55, 62*
2:25   *167, 174*
2:27   *43*
3:1   *468*
3:2   *261*
3:4   *260*
4:7   *125*
4:9–11   *468*
4:15   *198*
4:19   *67, 189*
5:6–8   *263*

2 JOHN

1:6   *67, 242*

JUDE

6   *230, 279, 370*
14   *56*
16   *128*

REVELATION

1:16   *345*
2:4   *323*
2:26   *88*
3:21   *167, 174*
4:11   *88*
5:5   *344*
5:9   *102*
5:10   *161*
5:12   *89*
6:11   *238*
6:17   *199*
7:9   *228, 279*
7:16   *315*
8:4   *402*
8:8   *345*
11:15   *88*
12   *370*
12:3   *366*
12:4   *345*
13:8   *74, 278*
14:11   *230*
14:15–16   *102*
16:15   *346, 375*
17:5   *370*
18:4   *385, 391*
19:7–9   *127, 444*
19:8   *189, 229*
19:15   *345*
19:16   *127, 242*
20:1–3   *75, 279*
20:2   *366*
20:5   *345*
20:10   *366, 431*
20:11–15   *344*
20:12–13   *127*
20:15   *230*
21:2   *444*
21:3   *169*
21:4   *230*
21:8   *230, 279*
21:9   *127*
22:2   *30*
22:4   *189*
22:18   *44*
22:20   *346*

SUBJECT INDEX

A

Abba *111*
Abraham *221, 405*
    Abraham's Bosom *153*
Adam *69, 139, 359, 411, 477*
Adoption *53, 111, 117, 135, 235, 387, 389, 461*
Adoration *237*
Adullam *349*
Adversity *117, 465*
Affections *491*
Affliction(s) *47, 55, 187, 357, 417*
Agag *385*
Almighty *273, 303, 483*
Altar *133, 155*
Ambassador(s) *87, 133, 227, 293*
Amen *52, 97, 135, 227, 251, 259, 297, 321, 333, 343, 357, 365, 379, 401, 437, 443, 449, 487, 495*
Angel(s) *53, 85, 152, 153, 193, 233, 235, 237, 339, 341, 359, 363, 411, 441, 443*
Anger *191, 193, 203, 385*
Anglican society *385*
Anguish *225, 273*
Antediluvians *361*
Anxiety *97, 233*
Apathy *329, 379*
Apollos *115*
Apostle(s(hip)) *41, 47, 51, 93, 111, 131, 297, 327, 329, 383*
Argument(s) *133, 145, 327, 385*
Ark *405, 423, 425, 427, 485, 487*
Army(ies) *259, 351, 355*
Assurance *36, 167, 247, 399*
Atonement *259, 293, 453*
Attribute(s) *55, 145, 233, 247, 359*
Author
    Author of evil *143*
    Author of good *143*

B

Babylon *273, 361, 405*
Backslider(s) *81, 287*
Baptize(s)(d)(ism)(ist) *93, 257, 295, 297, 361, 461*
    Baptismal Regeneration *259*
    Baptist Denomination *331*
    Baptist, [John the] *93*
Barren(ness) *319, 475*
Bath, [England] *259*
Battle *349, 413*
Beauty *47, 193, 319*
Beds of Spices *319*
Beelzebub *361*
Believe(f)(s)(d)(er(s))(ing) *55, 91, 93, 107, 139, 201, 215, 237, 287, 303, 305, 311, 329, 331, 339, 343, 363, 365, 385, 475, 483, 485, 487*
Beloved *185, 191, 249*
Belshazzar(s) *105*
Benefits *331, 435*
Benevolence *167, 359*
Benjamin *185*
Berea(n) *327, 329*
Bible(s) *41, 117, 201, 293, 303, 305, 309, 317, 329, 331, 333, 363, 397, 447*
Bigotry *331, 413*
Birth *35, 155, 235*
Bitter(s)(ness) *259, 413, 461*
Black Prince *349*
Blasphemous *153, 413*
Bless(ed)(ing(s)) *51, 53, 143, 177, 179, 185, 187, 191, 195, 201, 285, 287, 311, 317, 319, 321, 357, 387, 397, 407, 417, 427, 435, 443, 447, 453, 455, 473, 485, 503*
Blight *97, 319*
Blind(ness) *115, 133, 435, 495*
Blood(y) *119, 257, 259, 297, 401, 405, 495*
    Blood of Jesus *227, 387, 435*
Boast(ing) *191, 213, 271, 273, 343, 433, 447*

SUBJECT INDEX

Body   *131, 205, 225, 233, 251, 253, 255, 257*
Books   *309, 493*
Born Again   *235, 389*
Branches   *319, 405*
Bread   *27, 213, 331, 437, 461*
Bridegroom   *117*
Brother   *119, 133, 287, 365, 401*
Bunyan, [John]   *153*
Burden(s)   *35, 187, 255, 271, 447*

C

Caiaphas   *155*
Calling   *27, 95, 111, 135, 139, 383*
Calvary   *119*
Canaan   *205, 385*
Captive(ity)   *351*
Care(less(ness))   *51, 117, 185, 233, 309, 327, 379, 407, 475*
Carnal(ity)   *233, 245, 309*
Catholic(s)   *71, 79, 133, 385*
Cephas   *115*
Certain(ly)(ty)   *53, 71, 87, 111, 157, 195, 221, 245, 257, 275, 447*
Charity   *413*
Cherubim   *153*
Child(ren)   *41, 115, 177, 185, 223, 227, 251, 259, 283, 319, 461, 463, 465, 491, 493*
   Children, God's   *245*
   Children of Israel   *397*
   Children of Wrath   *389*
Chosen   *191, 273, 349, 387, 443*
   Chosen of God   *455, 461*
Christ   *51, 55, 119, 121, 135, 139, 153, 155, 167, 177, 191, 193, 195, 203, 247, 259, 271, 283, 297, 305, 327, 329, 331, 349, 365, 417, 425, 441, 449, 453, 475*
   Christ's Sake   *343, 417, 437*
Christian(s)   *35, 41, 53, 69, 97, 131, 135, 157, 167, 177, 235, 237, 249, 283, 287, 303, 317, 319, 321, 333, 339, 383, 387, 389, 397, 417, 425, 427, 435, 447, 449, 487, 493*
Church(es)   *47, 97, 105, 117, 119, 165, 167, 281, 287, 297, 327, 349, 361, 385, 413, 433, 441, 455, 473*
   Church of Christ   *283*
   Church of Corinth   *115, 411*
   Church of England   *191, 283*
City   *329, 355, 399, 405, 407, 473*

Clouds   *317, 341, 433*
Comfort   *79, 111, 117, 177, 179, 223, 281, 321, 357, 401, 419, 477*
Commission   *293, 297, 397*
Communion   *79, 155, 157, 179, 295*
Compassion   *399*
Condemn(ed)(ing)   *69, 213, 233, 253, 339, 401, 407, 411*
Conduct   *281, 327, 331, 343, 377, 389, 411*
Confess(es)(ed)(ion)   *91, 135, 379, 385, 493*
Confidence   *35, 165, 245, 247, 249, 251, 275, 351, 357, 419*
Confirmation   *117, 361, 371*
Congregation(s)   *51, 95, 223, 329, 407*
Conscience   *53, 87, 179, 201, 215, 283, 309, 475*
Conversation   *95, 203, 223, 319, 385, 443*
Convert(ed)(sion(s))   *35, 36, 47, 49, 51, 79, 91, 93, 111, 177, 201, 203, 205, 223, 233, 293, 327, 385, 389, 413, 425, 443*
Conviction(s)   *79, 331, 333*
   Conviction of Sin   *51, 79*
Corner Stone   *455*
Counsel   *191, 193, 303*
Covenant   *93, 235, 353, 383, 385, 441, 477*
   Covenant of Redemption   *27, 53, 221*
Creator   *143*
   Creation   *135, 273, 317*
Creed   *247*
Crime(s)   *139, 221, 235, 309*
Cross   *25, 97, 253, 419*
Crown   *85, 167, 237, 349, 413, 417, 419, 483*
   Crown, Laurel   *419*
   Crown of Life   *417, 419*
Crucify(ied)   *69, 71, 91, 253, 259*
Cure   *259, 309, 349, 437*
Curse(d)   *177, 225, 357*

D

Dagon(s)   *423, 424, 425, 427, 487*
Damn(ed)(ation)   *115, 225, 227, 333, 401, 407*
   Damned Souls   *53, 223*
Danger(s)   *245, 293, 311, 397, 401*
Daniel   *105*
Darkness   *177, 223, 435*
David   *191, 273, 349, 405, 411, 453*
Day(s)   *51, 53, 65, 69, 71, 87, 105, 131, 153, 155,*

SUBJECT INDEX

157, 193, 195, 213, 221, 273, 283, 295, 305, 311, 341, 343, 349, 361, 389, 399, 401, 425, 427, 449, 463, 465, 473, 485, 487, 491, 495, 503
    Day, Last   71, 485
    Day of Grace   105
    Day of Jesus   53
    Day of Judgment   105, 187, 237
    Day of Plague   385
    Day of the Lord   339
Dead   35, 131, 251, 253, 255, 341, 363, 389, 407
    Dead Sea   259
Death(Die(d))   65, 69, 71, 91, 117, 131, 139, 153, 177, 179, 185, 205, 213, 221, 247, 251, 253, 255, 257, 259, 275, 293, 311, 339, 387, 417, 423, 435, 437, 449, 465, 493, 495
Debauchery   309, 377
Debt(or)   167, 351, 401
Decay   319
Deceive(s)(d)   35, 305
    Deception   35
Defiled   424
Deist   339
Deliver(ed)(er)(ance(s))   117, 163, 235, 273, 275, 349, 401, 437
Depraved(ity)   27, 79, 87, 91, 138, 359
Depressed   285
Despair   93, 411, 413
Despise(d)   47, 71, 123, 227, 303, 327, 437, 475, 485
Destruction   193, 195, 213, 275, 377, 413, 485
    Destruction of Jerusalem   157
Devil(s)   27, 51, 65, 115, 119, 187, 221, 223, 225, 259, 305, 327, 343, 351, 357, 361, 363, 377, 425, 441
Devotion   36, 69, 237
Dignity   69, 221, 359, 417
Disciple(s)   51, 91, 119, 257, 271, 293, 295
Dispensation   47, 93, 135, 297, 435
Distress   201, 215, 245, 351, 377
Dives   225
Divine(ity)   93, 163, 201, 247, 249, 317, 473, 495
    Divine Character   311
    Divine Command   165
    Divine Generation   193
    Divine Grace   363
    Divine Guidance   165
    Divine Institution   51

    Divine Love   115, 317
    Divine Ordinance   51
    Divine Power   271, 419
    Divine Presence   441
    Divine Purposes   191
Doctrine(s)   47, 53, 107, 115, 223, 483
    Doctrines of Grace   131
Doubt(ing)   47, 247, 339, 419
Dragon   349, 361
Drunk(ard(s))(enness)   107, 305, 309, 361, 375, 377, 407, 495
Duty(ies)   287, 293, 311, 331, 399, 443, 477

E

Earth(ly)   47, 53, 85, 97, 105, 117, 121, 153, 155, 179, 193, 195, 221, 233, 275, 305, 329, 339, 341, 343, 361, 405, 425, 447, 449, 455, 461, 465
Education   35, 79, 293
Effect(s)(ual)   257, 317, 321
    Effectual Calling   27, 135, 139, 383
    Efficacious Grace   453
Egypt(ian)   223, 273, 405
Elect(ion)   27, 53, 95, 131, 133, 135, 185, 213, 215, 221, 235, 247, 317, 349, 383, 387, 423, 441, 443, 455, 475
Emmanuel   87, 117, 355
End   41, 95, 115, 167, 205, 215, 271, 297, 300, 311, 503
Endurance   419
Enemy(ies)   71, 163, 237, 255, 275, 305, 355, 385, 387, 441, 447, 475, 487
    Enemies of God   193
Enjoy(ed)(ing)(ments)   36, 65, 91, 115, 117, 157, 195, 201, 205, 221, 223, 309, 321, 387, 433
Enoch   51
Envy(ied)   143, 309
Ephraim   461
Epistle   111, 411
Eternal(ly)   27, 53, 145, 193, 249, 275, 285, 305, 359, 387, 401, 411, 417, 419, 437, 447, 465, 483
    Eternal Covenant   383, 384
    Eternal Life   167, 477
    Eternally Secure   193
Eternity   53, 87, 117, 225, 233, 237, 339, 359, 495
Evangelical   131
    Evangelical Obedience   387
Evangelist   93, 251, 297

SUBJECT INDEX

Evil(s)   *51, 59, 65, 139, 143, 191, 275, 383, 385, 441, 473, 485*
Exalt(ed)(ing)(ation)   *193, 275, 305, 453, 455*
Example   *319*
Exhortation   *281, 285, 383, 385*
Expectation(s)   *71, 165, 225, 287, 311, 449*
Ezekiel   *397*

F
Faith(ful(ness))   *27, 36, 41, 55, 91, 93, 97, 111, 133, 179, 201, 205, 215, 223, 233, 237, 245, 247, 251, 271, 275, 281, 283, 285, 287, 293, 309, 329, 333, 357, 359, 363, 401, 419, 449, 453, 477, 484, 485, 487, 503*
Fall(en)   *35, 69, 87, 359*
Father(s)   *85, 95, 111, 145, 179, 195, 225, 237, 245, 251, 305, 319, 331, 379, 387, 411*
    Father of Lights   *145*
    Father's Gift   *119, 377*
Fear(s)(ful)(ing)   *55, 79, 87, 185, 191, 195, 201, 205, 233, 245, 249, 251, 329, 343, 351, 355, 399, 419, 449, 463, 477, 493*
    Fear of God   *245, 311*
    Fear of Man   *245*
    Fear of the Lord   *245, 247, 249, 309*
Feast(s)   *105, 221, 225, 401, 427, 433, 435, 437*
Fellowship   *473*
Final Perseverance   *27, 53, 81, 135, 237, 247, 273, 275, 387, 455*
Fire(s)   *225, 341, 343, 353, 425*
Flesh(ly)   *69, 119, 233, 255, 339, 425*
Flock   *221*
Flood   *385*
Folly   *35, 115, 423, 485*
Fool(s)(ish)   *35, 121, 227, 247, 305, 309, 331, 351, 361, 377*
Forbidden   *309, 405*
Free(d)(ly)   *27, 35, 111, 113, 119, 131, 143, 167, 201, 206, 319, 351, 399, 401*
Friend(ship)   *71, 221, 303, 383, 405*
Fruit(ful)(ition)   *95, 179, 203, 351, 319, 377, 477*
    Fruit, First   *69*

G
Gain(s)(ed)   *65, 79, 257, 321, 349, 351, 357, 377*
Galatian(s)   *111, 363*
    Galatian Spirit   *363*
Garden of Eden   *411*

Gentile(s)   *111, 133, 155, 221, 227, 295, 327, 435*
Gideon   *273*
Gift(s)   *55, 93, 105, 111, 119, 143, 167, 235, 237, 245, 377, 383, 433*
    Gift of God   *111, 167*
    Giving   *245*
Gladness   *97, 205*
Glory(ify)(ified)(ious)   *41, 47, 51, 53, 65, 69, 95, 97, 107, 117, 119, 121, 139, 143, 145, 163, 185, 205, 215, 221, 223, 225, 227, 233, 237, 255, 273, 275, 305, 333, 339, 341, 359, 383, 387, 419, 449, 455, 463, 477*
God(ly)   *35, 36, 47, 51, 53, 65, 69, 71, 79, 93, 105, 111, 115, 119, 121, 131, 133, 135, 139, 143, 145, 155, 157, 167, 179, 185, 187, 191, 215, 249, 251, 271, 273, 281, 283, 285, 287, 297, 303, 305, 309, 311, 317, 319, 321, 329, 331, 339, 343, 349, 357, 359, 363, 379, 383, 387, 389, 397, 399, 401, 417, 419, 423, 424, 427, 437, 443, 449, 453, 461, 463, 465, 473, 477, 483, 485, 491, 493, 495*
    God, Day of   *341*
    God-man   *153, 193*
    God, Day of   *341*
    God-Man   *153, 193*
    God's Acts   *453*
    God's Ambassador   *133*
    God's Anger   *191*
    God's Blessings   *317*
    God's Character   *247*
    God's Children   *36, 41, 461*
    God's Church   *433*
    God's Decree(s)   *275, 383, 423*
    God's Elect   *317, 423*
    God's Exaltation   *193*
    God's Favour   *79, 201, 317*
    God's Firstborn   *461*
    God's Glory   *115, 163, 341, 503*
    God's Grace(s)   *47, 327, 333, 401*
    God's Judgments   *399*
    God's Justice   *79*
    God's Love   *419, 503*
    God's Name   *227*
    God's Oath   *221*
    God's Omnipotence   *221*
    God's Omniscience   *221*
    God's People   *185, 317, 441*
    God's Power   *341, 441*

SUBJECT INDEX

God's Promise(s) *163, 179, 433*
God's Right Hand *71*
God's Sanctum Sanctorum *155*
God's Spirit *227*
God's Throne *401*
God's Will *203*
God's Word *333, 495*
God's Work(s) *117, 247, 397*
Good(s)(ness) *27, 36, 41, 51, 53, 69, 91, 97, 117, 135, 139, 143, 145, 167, 179, 187, 203, 221, 227, 233, 235, 237, 285, 293, 295, 303, 309, 319, 331, 339, 349, 351, 353, 363, 377, 387, 389, 411, 413, 435, 437, 441, 463, 483, 485, 493*
Good Work(s) *36, 53, 91*
Gospel *47, 51, 55, 71, 79, 81, 93, 115, 139, 155, 163, 191, 215, 221, 223, 247, 249, 257, 293, 297, 327, 329 363, 455, 483*
Gospel of Grace *221*
Government *441*
Grace(s)(ful)(ious) *27, 47, 51, 91, 93, 95, 111, 117, 135, 143, 153, 185, 201, 205, 215, 221, 235, 237, 247, 249, 271, 275, 287, 303, 319, 333, 383, 387, 413, 423, 424, 427, 483*
Grace, Sovereign *205, 387*
Gratitude *85, 87, 117, 135, 143, 165, 167, 179, 283, 387*
Greedy *425*
Grief *177, 179, 245, 319*
Grow(th)(ing) *205, 213, 273, 317, 319, 321 327, 333, 359, 473*
Guilt *201, 255, 257, 259*

H

Happy(ier)(iest)(iness) *85, 95, 121, 145, 167, 225, 411, 417, 447, 491*
Harvest *95, 97*
Hate(d)(r) *79, 185, 191, 305, 349, 411*
Heart(s) *35, 36, 41, 53, 81, 85, 91, 107, 111, 121, 133, 177, 187, 203, 215, 233, 257, 259, 283, 309, 333, 351, 355, 417, 423, 425, 427, 465, 475, 491*
Heathen(s) *79, 191, 193, 339, 385, 447*
Heaven(ly) *41, 65, 85, 91, 97, 117, 121, 143, 145, 153, 155, 157, 163, 167, 179 201, 221, 223, 227, 271, 273, 285, 305, 339, 359, 361, 365, 387, 437, 443, 455, 463, 465, 495*
Hebrew *111*
Heir(s) *119*
Hell *65, 85, 115, 201, 223, 225 227, 275, 305, 309, 339, 359, 361, 397, 401, 407, 427, 435*

Hobab *165, 167*
Holy(ier)(iness) *51, 85, 117, 131, 133, 135, 145, 153, 195, 203, 215, 221, 237, 243, 273, 309, 339, 359, 365, 433, 443, 447*
Holy Ghost *139, 249, 473*
Holy Spirit *51, 213, 235, 273, 297, 387, 441*
Honour(s)(ed) *85, 87, 115, 145, 237, 315, 341, 397, 423*
Hope(s)(ful)(less) *35, 36, 53, 71, 87, 139, 157, 195, 213, 223, 227, 273, 295, 351, 363, 377, 407, 419, 49, 453, 483*
House(hold) *157, 163, 177, 281, 283, 349, 397, 423, 473, 477, 491, 493, 495*
House of God *157*
Human(ly)(ity) *69, 107, 245, 253, 271, 309, 423*
Humble(d)(y) *65, 87, 91, 119, 121, 213, 319, 379, 397, 483*
Hypocrite(s)(ical) *65, 305, 317, 397, 407, 413, 433*

I

Idol(ize)(atry)(aters)(atrous) *71, 115, 423, 487*
Ignorance *35, 333*
Immortal *339, 399, 419*
Immutable *145*
Imputed Righteousness *27, 201, 357, 365, 463*
Incarnate *441*
Infallibility *35*
Infants *295*
Infidel(s)(ity) *247, 305, 331, 413, 449*
Ingratitude *193, 377, 443*
Inherit(ance) *119, 177, 193, 303, 305, 465*
Inspired *163, 169, 309*
Intercession *53, 441*
Isaac *221, 405*
Israel(ites) *165, 167, 185, 317, 321, 349, 397, 423, 453*

J

Jacob *185, 221, 273*
James *143*
Jason *327*
Jehovah *255, 341*
Jeremiah *85*
Jericho *483, 485, 487*
Jerusalem *157, 163, 405, 433*
Jerusalem, New *233*
Jerusalem, Old *163*

525

SUBJECT INDEX

Jesus   27, 36, 41, 51, 53, 65, 69, 71, 87, 91, 95, 105, 107, 117, 121, 133, 135, 143, 153, 193, 195, 203, 205, 213, 221, 223, 227, 237, 247, 249, 251, 253, 255, 257, 271, 273, 281, 285, 293, 295, 303, 305, 309, 319, 327, 333, 349, 353, 359, 361, 363, 365, 377, 379, 383, 387, 397, 399, 401, 405, 407, 411, 413, 435, 441, 453, 475, 477, 487, 503
Jesus's Sake   343, 389, 437
Jesus's Work   139, 411
Jethro   165
Jew(s)(ish)   133, 155, 191, 221, 223, 227, 249, 253, 259, 273, 283, 295, 327, 329, 383, 453
Job   357, 411
Joe Smith   361
John   251
Jonah   111
Jordan   185
Joseph   273, 309
Josiah   405
Joy(s)(ful(ly))   53, 55, 65, 87, 117, 195, 205, 223, 235, 237, 311, 339, 351, 405, 417, 433, 437, 473, 483
Judea   473
Judge(s)(d)   51, 107, 331, 341, 447, 449
Judgment(s)   42, 65, 105, 117, 157, 191, 247, 251, 275, 303, 305, 311, 339, 341, 385, 387, 397, 399
  Judgment, Day of   187, 237
Just(ness)   87, 89, 91, 177, 180, 193, 331, 339, 399
Justice   69, 79, 85, 187, 235, 247, 273, 343, 357, 359, 363, 365, 447
Justify(ied)(ing)(ication)   53, 65, 91, 93, 117, 135, 177, 201, 203, 205, 215, 235, 237, 357, 359, 363, 443, 455
  Justification by Faith   27, 111, 247

K

King(s)(ly)(dom(s))   69, 85, 91, 105, 117, 119, 157, 167, 191, 193, 195, 203, 221, 223, 227, 271, 273, 275, 309, 341, 349, 411, 443, 453
  King of Kings   237, 349
Knowledge   36, 93, 157, 303, 317, 443, 483

L

Lamb   131, 139
  Lamb of God   255
Lament(ably)(ation)   115, 397
Language   435, 463
Law(s)(ful)(lessness)   51, 115, 131, 133, 135, 157, 179, 201, 213, 215, 253, 309, 355, 357, 359, 363, 365, 399, 401, 423, 447, 463
  Law of God   107
Lazarus   225, 405
Legalists   377
Levites   281, 283
Liberty   213, 215
Life(less)   47, 65, 69, 95, 97, 117, 131, 155, 177, 179, 205, 227, 255, 321, 339, 349, 353, 357, 387, 417, 441, 443, 483, 487, 491, 503
Light(s)(ly)   41, 47, 93, 107, 145, 157, 193, 223, 235, 285, 363, 401, 435
Lion
  Lion of Judah   341
  Lion's Den   273
Lord   41, 47, 68, 91, 97, 117, 163, 185, 187, 193, 203, 227, 235, 245, 247, 249, 251, 297, 309, 321, 339, 365, 385, 423, 427, 433, 487, 491, 495
  Lord of Hosts   87, 285, 435
  Lord Jesus   349
  Lord's Supper   257, 297, 361
Lost   35, 105, 121, 139, 201, 223, 225, 227, 305, 349, 351, 405, 477, 495
Lot   249
Love(s)(d)(ly)   25, 27, 36, 41, 55, 65, 69, 79, 81, 85, 87, 97, 115, 131, 133, 145, 185, 187, 191, 193, 225, 233, 235, 237, 245, 249, 251, 257, 271, 275, 283, 311, 317, 319, 341, 351, 355, 383, 387, 411, 419, 447, 461, 463, 475, 477, 483, 503
  Love of God   79, 249
Lucifer   363
Luke   153, 167
Lust(s)   41, 105, 135, 385, 387, 495

M

Mahommetans   71
Malachi   281
Malice   225, 253, 411
Marriage Banquet   225
Master   117, 203, 319, 351, 357, 377, 397
Mediator(ial)   93, 477
Mercy(ies)   71, 93, 95, 139, 145, 179, 191, 213, 215, 221, 223, 235, 273, 343, 363, 377, 399, 401, 424
  Mercy(ies) of God   135, 247
Messiah(ship)   255, 271, 475

526

SUBJECT INDEX

Mind(s)   *115, 247, 253, 273, 237, 239, 343, 374, 397, 405, 425, 437*
Minister(s)   *51, 115, 119, 135, 227, 293, 297, 319, 331, 397, 399, 401, 413, 419*
    Ministry   *91, 397*
Miracle   *221, 253, 461*
Mission   *41, 453*
Moabites   *385*
Money   *283, 361, 377*
Moral(ity)(izes)   *35, 36, 47, 107, 365, 491, 493*
Mormon(s)(ite)   *71, 293, 361*
Mortification   *133*
Moses   *93, 111, 165, 167, 185*
    Mosaic   *155, 213, 281, 435*
    Moses's Face   *319*
Most
    Most High   *233*
    Most Holy Place   *153*
Mountain(s)   *95, 105, 139, 433, 437*
    Mountain Lebanon   *319*
    Mount of the Lord   *433*
    Mount Zion   *433*
Murder(s)(ed)(er(s))   *91, 153, 213, 309*

N

Nation(s)   *27, 133, 191, 221, 223, 275, 293, 295, 339, 341*
Nature   *41, 69, 107, 139, 145, 163, 191, 215, 233, 247, 271, 295, 321, 339, 461*
Nehemiah   *281*
New(ly)   *331, 361, 461*
    New Jerusalem   *233*
Night   *213, 317, 399*
Noah   *51*

O

Oath   *55, 195, 433*
Obedience   *65, 87, 131, 359, 363, 387, 463*
Offering   *69, 131, 133, 237, 259, 441*
Old(er)   *51, 119, 131, 135, 185, 203, 215, 237, 255, 305, 321, 351, 355, 361, 377, 389, 397, 399, 407, 425, 427, 435, 447, 449, 465, 485, 491, 493*
    Old Jerusalem   *163*
Omnipotent(ce)   *221, 271, 275, 285*
Omniscience   *359, 379*
Ordinance(s)   *51, 79, 117, 157, 163, 235, 295, 297, 385*

P

Pain(s)   *225, 253, 385, 427, 495*
Palestine   *405, 473*
Paradise   *359*
Pardon(ed)(ing)   *53, 93, 95, 201, 235, 361, 365, 387*
Parent(s)   *177, 223, 247, 309, 377, 419, 493*
Passover   *221, 255, 405*
Pastor   *383*
Patient(ce)   *355, 357, 463*
Paul   *47, 115, 133, 273, 281, 327, 331, 361, 383, 411, 427*
Peace   *41, 163, 201, 425, 443, 473, 503*
Penitent(ce)   *225, 365, 377, 399, 411*
Perish(ed)(ing)   *167, 251, 303, 317, 377, 401, 433, 477*
Persecute(d)(ing)(ion)   *165, 191, 247, 327, 329, 413, 433, 453*
Persevere(ing)(ance)   *27, 53, 93, 111, 135, 247, 273, 443, 455, 485*
    Perseverance, Final   *27, 53, 81, 135, 237, 247, 273, 275, 387, 455*
Peter   *115, 251, 273, 281, 411*
Pharisee(s)   *107, 273, 317, 361, 377, 453*
    Pharasaical   *203*
Philistines   *423, 425*
Philosophy   *327*
Piety   *27, 167, 233, 245*
Pilate   *91*
Pilgrim(s)(age)   *41, 153, 385*
Pleasure(s)   *177, 185, 309, 433, 435*
    Pleasures of Religion   *305*
    Pleasure of Sin   *413*
Pledge   *71*
    Pledge of the Spirit   *477*
Poor(est)   *47, 53, 95, 107, 157, 215, 227, 293, 441, 475, 487*
Pope(s)(ry)   *35, 361, 385, 427*
Poverty   *247*
Power(s)(ful)(less)   *41, 47, 71, 85, 87, 173, 251, 255, 271, 273, 275, 283, 341, 351, 383, 411, 419, 423, 425, 433, 477, 483, 493, 503*
    Power, Spirit's   *221*
Praise   *27, 87, 233, 237, 453*
Pray(s)(er(s))(ing)   *51, 53, 91, 93, 95, 97, 133, 187, 203, 233, 235, 237, 283, 285, 287, 311, 359, 363, 401, 441, 443, 473*
Preach(es)(ed)(er(s))(ing)   *47, 51, 97, 227, 247, 293, 297, 327, 329, 361, 397, 407, 491, 493*
Precious   *51, 247, 251, 317, 455, 477*

527

SUBJECT INDEX

Pride *341, 361, 377*
Priest(s) *51, 69, 117, 119, 133, 153, 155, 157, 281, 359, 361, 427*
    Priest, High *153, 157*
Prince *87, 349, 355, 385*
    Prince, Black *349*
    Prince of Heaven *143*
Prison(er(s)) *213, 215, 341, 349, 461*
Prodigal *377, 379, 387*
Profane(s) *105, 413*
Profess(es)(ing)(ion)(ors)(edly) *223, 227, 293, 295, 319, 401*
Promise(s)(d) *87, 167, 179, 193, 201, 205, 221, 235, 245, 247, 249, 273, 275, 287, 293, 297, 317, 321, 387, 419, 433, 447, 483, 487*
Prophecy *91, 157, 163, 251*
Prophet(s)(ic) *51, 119, 155, 281, 397, 405*
Providence(s) *27, 117, 179, 193, 247, 253, 255, 475*
Psalm *191, 453*
Publicans *227*
Punish(ing)(ment) *53, 55, 91, 245, 293, 339, 359, 411, 413, 437*
Pure(ity)(ification) *117, 363, 365, 387*
Puritans *55*
Pusey(ism) *361, 385*

Q
Quakers *383*

R
Rabbis *153, 271, 309*
Race *107, 273, 339, 359*
Raquel *165*
Rationalist *247*
Reason *235, 329, 495*
Rebel(ed)(lion) *191, 213, 309, 453*
Receive(s)(ed) *51, 135, 157, 247, 285, 319, 327, 329, 331, 357, 379, 383, 387, 417*
Redeem(ed) *235, 387, 443, 465*
    Redemption *95, 135, 257, 327, 425, 435*
    Redemption, Covenant of *27, 53, 221*
Red Sea *273*
Reform(s)(ation) *79, 95, 133, 245, 453*
Refuge *245, 249, 251*
Regenerate(ation) *95, 111, 213, 235, 385, 425, 461*

Regeneration, Baptismal *259*
Rejoice *195, 215, 257*
Religion *35, 65, 107, 245, 247, 251, 275, 305, 311, 319, 327, 331, 383, 413, 427, 433, 465*
    Religion, True *245, 249, 311*
Remember(s)(ing) *71, 135, 257, 287, 293, 311, 357, 379, 385, 387, 397, 413, 491, 493, 495*
Remnant *133, 327*
Repent(s)(ing)(ance) *53, 65, 105, 303, 333*
Reproach *437*
Reprobate *107, 407*
Resurrection *69, 117, 255, 257, 387*
Return(ing) *139, 273, 319, 329, 343, 371, 387*
Reul *165*
Revelation(s) *55, 155, 157, 247*
Reverence *253, 463*
Revive *319, 321*
Reward *143, 339, 437*
Rich(es(t)) *27, 185, 227, 271, 295, 309, 349, 417, 465*
Righteous(ness) *27, 35, 65, 357, 363, 365, 377, 401, 425, 435, 443, 465*
    Righteousness of God *365*
    Righteousness of Jesus *273, 353, 365*
    Righteousness, Imputed *27, 201, 357, 365, 463*
    Righteousness, Inwrought *463*
    Righteousness, Robe of *223*
Right Hand
    Right Hand of God *69*
    Right Hand of Power *71*
Romans *55, 253, 365*
Rome *111*
    Rome, Babylonish *487*
    Romish *191*
Rule(s) *85, 213, 309, 349, 353, 355, 425, 463*
    Rule of Faith *329*
    Rule of Practice *329*

S
Sabbath(s) *117, 253, 283, 327, 455, 463, 495*
Sacred *155, 193, 437, 493*
Sacrifice(ing) *69, 131, 135, 155*
Safe(ty) *55, 111, 167, 185, 233, 387, 399, 447, 477*
Saint(s) *35, 47, 51, 55, 81, 105, 107, 111, 117, 145, 157, 225, 233, 259, 275, 295, 339, 341, 343, 363, 387, 401, 443, 447, 455*

Salt Lake   *293, 361*
Salvation   *53, 91, 139, 167, 195, 215, 221, 227, 247, 275, 333, 349, 377, 443, 453, 477, 483, 485*
   Salvation by Faith   *454*
   Salvation by Grace   *215*
   Salvation by Workings   *215*
Samson   *273*
   Sampson's Death   *423*
Samuel   *453*
Sanctify(ied)(ication)   *53, 179, 201, 203, 205, 235, 259, 353, 363, 365*
Sanctuary   *361*
Satan   *35, 41, 71, 275, 399, 411, 417, 419, 425, 427, 441*
   Satan's Accusing's   *441*
   Satan's Beer   *437*
   Satan's Blackamoors   *461*
   Satan's Devices   *413*
   Satan's Roaring   *65*
   Satan's Temptations   *433*
   Satan's Way   *413*
   Satan-Tempted   *107*
Satisfied   *69, 165, 225, 311*
Saul   *385, 453*
Save(d)   *27, 35, 47, 55, 85, 107, 119, 139, 157, 193, 215, 221, 225, 247, 251, 271, 317, 343, 361, 389, 485*
Saviour   *303*
Science   *35*
Scripture(s)   *55, 79, 107, 303, 327, 329, 331, 333, 359, 361, 363, 365, 423*
Second Adam   *411*
Second Death   *417, 435*
Secure(ity)   *163, 165, 167, 179, 191, 193, 195, 201, 237, 245, 247, 251, 399, 433, 477*
Seed   *53, 97, 187, 333*
Self-Denial   *131*
Selfishness   *79*
Self-Righteous(ness)   *35, 65, 79, 185, 213, 357, 377*
Sennacherib   *163*
Serpent   *255*
   Serpent's Head   *343*
Servant(s)   *51, 133, 143, 201, 203, 281, 305, 319, 379*
Serve(d)(s)(ice)   *85, 111, 117, 135, 179, 185, 193, 195, 215, 287, 349, 351, 353, 357, 365, 383 477*
   Service of God   *153*
Shame   *305, 477*

Ashamed   *305, 343, 447*
Sheep   *41, 81, 213, 385*
Shepherd   *349, 477*
Sick(ness)   *65, 93, 247*
Simon Magus   *259*
Sin(s)(ner(s))(ned)(ing)(ful(ness))(less)   *27, 35, 51, 55, 65, 69, 79, 85, 91, 93, 95, 97, 107, 115, 117, 133, 135, 139, 143, 157, 177, 185, 187, 191, 195, 201, 203, 213, 215, 221, 225, 227, 235, 245, 247, 257, 259, 273, 275, 281, 293, 295, 303, 305, 309, 311, 317, 333, 339, 341, 343, 349, 351, 359, 361, 363, 365, 377, 379, 383, 385, 389, 397, 399, 407, 411, 413, 417, 423, 425, 427, 435, 437, 441, 447, 473, 477, 485, 487, 491, 493, 505*
Slave(s)   *111, 213, 273*
Socinian   *297, 453*
Sodom   *259, 361*
Solomon   *245, 303, 309, 405*
Son(s(hip))   *53, 111, 115, 119, 143, 179, 185, 225, 419, 461*
   Son (Deity, see also Jesus)   *55, 95, 119, 193, 235, 273, 340, 349*
   Son, God's   *193*
   Son of God   *321*
   Sons of God   *157, 233, 245, 305, 465*
   Son of Man   *397*
   Son's Purchase   *119*
Sorrow(s)   *69, 79, 205, 221, 245, 281, 435, 437, 473*
Soul(s)   *51, 53, 79, 97, 111, 119, 131, 201, 205, 213, 223, 225, 233, 259, 293, 297, 305, 333, 339, 357, 399, 401, 407, 423, 437, 443, 453, 493*
Sovereign(ty)   *27, 255*
   Sovereign Grace   *27, 205, 387*
   Sovereign Power   *425*
Spirit(s)(ize)(ual(s))(ually)(uality)   *41, 69, 131, 143, 177, 179, 185, 213, 233, 245, 271, 275, 283, 317, 339, 359, 435, 441, 473, 475, 482, 491*
   Spirit (Deity, see also Holy Spirit)   *51, 53, 55, 91, 93, 111, 135, 139, 143, 185, 213, 221, 227, 235, 273, 297, 333, 353, 387, 397, 441, 473, 475, 477*
   Spirit, Galatian   *363*
   Spirit's Harvest   *97*
   Spirit's Power   *221*
   Spirit, Sword of the   *41*
Strength(en(s))   *85, 93, 117, 121, 135, 163, 179, 187, 203, 235, 244, 271*
Styx   *259*

SUBJECT INDEX

Submission   65, 87, 91, 195, 353
    Submit   203, 355
Suffer(s)(ed)(ing(s))   69, 191, 203,
    245, 327, 359, 377, 419, 477
    Sufferings of Jesus   105
Suicide   213
Sunday
    Sunday Man   107, 305
    Sunday School   463, 487
Supply(ies)(ied)(ing)(iant)   119,
    153, 163, 203, 221, 235, 293, 317
Sword(s)   41, 343, 359, 485
    Sword of the Spirit   41
Synagogue   327

T

Tabernacle   163
Teach(es)(er(s))(ing)   41, 53, 117,
    293, 295, 297, 423, 449, 463, 487
Tears   139, 225, 407, 437
Temple   153, 155, 157, 185, 405, 411, 423, 425, 427, 455
    Temple, Living   455
Tempt(s)(ed)(er)(ing)(ation(s))   107, 225,
    247, 355, 401, 411, 413, 417, 423, 425, 427, 433
Testimony   331, 419
Thank(s)(ful(ness))   87, 97, 237, 283, 453
Thessalonians   329
Thessalonica   327, 419
Thief   91, 93, 309, 493
Throne(s)   69, 71, 167, 341, 401
Tithe(s)   281, 283, 285, 287
Tower of Babel   487
Trespasses   407
Trial(s)   47, 105, 275, 387, 413, 417, 419, 447
Trinity   41, 295, 297
    Triune   341, 477
Triumph(ant)   343, 405, 419, 427
Trouble(s)   65, 117, 179, 233, 235, 247, 281, 311, 317, 417
Trust(ed)(ing)   87, 121, 145, 195,
    237, 251, 271, 293, 304, 483
Truth(s)   51, 85, 93, 115, 247, 251, 259, 297, 317,
    319, 327, 329, 397, 399, 411, 423, 435, 447
Tunbridge   259

U

Unbelief   41, 93, 119, 247, 309
Unchangeable   145
Unconverted   201, 407, 493
Unfaithful(ness)   399, 401
Ungodly   157, 287, 305, 333, 433
Unregenerate   213
Useful(ness)   41, 167, 303, 309, 319, 475

V

Vanity   295, 343, 355
Verse(s)   93, 139, 143, 233, 271, 287, 317, 453
Vessel(s)   47, 104, 193, 257, 321
Vice(s)   177, 225, 331
Victory   275, 435, 437, 483
Vile(r)(st)   47, 226, 274, 349, 351,
    358, 377, 407, 423, 435, 461

W

Wage(s)   79, 143, 305
Warn(s)(ing)   51, 223, 227, 281, 389
Warrant(ed)   251, 293, 295
Wash(ed)   201, 259, 295, 353, 385, 389, 495
Water(ed)   97, 213, 257, 259, 273, 295,
    317, 355, 424, 433, 447
Waterbeach   407
Way, The   333, 343, 359, 365
Weep(s)(ing)   139, 225, 257, 259, 351, 405, 407
Wicked(ness)   145, 153, 177, 255, 311,
    339, 401, 411, 413, 447, 465
Will(ing)   51, 85, 87, 105, 221, 379, 485, 491
Wine
    Wine of Comfort   321
    Wine of Lebanon   321
Wisdom   71, 85, 93, 145, 271, 309, 435
Wise(ly)   293, 295, 303, 305
Witness   247, 251, 257, 273, 295, 385, 399, 401
    Witness of the Spirit   53
Word   185, 191, 503
    Word of God   423
    Word, God's   333
Work(s)(ed)(ing(s))   53, 69, 79, 85, 91,
    191, 214, 215, 221, 273, 287, 303, 317, 327, 329,
    351, 353, 363, 395, 401, 441, 475, 485, 495
    Works of God   433
    Work(s), God's   117, 247, 397, 433

SUBJECT INDEX

Works, Jesus's *139, 441*
Works, Christ's *441*
World(ly)(liness)(lings) *35, 41, 51, 65, 105, 115, 119, 131, 135, 177, 185, 191, 193, 213, 221, 223, 233, 281, 285, 319, 327, 343, 349, 379, 383, 385, 387, 389, 411, 417, 423, 425, 427, 443, 453, 465, 491*
    World of Spirits *441*
Worship(pers) *153, 213, 233, 305*
Wound(s) *220, 255, 349, 357*
Wrath(ful) *71, 85, 115, 139, 157, 191, 193, 195, 225, 399, 433, 475*
    Wrath, Day of His *195, 343*
    Wrath, God's *255*
    Wrath of God *105, 201*
    Wrath, Children of *389*
Wretch *253, 309*

X

Xn *69, 235, 365*

Z

Zeal(ous) *115, 116, 329, 483*
Zion *191, 193, 433*
    See also Mount Zion *433*